Children, Childhood and Cultural Heritage

Children, Childhood and Cultural Heritage explores how the everyday experiences of children and their imaginative and creative worlds are collected, interpreted and displayed in museums and on monuments, and represented through objects and cultural lore. Young people constitute up to half the population of any given society, but their lives are inescapably influenced by the expectations and decisions of adults. As a result, children's distinct experiences are frequently subsumed within the broader histories and heritage of their families and communities. And while adults inevitably play a prominent role in children's lives, children are also active creators of their own cultures. As this volume so vividly demonstrates, the cultural heritage of children is rich and varied, and highly revealing of past and present attitudes to children and their work, play, creativity, and human rights.

The essays in this book span the experiences of children from classical Rome to the present moment, and examine the diverse social and historical contexts underlying the public representations of childhood in Britain, Europe, North America, Australia, North Africa and Japan. Case studies examine the heritage of schools and domestic spaces; the objects and games of play; the commemoration of child Holocaust survivors; memorials to Indigenous child-removal under colonial regimes; children as collectors of objects and as authors of juvenilia; curatorial practices at museums of childhood; and the role of children as visitors to historical sites.

Until now, the cultural heritage of children and the representations of childhood have been largely absent from scholarly discussions of museology, heritage places and material culture. This volume rectifies that gap, bringing together international experts in children's histories and heritage. Aimed at a wide readership of students, academics, and museum and heritage professionals, *Children, Childhood and Cultural Heritage* authoritatively defines the key issues in this exciting new field.

Kate Darian-Smith is Professor of Australian Studies and History at the University of Melbourne, and a Fellow of the Academy of the Social Sciences in Australia. She has published widely on Australian and imperial history; on memory studies, material culture and heritage; and the historical and contemporary dimensions of children's play. She has held advisory positions with many cultural institutions, and led major research projects in partnership with government, museums and heritage organisations.

Carla Pascoe is a Research Fellow at the University of Melbourne, an Honorary Associate at Museum Victoria and a professional historian. She has published a monograph *Spaces Imagined, Places Remembered: Childhood in 1950s Australia* (2011) and in leading Australian and international journals.

Key Issues in Cultural Heritage
Series Editors:
William Logan and Laurajane Smith

Also in the series:

Heritage and Globalisation
Sophia Labadi and Colin Long

Intangible Heritage
Laurajane Smith and Natsuko Akagawa

Places of Pain and Shame
William Logan and Keir Reeves

Cultural Diversity, Heritage and Human Rights
Michele Langfield, William Logan and Máiréad Nic Craith

Heritage, Labour and the Working Classes
Laurajane Smith, Paul Shackel and Gary Campbell

The Heritage of War
Martin Gegner and Bart Ziino

Managing Cultural Landscapes
Ken Taylor and Jane L. Lennon

Coming soon:
Heritage and Tourism
Russell Staiff, Robyn Bushell and Steve Watson

Children, Childhood and Cultural Heritage

Edited by
Kate Darian-Smith and
Carla Pascoe

Routledge
Taylor & Francis Group

LONDON AND NEW YORK

First published 2013
by Routledge
2 Park Square, Milton Park, Abingdon, Oxon OX14 4RN

Simultaneously published in the USA and Canada
by Routledge
711 Third Avenue, New York, NY 10017

Routledge is an imprint of the Taylor & Francis Group, an informa business

British Library Cataloguing in Publication Data
A catalogue record for this book is available from the British Library

Library of Congress Cataloging-in-Publication Data
   Children, childhood and cultural heritage / edited by
   Kate Darian-Smith and Carla Pascoe. — First [edition].
   pages cm — (Key issues in cultural heritage)
   Includes bibliographical references and index.
   1. Children. 2. Cultural property. I. Darian-Smith,
   Kate, editor of compilation. II. Pascoe, Carla, editor of compilation.
   HQ781.C543 2012
   305.23—dc23
   2012021434

ISBN: 978-0-415-52994-5 (hbk)
ISBN: 978-0-415-52995-2 (pbk)
ISBN: 978-0-203-08064-1 (ebk)

Typeset in Garamond
by Swales & Willis Ltd, Exeter, Devon

Printed and bound by CPI Group (UK) Ltd, Croydon, CR0 4YY

Contents

List of illustrations   viii
List of contributors   x
Acknowledgements   xiv
Series general co-editors' foreword   xvi

1 Children, childhood and cultural heritage: mapping the field   1
   KATE DARIAN-SMITH AND CARLA PASCOE

PART I
Stories, games and memories: the intangible
cultural heritage of children   19

2 Patrimonito leads the way: UNESCO, cultural heritage, children
   and youth   21
   WILLIAM LOGAN

3 Playlore as cultural heritage: traditions and change in Australian
   children's play   40
   GWENDA BEED DAVEY, KATE DARIAN-SMITH AND CARLA PASCOE

4 The case of the Wildcat Sailors: the hybrid lore and multimodal
   languages of the playground   55
   ANDREW BURN

5 The hidden heritage of mothers and teachers in the making of
   Japan's superior students   74
   MARK A. JONES

6 Playing the author: children's creative writing, paracosms and the construction of family magazines 85

CHRISTINE ALEXANDER

PART II
Sites and places: the spatial heritage and commemoration of children 105

7 Taking the children: children, childhood and heritage making 107

LAURAJANE SMITH

8 'Let children be children': the place of child workers in museum exhibitions and the landscapes of the past 126

SIMON SLEIGHT

9 Roman children and childhood and the perception of heritage 144

MARY HARLOW

10 Children, colonialism and commemoration 159

KATE DARIAN-SMITH

11 The last remnant of the Holocaust: the representation and reality of child survivors' lives 175

BETH B. COHEN

12 School buildings and the architectural heritage of childhood: designing mid-twentieth-century schools in England 190

ELAIN HARWOOD

PART III
Objects and collections: the material culture of children 207

13 Putting away the things of childhood: museum representations of children's cultural heritage 209

CARLA PASCOE

14 Museums and representations of childhood: reflections on the Foundling Museum and the V&A Museum of Childhood 222

RHIAN HARRIS

15 Children as collectors of cultural heritage: Leland Stanford, Jr and
    his museum   240
    KAREN SÁNCHEZ-EPPLER

16 Home and hearth: representing childhood in fin de siècle Russia   257
    REBECCA FRIEDMAN

17 Material culture in North African children's play and toy heritage 270
    JEAN-PIERRE ROSSIE

    Index   284

Illustrations

Figures

2.1 Patrimonito, mascot of the World Heritage Education Programme   22

2.2 Children tending the gardens around grass-roofed houses on the Vega Archipelago, 2010   26

2.3 Youth workers with professional carpenter, Røros summer camp, August 2011   26

2.4 Borobudur Patrimonito International Work Camp in Indonesia, 2010   27

2.5 Indonesian work camp for elementary school children, 2010   28

2.6 Safeguarding of traditional wooden toy-manufacturing skills in Hrvatsko Zogorje   31

3.1 Dorothy Howard documenting children playing marbles game in 1955   45

3.2 Fieldworker Judy McKinty interviews children about their games and play   47

3.3 Girls playing a skipping and rhyme game with elastics   49

4.1 A clapping game at Monteney Primary School, Sheffield   57

4.2 Boys playing marbles, Leyland, Lancashire   60

4.3 The homepage of the Playtimes website at the British Library, showing the categories of play around which the site is organized   60

6.1 Title page and editorial page of Lewis Carroll's *The Rectory Magazine*   90

6.2 A page from *Dick Doyle's Journal*, 1840   93

6.3 The earliest miniature hand-sewn books of the Brontës   96

6.4 Branwell Brontë's title page to *The History of the Young Men*   97

8.1 Lewis Hine, Boy with bare arms   135

8.2 Schoolchildren from Westholme School visiting Quarry Bank Mill, January 2010   136

8.3 *Melbourne's Newsboys* exhibition   138

9.1 Funerary altar for Q. Sulpicius Maximus, Palazzo dei Conservatori, Rome   145

9.2 Funerary altar for the infant son and *verna* of Publicia Glypte, Villa Albani, Rome   146

11.1 Child's shoe from Majdanek, Samueli Library, Chapman University   176

11.2   Butterflies. Outdoor Memory Wall at the Heschel School, Northridge,
        California   176
11.3   'They've Learned to Laugh Again', *New Neighbors*, 1950   187
12.1   Templewood Primary School, Welwyn Garden City   195
12.2   Bousfield Primary School, Kensington   196
12.3   Oldbury Wells School, former Girls' School, 1959–60   201
14.1   V&A Museum of Childhood exterior   223
14.2   A view of the Foundling Hospital, originally published in 1750   226
14.3   Court Room at the Foundling Museum   228
14.4   Mr F. Wilson, guide lecturer, teaching a school party in 1926   232
14.5   Museum of Childhood interactive   235
15.1   Stanford Family, 1880   241
15.2   The 'Pompeiian Room' of the Stanfords' San Francisco mansion   244
15.3   'San Francisco residence Museum' is written on the back of this
        photograph   252
15.4   Leland Stanford, Jr Museum in 1905   254
17.1   Ghrib girls making an enclosure before their tent, Tunisian Sahara   276
17.2   Reconstruction of a scene of village girls' wedding play   277
17.3   Boys making a skateboard, Sidi Ifni   279

Tables

4.1   Multimodal analysis grid of four minutes of the cheerleaders'
        sequence   67
14.1   Collections at the V&A Museum of Childhood   225

Contributors

Christine Alexander is Scientia Professor of English at the University of New South Wales, Fellow of the Australian Academy of the Humanities, and general editor of the Juvenilia Press. She has published extensively on the Brontës, including *The Early Writings of Charlotte Brontë* (1983), *The Art of the Brontës* (1995), *The Oxford Companion to the Brontës* (2003), and a number of critical editions; and she has co-edited, with Juliet McMaster, the first book on literary juvenilia, *The Child Writer from Austen to Woolf* (2005). She has recently completed an Oxford World Classics edition entitled *The Brontës: Tales of Glass Town, Angria, and Gondal: Selected Writings* (2010).

Andrew Burn is Professor of Media Education at the Institute of Education, University of London, and a pioneer of the use of new media for creative production with young people, conducting many funded research projects on children's play, creativity and culture. His published work on the media includes studies of media literacy in schools, the semiotics of the moving image and computer games, and young people's media production. His recent books are *Making New Media: Creative Production and Digital Literacies* (2009), and, with J. Durran, *Media Literacy in Schools: Practice, Production and Progression* (2007). He was principal investigator for the recent UK research project 'Children's Playground Games and Songs in the Age of New Media'.

Beth B. Cohen is Gold/Weinstein Visiting Professor of Holocaust History at Chapman University, Orange, CA. She received her PhD from the Strassler Family Center for Holocaust and Genocide Studies, Clark University. In 2004, she was a 'Life Reborn' Postdoctoral Fellow at the United States Holocaust Memorial Museum, completing research for her book *Case Closed: Holocaust Survivors in Postwar America* (2007). She has contributed chapters to numerous edited volumes including *'We Are Still Here': Current Research on Jewish Displaced Persons in Postwar Germany* (2010) and *After the Holocaust: Challenging the Myth of Silence* (2011) and consulted on Holocaust education projects.

Kate Darian-Smith is Professor of Australian Studies and History at the University of Melbourne, and has published on Australian history, the culture of British colonialism, and memory and museum studies. She is currently involved in cross-disciplinary research projects on rural communities; the cultural histories of conciliation between Indigenous and non-Indigenous peoples; and on post-war modernist design and schooling; and was the lead investigator on the 'Childhood, Tradition and Change' study of Australian children's playlore. She is an elected Fellow of the Academy of the Social Sciences in Australia, on the Council of the Museum of Australian Democracy at Old Parliament House, a Senior Research Associate at Museum Victoria, and has served in many advisory capacities on Australian studies and heritage issues.

Gwenda Beed Davey is a Visiting Fellow in the Cultural Heritage Centre for Asia and the Pacific at Deakin University. She is an Associate of Museum Victoria, serves on the Museum's reference committee for the Australian Children's Folklore Collection and has been awarded a Member of the Order of Australia (AM) for her contribution to folklore studies. Her publications are numerous, and include, as co-editor, *The Oxford Companion to Australian Folklore* (1993) and *A Guide to Australian Folklore* (2003). She was principal researcher on the 'Childhood, Tradition and Change' study of children's play.

Rebecca Friedman is Associate Professor of History at Florida International University in Miami, and the Co-Director of the Miami-Florida European Union Center of Excellence and the Director of European Studies. Her research focuses on gender and the family in modern Russia in the context of Russia's relationship to European institutions and ideologies. She is the author of *Masculinity, Autocracy and the Russian University, 1804–1863* (2005) and (with B. Clements and D. Healy) *Russian Masculinities in History and Culture* (2002). She recently edited (with M. Thiel) *European Identity and Culture: Narratives of Transnational Belonging* (2012). She is currently working on a major study of gender, childhood and domestic interiors in Russia from the mid-nineteenth century to the first decades of Bolshevik rule.

Mary Harlow is Senior Lecturer in Roman History at the University of Birmingham. Her research interests are in the Roman life course and family history and in Roman dress. Recent publications include *Growing Up and Growing Old in Ancient Rome: A Life Course Approach* (co-written with R. Laurence, 2002); the edited volume *A Cultural History of Childhood and the Family, Vol. 1 800 BC–AD 800* (with R. Laurence, 2010) and *Families in the Roman and Late Antique Worlds* (with L. Larsson Loven, 2011).

Rhian Harris is Director of the V&A Museum of Childhood. A graduate in Art History and of the City University, London's Museum and Gallery Management MA programme, she has extensive experience running major projects, including the establishment of the Foundling Museum. She has written, published and lectured extensively on the Foundling Hospital and its art, music and social history collections; on William Hogarth and his contemporaries; and on eighteenth-century childcare and childhood. She also has a keen interest in the issues surrounding contemporary childhood, as well as in eighteenth-century British art, the visual representation of children, and visual culture in Wales.

Elain Harwood is a historian with English Heritage specializing in buildings designed after 1940, and is a Trustee of the Twentieth Century Society. She was responsible for English Heritage's research and listing programme for many years. Her publications include the books *England: A Guide to Post-war Buildings* (1999), *England's Schools* (2010) and *Chamberlin, Powell and Bon* (2011). Her PhD, completed in 2010, examined London's South Bank. A fuller study of the architecture of the post-war period, *Space, Hope and Brutalism*, is forthcoming from Yale.

Mark A. Jones is Associate Professor of History at Central Connecticut State University. His research interests are in the history of modern Japan, East Asian Studies and the history of childhood. He has recently published *Children as Treasures: Childhood and the Middle Class in Early Twentieth Century Japan* (2010).

William Logan is Alfred Deakin Professor and UNESCO Chair of Heritage and Urbanism at Deakin University, Melbourne, Australia, where he was founding director of the Cultural Heritage Centre for Asia and the Pacific (CHCAP) from 2001 to 2009. He was President of Australia ICOMOS in 1999–2002 and is currently a member of the Heritage Council of Victoria and a Fellow of the Academy of the Social Sciences in Australia. His research focuses on world heritage, heritage and human rights, intangible heritage, heritage education, and the cultural heritage and history of Vietnam.

Carla Pascoe is a Research Fellow at the University of Melbourne, an Honorary Associate at Museum Victoria and a professional historian. She has published a monograph *Spaces Imagined, Places Remembered: Childhood in 1950s Australia* (2011) and has published on children's history in leading Australian and international journals. From 2005 to 2009 she had curatorial responsibility for the childhood collections at Museum Victoria. She is currently completing a social history of Melbourne's tram workers, contributing to a biography of eminent Australian H.V. Evatt and teaching undergraduate history courses.

Jean-Pierre Rossie holds a PhD in African history and philology, and his long-term research has focused on North African children's toys and play culture. He is a research associate at the Musée du Jouet in Moirans-en-Montagne, France and a member of the International Network Forum UNESCO-University and Heritage.

Karen Sánchez-Eppler is Professor of English and American Studies at Amherst College. Her work explores how literature interacts with social structures and participates in social change, recognizing literary production as a form and site of enfranchisement. Her publications include *Dependent States: The Child's Part in Nineteenth-Century American Culture* (2005) and *Touching Liberty: Abolition, Feminism and the Politics of the Body* (1993; 1997). She is one of the founding co-editors of *The Journal of the History of Childhood and Youth* and is presently at work on two book projects: *The Unpublished Republic: Manuscript Cultures of the Mid-Nineteenth-Century U.S.* and *In the Archives of Childhood: Personal and Historical Pasts*.

Simon Sleight is Lecturer in Australian history at King's College London and also an adjunct research associate at Monash University. Simon's research explores the processes of 'making place', the evolution of youth cultures and the Australian presence in Britain. He is particularly interested in understanding the lived experience of the past, and uses a wide range of source material and interdisciplinary perspectives to do so. His forthcoming book analyses the relationship between young people's activities in the public domain and the shaping of the modern city.

Laurajane Smith is Australian Research Council Future Fellow in the School of Archaeology and Anthropology, Research School of Humanities and the Arts, the Australian National University, Canberra. She has authored *Uses of Heritage* (2006) and *Archaeological Theory and the Politics of Cultural Heritage* (2004), and her edited books include *Heritage, Labour and the Working Classes* (2011 with P.A. Shackel and G. Campbell), *Representing Enslavement and Abolition in Museums* (2011, with G. Cubitt, R. Wilson and K. Fouseki) and *Intangible Heritage* (2009, with N. Akagawa). She is editor of the *International Journal of Heritage Studies*.

Acknowledgements

Many people have contributed to the development of this volume over the past two years. We thank the series editors of the Key Issues in Cultural Heritage series, Bill Logan and Laurajane Smith, for their advice and encouragement from the inception of this volume. Matthew Gibbons and Amy Davis-Poynter at Routledge have always been responsive and supportive throughout the preparation process, and we are most appreciative of their efforts.

At Museum Victoria, Richard Gillespie and Deborah Tout-Smith and the members of the Reference Committee of the Australian Children's Folklore Collection, have been an invaluable source of ideas and practical suggestions. Museum Victoria also granted permission to reproduce the image of dolls' house 'Pendle Hall' which graces the cover of this book. 'Pendle Hall' incorporates 612 components which were painstakingly created by Felicity A. Clemons in the 1940s.

Julie Willis generously provided insight on architectural heritage. Bronwyn Lowe, Nikki Henningham, Leanne Howard and especially Kelly Jean Butler have cheerfully assisted with various research tasks. We are particularly grateful to Sharon Harrison for her excellent editorial and other organisational assistance. Zoe and Eirene Vlahogiannis and Nina Pascoe kept us in touch with the rich culture of children.

Finally, we are grateful to all the contributors, strewn across the globe and across disparate disciplines, for their excellent contributions to this field-defining volume.

Some of the illustrations in this volume are photographs taken by chapter contributors. Others are produced courtesy of the World Heritage Program, UNESCO (Fig. 2.1), Vega Archipelago Foundation (Fig. 2.2), Røros Upper Secondary School (Fig. 2.3), Indonesia International Work Camp (Figures 2.4 and 2.5) the Croatian Ministry of Culture, by permission of UNESCO (Fig. 2.6), Museum Victoria (Fig. 3.1), the Damien Webb Collection, Pitt Rivers Museum Oxford (Fig. 4.2), the British Library (Figures 4.3 and 6.4), the Ransom Humanities Research Center (Fig. 6.1), the Brontë Parsonage Museum (Fig. 6.3), the University of Maryland (Fig. 8.1), City Gallery, Melbourne Town Hall (Fig. 8.3), German Archaeological Institute Rome (Figures 9.1 and 9.2), Samueli Library, Chapman University (Fig. 11.1), Heschel School,

Northridge, California (Fig. 11.2), James O. Davies, English Heritage (Figures 12.1, 12.2 and 12.3), the Victoria and Albert Museum (Figures 14.1, 14.4 and 14.5), the Foundling Museum (Figures 14.2 and 14.3), Stanford University Archives (Figures 15.1, 15.2, 15.3 and 15.4).

Kate Darian-Smith and Carla Pascoe
Editors

Series general co-editors' foreword

The interdisciplinary field of Heritage Studies is now well established in many parts of the world. It differs from earlier scholarly and professional activities that focused narrowly on the architectural or archaeological preservation of monuments and sites. Such activities remain important, especially as modernization and globalization lead to new developments that threaten natural environments, archaeological sites, traditional buildings and arts and crafts. But they are subsumed within the new field that sees 'heritage' as a social and political construct encompassing all those places, artefacts and cultural expressions inherited from the past which, because they are seen to reflect and validate our identity as nations, communities, families and even individuals, are worthy of some form of respect and protection.

Heritage results from a selection process, often government-initiated and supported by official regulation; it is not the same as history, although this, too, has its own elements of selectivity. Heritage can be used in positive ways to give a sense of community to disparate groups and individuals or to create jobs on the basis of cultural tourism. It can be actively used by governments and communities to foster respect for cultural and social diversity, and to challenge prejudice and misrecognition. But it can also be used by governments in less benign ways, to reshape public attitudes in line with undemocratic political agendas or even to rally people against their neighbours in civil and international wars, ethnic cleansing and genocide. In this way there is a real connection between heritage and human rights.

This is time for a new and unique series of books canvassing the key issues dealt with in the new Heritage Studies. The series seeks to address the deficiency facing the field identified by the Smithsonian in 2005 – that it is 'vastly under-theorized'. It is time to look again at the contestation that inevitably surrounds the identification and evaluation of heritage and to find new ways to elucidate the many layers of meaning that heritage places and intangible cultural expressions have acquired. Heritage conservation and safeguarding in such circumstances can only be understood as a form of cultural politics and this needs to be reflected in heritage practice, be that in educational institutions or in the field.

It is time, too, to recognize more fully that heritage protection does not depend alone on top-down interventions by governments or the expert actions of heritage industry professionals, but must involve local communities and communities of interest. It is critical that the values and practices of communities, together with traditional management systems where such exist, are understood, respected and incorporated in heritage management plans and policy documents so that communities feel a sense of 'ownership' of their heritage and take a leading role in sustaining it into the future.

This series of books aims then to identify interdisciplinary debates within Heritage Studies and to explore how they impact not only on the practices of heritage management and conservation, but also the processes of production, consumption and engagement with heritage in its many and varied forms.

William S. Logan
Laurajane Smith

Chapter 1

Children, childhood and cultural heritage

Mapping the field

Kate Darian-Smith and Carla Pascoe

When Lillian Boyd died, her son Bill journeyed to her small, humble home in an Australian country town to sort through her possessions. One room of the four-room dwelling was crammed to the ceiling with objects. Having lived through the austerity of the 1930s Depression and the Second World War, Lillian was unable to throw anything away (including rubber bands and plastic bags) in case it proved useful.

Lillian's hoarding proved to be a rare and valuable treasure trove. She had kept every single item that her son had owned, used or played with during his upbringing. The material culture of Bill's childhood included school exercise books and chewed pencils; clothing such as knitted baby jackets and booties; sporting equipment including a homemade cricket bat; manufactured toys such as tiny plastic spacemen and tin animals; and his own juvenile collections of hand-blown birds' eggs, 'swap' cards and matchboxes. Alongside the mass-produced playthings common to post-war Australian childhoods were several items that spoke poignantly of the straitened circumstances in which the Boyd family lived. Whilst museum collections of children's material culture have traditionally featured the toys of wealthy or elite children, the objects preserved from Bill's childhood include a scrapbook of his favourite pictures cut from birthday cards and magazines; a crudely fashioned balsa wood imitation knife emblazoned with the misspelt words 'Davy Croket'; and a 'Red Indian' dress-up costume made from hessian sacks and dyed chicken feathers.

This extraordinary collection of some 700 artefacts highlights the tension between the particular and the general when preserving the heritage of children. To some extent, Bill's juvenile artefacts are typical of baby boomer childhoods: they depict the growing availability of cheap, manufactured toys; the rising influence of American popular culture; and the polarized gender roles of the 1950s. But other aspects of the collection speak of the unique circumstances of Bill's story, particularly the predominance of quiet, indoor games which reflect the debilitating kidney problems of his early years.[1]

The William Boyd Childhood Collection, now housed in Museum Victoria, is also unusual because it comprises an entire slice of one child's life. Whilst institutional and private collections have long cherished exquisite or nostalgic artefacts associated with childhood, such indiscriminate and comprehensive collecting is highly uncommon. In other respects, however, the William Boyd Childhood Collection is an excellent entry point into this volume, as it encapsulates many of the recurring themes that characterize the heritage of children and childhood. Clearly on one level it is a collection of material culture of all descriptions. Bill has also related the intangible cultural heritage of his childhood through oral history interviews: the stories, songs and games that characterized his youth. In addition, both the interviews and the objects themselves reveal the prominence of particular places in Bill's early years, from the intimate domestic spaces of his home to the mullock heaps and waterways around which local children played.[2]

The cultural heritage of children and childhood is complex and varied, incorporating material objects such as toys, intangible heritage such as songs and games and the spatial heritage of the buildings, environments and landscapes that children inhabit. Yet despite an increasing scholarly and public interest in the past and present experiences of children in a variety of chronological and geographical locations, alongside pressing contemporary concerns about children's welfare and well-being (for instance, Fass 2003; James and James 2008; Wells 2009), the examination of the cultural heritage of children has been relatively limited. This may be because the circumstances of children are contained within the wider contexts of the adult world: children are, to put it simply, everywhere. Their universal presence in all human societies has often obscured, or even rendered invisible, the specificity of children's lives and cultures.

Children and teenagers can constitute up to, or even more than, 50 per cent of any given society, and the range of their experiences are as determined by the spectrum of social, economic, legal and environmental factors as those of adults. But it is rare for children to be accorded the same powers, privileges and responsibilities as 'grown-ups', and their lives are always influenced by the expectations of the adult world about how 'children' and the period of 'childhood' may be defined and understood.

There has been too little interrogation of the cultural heritage of children, and the representations of childhood, in discussions of museology, heritage sites and material culture. This volume thus constitutes the first scholarly attempt to map key issues in the complex and emerging field of the cultural heritage of children and childhood. Establishing a coherent body of knowledge about such cultural heritage requires bringing together a range of disciplinary approaches across the humanities and social sciences, and the contributors to this volume speak from a range of scholarly and professional perspectives. Through case studies drawn from across the globe, stretching from ancient times to the present day, we explore how children's cultural heritage may be recognized, represented and received in such forms as museum exhibitions and built heritage and landscapes, and through memorials and children's own creative production.

Cultural heritage

But what do we mean when we speak of the cultural heritage of children and childhood?

David Lowenthal has famously claimed that from the late twentieth century, heritage has become a 'new religion'. He argues that people incorporate selective elements of the past into their own sense of individual and collective identity, sometimes stak-ing ownership over tangible traces of history to ward off other claimants (Lowenthal 2010). This may be true for certain cultural, national or ethnic groups, but the case of children is different. Children rarely agitate for the preservation of their own heritage. Instead, the conservation, display or study of the heritage of children and childhood is generally undertaken by adults – purportedly on behalf of children, but perhaps also on behalf of their own childhood selves.

Heritage is closely aligned to history, but there is an important distinction between the two. Historians increasingly recognize that the values and conditions of the past may be very different from our present times, whereas a key ideological underpinning of heritage is that the past is closely aligned to our own circumstances. In the formu-lation of Brian Graham and Peter Howard, heritage refers to 'the ways in which very selective past material artefacts, natural landscapes, mythologies, memories and tra-ditions become cultural, political and economic resources for the present' (Graham and Howard 2008: 2). Indeed as R.S. Peckham points out, cultural heritage is always present-centred (2003). As a form of collective memory about historical events, the values and politics of heritage may be created to serve contemporary needs, and are thus subject to change if these priorities are revised. The social and cultural values ascribed to heritage sites, customs and objects are often conflicted as different groups or nations may contest the ownership or the meaning attached to particular elements of the past. The constructed political and cultural meanings of children's heritage are firmly embedded in the heritage of the families, communities and nations where chil-dren are located. However, the ways that we acknowledge the heritage and cultures of children are constantly evolving in dialogue with the changing status of children in today's society.

Children's heritage, like that of adults, is protected by UNESCO conventions including the 1972 *Convention Concerning the Protection of the World Cultural and Natural Heritage* and the 2003 *Convention for the Safeguarding of the Intangible Cultural Heritage*. Bill Logan's chapter in this volume explains the ways in which UNESCO is seeking to involve young people in identifying and managing their own heritage, in a field which has largely been governed by the views of adults. But whilst the heritage of children and childhood is to some extent protected by international frameworks, examples of such heritage need to be recognized as such before they can even begin to enjoy pro-tection. Many manifestations of children's heritage are not necessarily acknowledged if they do not fit easily with prevailing understandings of childhood.

Contemporary representations of children

Given that heritage serves the purposes of the present, contemporary definitions of childhood have a profound influence on our understandings of that heritage. In the early twenty-first-century Western world, children are commonly represented as innocent and vulnerable. The figure of the child becomes the container for a number of adult anxieties and concerns. Popular media, for example, worries that children enjoy less spontaneous play than they once did; are more pressured by parents and teachers to perform; experience less unmediated contact with natural environments; are subject to a greater number of physical dangers including violent crimes; and are more overtly sexualized and commercialized. Whether such claims are objectively accurate is not our concern here. Rather, the point is that the notion of the vulnerable child, coupled with adult attempts to protect that child from risk, dominate contemporary representations of children (see, for example, Stearns 2009).

Current sociological thinking draws upon self-reflexive definitions of children and childhood, demonstrating that the views of childhood are both socially constructed and temporally specific. Central to this 'sociology of childhood' is the rejection of definitions of the child based purely on biology, with a 'natural' set of behaviours and attitudes that are distinctively childish (James and James 2004, 2008; James *et al.* 1998; James and Prout 1997; Jenks 2005; Prout 2000). Such insights have been invaluable in demonstrating that definitions of childhood must be understood as constructed within particular historical and cultural contexts. John R. Morss takes the argument a step further: he raises the question of whether children should be treated simply as 'humans'.

> The proposal to treat children as humans might not be as banal as it may seem; it seems to imply that there are no children's rights as such and therefore raises challenging questions concerning the United Nations Convention on the Rights of the Child, not to mention enormously problematic questions about sexuality.
>
> (Morss 2002: 52)

In support of his case, Morss cites Berry Mayall's suggestion that perhaps children are not different from adults except by virtue of the different ways they are treated (Mayall 1994). The issue of whether there is a substantive ontological difference between children and adults is beyond the scope of this discussion, but it is important to note that if definitions of childhood are recognized as historically and culturally contingent, then many of our taken-for-granted assumptions about the young and the rights of children are also subject to question. There is a vast diversity of experiences of childhood, and while children may be subjected to adult directives, they are also active agents in their own lives. As Nick Lee points out, researchers need 'to see children as human beings, active in social life, rather than as human becomings, passive recipients of socialisation' (Lee 2001: 47).

This view that children can be both independent agents and also influenced by adult expectations and behaviour has consequences for our analysis in this volume. An important distinction can be made between examples of cultural heritage constructed by children and those constructed by adults. For example, the chapter by Carla Pascoe distinguishes between objects made by children and by adults, discussing the ramifications of this distinction for museum collecting and exhibiting.

Children are not just producers of cultural heritage but also the audience for heritage displays. A significant body of work has been generated analysing children as visitors to museums or other heritage sites. Indeed, this is how children are most commonly discussed in the museological and heritage literature: as an important segment of the market for heritage in its institutional and educational forms. Research into museum audiences has argued that exhibitions appear to be spaces where children have considerable autonomy within family groups, choosing where to go, what to pay attention to and how much time to spend in different areas (Beaumont and Sterry 2005). Indeed, it appears that children may retain memories of visits to museums and other heritage sites for many years (Hicks 2005). Other research argues that the most effective strategy to ensure that children enjoy visiting museums and engage with their content is to intimately involve them in exhibition development and design (McRainey and Russick 2010).

In this volume Laurajane Smith analyses the experiences and perspectives of children visiting heritage sites, finding that they do not necessarily conform to the expectations of heritage professionals. Rhian Harris details the ways in which the V&A Museum of Childhood has tried to deepen its engagement with juvenile audiences, through strategies such as adapting interpretation panels so they are more child friendly, lowering display cases to improve accessibility for child viewers and introducing a range of interactive displays and activities especially intended for younger children who learn through play. Such methods are increasingly employed by museums around the world in an attempt to heighten their appeal for younger audiences.

Historiography of children and childhood

Part of the recent increase in museum exhibitions and heritage sites relating to children has stemmed from the growing body of scholarship on the histories of children and childhood over the past decades. This emergent interest in children amongst historians can be understood as a consequence of the redress of prior scholarly neglect, the strength of social and personal nostalgia about the state of childhood, and increasingly urgent contemporary concerns about children's welfare and development. Following scholarly interest in previously marginalized histories of women, the working classes or ethnic minorities, children were one of the last neglected groups to come under the scrutiny of historians. Partially this was due to a lack of sources authored by the subjects themselves, but it was also a consequence of the lack of scholarly and social importance attached to the experiences and pasts of children. Nostalgia has undeniably contributed to this recent surge of historical attention – we were all children once – and has permeated some of the historical research.

Many scholars in this field fail to differentiate histories of *children*, which concern the actual experiences and practices of young people in the past, and histories of *childhood*, which denote the ideological concepts that adults have held of children. Due to the enormously problematic nature of uncovering source material authored by children themselves, many early works were much more about adults and their views than about children themselves (see, for example, Shorter (1975) and Stone (1979)). In trying to write the history of the child, historians are forced in large measure to rely upon what adults have said about children or what adults remember of their own pasts (Hiner and Hawes 1985; Kociumbas 1997).

Since publication of the 1962 English translation of Philippe Ariès' *Centuries of Childhood*, historians have concurred that understandings of childhood are not a biological given but a sociohistorical construct (Ariès 1962; first published 1960). But the early historiography of childhood was largely mired in debates about whether childhood had become better or worse. Lloyd deMause's 'psychogenic' approach claimed that widespread child abuse existed in the past, but had diminished with the improvement of parent–child relations. Arguing that the human psychic structure pre-determines all other cultural developments, deMause viewed the parent–child relation-ship as the fundamental cause of historical change (deMause 1974). This contradicts Ariès, who claimed children were happier before the social concept of childhood was invented in the Western world during the seventeenth century, leading to the tightened regulation of children through the institutions of the family and the school.

In the 1970s most historians accepted the teleological view that the experience of being a child had improved over time, but by the late 1980s the emphasis was on his-torical continuity (Cunningham 2005; see also Cox 1996). Linda Pollock challenged the concept that the treatment of the child had changed dramatically over time. She argued that a concept of childhood had existed before the seventeenth century, but that parent and child relations were formal and children were often cruelly exploited (Pollock 1983). More recent historical work has explored the histories of children in particular nations, including Catriona Kelly's detailed account of growing up in Soviet Russia (Kelly 2007) to numerous works on childhood and children in the US (Fass and Mason 2000; Illick 2002; Mintz 2004; Chudacoff 2007) and elsewhere around the world. Such national perspectives argue that the legal, social and policy attitudes of the state towards its children offer key insights into a country's politics and priori-ties, as well as a unique view on public and private life. Nor are national experiences isolated from the global flows of ideas about children and childhood and the forces of globalization (Wells 2009).

This expanding historical interest in children and their social and political role at different times and places has certainly enriched how children's cultural heritage is perceived and represented through museum exhibitions, the interpretation of heritage sites and the appreciation of material culture. Several chapters in this book add to our understandings of both the history and the cultural heritage of children across a range of contexts, including the lives of free and slave children in classical Rome (Mary Harlow); the educational ideal in twentieth-century Japan (Mark A. Jones); children and domestic life in fin-de-siècle Russia (Rebecca Friedman); child survivors of the Holocaust in post-war America (Beth B. Cohen); and the experiences of Indigenous children and European child migrants in the British Empire (Kate Darian-Smith). Such accounts recognize how historical knowledge shapes our understandings of the cultural heritage of children, forging a dynamic link between the two. Mary Harlow, for example, argues that we lack the cultural and historical framework to fully inter-pret classical Roman practices and attitudes concerning children, including those who were slaves. Heritage tends to reflect popular understandings of history, including the implicit conviction that human society is always progressing, whether that be in terms of medical advances, technological enablers or cultural sophistication. However, historical research may both confirm and complicate this assumption, pointing to a difficult past for children – and one deserving of acknowledgement and public commemoration – if not always providing assurance that the present circumstances of children, in the developed and developing world, have dramatically improved.

Material culture of children

Given the limited documentary traces of children's lives in the past, material culture analysis offers an alternative entry point to the cultural heritage of children and childhood. But as Carla Pascoe's chapter in this volume explains, material artefacts illuminating the history of children and childhood are characterized by similar issues to those which plague documentary sources. Many objects associated with children were in fact made by adults and are much more representative of adult views of childhood than they are of children's own experiences.

The objects associated with children include all manner of items – such as nappies, cribs, canes, slates, and bottles – but analysis of the material culture of children has tended to focus upon toys as the archetypal symbols of childhood. From simple handmade objects made from clay or natural materials, discussed by Jean-Pierre Rossie in his chapter on the material culture of North African children, through to today's sophisticated electronic devices, both toys, and the play that they encourage, mimic and subvert the social and gender roles of the adult world. Spreading industrialization in the nineteenth century enabled the mass production of toys and a growing culture of consumption directed at children and parents. Rebecca Friedman's chapter discusses how modern consumer behaviours and expectations about the management of children and the home were evident in new forms of material goods for children, such as clothes and furnishing, in early twentieth-century Russia.

Historian Thomas Schlereth has asserted that 'most manufactured toys are objects made by adults to appeal and to sell to other adults, ostensibly, of course, for children' (Schlereth 1990: 91). However, histories of the production, advertising, consumption and use of everyday toys are as revealing of the broader racial, class and gender ideologies of societies at particular historical moments as they are about the play choices of children (Seiter 1993). For instance, as the American doll industry expanded from the mid-nineteenth century, the types of dolls produced differed from those of European manufacturers. There were further distinctions in the dolls produced by male and female entrepreneurs, with male dollmakers emphasizing realism and mechanical features while women favoured durable dolls likely to meet the sensory needs of children (Formanek-Brunell 1993). 'Playing house' also reflects contemporary values and attitudes, especially in relation to gender; in the twentieth century girls were encouraged to 'learn' methods of scientific home and child management through playing with dolls. More recently, the influence of more sexualized dolls, such as the internationally popular Barbie, on children's understandings of gender roles and personal appearance have attracted scholarly and public attention.

Some toys such as dolls and teddy-bears have had a particular appeal for adults, and have long been collected by institutions and individuals. So too have model villages, electric train models and automobile sets, all illustrative of how technological and social changes in the wider world are evident in children's material and play cultures. There is also a fascination, seemingly by adults and children alike, in the miniaturization of the everyday (see Stewart 1984). Elaborate dolls' houses, such as that made by Faith Bradford and now displayed at the National Museum of American History, illustrate this captivation. The Bradford Dollhouse, occupied by Mr and Mrs Doll and their 10 children, has 23 rooms and incorporated 1,354 items in its construction.[3] Pendle Hall, which graces the cover image of this book, incorporates 612 components which were painstakingly created by Felicity Clemons.[4] Such intricate collections of objects carefully crafted by adults over many years speak to the continuing emotive connection with toys long after the official years of childhood are over. In contrast, fewer objects made or used according to children's own desires have been formally collected. Indeed, as Schlereth notes, 'the physical evidence of past childhood, flawed as it is by the fecklessness in collection, romanticism in exhibition, and gender and age bias in generation, offers material culture researchers a special methodological challenge' (Schlereth 1990: 106).

As the objects that pervade a child's life are often made, purchased or gifted by adults, they offer insight into such adult aspirations for children. The everyday things used in child-raising may highlight the social values attached to childhood and parenting considered too obvious to be explicitly recorded (Calvert 1992). Yet children have also created their own meanings through idiosyncratic use or manufacture of objects, which may contradict adult intentions. Analysis of material culture can therefore offer insights into the perspectives of both adults and children. Archaeologist Jane Eva Baxter explains that by looking at toys:

> archaeologists may be able to ascertain the types of lessons and behaviour adults are trying to encourage in their children, and the types of messages they are trying to convey through their children to the broader community. At the same time, archaeologists may be able to infer how children are perceiving, accepting, and altering these adult ideas through their own manipulation and use of material culture.
>
> (Baxter 2005)

Whilst studying artefacts offers this potential, researchers need to be self-reflexive in order to separate contemporary cultural constructs from those of the past. Joanna Sofaer Derevenski points out that children are sentimentalized as dependent, asexual and cheerful in modern Western culture. Scholars approaching the materiality of children must suspend these preconceived notions in order to 'use the relationship between children and material culture to construct interpretations' (Sofaer Derevenski 2000).

If the material culture of children often reveals as much about adults as it does children, the study of children's own collections offers rare insights into the minds of children in the past. Christine Alexander's chapter in this volume engages with the writings of children as a window into the dreams, desires and aspirations of historical children. Her chapter examines a range of literary juvenilia across various historical periods, arguing that juvenile writing is more than solely material culture: it is also a means of understanding the creative imagination of children.

In a similar vein, Karen Sánchez-Eppler has examined juvenilia as an example of children's cultural heritage. Her study of two generations of children from the same wealthy Boston family explored their production of lending libraries of hand-made books. Through their play, these children imitated and re-invented adult literary traditions. Sánchez-Eppler explains that 'the Hale children's extraordinary literary engagement and productivity help us to recognize children not simply as passive consumers of culture . . . but also as cultural actors – interpreting, redefining, and making meaning and institutions' (Sánchez-Eppler 2008: 194–5). With a similar focus on children as cultural producers, Sánchez-Eppler's chapter in this volume studies the private museum created by Leland Stanford, Jr in order to better understand the personal perspectives and cultural milieu of one juvenile collector.

Museums like that of Leland Stanford, Jr that have been shaped by a child's priorities are extremely rare. Unsurprisingly, museums are generally established and staffed by adults, resulting in collections and displays largely representative of adult views of childhood. However, cultural institutions are increasingly seeking to engage with the child as visitor. In some respects this can be understood as a softening of the boundaries between museums of childhood and children's museums. Both types of institution take the child as their focus. But whereas museums of childhood privilege the history of children and childhood, children's museums focus on the way the child learns (Lewin 1989; Hodges 1978).

The emergence of children's museums can be understood as linked to the growth of a broader cultural interest in children and their needs across the Western world from the late nineteenth century. Children's museums developed initially in the US, and from the 1970s their popularity has exploded worldwide. The main aim of a children's museum is the creation of a stimulating, enjoyable learning environment for children (Lewin 1989: 55). By contrast, for museums of childhood, it is children who are the subject rather than the primary audience. (Rhian Harris's chapter in this volume, however, explains the imperatives which often lead museums of childhood to aim to appeal to children as part of their audience.) Museums of childhood are often rather nostalgic in their depiction of children's lives in the past, largely due to their origins in sentimental private collections (Brookshaw 2009; Burton 1997; Roberts 2006). In contrast, children's museums generally focus on technological development and demonstrations of scientific phenomena, encouraging children to actively discover their social and natural environments.

Intangible cultural heritage and children's folklore

If material culture constitutes an important part of the heritage of children and childhood, intangible heritage offers another way into understanding children's lives in the past. Heritage practitioners and scholars often portray their field as a relatively new discipline, particularly intangible cultural heritage (see Smith and Akagawa 2009). But the concern to preserve elements of children's intangible heritage – the transmission by children of their own culture – is at least two centuries old, as discussed in the chapter by Gwenda Davey *et al.* in this volume. The study of folklore emerged in the nineteenth century, driven by an antiquarian fascination for traditional cultural customs considered to be disappearing (Davey 1982). Most folklorists would agree with Mary and Herbert Knapp that folklore is orally transmitted and anonymously authored, with verbal folklore using memorable phrases repetitively to aid oral transmission. Folklore is strongly connected with group identity, and 'connects us to the past and to each other, because it requires face-to-face contact' (Knapp and Knapp 1976).

Scholars of children's folklore have studied the games, songs, rhymes and rituals that circulate amongst children. Folklore studies are different from other domains of research in being genuinely concerned with children's own culture, rather than adult perspectives (Davey and Factor 1980). Strikingly, much of children's folklore, also known as playlore, appears to be universal in scope, though with important regional, ethnic and class variations. June Factor explains that children's folklore exists within children's traditional play as 'part of a continuum of folklore, sometimes shared with adults, more often learnt from other children in the long, anonymous chain of oral tradition, subject to the processes of decay, preservation, adaptation and innovation' (Factor 1988).

Early collections of children's folklore from the late nineteenth century focused on documenting children's traditional and street games before they disappeared, emphasizing the continuity of folkloric traditions (Gomme 1984, first published 1894–8; Douglas 1931, first published 1916). But as children's folklore survived into the twentieth century, folklorists began to perceive that alongside longevity and conservatism in children's games and rhymes there exists considerable innovation (Turner 1969). Moreover, the transmission of children's folklore is not insulated from the influence of adults (Lowenstein 1988; see also Factor 1988). Chapters by Andrew Burns and by Davey *et al.* in this volume explore the different ways in which the intangible cultural heritage of children, whilst drawing on traditional games for inspiration, continues to adapt to suit the needs of twenty-first-century children – including through active and creative engagement with media technologies and popular culture.

Sites of childhood

Whilst aspects of children's cultural heritage take immaterial form, other aspects are very much grounded in the physical environment. Alongside material culture and intangible culture, sites and spaces are important to the history and heritage of children. These include the domestic space of the home, as well as the street, village or neighbourhood, and other modern institutional sites such as the school. Since the 1970s geographers have been identifying and analysing the types of spaces that are important in children's lives (Ward 1978; Hart 1979; Holloway and Valentine 2000; Christensen and O'Brien 2003). More recently, historians have begun to extend such spatial research along temporal axes (Pascoe 2011; Gutman and Coninck-Smith 2008). But as Kim Rasmussen contends, a crucial differentiation can be made between 'places of children', which are designated by adults, and 'children's places' which are chosen by children themselves. Sometimes overlap between these categories occurs, but often children's places – which may be imbued with symbolic meanings by children – appear disordered, dangerous or dirty to adults (Rasmussen 2004).

In other words, the research undertaken on the geographies of children reveals that the spaces created for children by adults might not be those which children value most. For example, the thrill of playing in derelict or wild sites often cannot be replicated in the safe spaces of a designated suburban playground. As Claire Cooper Marcus's research into childhood environmental memories has revealed, generally the places valued by children are makeshift and ephemeral, such as a cubby house in the forest or a sandcastle at the beach (Cooper Marcus 1992). How and why would such spaces be preserved as representative of children's heritage? Who would agitate for their preservation?

Childhood is the period of the life cycle closely associated with the acquisition of knowledge, either informally or formally, so the child is equipped to enter the adult world. With the gradual introduction of universal education throughout the world, such education has been spent in the schoolroom. The culture of children is thus shaped by the ideologies, regulations and experiences of the school. Mark A. Jones's chapter in this volume looks at the importance of ideas about education and mothering in the creation of the 'superior student' in modern Japan. The cultural heritage of children is also evident in the spatial and built environment of the school, and how this environment may influence their play, social interactions and learning (see chapters by Davey *et al.* and Burn in this volume). In an examination of the architectural heritage of post-Second World War English schools, Elain Harwood outlines the innovation evident in the design of 'child-centred' school buildings, including the interiors of the classroom. Yet it is the 'everyday' or 'ordinary' nature of these buildings that has raised questions about whether they are of social or design significance, and hence worthy of preservation.

The architectural heritage of children and childhood is encompassing, for children are present in all aspects of adult life and locales. Apart from schools, there are particular institutional sites associated with the adult management of children, including orphanages, reformatories or children's hospitals. Rhian Harris and Simon Sleight discuss the Foundling Hospital in their chapters in this volume as an example of a particular site, now a museum, associated with the fortunes of children. It is clearly far easier to preserve the institutional heritage sites associated with children or to ensure children are included in the historical interpretation at heritage sites which carry multiple significations (such as house museums), than it is to commemorate the more ephemeral play spaces children create. As with other aspects of heritage, it will always be a challenging undertaking to decipher the ways in which historical children engaged with the landscapes and buildings they inhabited.

Human rights and romanticism in children's cultural heritage

As Hilary Charlesworth has argued, 'A human rights approach to cultural heritage argues that human rights themselves should be understood as heritage' (Charlesworth

2010: 28). This view has particular relevance to the cultural heritage of children, for the lives of children, both in the past and today, are often harsh and traumatic. Many chapters in this volume attest to the realities of childhoods that are dominated by work, inadequate food and clothing, and cruelty. Simon Sleight points to the past and present experiences of children as workers, including exploitative arrangements, and how these experiences are represented in museum displays and heritage sites. Kate Darian-Smith documents the commemorations, through such forms as memorials and government apologies, for the suffering of Indigenous children separated from their families as a result of colonial policies in Australia and elsewhere.

In another key example, the experiences of children are central to the public memories and commemorations of the Holocaust. Those Jewish children who perished are represented in museums and memorial sites by such objects as shoes. The experiences of Anne Frank have become universally associated with the suffering of children in the Holocaust, with the Anne Frank House Museum in Amsterdam now receiving a million visitors annually, many of them young people. However, as Beth B. Cohen points out in this volume, the Jewish children who survived the Holocaust have been frequently overlooked in the representation of its history, despite being viewed at the time as the physical and symbolic embodiment of the future of Jewish culture and heritage.

The experiences of children as victims of war, genocide and natural disasters has led to attempts to explicitly enshrine their rights. The formation of the United Nation's Children's Fund (UNICEF) after the Second World War indicated that at the global level there was increasing recognition of the rights of children as a special group requiring protection. In 1959, the United Nations General Assembly adopted the Declaration of the Rights of the Child which enshrined the rights of children to health care, education, food and shelter. In 1989, these rights were expanded when the United Nations General Assembly adopted the Convention on the Rights of the Child, which quickly became the most widely accepted international human rights treaty in history. The Convention takes a 'whole child' approach to the heritage of children, recognizing the full range of social, economic, civic, social, political and cultural human rights regardless of gender, race, religion and ethnicity. Its core principles include the right to life, survival and development and respect for the views of children. In a broader framework, human rights issues associated with tangible and intangible heritage and cultural diversity are emerging as a key challenge for heritage professionals (Langfield *et al.* 2010). The rights of children have a distinct place within this heritage environment, especially as they are a particularly powerless group who, by nature of their status as children, have little access to a social or political voice.

However, despite the special status of children's human rights in international law, the view of children as particularly vulnerable and in need of adult protection has continued to have strong resonance. Whilst the cultural heritage of children and childhood takes different forms – from material to intangible to spatial – each of these categories demonstrates the emotive impact of the figure of the child. In contemporary Western culture, the child is the symbol of vulnerability, which is why debates about children can slip easily into moralizing, whether they concern child labour or children's play. As Peter Kraftl has cogently argued, childhood and utopia are often connected in public discourse. Images of children are represented as images of hope and of the future, connected with an implicit biological essentialism underlining the view of children as naturally innocent and playful. Kraftl writes that

> whether deliberate or not, my reading is that such tendencies . . . leave to varying degrees untouched an association between four ideas(l)s: the romanticisation of childhood as a biological and social time-space of innocence; nostalgias for childhoods past, whether in the city or the country; the free play, creativity and imagination demonstration by (some) children themselves; and, the utopian possibilities of (child-like) free play, creativity and imagination.
>
> (Kraftl 2009: 72)

Imagery of childhood has a deep emotional influence not only because of collective aspirations for a utopian society, but also because on an individual level there are implications for personal self-identity. Paula Fass explains that the Enlightenment bequeathed the notion that the self is made of collected memories, particularly early recollections, so that childhood becomes the foundation of the self. Across the twentieth century, this view that childhood memory is crucial to adult personality has only deepened. Because of such cultural associations, Fass argues that the study of children's history – and implicitly children's heritage – has far-reaching implications. This is because 'we are not only questioning a grand integrated adult-based narrative, we are making possible the unravelling of the coherent individual and asserting that this individual has engaged in a number of separately investigable lives . . . that could change over time' (Fass 2010: 161).

Conclusion

Given that the child carries profound individual and social associations in contemporary Western culture, the heritage of children and childhood cannot but be affected by such strong cultural views. Chapters in this volume reflect and acknowledge this cultural framework, but simultaneously strive to be self-reflexive about the implicit assumptions of the author(s). We have endeavoured throughout to emphasize the agency of children in determining their own experiences, cultures and creativity. In particular, we have attempted to maintain a distinction between the heritage of children and the heritage of childhood. In other words, to analyse the difference between folklore, toys or places created by children and those created by adults *for* children.

This, really, is the critical question for the heritage of children and childhood: what types of sites, objects or folklore do we choose to preserve in representing the histories of children in the past? Ultimately, such decisions reflect the types of narratives we wish to emphasize about children, as well as the extent to which we wish to involve children in the preservation and interpretation of their own experiences and material and immaterial heritage.

To be truly representative of children's experiences, cultural heritage needs to encompass more than solely sentimental or nostalgic visions of children's history that privileges wealthy or fortunate childhoods. As the chapters in this volume attest, some examples of the heritage of children and childhood are attempting just that. But more radically, some scholars and heritage professionals call for a move beyond adult visions of children's heritage to allow children to decide what to preserve and how it should be displayed. Some precedents already exist, as Bill Logan's chapter herein discusses in relation to UNESCO programmes. Similar work has been done through the UNICEF Child Friendly Cities initiative, which encourages children to influence the kinds of urban spaces they wish to inhabit.[5]

As has been argued in relation to juvenile involvement in designing museum displays 'it is both difficult and unnecessary for adults to try to imagine and/or predict what children will think. Rather, children should be involved in the planning and evaluation of exhibits and simply be asked for their input and opinions' (McRainey and Russick 2010). Whether or not we accord children an active role in selecting and exhibiting heritage, the primary challenge for this emerging field of heritage practice is to consistently interrogate and complicate definitions of children and childhood that are represented as self-evident. With rapidly growing interest in both childhood studies and heritage studies around the globe, it is certain that the cultural heritage of children and childhood will continue to expand in exciting new directions in the future.

Notes

1 The William Boyd Childhood Collection is preserved at Museum Victoria. For more information see http://museumvictoria.com.au/collections/themes/1622/william-boyd-childhood-collection
2 Interview with Bill Boyd in Perth by Carla Pascoe, 28 September 2006.
3 See http://americanhistory.si.edu/exhibitions/small_exhibition.cfm?key=1267&exkey=376
4 See http://museumvictoria.com.au/about/mv-blog/mar-2011/introducing-pendle-hall/
5 See http://childfriendlycities.org/

References

Ariès, P. (1962) *Centuries of Childhood: A Social History of Family Life*, trans. Robert Baldick, New York: Knopf.

Baxter, J.E. (2005) *The Archaeology of Childhood: Children, Gender, and Material Culture*, Walnut Creek, CA: AltaMira Press.

Beaumont, E. and Sterry, P. (2005) 'A Study of Grandparents and Grandchildren as Visitors to Museums and Art Galleries in the UK', *Museum and Society*, 3(3): 167–80.

Brookshaw, S. (2009) 'The Material Culture of Children and Childhood: Understanding Childhood Objects in the Museum Context', *Journal of Material Culture*, 14(3): 365–83.

Burton, A. (1997) 'Design History and the History of Toys: Defining a Discipline for the Bethnal Green Museum of Childhood', *Journal of Design History*, 10(1): 1–21.

Calvert, K. (1992) *Children in the House: The Material Culture of Early Childhood, 1600–1900*, Boston, MA: Northeastern University Press.

Charlesworth, H. (2010) 'Human Rights and the UNESCO Memory of the World Programme', in M. Langfield, W. Logan and M. Nic Craith (eds), *Cultural Diversity, Heritage and Human Rights: Intersections in Theory and Practice*, London and New York: Routledge.

Christensen, P. and O'Brien, M. (eds) (2003) *Children in the City: Home, Neighbourhood and Community*, London: Routledge.

Chudacoff, H.P. (2007) *Children at Play: An American History*, New York: New York University Press.

Cooper Marcus, C. (1992) 'Environmental Memories', in I. Altman and S.M. Low (eds), *Place Attachment*, New York and London: Plenum Press: 87–112.

Cox, R. (1996) *Shaping Childhood: Themes of Uncertainty in the History of Adult-Child Relationships*, London and New York: Routledge.

Cunningham, H. (2005) *Children and Childhood in Western Society since 1500*, 2nd edition, Harlow: Pearson/Longman.

Davey, G. (1982) 'Folklore and the Enculturation of Young Immigrant Children in Melbourne', Master of Education thesis, Monash University.

—— and Factor, J. (1980) 'Cinderella and Friends: Folklore as Discourse', paper presented at the ANZAAS Conference, 1980.

deMause, L. (1974) 'The Evolution of Childhood', in L. deMause (ed.) *The History of Childhood*, New York: Psychohistory Press.

Douglas, N. (1931) *London Street Games*, 2nd rev. edn, London: Chatto and Windus.

Factor, J. (1988) *Captain Cook Chased a Chook: Children's Folklore in Australia*, Ringwood, Victoria: Penguin.

Fass, P.S. (2010) 'Childhood and Memory', *The Journal of the History of Childhood and Youth*, 3(2): 155–64.

—— (ed.) (2003) *Encyclopedia of Children and Childhood in History and Society*. 3 vols. New York: Macmillan Reference USA.

—— and Mason, M. (eds) (2000) *Childhood in America*, New York: New York University Press.

Formanek-Brunell, M. (1993) *Made to Play House: Dolls and the Commercialization of American Girlhood, 1830–1930*, New Haven and London: Yale University Press.

Gomme, B. (1984) *The Traditional Games of England, Scotland, and Ireland*, reprinted edn, London: Thames and Hudson.

Graham, B. and Howard, P. (2008) 'Introduction: Heritage and Identity', in B. Graham and P. Howard (eds) *The Ashgate Research Companion to Heritage and Identity*, Farnham: Ashgate.

Gutman, M. and Coninck-Smith, N. (2008) *Designing Modern Childhoods: History, Space, and the Material Culture of Children*, New Brunswick, NJ and London: Rutgers.

Hart, R. (1979) *Children's Experience of Place*, New York: Irvington Publishers.

Hicks, M. (2005) '"A Whole New World": The Young Person's Experience of Visiting Sydney Technology Museum', *Museum & Society*, 3(2): 66–80.

Hiner, N.R. and Hawes, J.M. (eds) (1985) *Growing up in America: Children in Historical Perspective*, Urbana and Chicago: University of Illinois Press.

Hodges, D.J. (1978) 'Museums, Anthropology, and Minorities: In Search of a New Relevance for Old Artifacts', *Anthropology & Education Quarterly*, 9(2): 148–57.

Holloway, S.L. and Valentine, G. (eds) (2000) *Children's Geographies: Living, Playing, Learning*, London: Routledge.

Illick, J.E. (2002) *American Childhoods*, Philadelphia: University of Pennsylvania Press.

James, A. and James, A. (2004) *Constructing Childhood: Theory, Policy, and Social Practice*, New York: Palgrave Macmillan.

—— (2008) *Key Concepts in Childhood Studies*, London: Sage.

James, A. and Prout, A. (1997) *Constructing and Reconstructing Childhood: Contemporary Issues in the Sociological Study of Childhood*, 2nd edn, London and Washington, DC: Falmer Press.

James, A., Jenks, C. and Prout, A. (1998) *Theorizing Childhood*, Cambridge: Polity Press.

Jenks, C. (2005) *Childhood*, 2nd edn, London: Routledge.

Kelly, C. (2007) *Children's World: Growing up in Russia, 1890–1991*, New Haven, CT: Yale University Press.

Knapp, M. and Knapp, H. (1976) *One Potato, Two Potato: The Secret Education of American Children*, New York: W.W. Norton & Company.

Kociumbas, J. (1997) *Australian Childhood: A History*, St Leonards, NSW: Allen & Unwin.

Kraftl, P. (2009) 'Utopia, Childhood and Intention', *Journal for Cultural Research*, 13(1): 69–88.

Langfield, M., Logan, W. and Nic Craith, M. (eds) (2010) *Cultural Diversity, Heritage and Human Rights: Intersections in Theory and Practice*, London and New York: Routledge.

Lee, N. (2001) *Childhood and Society: Growing Up in an Age of Uncertainty*, Buckingham: Open University Press.

Lewin, A. (1989) 'Children's Museums', *Marriage & Family Review*, 13(3): 51–73.

Lowenstein, W. (1988) *Improper Play Rhymes of Australian Children*, 3rd edn, Kuranda: Rams Skull Press.

Lowenthal, D. (2010) *The Heritage Crusade and the Spoils of History*, 8th edn, Cambridge: Cambridge University Press.

Mayall, B. (ed.) (1994) *Children's Childhoods: Observed and Experienced*, London: Falmer Press.

McRainey, D.L. and Russick, J. (eds) (2010) *Connecting Kids to History with Museum Exhibitions*, Walnut Creek, CA: Left Coast Press.

Mintz, S. (2004) *Huck's Raft: A History of American Childhood*, Cambridge, MA: Belknap.

Morss, J.R. (2002) 'The Several Social Constructions of James, Jenks, and Prout: A Contribution to the Sociological Theorization of Childhood', *The International Journal of Children's Rights*, 10: 39–54.

Pascoe, C. (2011) *Spaces Imagined, Places Remembered: Childhood in 1950s Australia*, Newcastle upon Tyne: Cambridge Scholars Publishing.

Peckham, R.S. (2003) 'Introduction: The Politics of Heritage and the Public Culture', in R.S. Peckham (ed.) *Rethinking Heritage: Cultures and Politics in Europe*, London: I.B. Tauris: 1–13.

Pollock, L.A. (1983) *Forgotten Children: Parent-Child Relations from 1500–1900*, Cambridge: Cambridge University Press.

Prout, A. (ed.) (2000) *The Body, Childhood and Society*, New York: St Martin's Press.

Rasmussen, K. (2004) 'Places for Children – Children's Places', *Childhood*, 11(2): 155–73.

Roberts, S. (2006) 'Minor Concerns: Representations of Children and Childhood in British Museums', *Museum and Society*, 4(3): 152–65.

Sánchez-Eppler, K. (2008) 'Practicing for Print: the Hale Children's Manuscript Libraries', *The Journal of the History of Childhood and Youth*, 1(2): 188–209.

Schlereth, T.J. (1990) 'The Material Culture of Childhood: Research Problems and Possibilities', in T.J. Schlereth *Cultural History and Material Culture: Everyday Life, Landscapes, Museums*, Ann Arbor, MI: UMI Research Press.

Seiter, E. (1993) *Sold Separately: Parents and Children in Consumer Culture*, New Brunswick, NJ: Rutgers University Press.

Shepherd, B.W. (1996) 'Making Children's Histories', in G. Kavanagh (ed.) *Making Histories in Museums*, London and New York: Leicester University Press: 257–69.

Shorter, E. (1975) *The Making of the Modern Family*, New York: Basic Books.

Smith, L. and Akagawa, N. (2009) 'Introduction', in L. Smith and N. Akagawa (eds) *Intangible Heritage*, London: Routledge.

Sofaer Derevenski, J. (2000) 'Material Culture Shock: Confronting Expectations in the Material Culture of Children', in J. Sofaer Derevenski (ed.) *Children and Material Culture*, London and New York: Routledge.

Stearns, P.N. (2009) 'Analyzing the Role of Culture in Shaping American Childhood: A Twentieth-Century Case', *European Journal of Developmental Psychology*, 6(1): 34–52.

Stewart, S. (1984) *On Longing: Narratives of the Miniature, the Gigantic, the Souvenir, the Collection*, Baltimore, MD: Johns Hopkins University Press.

Stone, L. (1979) *The Family, Sex and Marriage in England 1500–1800*, abridged edition, Harmondsworth: Penguin.

Turner, I. (1969) *Cinderella Dressed in Yella: Australian Children's Play-Rhymes*, Melbourne: Heinemann Educational.

Ward, C. (1978) *The Child in the City*, New York: Pantheon Books.

Wells, K. (2009) *Childhood in a Global Perspective*, Cambridge: Polity Press.

Part I

Stories, games and memories

The intangible cultural heritage
of children

Chapter 2

Patrimonito leads the way

UNESCO, cultural heritage, children and youth

William Logan

At the global level, the United Nations Educational, Scientific and Cultural Organization (UNESCO) is the peak body in the cultural heritage field. It works with its member states to shape attitudes to, form statements of principle about and administer conservation programmes aimed at protecting the world's cultural diversity and heritage. Since at least the 'Linking Universal and Local Values' conference UNESCO ran in Amsterdam in 2003, it has promoted the view that heritage protection does not depend alone on top-down interventions by governments or the expert actions of heritage industry professionals, but must involve local communities (UNESCO 2004: 9). This reflects many factors, among which has been successful lobbying by Indigenous peoples from around the world for better representation in the World Heritage listing and management processes. By comparison, efforts to accommodate the interests of another part of 'the local community' – young people – have not been so concerted nor so apparently successful. This is despite the fact that 1.8 billion or 26 per cent of the world's total population of 7 billion are under the age of 15 years (the United Nations definition of 'children') and another 1.2 billion, or 17 per cent of the world's total population, are in the 15–24 years age bracket (UN definition of 'youth').

Clearly children and youth lack the political clout now being won by the world's far less numerous Indigenous population (370 million) (UN 2008a). Of course young people, especially children, depend on others to speak for them in public forums and to uphold their rights. Nevertheless a start has been made in acknowledging the important connection between young people and heritage and, in this, UNESCO has been at the forefront. The record has, however, been slow and patchy. While UNESCO claims to be the first agency in the United Nations system to develop a programme for youth (UNESCO Executive Board 1999: paragraph 7), little progress was made until the 1990s. The early lack of urgency is perhaps surprising. If the world's cultural heritage and diversity are to survive beyond the current generation of decision-makers and professionals, it would seem critically important to enable the next generation – today's young people – to appreciate the value of maintaining heritage in its various tangible and intangible forms and to bring them into the work of heritage protection and maintenance. The comparative reticence to focus on children and youth heritage issues is also surprising given that UNESCO's largest sector is

Education. Young people have always been a main, if not *the* main priority for UNESCO. The Culture sector, in which heritage programmes are located, is far smaller but one might have expected cross-sectorial cooperation to ensure that the heritage message was picked up in the mainstream of the Education sector's global programmes.

Clearly UNESCO has a large role to play in issues related to young people and heritage and, in fact, the organization has taken some valuable initiatives in the last 20 years. These have been in the World Heritage system that deals with places of 'Outstanding Universal Value', in the Memory of the World programme that focuses on documentary heritage, and in the system that has been more recently created under the Intangible Heritage Convention (UNESCO 2003a). It was during the 1990s – 1995 to be precise – that a cartoon character, Patrimonito, was introduced to give a visual focus to UNESCO's efforts in the World Heritage area. With a name derived from the Spanish word for heritage, *patrimonio*, the character is based on the World Heritage emblem which symbolizes the interdependence of cultural heritage (the square) and natural heritage (the surrounding circle). He quickly became the mascot of a burgeoning World Heritage Education Programme and its World Heritage Volunteers sub-programme that developed in the 2000s and he now appears on websites and teaching kits and other publications. While officially symbolizing UNESCO's involvement with young people in the World Heritage field, particularly those of school age, Patrimonito is taken in this chapter to reflect UNESCO's interest in linking young people and cultural heritage more broadly defined.

While the World Heritage arena has witnessed the most UNESCO activity, these efforts are almost entirely related to involving young people in UNESCO's work of

Figure 2.1 Patrimonito, mascot of the World Heritage Education Programme (© UNESCO).

protecting heritage places. Those aspects of heritage that are significant specifically to children and youth also need protection and to date UNESCO has paid little attention to identifying and safeguarding the intangible and tangible cultural heritage of young people. This chapter looks at these two dimensions: young people's heritage and young people acting for heritage. It provides an overview of UNESCO's heritage programmes that aim to give young people the motivation, knowledge, skills and contacts needed to take part in protecting, preserving and presenting heritage as well as the more limited attempts to safeguard the kinds of cultural heritage that young people find significant. Since UNESCO is an intergovernmental organization its programmes can only be carried out with the good will and collaboration of its member states. The chapter, therefore, outlines some initiatives at the national and local levels to translate the UNESCO objectives into action on the ground.

World Heritage Education Programme

It was a wise move on the part of those who drafted the 1972 *Convention Concerning the Protection of the World Cultural and Natural Heritage* (The World Heritage Convention) to require that places inscribed on the World Heritage List be given 'a life in the community', particularly through educational and information activities (Article 27.1). However, as the UNESCO World Heritage Centre (WHC) itself admits (UNESCO 2007a: 53), Article 27 of the convention has not been used as extensively as might have been hoped. For the first two decades of the convention's existence attention was focused on constructing the mechanics of the global World Heritage system.

As previously noted, however, the situation took a turn for the better in the 1990s when, after consultations with archaeologists, architects, historians and lawyers in a number of countries, the WHC decided it was time to involve young people in the work of protecting and promoting World Heritage (Kvisterøy 1997: 27). The Centre began collaborating in 1994 with the UNESCO Associated Schools Project Network (ASPnet) in UNESCO's Education Sector to create a World Heritage Education Programme (WHE Programme). ASPnet itself had been launched in 1953 to promote peace and international cooperation and it now covers more than 9,000 schools in 180 countries. The objectives of the collaborative WHE Programme relate to young people acting for heritage rather than identifying and safeguarding what is significant to them. These goals remain in place today – to 'encourage young people to become involved in heritage conservation on a local as well as on a global level' and 'to promote awareness among young people of the importance of the UNESCO 1972 World Heritage Convention and a better understanding of the interdependence of cultures among young people' (UNESCO WHC n.d.(a)). Drawing on Education sector expertise, the programme also seeks to 'develop new and effective educational approaches, methods and materials to introduce/reinforce World Heritage Education in the curricula in the vast majority of UNESCO Member States'. It should be noted that by 'young people' the programme has in mind secondary school children aged between 12 and 18 years, and there remains little done so far for younger, elementary school children.

The WHE Programme was formally established in 1994 as a two-year pilot project entitled 'Young People's Participation in World Heritage Protection and Promotion'. UNESCO's General Conference endorsed the project in November 1995 and subsequently approved its continuation as a five-year 'Special Project' (1996–2001). In the first stage Ingunn Kvisterøy, then Deputy Secretary-General of the Norwegian National Commission for UNESCO, worked with Breda Pavlic and Sarah Titchen from the WHC and Elisabeth Khawajkie from ASPnet to organize the programme's first international forum. ASPnet secondary schools in 25 countries were invited to send one teacher and one student representative to the inaugural World Heritage Youth Forum in Bergen, Norway, in June 1995. It was in a media workshop at this forum that the character Patrimonito was created to represent and promote World Heritage. The first African regional World Heritage Youth Forum at Victoria Falls, Zimbabwe, in 1996 and the five major regional forums over the next decade enthusiastically endorsed the use of Patrimonito to represent young heritage guardians. The character was further popularized in 2002 when a multi-lingual cartoon series called 'Patrimonito's World Heritage Adventures' was launched. In it Patrimonito introduces viewers to World Heritage sites and the threats they are confronting and canvasses possible solutions. The storyboards were selected following a competition among secondary school students that was organized by UNESCO at a workshop held in 2002 at Treviso, Italy, on the theme of 'Mobilizing Young People for World Heritage', as part of the celebrations for the 30th anniversary of the World Heritage Convention.

In the second stage of the WHE Programme the focus turned to producing and promoting World Heritage educational materials specially designed to meet children's interests and ability levels and to assist teachers. The most important of these is the *World Heritage in Young Hands*, an educational resource kit for teachers that demonstrates how to inject World Heritage into subjects across the curriculum, as well as through field trips and extra-curricular activities. Following a European regional forum in Dubrovnik, Croatia, in 1997, a UNESCO workshop was held where heritage education specialists Ingunn Kvisterøy from Norway and Peter Stone from the United Kingdom presented a concept proposal for a kit and, with others from Bulgaria, Croatia and New Zealand, formed a steering group for the kit's development (Kvisterøy pers. comm. 1 March 2012). Kvisterøy and Stone drafted most of the original texts and these were revised in-house by UNESCO staff. The project was supported financially by the Rhône-Poulenc Foundation and the Norwegian Agency for Development Cooperation (Norad). The kit was published in 1998 and by the end of 2011 had been translated into 32 languages starting with the six official UN languages (Arabic, Chinese, English, French, Russian and Spanish) and then moving to 26 others as well as a regional adaptation for the Pacific. Since 1998 other WHE materials have been added covering issues such as peace, identity, the environment and tourism. The kit is used by almost 1,000 ASPnet schools in more than 130 countries (UNESCO WHC n.d.(b)). The kit is also being made available on the World Heritage website free of charge and UNESCO hopes that more than a million young students will eventually be reached.

With the kit finished, UNESCO decided to start regional workshops to train teachers to use it. Peter Stone and Ingunn Kvisterøy sought to persuade UNESCO to identify key teacher training institutions in each region where World Heritage courses/ training would be inserted into their curriculum. Their idea was to initiate three-region-cooperation involving both developed and developing countries in teacher exchange and student exchange programmes (Kvisterøy pers. comm. 1 March 2012). This notion of engaging more directly with teacher training institutions was picked up in one of the recommendations coming out of the 2002 Treviso workshop (UNESCO 2003b: 29). However, the original WHE Programme objective of promoting synergy between educators, decision-makers and heritage experts remains largely unachieved. Financial support from the governments of Norway, Netherlands and Italy and from the World Heritage Fund has allowed the WHE Programme to continue beyond 2001 (UNESCO WHC n.d.(a)) but this has focused mainly on further development of the kit for teachers and holding forums for students and teachers. UNESCO does not appear to have succeeded in institutionalizing the expertise that was and is still being developed through the regional workshops.

The various UNESCO member states range considerably in the seriousness with which they have moved to link heritage and young people. Norway is at the better end of the scale. The role of Ingunn Kvisterøy and the Norwegian aid agency, Norad, in the development and promotion of the WHE kit has already been mentioned. A number of primary and secondary schools, including those around most of Norway's seven World Heritage sites, have adopted elements of the kit in their teaching programme. For instance, at the Vega Archipelago World Heritage site on the Arctic Circle, a cluster of islands housing fishermen and their families for 1,500 years and now the centre of eider down harvesting, mainly by women, all students in grades 4 to 10 have World Heritage as part of their curriculum. Summer schools have also been a regular feature in Norway's World Heritage efforts since 1998, all being located in the copper mining town of Røros in the mountains of central Norway. The most recent summer camp here – the Sixth International Course in Restoration for Youth – was held over 10 days in August 2011. Young people aged 16–18 from European ASPnet schools were invited to come to the World Heritage-listed town and 'assist in preserving this wooden town for future generations' (Norwegian National Commission for UNESCO 2011). The work included building restoration, fencing and haymaking. All the young people were supervised by professionals and stayed with host families. The organizers were the Røros Upper Secondary School, the local municipality, Røros Museum, the Norwegian Directorate for Cultural Heritage Management and the National Commission for UNESCO.

Other UNESCO member states have taken on the summer school idea and hosted international or regional forums. Indonesia, for example, has conducted two 'Patrimonito International Work Camps' in 2009 and 2010 at Borobudur, a magnificent World Heritage property in central Java. Both camps were arranged by Indonesia International Work Camp (IIWC), the organization responsible for international volunteering services in the country. The senior high school students at the camps focused on providing better information about the site's global and local significance

Figure 2.2 Children tending the gardens around grass-roofed houses on the Vega Archipelago, 2010.

Source: Vega Archipelago Foundation.

Figure 2.3 Youth workers with professional carpenter, Røros summer camp, August 2011.

Source: Røros Upper Secondary School.

and building up a sense of pride in the monument. In this way it was hoped to discourage the mostly national visitors from littering the site, climbing the stupa or touching and scratching the bas reliefs. In 2011 the follow-up work camp at Borobudur was organized on a bi-lateral basis with Taiwan. Other camps have been designed for elementary school children.

An Arab region workshop for secondary school teachers that was held in Jordan in 2002 led to the production of English- and Arabic-language versions of a practical teacher's manual and a series of training workshops in Tunisia, Syria and other Arab countries. The success of the manual prompted UNESCO to print a revised second edition a few years later, this time in collaboration with the International Centre for the Study of the Preservation and Restoration of Cultural Property (ICCROM) (UNESCO-ICCROM 2006–7). Meanwhile, in the Asia-Pacific region, Australia has focused on developing online materials for teachers of grades 5–10 in upper elementary and lower secondary schools. Launched in 2010, the website www.heritage.gov.au/education provides model lessons and activities, teacher's notes, information sheets on each of Australia's World Heritage properties and useful web links that enable teachers to use the materials within their state (provincial) curriculum.

Figure 2.4 Borobudur Patrimonito International Work Camp in Magelang, Indonesia, 2010.

Source: Indonesia International Work Camp.

Figure 2.5 International work camp for elementary school children in Blora, Indonesia, 2010.

Source: Indonesia International Work Camp.

Older 'young people'

Although the WHE Programme uses the term 'young people' (as distinct from 'grown-ups'), the kit and the Patrimonito mascot have in fact largely targeted secondary school children and their teachers. Pre-school and elementary school children have been relatively overlooked. The current UNESCO Director-General Irina Bokova (2011: 5), however, takes a different view on the term 'young people', making it clear that she follows the UN definition in which young people range from 15 up to 24 years. What is more, she notes, they number more than a billion world-wide and need UNESCO's help and support. Their innovative role in society, she says, is immense: 'With or without academic degrees, free or determined to become free, young people are reinventing culture, taking control of the new media, recreating how we relate to each other.'

UNESCO looked to developing links with older 'young people' in universities and other tertiary education institutions in 1996 when Director-General Federico Mayor signed an agreement with the Polytechnic University of Valencia, Spain, to establish 'Forum UNESCO: Universities and Heritage' (FUUH), an informal network of universities teaching and researching in the cultural heritage field. The FUUH mission is broad and emphasizes supporting UNESCO action in favour of cultural and natural heritage protection, conservation and enhancement. Its main collaborative activity has been the initially annual, now biennial international conferences that it has run in 13 university locations across the world. It has a youth wing, Students Association for Heritage Defence (SAHD), which is designed to assist the intergenerational transfer of responsibility for studying and protecting heritage. A number of SAHD events have occurred in the ensuing 15 years, mostly in the Spanish- and Portuguese-speaking world. In March 2001 students from senior high schools and universities in 12 countries came together in Australia for a training workshop conducted by Deakin University at Walhalla, a nineteenth-century gold-mining town 180 kilometres to the east of Melbourne.

There is considerable potential for further SAHD activities hosted by universities in UNESCO member states around the world. Some of the gap has been filled by National Commissions for UNESCO in several member states where conferences, seminars and workshops have been organized in support of UNESCO's youth and World Heritage ambitions. One such meeting was the International Youth Culture Camp conducted by the National Commission of the Republic of Korea at Kyongju in association with the Kyongju EXPO 2000. At the Kyongju workshop my own presentation had 'Passing the baton' as its main title (Logan 2000: 20), playing on the fact that Sydney in my country, Australia, was about to host the 27th Summer Olympic Games, only 12 years after Seoul, the Korean capital, hosted the 24th, and making parallels between the need for effective baton passing in foot races and the transmission of the responsibility for protecting the world's cultural heritage from one generation to the next.

Intangible heritage

In 2003 UNESCO adopted another heritage convention that dealt with 'living', intangible heritage as distinct from the tangible heritage of places and artefacts. This *Convention for the Safeguarding of the Intangible Cultural Heritage* (the Intangible Heritage Convention) (UNESCO 2003a) focuses on 'practices, representations, expressions, knowledge, skills' – in other words, in heritage that is embodied in people rather than in inanimate objects (Logan 2007: 33). Under the system UNESCO has now put in place to operationalize the convention, efforts are being made to create opportunities for children to appreciate, safeguard and promote their own and other countries' heritage of artistic and artisan skills, festivals and other forms of living heritage. An article in *The Intangible Heritage Messenger* in 2007 (UNESCO 2007b) reviewed two publications designed to introduce children to the intangible heritage concept and explain why such heritage should be safeguarded. The first of these is *Animals in Asian Tradition: Intangible Cultural Heritage around Us* produced by the Asia/Pacific Cultural Centre for UNESCO in Japan (ACCU 2007). The second, published by UNESCO itself, is *Tell Me about Living Heritage* (UNESCO 2008). Rik Smiets, former Chief of UNESCO's Intangible Heritage Section, explains in the preface that many of the traditions and practices expressing the spirit of peoples and communities have survived centuries but now face the globalized and industrialized twenty-first century in a critical condition. International solidarity and government action are essential, he argues, but in particular

> we must also be able to count on a younger generation that . . . will refuse to accept uniformity and the disappearance of memory. This little book will help you discover the wonders of our living heritage. You will learn how important they are not only for future generations, but also for each of us today and why, as world citizens, you must do your utmost to protect them.
>
> (UNESCO 2008: 5)

There is an overtly top-down attitude of teaching children and youth how to think and behave in much of the UNESCO and related discourse. It is a fine balance, of course, between being patronizing and engaging with young people on their own terms. Educators have a responsibility to introduce young people to their culture and the culture of others and foster sensitivity towards the maintenance of cultural diversity, but it is also important that the voices of young people be heard and that they have opportunities to explain which elements of the past constitute significant heritage for them. As the Youth component of the UN's *State of World Population Report 2008* observed:

> Young people do not share their elders' experiences and memories. They develop their own ways of perceiving, appreciating, classifying and distinguishing issues, and the codes, symbols and language in which to express them. Young people's responses to the changing world, and their unique ways of explaining and communicating their experience, can help transform their culture and ready their societies to meet new challenges.
>
> (UN 2008b)

Valuable initiatives have been taken by some countries to include young people's heritage in their national intangible heritage inventories. Nepal, for instance, referred to children's use of riddles in documentation prepared in the lead up to ratification of the convention (UNESCO 2007c: 12). Some 17 States Parties to the Convention have included children's interests in their nominations to the Representative List of the Intangible Heritage of Humanity (UNESCO 2012). Colombia, for example, included a children's festivity in its Carnival of Barraquilla nomination (inscribed 2008), while the traditional wooden toy-making skills developed in the villages of northern Croatia were inscribed on the Representative List in 2009 and the Makishi masquerade, a performance that ends the *mukanda*, an annual initiation ritual for boys between the ages of 8 and 12, was also inscribed in 2009.

Another UNESCO programme – the Goodwill Ambassadors – also seeks to benefit intangible heritage. Of the 46 ambassadors currently appointed, nine indicate their support for projects to safeguard intangible cultural heritage, while a further three focus on World Heritage and one on cultural heritage in general (UNESCO 2011b).

Figure 2.6 Safeguarding of traditional wooden toy-manufacturing skills in Hrvatsko Zogorje (northern Croatia) (© 2008 Croatian Ministry of Culture, by permission of UNESCO).

Often these interests are linked with the promotion of peace, support for human rights or protection of Indigenous people's rights. One ambassador whose interests are particularly relevant to this discussion is HRH Princess Maha Chakri Sirindhorn of Thailand who was appointed in 2005 in recognition of her 'outstanding commitment to education and to the welfare of children in remote areas': her particular ambition is to promote the empowerment of minority children through education and through the preservation of their intangible cultural heritage (UNESCO 2011b).

Cultural heritage and human rights

This emerging emphasis on heritage and young people links with the growing focus on human rights in the 2000s within UNESCO and the heritage profession and in university heritage studies. Within human rights, the sub-set of cultural rights – once scarcely regarded – has begun to emerge strongly as a key element (Logan 2007: 38). The UN's *Convention on the Rights of the Child* (UN 1989) clearly gives high priority to education and, although it does not use the term, makes an important connection to cultural heritage. In this normative international instrument States Parties to the Convention are called upon to recognize the right of children to education (Article 28) and, further, to an education that develops their personality, talents and mental and physical abilities to their fullest potential and inculcates respect for their cultural identity, language and values as well as those of their parents, country of residence, country of origin and for civilizations different from their own (Article 29).

Two other normative statements, both flowing recently out of the Office of the UN High Commissioner for Human Rights (OHCHR) in Geneva, also help to set a stronger context for assuring that the rights of children and youth in the heritage field are heeded. The first comes from the Committee on Economic, Social and Cultural Rights, an expert body belonging to the UN Economic and Social Council (ECOSOC), which was itself set up in 1985 to monitor the implementation of the ground-breaking *International Covenant on Economic, Social and Cultural Rights* (UN 1966). The Committee publishes from time to time its interpretations of the provisions of the covenant, known as 'General Comments'. In December 2009 it issued General Comment No. 21 (UN ECOSOC 2009), one paragraph of which – number 26 – deals with children. This may be only one of the total 76 paragraphs but it was the first time outside of the *Convention on the Rights of the Child* that such a clear statement had been made, especially with regard to the intergenerational transmission of cultural values and to the link between culture, cultural identity and individual worth:

> Children play a fundamental role as the bearers and transmitters of cultural values from generation to generation. States Parties should take all the steps necessary to stimulate and develop children's full potential in the area of cultural life, with due regard for the rights and responsibilities of their parents and guardians ... Thus, education must be culturally appropriate, include human rights education, enable children to develop their personality and cultural identity and learn and understand cultural values and practices of the communities to which they belong, as well as those of other communities and societies.

The second statement comes from Farida Shaheed, a Pakistani sociologist who was appointed as Independent Expert to the OHCHR in August 2009 to investigate cultural rights over a three-year period. In 2011, she chose to focus on access to and enjoyment of cultural heritage as a cultural right. Ms Shaheed's report (UN HRC 2011) was presented to the Human Rights Council in Geneva in March 2011 and launched publicly at the end of May. In it she insisted that 'the right to education is crucial in fostering respect for the diversity of cultural heritages and expressions, and in ensuring access to one's own cultural heritage and that of others' (Article 46), while her Recommendation proposed that

> States should include in their periodic reports to treaty bodies, in particular the Human Rights Committee, the Committee on Economic, Social and Cultural Rights, and the Committee on the Rights of the Child, information on action taken to ensure the full participation of concerned individuals and communities in cultural heritage preservation/safeguard programmes, as well as on measures taken, particularly in the field of education and information, to ensure access to and enjoyment of cultural heritage.

In order to find further ways to put these principles into practice on the ground, Farida Shaheed has since met with officers from UNESCO and the International

Council on Monuments and Sites (ICOMOS). While these activities are not, of course, specifically directed at children and youth, it is clear that the right to access and enjoy their cultural heritage should be a significant concern. Many of the gross abuses of young people's rights fall in the intangible cultural heritage area and therefore largely lie outside ICOMOS's purview. But it was important for Ms Shaheed to engage UNESCO in discussions from the outset. Too often the human rights of children and youth have been infringed, sometimes in the name of protecting cultural traditions and expressions. As I have outlined elsewhere (Logan 2007), many such cultural practices have been eradicated but others remain. West Asian rugs and carpets, much prized by affluent buyers around the world, continue to be made using child labour. Female and male circumcision is actively discouraged by some sections of the world community but is justified by others on cultural grounds, including religious. Child gods in Tibet are effectively denied their right to childhood itself. The use of children as soldiers in Africa and as suicide bombers in Afghanistan denies both childhood and, in many cases, life – and without even the justification of upholding longstanding cultural tradition. The treatment of ethnic minorities such as the Roma in Europe, the Shan in Myanmar and the Tibetans and Uighur in China is the focus of recent heritage scholarship (Aygen in press: ch. 7; Sinding-Larsen 2012) and international efforts are afoot to establish a rights-based approach to the management of UNESCO World Heritage sites (Ekern *et al.* 2012). It will be important to ensure that such an approach to heritage protection encompasses the rights of children.

Some salutary initiatives have been taken. In 2008 the European Commission (EC) conducted a study on the access of young people to culture (including cultural heritage) across its 27 member states. The final report (EC 2008) indicated that most member states have arts and culture education as a primary focus of youth policy priorities related to access to culture and referred to a diverse range of projects aimed at enabling young people to access local heritage or cultural community, mostly through the use of new technologies. By contrast, UNESCO has yet to address young people's cultural rights as a priority programme area. Its 'Growing Up in Cities' project, which comes under the umbrella 'Management of Social Transformations and the Environment' (MOST) Programme, perhaps came closest but is now terminated. Building on the ideas of the prominent architect and urban planner, Kevin Lynch, and in particular the findings of his 1970 UNESCO-funded project (Lynch 1977), the 'Growing Up in Cities' project operated from 1994 to 2000 under the principal leadership of Louise Chawla at Kentucky State University. Chawla had persuaded UNESCO to revisit Lynch's findings in order to take into account the economic and demographic changes since the 1970s that were leading to increasing numbers and proportions of children being raised in urban areas (Moffatt 2002: 46). It was an international participatory action-research project designed to involve children, youth and governments in evaluating and improving local environments. Eight countries – Argentina, Australia, India, Norway, Poland, South Africa, UK and USA – were sampled and activities included training workshops, development of a manual on 'Creating Better Cities with Children and Youth' and production of a video, exhibitions, websites and an electronic discussion room (UNESCO n.d.).

In her edited book (2002) summarizing the extended project, Chawla identified the key trends impacting on children's lives in cities in the following way:

> [T]he realities of most urban areas are that traffic dominates the streets; waste places and public open spaces are often barren or dangerous; children's hunger for trees does not appear to be shared by most developers and city officials; communities still have to fight to maintain their heritage and identity in the face of development pressures; most children have narrowly limited ranges of movement; and research with children and attention to their needs are emphatically not part of most urban policy planning and design and management practices.

Heritage protection is part of children's needs because it underpins individual and group identity. Moffatt (2002: 46) noted Chawla's gloomy picture but reported that the project team believed nevertheless that several advances have been made since Lynch's time, including the United Nations' adoption in 1989 of the *Convention of the Rights of the Child*. UNESCO's Director-General Irina Bokova (2011: 5) also remains optimistic about young people's rights to culture and recognizes their strong attachment to culture. Referring to the 'Arab Spring' and Egypt in particular, Mrs Bokova expresses amazement at the 'capacity of young people to widen the horizons of possibility', 'to take up the torch of human dignity'. Culture, she notes,

> is a strong foundation for the new democratic society. Young Egyptians proved to be particularly concerned with safeguarding their culture during the demonstrations, spontaneously forming a human chain around the Library of Alexandria to protect it from looters. UNESCO wants to encourage this consciousness among young people, the collective maturity they displayed.

She went on to announce that she would launch a Heritage and Dialogue initiative in September 2011. A global programme has yet to appear, although a regional initiative was discussed at the First South-East Europe World Heritage Youth Forum *World Heritage Education: Networking for a Better Common Future*, held in Croatia, 22 May 2011 (UNESCO 2011a) and again in June 2011 at the Seventh Ministerial Conference on Cultural Heritage in South-Eastern Europe, held in Belgrade, Serbia. At the Croatia meeting she outlined her vision:

> The *Heritage and Dialogue* initiative focuses on young people across the region. It will encourage them and it will encourage you to share cultures and to deepen our common history by building new forms of dialogue to foster understanding and mutual respect. It will create innovative networks and platforms that span across the region – with the aim to imbue young people with the values of shared cultural heritage, in both its tangible and intangible forms . . . We are seeking to focus on youth at UNESCO. Every young person in the room this morning is a custodian of their country's and region's heritage. I am convinced that youth

heritage education is *the* way to prepare for the future. It is the best way to safe-guard and to promote cultural heritage on the basis of respect and dialogue.

We await the full implementation of the Director-General's plan.

Conclusion

Interest in exploring the relationship between young people and cultural heritage seems to have flourished at different times across the 65 years of UNESCO's life and in different parts of the organization. Reflecting the fact that young people, children especially, have to rely on others to speak for them in most public forums, the promo-tion of their interest within UNESCO seems to be related to the presence of champi-ons at leadership level. Ideally the relationship should lead to two complementary sets of activities – the safeguarding of young people's heritage on the one hand and, on the other, young people taking on a role in safeguarding the heritage of significance to their community, nation and the world. To date most of UNESCO's initiatives have related to the latter; that is, to give young people the motivation, knowledge, skills and contacts needed to take part in protecting, preserving and presenting heritage. Much less attention has been given to listening to what children and youth consider to be the important heritage they would like to see protected.

Of UNESCO's efforts to bring together cultural heritage and young people the WHE Programme is the most widely applied and successful, having overcome the organization's internal structural barriers to achieve genuine collaboration and sharing of expertise between its Education and Culture sectors. The *World Heritage in Young Hands* kit is widely used and the World Heritage Volunteers (WHV) sub-programme, which commenced in 2008, has already involved 78 projects at 43 sites in 23 countries and nearly 1,000 young volunteers. The WHV programme for 2011, sub-titled 'Patrimonito Voluntary Action', demonstrates the geographical extent achieved with activities from Kenya, Malawi, Togo and Zambia in Africa to Mexico and Peru in South America, India, Indonesia, South Korea and Vietnam in Asia, and Arme-nia, Austria, Estonia, France, Russia and the United Kingdom in Europe (UNESCO WHV 2011).

While Patrimonito has signalled UNESCO's increasing involvement with young people and their heritage, gaps remain. UNESCO's 'Challenges for the Millennium' report (UNESCO 2007a) admits deficiencies with regard to World Heritage specifi-cally, although many of its conclusions apply to heritage more broadly defined. In relation to the education of young people in heritage matters, the report defines three challenges: to encourage schools to integrate World Heritage into the curriculum, to create new resource materials geared to elementary schools, and to provide for the 'sustained empowerment of young people . . . by ensuring their inputs to World Heri-tage Committee meetings and to World Heritage promotional campaigns' (p. 55).

There is also a need to listen to and work more regularly with teachers in schools, colleges and universities. This is not a new point but it continues to go unheeded in many quarters. There is more than one agenda for heritage education, as Zimmerman *et al.* found 20 years ago (1994: 369) in relation to efforts to implant archaeology education in American schools. The teachers were clearly interested but, feeling overwhelmed by the professional archaeologists, ended up only lukewarm to the proposals put forward.

> As we probed the reasons, we discovered that the agenda for archaeologists for archaeological education is not necessarily the same as the agendas of teachers for it . . . The archaeologists had spent a great deal of time outlining what they could provide for teachers, but they paid little attention to the needs or concerns of teachers themselves.

Other forms of heritage have undertaken smaller projects but they have been expanding over the last decade. In the Memory of the World programme, for instance, representatives of more than 30 countries meeting in the Third International Conference in Canberra in February 2008 sent a number of recommendations to UNESCO headquarters in Paris, one of which was to 'develop strategies for involving children and young people in Memory of the World so as to build intergenerational equity in the programme and so as to ensure the sustainability of the world's documentary heritage' (MOW National Committee of Australia 2008). The Intangible Heritage system, while relatively new, has taken useful steps towards identifying the skills relevant to children, such as the making of toys and musical instruments. The extent to which children and youth were involved in identifying traditional expressions or in their subsequent safeguarding is not known. In general, of course, such expressions need to be transmitted from the older generations to the young and some nomination documents make a strong point of this. However, it is quite likely – and perhaps inevitable – that the complex inscription and management processes were initiated and led by adults in culture or heritage bureaucracies.

Perhaps we expect too much of UNESCO. Even though it is the peak global organization in the heritage field, it is an international government organization made up of nation states. It lacks the power to do more than inspire and encourage its member states to behave according to the various normative statements. In a recently published paper (Logan 2012), I pointed out that much of the criticism directed at UNESCO should, rather, be aimed at the various member states which abuse the UNESCO system for their own narrowly nationalistic economic and political purposes. The anticipatory burden placed on UNESCO by scholars and commentators has to be relieved by the member states developing their own internal heritage system as is required, indeed, by ratification of the World Heritage and Intangible Heritage conventions.

That is not to say that UNESCO could not do its job better. The almost universal membership of UNESCO shows that there is ostensible general support for its mission of using education, science and culture to build bridges to intercultural understanding, tolerance and peace. More and more, the potential of culture to overcome discrimination, enhance social cohesion and to create opportunities is being recognized. The previously mentioned EC report of 2008 concluded that policymakers at international, European, national, regional and local levels are show-ing increasing interest in improving the access of young people to culture. As we have seen, UNESCO under Director-General Irina Bokova seems to be putting greater stress on the cultural heritage/young people relationship. The biggest cloud hanging over extended programming in the area is, of course, the financial crisis both within UNESCO itself due to the loss of American funding and, outside, with European and American financial woes now going global. It may be that the energy we have seen since the 1990s in heritage programmes with and for children and youth could dissipate as governments everywhere give greater attention than ever to regenerating economies, protecting jobs and maintaining incomes and basic living standards for people of all ages, young people included.

Acknowledgement

I am grateful to Vilia Dukas, Research Assistant in the Deakin University Cultural Heritage Centre for Asia and the Pacific, for locating and summarizing many of the materials used in the preparation of this chapter.

References

Asia/Pacific Cultural Centre for UNESCO (ACCU) (2007) *Animals in Asian Tradition: Intan-gible Heritage around Us*, Tokyo: ACCU. Online. Available http://www.accu.or.jp/ich/en/materials/ (accessed 25 February 2012).

Aygen, Z. (in press) *International Heritage and Historic Building Conservation*, London: Routledge.

Bokova, I. (2011) 'Editorial', *The UNESCO Courier*, 64(3): 5. Online. Available http://unesdoc.unesco.org/images/0019/001937/193773e.pdf (accessed 2 September 2011).

Chawla, L. (ed.) (2002) *Growing Up in an Urbanizing World*, Paris: UNESCO Publishing.

Ekern, S., Logan, W., Sauge, B. and Sinding-Larsen, A. (2012) 'Human Rights and World Herit-age: Preserving Our Common Dignity through Rights-Based Approaches to Site Manage-ment', *International Journal of Heritage Studies*, 18(3): 213–25.

European Commission (EC) (2008) *Access of Young People to Culture: Final Report*, Barcelona: Interarts. Online. Available http://ec.europa.eu/youth/documents/study-on-youth-access-to-culture-full-report_en.pdf (accessed 27 February 2012).

Kvisterøy, I. (1997) 'In Youthful Hands', *The UNESCO Courier*, 50(9): 27–8. Online. Available http://unesdoc.unesco.org/ulis/cgi-bin/ExtractPDF.pl?catno=109600&look=default&ll=1&display=1&lang=eo&from=&to= (accessed 28 February 2012).

Logan, W. (2000) 'Passing the Baton: the Role of Youth in Preserving the Cultural Herit-age and Its Environment', in Kyongju World Culture EXPO Organizing Committee and Korean National Commission for UNESCO, *Kyongju World Culture EXPO 2000. International Youth Culture Camp 2000; Youth, Culture and Encounter*, Korean National Commission for UNESCO: Kyongju.

—— (2007) 'Closing Pandora's Box: Human Rights Conundrums in Cultural Heritage Protec-tion', in H. Silverman and D. Ruggles Fairchild (eds) *Cultural Heritage and Human Rights*, New York: Springer.

—— (2012) 'States, Governance and the Politics of Culture: World Heritage Places in Asia', in P. Daly and T. Winter (eds) *The Routledge Handbook of Heritage in Asia*, London: Routledge.

Lynch, K. (ed.) (1977) *Growing Up in Cities*, Cambridge, MA: MIT Press.

Moffatt, D. (2002) 'Growing Up in Cities', *Places* (The Design Observer Group), 15(1): 46–9. Online. Available http://places.designobserver.com/toc.html?issue=537 (accessed 24 February 2012).

MOW National Committee of Australia (2008) *Communities and Memories: A Global Perspective. Third International Conference of the UNESCO Memory of the World Programme*. Online. Available: http://pandora.nla.gov.au/pan/83301/20080415–1354/www.amw.org.au/mow2008/mow/proclamation.html (accessed 17 August 2012).

Norwegian National Commission for UNESCO (2011) Sixth International Course in Restoration for Youth, Røro, Norway, 15–26 August 2011. Information sheet. Oslo: Norwegian National Commission for UNESCO.

Sinding-Larsen, A. (2012) 'Lhasa Community, World Heritage and Human Rights', *International Journal of Heritage Studies*, 18(3): 297–306.

United Nations Organization (UN) (1966) *International Covenant on Economic, Social and Cultural Rights* (CESCR). Online. Available http://www2.ohchr.org/english/law/cescr.htm (accessed 21 December 2011).

—— (1989) *Convention on the Rights of the Child*. Online. Available http://www2.ohchr.org/english/law/crc.htm (accessed 23 February 2012).

—— (2008a) *International Day of the World's Indigenous Peoples*. Online. Available http://www.un.org/events/indigenous/2008/forumpresmes.shtml (accessed 27 February 2012).

—— (2008b) *State of World Population. Youth Report*. Online. Available http://www.unpfa.org/swp/2008/en/youth_preface_introduction.html (accessed 1 March 2012).

UN Economic and Social Council (ECOSOC) (2009) *General Comment No. 21*. Online. Available http://www2.ohchr.org/english/bodies/cescr/docs/gc/E-C-12-GC-21.doc (accessed 27 February 2012).

UN Human Rights Council (HRC) (2011). *Report of the Independent Expert in the Field of Cultural Rights*, Human Rights Council, UN General Assembly. Online. Available http://indigenouspeoplesissues.com/attachments/article/10227/A-HRC-17-38.doc (accessed 5 March 2012).

UNESCO (1972) *Convention Concerning the Protection of the World Cultural and Natural Heritage* (The World Heritage Convention). Online. Available http://whc.unesco.org/en/conventiontext (accessed 22 October 2011).

—— (2003a) *Convention for the Safeguarding of the Intangible Cultural Heritage* (The Intangible Heritage Convention). Online. Available http://unesdoc.unesco.org/images/0013/001325/132540e.pdf (accessed 21 February 2012).

—— (2003b) *Mobilizing Young People for World Heritage*, World Heritage Papers 8, Paris: UNESCO WHC. Online. Available http://whc.unesco.org/documents/publi_wh_papers_08_en.pdf (accessed 28 February 2012).

—— (2004) *Linking Universal and Local Values*, World Heritage Papers 13, Paris: UNESCO WHC. Online. Available http://whc.unesco.org/documents/publi_wh_papers_13_en.pdf (accessed 28 February 2012).

—— (2007a) *World Heritage: Challenges for the Millennium*, Paris: UNESCO WHC, 53–5. Online. Available http://whc.unesco.org/documents/publi_millennium_en.pdf (accessed 28 February 2012).

—— (2007b) 'Introducing Young People to Intangible Heritage', *The Intangible Heritage Messenger*, 7: 4. Online. Available http://www.unesco.org/culture/ich/doc/src/00244-EN.pdf (accessed 25 February 2012).

—— (2007c) *The Intangible Cultural Heritage of Nepal: Future Directions*, Kathmandu: UNESCO

Kathmandu Office. Online. Available http://unesdoc.unesco.org/images/0015/001567/156786e.pdf (accessed 27 February 2012).

—— (2008) *Tell Me about Living Heritage*, Paris: UNESCO.

—— (2011a) *World Heritage Education: Networking for a Better Common Future. Address by Irina Bokova, Director-General of UNESCO on the Occasion of First South-East Europe World Heritage Youth Forum, Croatia, 22 May 2011*. Online. Available http://unesdoc.unesco.org/images/0019/001925/192523e.pdf (accessed 27 February 2012).

—— (2011b) *UNESCO Goodwill Ambassadors*. Online. Available http://portal.unesco.org/en/ev.php-URL_ID=4053&URL_DO=DO_TOPIC&URL_SECTION=201.html (accessed 1 March 2012).

—— (2012) *Intangible Heritage Lists*. Online. Available http://www.unesco.org/culture/ich/index.php?lg=en&pg=00011#tabs (accessed 27 February 2012).

—— (n.d.) *Growing Up in Cities*. Online. Available http://www.unesco.org/most/guic/guicmain.htm (accessed 25 February 2012).

UNESCO Executive Board (1999) *Evaluation of Unesco's Youth Activities 1994–1997 and Proposals for a New UNESCO Strategy on Youth* (156 EX/45). Online. Available http://unesdoc.unesco.org/images/0011/001155/115579e.pdf (accessed 28 February 2012).

UNESCO World Heritage Centre (n.d.(a)) *World Heritage Education Programme*. Online. Available http://whc.unesco.org/en/wheducatioin/ (accessed 4 October 2011).

—— (n.d.(b)) *The KIT: World Heritage in Young Hands*. Online. Available http://whc.unesco.org/en/wheducatioin/ (accessed 4 October 2011).

UNESCO World Heritage Volunteers (WHV) (2011) *World Heritage Volunteers 2011. Patrimonito Voluntary Action*. Online. Available http://www.whvolunteers.org/pdf/2011WHVBooklet_version9.pdf (accessed 3 March 2012).

UNESCO-ICCROM (2006–7) *Introducing Young People to the Protection of Heritage Sites and Historic Cities. A Practical Guide for Secondary School Teachers in the Arab Region*. Online. Available http://www.iccrom.org/eng/02info_en/02_04pdf-pubs_en/ICCROM_doc09_ManualSchoolTeachers_en.pdf (accessed 2 March 2012).

Zimmerman, L.J., Dasovich, S., Engstrom, M. and Bradley, L.E. (1994) 'Listening to Teachers: Warnings about the Use of Archaeological Agendas in Classrooms in the United States', in P.G. Stone and B.L. Molyneaux (eds) *The Presented Past: Heritage, Museums and Education*, London: Routledge.

Chapter 3

Playlore as cultural heritage

Traditions and change in Australian children's play

Gwenda Beed Davey, Kate Darian-Smith and Carla Pascoe

In 1560 Flemish Renaissance artist Pieter Brueghel created the famous oil painting *Children's Games*. This elaborate composition depicts myriad children playing games in a town square, with over 80 forms of play portrayed in meticulous detail. What is striking is the rich variety of children's games: leapfrog, marbles, piggyback, tree-climbing, hoops, ball games and much more. Even more arresting is that almost every game Brueghel documented in the sixteenth century is still played by children half a millennium later. How is this remarkable persistency of children's play activities possible, given the vast social and economic shifts over this period?

The continuity and change of children's games over time and across cultures is one of the most intriguing facets of their playlore and heritage, and such issues have fascinated scholars from a range of disciplines and across a variety of cultures. This chapter considers how children's play has been interpreted across the past two centuries and the impulses that have prompted the study of children's playlore. From this broad international overview of research into playlore, it examines specific Australian examples of the collection, display and analysis of children's games.

Playlore as the cultural heritage of childhood and children

Playlore can be understood as a form of cultural heritage in both its tangible and intangible manifestations. The tangible facets of children's play are perhaps most obvious, and include the objects of play such as balls, dolls and other toys as well the structures that children play upon, such as playground equipment. However, playlore is also intangible, in the sense that its heritage and culture are embodied in the knowledge and practices of people. The everyday experiences of play can be seen to demonstrate four of UNESCO's five key 'domains' which characterize the traditions it has classified as Intangible Cultural Heritage (UNESCO 2003: Article 2). The domain of 'oral traditions and expressions' includes play rhymes and chants, as well as the taunts, jokes, riddles and nicknames that are incorporated into children's play language. That of 'performing arts' encompasses handclapping, skipping and string games. In counting-out rhymes, divinations, role-playing and other imaginative games, children combine 'social practices' with 'rituals'. The UNESCO domain of 'traditional craftsmanship' is evident in children's processes in the constructions of toys and play settings, from simple handmade dolls and balls, through to cubby houses built from various materials in a multitude of forms.

Playlore also constitutes cultural heritage through its transmission of games and other activities. Children pass on play traditions to each other, such as the rules of ball-bouncing games, the construction methods of handmade toys, the words and gestures of clapping games, or the tunes and rhythms of songs. In this sense, playlore is cultural heritage that both belongs to and is created by children themselves. Although children's play often draws upon instructions and other influences from the adult world, through such adaptive processes as mimicry and imitation of adult activities through role-playing, children will fashion and refashion play activities so that these represent their own understandings of the world around them.

Within the growing international field of childhood studies today, research into children's play has offered a significant contribution in that it genuinely engages with children's own culture rather than simply adult views of children's lives. This is a relatively new development. The growth of ethnography as a discipline from the late nineteenth century meant that children's play was studied by Western scholars as part of the documentation of non-Western cultures, though generally it attracted little attention in its own right. Scholarly interest in the playlore of Western societies was also limited, no doubt because of what Brian Sutton-Smith terms 'the triviality barrier': adults rarely take seriously the whimsical play traditions of children (Sutton-Smith 1972: 532). Early British investigations into children's play such as Lady Alice Gomme's *Traditional Games of England, Scotland and Ireland* (first published 1894–8) or Norman Douglas's *London Street Games* (first published 1916) were motivated by the assumption that traditional games were disappearing and thus needed to be recorded (Gomme 1984; Douglas 1931).

By the mid-twentieth century, the study of children's play was becoming a more serious and scholarly exercise. In their detailed studies of English children in each of the 1950s, 1960s and 1970s decades, pioneers Iona and Peter Opie demonstrated the dynamism and tenacity of children's play traditions (Opie and Opie 1959, 1969; Opie 1993). Mary and Herbert Knapp researched children's unsupervised play across the United States in the 1960s and 1970s, claiming that children's play functioned to instil a sense of collectivism, release the tension created by school discipline, parody popular culture and lessen childhood fears (Knapp and Knapp 1976). The school playground, as a regulated space which brought together all the children of a local community, was increasingly to be a site of play observation and research (see Bishop and Curtis 2001).

The writings of both the Opies and the Knapps typify the approach of many folklorists in describing childhood as a cooperative, tolerant, liberated and creative state that is slowly corrupted by the learning of adult traits. By the late 1960s and 1970s, however, some Australian research was beginning to counteract this trend to sentimentalize childhood by including vulgar, sexist and/or racist examples of children's playlore (Turner 1969; Lowenstein 1988; Factor 1988). Studies of children's play also became more concerned with a wider range of demographic, technological and environmental changes in Western and non-Western societies more generally, such as the influences of migration and cultural diversity or urban development or the role of television and popular culture on children's play activities. These changes were observed in the school playground, the site of much research on play across the twentieth century.

By the early twenty-first century, however, the place of children's play in our contemporary world has become a pressing public issue. The opportunities for children to play, and the activities that they undertake, are taken seriously by education and health professionals increasingly anxious about children's well-being and learning capacities. In the public arena, the work of authors including Tim Gill (2007) and activist organizations such as Play England, have highlighted the importance of play in the development of risk-taking and creativity among children. At an international level, government and medical studies are examining the relationship of children's games and play to such vexed issues as the growth of childhood obesity, how to provide optimum learning and teaching strategies, and the significance of the built environment and outdoor spaces on play and children's mental and physical development (e.g. Burdett and Whittaker 2005; Ginsberg 2007; Woolley *et al.* 2009; *The Future of Children* 2008).

From this broad international context of changing attitudes to play, we turn in the remainder of this chapter to look at the Australian context. Since the mid-twentieth century, Australian studies of playlore have both reflected and engaged with similar research occurring overseas, whilst Australian cultural institutions have been at the forefront of attempts to preserve and exhibit examples of children's intangible cultural heritage.

Collecting and displaying playlore

Despite an academic tradition in Australian universities that neglects the significance of folklore and its relations to cultural knowledge and evolving social practices, Australian research into playlore and Australian museum collections of play objects and the documentation of play have been highly significant in international terms. The National Library of Australia has an extensive repository of archival materials and sound recordings of playlore, as well as oral interviews with Australians reflecting on their childhood lives, in its Oral History and Folklore Collection (Davey 2002, 2011). Museum Victoria holds one of the world's largest collections of playlore, the Australian Children's Folklore Collection (ACFC). In 2004, this collection was placed on the UNESCO Australia Memory of the World Register as an essential element in the documentary heritage of the Australian nation, and by extension the cultural heritage of humanity.

The ACFC classifies children's folklore as either the folklore *of* children, or folklore *for and about* children, depending on whether the main persons transmitting such lore are children or adults. Folklore *of* children consists largely of playground lore, such as rhymes, games, taunts, jokes and riddles, which are passed on from one generation of children to another, adapted, altered, lost and resurrected. Folklore *for* and *about* children has many forms, including nursery rhymes, folk tales, finger and body plays, stories, proverbs, sayings, and pencil and paper games, that are passed on informally by adults and, like all traditions, are subject to change over time. The breadth and range of holdings in the ACFC serves as a potent illustration of the myriad ways children's folklore can be categorized under the more specific term 'playlore'. The collection contains more than 10,000 card files and other documents listing children's games, rhymes, riddles, jokes, superstitions and other kinds of children's folklore, together with photographs, audio-visual materials, play artefacts and a number of specialist collections of children's lore.[1]

These include, for example, the findings of the first major research project into the play of Indigenous Australian children, undertaken in the 1990s. The Aboriginal Children's Play Project involved oral history interviews with Indigenous Australians, who had mostly grown up in the state of Victoria, about their childhoods and the games that were played (Darian-Smith 2008). Ethical guidelines for the project, including a follow-up project to clarify permissions for the use of the materials, were carefully constructed in an attempt to avoid some of the cultural insensitivities that have plagued many projects involving Indigenous Australians (Fredericks 2008). The interviews crossed generations, and incorporated elderly people and children, thus providing glimpses of playlore that spanned several decades and occurred in a variety of urban and rural communities. In addition to these recordings, the Aboriginal Children's Play Project includes photographs of participants and some examples of children's handmade toys.

Museum Victoria has drawn upon the ACFC materials in a number of ways in its recent exhibitions. A children's playground was included in *Stories From a City* in the Australia Gallery at Melbourne Museum, which ran from 2000 to 2007. This included a structure that resembled the 'shelter shed', a common feature of school playgrounds in Australia, and a display of the containers and contents of school lunchboxes, as a means of narrating a story about the cultural diversity of Melbourne's population. A soundscape of children chanting counting-out rhymes also evoked the schoolyard, and there was a capacity for museum visitors to contribute details of the games and rhymes present in their childhood, adding to the development of the overall collection. In audience surveys, the 'Children's Playground' was rated one of the most popular of all segments in the larger exhibition, possibly because it provided the opportunity for adult visitors to reminisce about their own experiences of the schoolyard and share these with their children or grandchildren. A subsequent exhibition on the history of Melbourne, *The Melbourne Story*, also includes soundscapes of children's play, set this time in a late-nineteenth-century laneway. Adjacent displays include children's toys uncovered during archaeological excavations of inner Melbourne.

At the Immigration Museum, a campus of Museum Victoria, an exhibition that opened in 2011 entitled 'Identity: yours, mine, ours' incorporated children's songs and rhymes as a way of highlighting the everyday racism and name-giving that is part of children's culture. The redevelopment of Museum Victoria's Indigenous Cultures gallery, Bunjilaka, scheduled to open in 2013, will include a range of children's playthings and activities aimed at passing on, illustrating or supporting the transmission of Indigenous children's playlore. Other smaller, temporary showcases have highlighted other aspects of the collection at Melbourne Museum, including toys and other objects.

The ACFC grew out of research undertaken in the 1970s by scholars June Factor and Gwenda Davey, and remains a collection that has developed in line with ongoing research on the tangible and intangible cultural heritage of Australian children's playlore. Ongoing research into playlore has built upon and made active comparisons and contrasts with a rich vein of playlore research in Australia and internationally stretching back to the nineteenth century. *Play and Folklore*, the journal associated with the ACFC, has continued to provide a forum for international research into playlore for over 30 years.[2]

Australian research on play

Just as the repositories of playlore at major collecting institutions in Australia are significant in world terms, Australian research into the lore of the playground and children's games has also been internationally important. A survey of these Australian investigations reveals not just how the games of children have changed and remained constant across time, but also how the questions and methods of play researchers have shifted in response to wider social and educational concerns and conditions.

American scholar Dorothy Howard was the first to carefully document the play-lore of Australian children. She visited Australia in 1954–5, on a Fulbright Fellowship, with the aim of gathering information on children's games and culture and contrasting this with her ongoing research on play in the United States. Howard travelled extensively around the Australian continent in 1954–5, observing children at play in school playgrounds and speaking to their parents and teachers about games past and present. Her research was meticulously transcribed onto thousands of tiny index cards, which are preserved in the ACFC. Howard found an Australia on the cusp of change in the post-Second World War world, with children's culture shaped by the increasing production and consumption of toys, games, swap cards and magazines that were aimed specifically for them. One example of this was the way that plastic jacks were quickly replacing the real sheep's bones traditionally used in the game of knucklebones, despite the latter being preferred by children.

Alongside this child-centred consumer culture, the impact of popular culture on children's imaginative and language play was evident. Howard also found that there was a remarkable diversity in the rules of games and playground rhymes between geographical locations, reflecting very localized influences. Her published articles, anthologized in 2005, discussed the folklore of Australian children with studies of knucklebones, hopscotch, ball-bouncing, customs and rhymes, counting out, marbles and string games (Darian-Smith and Factor 2005).

Howard was a pioneer of playlore research, but by the 1960s and 1970s interest in folklore of all types had begun to grow around the world. In Australia the growth of more general folklore studies (Davey and Seal 2003) included increased attention on children's own culture and play. In 1969, the Melbourne academic Ian Turner published *Cinderella Dressed in Yella: Australian Children's Play-rhymes* (Turner 1969), the first

Figure 3.1 Dorothy Howard documenting children playing marbles game in 1955, from the Australian Children's Folklore Collection.

Source: Museum Victoria, photographer unknown.

major collection of Australian children's lore. Despite Turner's scholarly imprimatur, and his careful documentation of each entry, the book caused a furore because of its inclusion of 'improper rhymes'. Its authentic replication of the full frankness of language which is transmitted between children in the playground met with government disapproval, resulting in *Cinderella* being briefly banned by Australia's national postal service, a dramatic event which undoubtedly increased the book's impact in Australia. A second enlarged edition of *Cinderella* followed (Turner *et al.* 1978). In 1988 June Factor published a major scholarly study of the history of children's folklore, *Captain Cook Chased a Chook*.

If folklorists had begun taking an interest in playlore, educationalists slowly realized that a vibrant source of children's learning and development was occurring right under their noses, albeit outside the boundary of formal classroom learning. In the 1970s two physical education lecturers, Peter Lindsay and Denise Palmer, carried out extensive research into schoolyard play (Lindsay and Palmer 1981). Their significant study of nearly 5,000 children in 21 Brisbane primary schools indicated that among other findings, children's traditional games such as skipping were more beneficial than formal syllabus games on a number of measures, such as cardio-vascular endurance and rhythm.

As an ethnographer, Heather Russell approached her research with a slightly different emphasis. She conducted an anthropological study of an inner-Melbourne school in the 1980s, with a particular focus upon the role of cultural influences on play and friendship (Russell 1986). This ground-breaking work documented the transmission of new practices such as 'the Chinese flick' in marbles, and elaborated games of elastics in a multiethnic playground. In the 1990s, the Moe Folklife Project signalled the first detailed study of Australian playlore outside of major metropolitan cities, and involved fieldwork in primary schools in a brown-coal mining area of regional Victoria. Research highlighted the importance of chasing games. Twenty-six variations of 'pursuit games' were noted, some using physical features of the playground such as poles, barrels, seats and posts (Davey 1996).

Whilst the playlore studied by researchers in Australia from the 1950s encompassed many forms, including material artefacts such as handmade toys and somatic movements like dance routines, verbal play is also a primary aspect of children's cultural heritage. June Factor's dictionary *Kidspeak* (2000) added enormously to the body of knowledge about Australian children's vernacular speech and its uses. In the foreword to *Kidspeak*, Iona Opie wrote that 'perhaps the most fascinating aspect of the dictionary is the picture it gives of the social values of the child and teenage world ... The deployment of the latest slang can be a game in itself' (Factor 2000: vii). Factor commented on the influence of American television, films and music on children's slang: 'Australian adolescents in large numbers ... call each other *bro, dude* and *guy,* and words such as *mondo* and *carumba*, originally Italian and Spanish respectively, have entered our children's vocabulary' (Factor 2000: xxix).

Factor's research into 'kidspeak' and Russell's research into the transmission of games such as marbles and elastics within the school playground, noted the ways in which shifting cultural influences are reflected in Australian children's play, as the result of migration and the global transmission of media formats. One of the reasons that children's playlore is so susceptible to taking on and adapting a variety of cultural influences is that playlore itself is truly an international phenomenon, taking broadly similar forms in widely varying cultural contexts around the globe. Musicologist Kathryn Marsh has explored some of these similarities and differences in her work, which studies children's play in school playgrounds in many parts of the world, including Australia, the United Kingdom, the United States and Korea (Marsh 2008).

Since the collection of children's culture by Gomme and Douglas in Britain over a century ago, and Howard in 1950s' Australia, generations of folklorists have feared the demise of children's play rituals. In both past and contemporary times, this has been attributed to many influences, such as the disappearance of open spaces, adult interference and supervision, the 'couch potato' draw of television and the seduction of the computer, the increasing dominance of organized sports and physical education, and the general commodification of childhood.

But as Factor points out, children's playlore has always been characterized by both conservation and creativity, ever managing to reinvent tradition in the face of threats. It has remained resilient in the face of changing social contexts. Indeed children have always played, across all cultures and time periods (Factor 1988: 13–16). Even when the adult world undergoes economic and political crises, children obstinately retain and reinvent their play traditions. Through their playlore, children visibly demonstrate that they are engaged social actors, not passive subjects who are directed by adults – and children's agency is central to sociological studies of the changing world of childhood and the identity of children (James 1993; James *et al.* 1998; James and James 2004; Jenks 2005). Thus one of the important contributions of twenty-first-century studies of playlore is to demonstrate that despite pessimistic predications, the cultural heritage of children's play remains vibrant.

The *Childhood, Tradition and Change* project

The most recent study of Australian children's playlore is the *Childhood, Tradition and Change* project, the first publicly funded survey of play in Australian primary school playgrounds. The research involved fieldwork at 19 primary schools across every state and territory in Australia, where children's activities during free play periods were

Figure 3.2 Fieldworker Judy McKinty interviews children about their games and play.

Source: *Childhood, Tradition and Play* project.

recorded. The multidisciplinary research team included historians, folklorists, early childhood educators, heritage experts and ethnographic fieldworkers, with support from the National Library of Australia and Museum Victoria. With a focus on investigating the questions of 'tradition' and 'change' in play practices and language, the project aimed to compare its findings with those of previous research studies on play and the existing documentation of playlore held in public collections (see Darian-Smith and Henningham 2011). The data gathered will be preserved alongside existing collections of children's material, cultural and ephemeral heritage in the National Library of Australia and Museum Victoria.[3]

The final report for the project analysed both dynamism and continuities in Australian playlore. Since the 1950s, a plethora of factors have changed the conditions for play at school, including the transformation of physical environments of school grounds through landscaping or play equipment, and the school regulations concerning what games are played. Although gender segregation was common in the schoolyards of the 1950s and 1960s, this practice has largely been abandoned by school authorities in favour of age-based segregation, to protect younger children from the rougher play of older children. Some contemporary school rules contain an imposing list of forbidden activities, such as playing with sticks or climbing trees. But other schools have expansive philosophies of play that explicitly recognize the developmental outcomes of children's games.

Some variations to playlore are representative of wider changes to Australian society, such as the increasing cultural and ethnic diversity of the nation. The repertoire of schoolyard games has expanded with successive waves of migration, such as the introduction of a game involving rocks and pebbles which girls of Sudanese origin have brought to Australian schools. Play is often an important means by which migrant children are socialized.

New media and technologies have also influenced Australian playlore. Howard conducted her research in the mid-1950s, immediately prior to the introduction of television to Australia in 1956. In the early twenty-first century, children regularly borrow from contemporary popular culture as the inspiration for their imaginary play, including television shows such as *Australian Idol* or movies such as the *Harry Potter* series. New technology and computers also inform play, creating a new language for traditional games. At one school, the favoured method to ask for a break in a game is to hold up the index and middle fingers together and yell 'Pause' (like the pause button on a DVD player). Similarly, if something needs to be repeated the players shout 'Rewind'.

Certain aspects of playlore remained strikingly consistent over time. Games such as hopscotch and marbles were still observed in Australian playgrounds, though with lesser frequency than previously. Active running play such as chasey and ball games remain central to play, though the rules of some schools place restrictions on their occurrence due to safety concerns. Across Australia clapping, chanting and rhyming games are still a feature of most playgrounds, though each generation varies the popular cultural references.

The rich literature of earlier playlore research, Australian and international, enables comparisons and contrasts in children's play to be drawn across time. For example,

Figure 3.3 Girls playing a skipping and rhyme game with elastics.
Source: *Childhood, Tradition and Play* project.

the *Childhood, Tradition and Change* project found that the form and prevalence of 'acting' or 'story' games have changed over recent decades. In their 1969 classic, *Children's Games in Street and Playground*, the Opies described 'acting games' – what we have called 'story games' – as 'games in which particular stories are enacted with set dialogue'. Such games include 'Old Man in the Well', 'Ghosties in the Garret', 'Old Mother Grey' and 'Fox and Chickens' (Opie and Opie 1969: 305–17). Howard also identified a number of story games. Following her visit to a Tasmanian school in 1954, a number of Year 6 pupils sent her compositions about their favourite game. A number of these games involved complex role-plays and routines, such as 'Three Jolly Welshmen', 'Zoo Train' and 'Stalking through the Light-houses'.[4]

Fewer story games were recorded in contemporary school playgrounds. Children today are inundated with stories generated by popular media channels, perhaps contributing to a decline in 'story games' devised by children themselves that have a set dialogue. Children do play games based on characters such as Harry Potter, but they are also likely to invent their own games, with allocated roles and activities. A particularly interesting activity in one school by four Year 3 and 4 boys involved both fantasy and physical activity: the boys had dug a 'city' with small caves and temples where invisible children would be taught spells and potions. Some, but not all, of the boys were wizards. The city had a mayor (an earthworm who had entered the site) and a military base. 'Digging in the dirt' is a favourite activity, one that is not always encouraged by schools.

There are other changes to the spaces in which play takes place. Even by the mid-1950s Howard noticed that 'Playways in Australia are changing as play space becomes more and more congested and disappears in city areas, and as open paddocks for unsupervised play become well-groomed playing fields for organized athletic activities and professional sports' (Darian-Smith and Factor 2005: 82). But whereas in the mid-twentieth century most children's play occurred on streets, the leading location for children's traditional play in the early twenty-first century is the primary school playground. Shifting physical environments for children's play are a result of increased motor vehicle traffic on streets, a trend towards smaller or non-existent backyards around Australian homes, and parental fears about 'stranger danger', which often inhibit children's independent mobility (Pascoe 2009).

One of the challenges facing the *Childhood, Tradition and Change* project was that children's playlore research now operates in a social context of considerably heightened concern around children's safety. Careful processes of establishing research credentials and appropriate ethical methodological procedures are important in projects that involve working closely with children. Scholars such as Frank Furedi (2002) have documented rising levels of fear in the Western world, one consequence of which is greater anxiety concerning children. This may also affect the conditions under which children play in the school playground, with some restrictions imposed by the fear of accidents and the potential threat of litigation. For example, playing with sticks is sometimes forbidden, which means that children can no longer construct cubby houses and other play structures. There are schools which have attempted to ban running in the playground, though in the words of one child observed in the *Childhood, Tradition and Change* project, 'they might as well try to stop us breathing'. Tim Gill, one of the United Kingdom's leading thinkers on childhood and a strong advocate for children's play, has written extensively on the impact of adult risk aversion upon children. He argues that children need some measure of risk and danger for their personal development and in keeping with this position he has actively agitated for adults to be wary of over-protecting children (Gill 2007).

The very real pitfall that has dogged studies of playlore since the nineteenth century is that through documenting children's play, adults may advocate nostalgic or romanticized understandings of childhood. These understandings may either ignore the perpetually dynamic nature of playlore or seek to censor the prejudices and vulgarities that also circulate amongst children. Gill is by no means a simple antiquarian, lamenting the 'good old days'. He is actively interested in children's electronic and online play. Children observed for the *Childhood, Tradition and Change* project played many computer, video and Wii games and used hand-held electronic toys such as Tamagotchis and Nintendo DS consoles. These new media forms are changing the nature of playlore, and perhaps to balance this some Australian schools are encouraging traditional children's play.

Indeed, pedagogical and behavioural management strategies currently in use in primary schools are actively incorporating forms of play as a tool. One school in a low socio-economic area which was studied as part of the *Childhood, Tradition and Change* project has undergone a deliberate transformation in its playground culture. This school operates a system of 'positive play', a program introduced by a new principal to manage a previously hostile playground environment where bullying and even violent behaviour regularly occurred. The playground gradually became a safe place for students, but the legacy of past practices had severely disrupted children's play patterns. There had been a break in the continuity of the transmission of cultural lore and play traditions between children. These forms of knowledge and cultural heritage were simply not being passed on, and many children did not know how to play any of the games usually found in schoolyards. Some of the teachers began teaching games they remembered from their own childhoods, including instructing the children on how to make rules and take turns in games. The physical education curriculum of this school now includes a component where students are taught the social skills and rules of games so that children can interact positively in the playground. There has been explicit encouragement for students to be actively and creatively engaged during recess and lunchtime, with some students taking on the role of peer-tutors. The school has a policy of some teacher-led physical activity every morning, which includes the playing of games.

More generally, in all primary schools in Australia there is an emphasis on children's safety and conflict management. Games deemed physically dangerous or having the potential to cause conflict are often banned (such as 'Brandy'). Forbidden activities may also include running or chasey, although children claimed that they played such games anyway. Although there remains an issue of whether adults should interfere in playlore, which at its core is children's own cultural heritage, there are a number of other Australian schools where active play programmes have successfully improved the culture of the playground. For example, Russell's *Play and Friendships* research from the mid-1980s had been carried out at the invitation of the school as an investigation into what was seen as a dysfunctional school playground. As a result of Russell's study, the school introduced a highly successful play programme which is still carried out today. Every classroom has a play box with balls, bats, ropes and elastics which children take outside at break times. The school also has a number of sandpits for creative play with 'loose materials' (Russell 1986).

As well as these rescue operations, there are many schools in Australia where children's playlore is flourishing unaided by adults, or sometimes assisted by adult provision of a sympathetic environment. One new school in rural Victoria, relocated after a fire, chose its new site because of the adjacent pine plantation. This was at the insistence of parents and teachers, who recognized this as a magical place for children to build cubby houses, as they had done at the old school.

One aspect of children's play which has not changed is the appreciation of a satisfying game, and the willingness to change rules to accommodate weaker players. Both the children who wrote to Howard in the 1950s and those who were recorded in the recent project indicated the cooperative nature of much play. In 1954 a 12-year-old boy explained the game of 'Donkey', where a ball must be caught on the first bounce.

He wrote that 'some of the little children play. They have two bounces, because they can't catch very well and they become Donkey quicker than the big ones do'. In 2009, two much younger girls (from Year 1) were heard discussing the rules of 'the ghost game', a game which they had invented: 'the game goes like there's bad dogs and there's good persons and they've got three chances and the kinders [kindergarten-aged children] that play they've got five because they're only young'.[5]

Children will also adjust the rules of a game if 'star players' are getting more than their fair share. Lindsay and Palmer described the game of 'continuous cricket':

> The layout and rules of the game are simple and the players readily adapt them to suit themselves . . . When the game slows down because individual players are difficult to get out, the players simply lengthen the distance of the run.
>
> (Lindsay and Palmer 1981: 25–6)

The four years of extensive documentation undertaken for the *Childhood, Tradition and Change* project have proven the persistence of a rich tradition of children's playlore in Australia, a tradition which is also international in its scope. Major playlore research projects conducted elsewhere, such as the UK study *Children's Playground Games and Songs in the New Media Age*,[6] certainly demonstrate that children's play has changed vastly over recent years, but also the many surprising ways in which playlore – despite its dynamism – conserves traditional elements from the past. The forms of playlore may change over time, as do the cultural references that children make to the adult world around them. But as far back as research has been conducted, playlore has consistently remained a vibrant expression of children's cultural heritage. Whilst the differing inputs of adults and children in material and spatial forms of heritage are sometimes difficult to separate, playlore remains a form of heritage that is expressive of children's own collective and individual cultures, operating alongside but largely autonomously from the strictures of adult interference.

Acknowledgements

Childhood, Tradition and Change: A national study of the historical and contemporary practices and significance of Australian children's playlore was funded in 2007–11 by the Australian Research Council (ARC) through the Linkage Project scheme (LP0663282), with additional financial support from the National Library of Australia and Museum Victoria. The research team included scholars at the University of Melbourne: Kate Darian-Smith (Chief Investigator), June Factor and Nikki Henningham (Project Officer); at Deakin University: William Logan and Gwenda Davey; at Curtin University: Graham Seal; at Museum Victoria: Richard Gillespie; at the National Library of Australia: Margy Burn and Kevin Bradley. The project website is located at: http://ctac.esrc.unimelb.edu.au/

We are grateful for the assistance of June Factor and Deborah Tout-Smith (Museum Victoria) in the preparation of this chapter.

Notes

1 For more information see http://museumvictoria.com.au/discoverycentre/infosheets/ australian-childrens-folklore-collection/.
2 The journal, *Play and Folklore*, has since 1981 published historical and contemporary material of Australian and overseas origin, and all back copies are fully indexed and available online. See http://museumvictoria.com.au/about/books-and-journals/journals/play-and-folklore/.
3 Fieldworkers described nearly 400 games, which have been organized into 38 categories of play. Games were documented using video and sound recordings, photographs and text descriptions. See http://ctac.esrc.unimelb.edu.au/.
4 These compositions are held in the Australian Children's Folklore Collection, Museum Victoria.
5 Data from Dorothy Howard Paper (1954–5), Australian Children's Folklore Collection, Museum Victoria; and from the Childhood, Tradition and Change (2007–11) research database.
6 This project is described by Andrew Burn in his chapter in the present volume.

References

Bishop, J. and Curtis, M. (2001) *Play Today in the Primary School Playground*, Buckingham: Open University Press.
Burdett, H. and Whittaker, R. (2005) Resurrecting Free Play in Young Children: Looking beyond Fitness and Fatness to Attention, Affiliation and Affect, *Archives of Pediatrics and Adolescent Medicine* 159. Online. Available: http://www.childrenandnature.org/downloads/ Burdette_LookingBeyond.pdf (accessed 6 January 2012).
Childhood, Tradition and Change (2011) Online. Available: http://ctac.esrc.unimelb.edu.au (accessed 16 April 2012).
Darian-Smith, K. (2008) Oral Histories of Childhood and Playlore: The Aboriginal Children's Play Project, Museum Victoria, *Aboriginal History*, 32: 146–50.
Darian-Smith, K. and Factor, J. (eds) (2005) *Child's Play: Dorothy Howard and the Folklore of Australian Children*, Melbourne: Museum Victoria.
Darian-Smith, K. and Henningham, N. (2011) *Childhood, Tradition and Change Final Report*. Available at http://ctac.esrc.unimelb.edu.au/objects/project-pubs/FinalReport.pdf (accessed 6 July 2012).
Davey, G. (1996) *The Moe Folklife Project: A Final Project Report prepared for the Department of Communication and the Arts and the National Library of Australia*, Melbourne: National Centre of Australian Studies, Monash University.
Davey, G. (2002) *Fish Trout, You're Out: Children's Folklore in the Oral History and Folklore Section*, Canberra: National Library of Australia.
Davey, G. (2011) 'Substance and Style in Electronic Recording of Australian Children's Folklore', in G. Seal and J. Gall (eds) *Antipodean Traditions: Australian Folklore in the 21st Century*, Perth: Black Swan Press.
Davey, G. and Seal, G. (2003) *A Guide to Australian Folklore: From Ned Kelly to Aeroplane Jelly*, Sydney: Kangaroo Press (Simon & Schuster).
Douglas, N. (1931) *London Street Games*, 2nd rev. ed., London: Chatto and Windus.
Factor, J. (1988) *Captain Cook Chased a Chook: Children's Folklore in Australia*, Ringwood, Victoria: Penguin Books Australia.
Factor, J. (2000) *Kidspeak: A Dictionary of Australian Children's Words, Expressions and Games*, Parkville: Melbourne University Press.

Fredericks, B.L. (2008) So, You Want To Do Oral History With Aboriginal Australians . . . Old Stories, New Ways (2), *Oral History Association of Australia Journal*, 30: 22–4.

Furedi, F. (2002) *Culture of Fear: Risk-taking and the Morality of Low Expectation*, London: Continuum.

Gill, T. (2007) *No Fear: Growing Up in a Risk-Aversive Society*, London: Calouste Gulbenkian Foundation.

Ginsberg, K.R. (2007) 'The Importance of Play in Promoting Healthy Child Development and Maintaining Strong Parent-Child Bonds', *Pediatrics* 119: 1. Online. Available: http://aappolicy. aappublications.org/cgi/content/full/pediatrics;119/1/182 (accessed 19 January 2012).

Gomme, B. (1984) *The Traditional Games of England, Scotland, and Ireland.* Reprinted. London: Thames and Hudson.

James, A. (1993) *Childhood Identities: Self and Social Relationships in the Experience of the Child*, Edinburgh: Edinburgh University Press.

James, A. and James, A.L. (2004) *Constructing Childhood: Theory, Policy, and Social Practice*, New York: Palgrave Macmillan.

James, A., Jenks, C. and Prout, A. (1998) *Theorizing Childhood*, Cambridge: Polity Press.

Jenks, C. (2005) *Childhood*, 2nd ed. London: Routledge.

Knapp, M. and Knapp, H. (1976) *One Potato, Two Potato: The Secret Education of American Children*, New York: W.W. Norton & Company.

Lindsay, P. and Palmer, D. (1981) *Playground Game Characteristics of Brisbane Primary School Children*, Commonwealth Department of Education, Education Research and Development Committee (ERDC) Report No. 28, Canberra: Australian Government Publishing Service.

Lowenstein, W. (1988) *Improper Play Rhymes of Australian Children*, 3rd ed. Kuranda: Rams Skull Press.

Marsh, K. (2008) *The Musical Playground: Global Tradition and Change in Children's Songs and Games*, New York: Oxford University Press.

Opie, I. (1993) *The People in the Playground*, Oxford: Oxford University Press.

Opie, I. and Opie, P. (1959) *The Lore and Language of Schoolchildren*, London: Oxford University Press.

Opie, I. and Opie, P. (1969) *Children's Games in Street and Playground: Catching, Seeking, Hunting, Racing, Duelling, Exerting, Daring, Guessing, Acting, Pretending*, London: Oxford University Press.

Pascoe, C. (2009) 'Be Home By Dark: Childhood Freedoms and Adult Fears in 1950s Victoria', *Australian Historical Studies*, 40(2): 215–31.

Russell, H. (assisted by G. Davey and J. Factor) (1986) *Play and Friendships in a Multi-Cultural Playground*, Melbourne: Australian Children's Folklore Publications, Institute of Early Childhood Development.

Sutton-Smith, B. (1972) *The Folkgames of Children*, Austin: University of Texas Press.

The Future of Children (2008) Children and Electronic Media Special Issue, 18(1).

Turner, I. (1969) *Cinderella Dressed in Yella: Australian Children's Play-Rhymes*, Melbourne: Heinemann Educational.

Turner, I., Factor, J. and Lowenstein, W. (eds) (1978) *Cinderella Dressed in Yella: Australian Children's Play-Rhymes*, 2nd ed., Melbourne: Heinemann Educational.

UNESCO (2003) *Convention for the Safeguarding of Intangible Cultural Heritage*. Online. Available: http://unesdoc.unesco.org/images/0013/001325/132540e.pdf (accessed 14 April 2012).

UNESCO. *Australia Memory of the World Register*. Online. Available: www.amw.org.au/register (accessed 2 February 2012).

Woolley, H., Pattacini, L. and Somerset Ward, A. (2009) *Children and the Natural Environment: Experiences, Influences and Interventions*, Natural England Commissioned Reports 026. Online. Available: http://publications.naturalengland.org.uk/file/61087 (accessed 25 August 2012).

Chapter 4

The case of the Wildcat Sailors

The hybrid lore and multimodal languages of the playground

Andrew Burn

Childlore is a contradictory, magpie culture. The picture that emerged from the work of British folklorists Iona and Peter Opie testifies to this (Opie and Opie 1959, 1985). The integrity and attention to detail of their research compels them both to celebrate the continuity of tradition, and to reveal the hybridity of cultural influences which children draw on to compose, adapt and ceaselessly transform the games, songs, rhymes and rituals they perform. The concept of 'childlore' is effectively a fusing of folklore with childhood, and it implies the passing on of a corpus of folkloric material through forms of oral transmission. However, when it becomes clear, as it did to the Opies, that this body of material draws as much on children's media cultures as on traditional games and songs, then notions of tradition and lore become problematic. Furthermore, the collection of this material has tended to privilege language: the words of the games, songs, chants and jokes. This is partly for practical reasons: the Opies began by noting down the words, and only later moved on to transcribe melodies of songs. It is partly also because of a linguistic approach to folklore, however, which seeks to establish the progress of tradition through historical comparison of textual variants. However, the culture of play and playgrounds combines many elements to make new meanings out of old resources: words, melody, gesture, dance, objects and artefacts both found and manufactured, and the built and natural environment. This complex mix of the intangible legacies of word, song and game structure with the tangible assets of the immediate context is what constitutes the cultural moment for the child.

This chapter will explore some of this odd combination of continuity and hybridity, from two angles. One will consider the provenance of the cultural forms found on today's playgrounds. The other will look at the combination of semiotic modes employed by the children. These considerations have been amongst those at the centre of a recent research project in the UK, which has both explored the Opies' legacy and sought to update the picture through ethnographies of two playgrounds. The project, entitled Children's Playground Games and Songs in the Age of New Media, was funded by the UK's Arts and Humanities Research Council. I will begin by describing the project, in order to provide a context for the chapter, and also to indicate briefly some main outcomes. I will then move on to consider one detailed example, of three girls working out a dance routine on the playground during a lunch break.

Children's playground games and songs in the age of new media[1]

This project was inspired initially by a collection donated by Iona Opie to the National Sound Archive at the British Library.[2] 'The Opie Collection of Children's Games and Songs' was created from the late 1960s through to the early 1980s and captures the songs, games, jokes, rhymes and voices of children from across the country.

One of the insights of the Opies' work was to look beyond earlier assumptions that the culture of the playground was purely a folkloric culture. While their dominant interest was, perhaps, in the traditions of oral culture, and to the folkloric elements of playground games and songs, they also recognized that children drew inventively on anything that came to hand, including their media cultures. In *The Lore and Language of Schoolchildren* (1959), various examples are cited, and they reflect, of course, the media of the time, including for example the 'Ballad of Davy Crockett', a hit song on the radio in 1955, and the theme song of the hugely popular TV mini-series imported from the US in the 1950s. By the 1980s, when *The Singing Game* was published (Opie and Opie 1985), the media influences reflect in particular the pop song culture of the time. The Opie archive at the British Library includes, for example, a group of girls in 1974 in London's Coram Fields, performing the 1974 hit 'Ma, He's Making Eyes at Me' by Lena Zavaroni, who won the popular television talent show *Opportunity Knocks* in the same year.

Taking our cue from the Opies' eclectic approach to the influences of playground lore, then, our project's central question asked what the relation was between playground games and songs and their media cultures. We assumed that, in the 30 years or so since the collection was made that media cultures would, like folkloric repertoires, have both remained the same in some respects (films, TV shows, pop songs, adverts and comics), and have changed markedly in others (computer games, social media and mobile phones) as a result of the expansion of new media technologies in children's lives, and a general social shift from outdoor play into the media cultures of the bedroom.

We went about the investigation into new media in children's play in four ways. First, we interrogated the Opie archive, looking for examples of the influence of media cultures beyond those cited in *The Singing Game*. The archive contains a good deal of material never published before, revealing some new themes: the more extreme scatological and taboo-busting songs and rhymes the Opies collected; the wide range of variations on 'classic' singing and other games; and the great variety of media influences that informed the culture of play. This revealed a considerably broader media landscape than emerges in the published work, making reference to what were then popular TV drama series (*The Saint*), peak-time game shows (Larry Grayson's *Shut That Door*), talent shows (*Opportunity Knocks*) and, of course, pop music such as Abba (Jopson 2010). It is not clear why these references to contemporary media cultures were not included in publications such as *The Singing Game*, though a reasonable assumption is that the Opies' interest lay in the development of tradition: the growth over time of durable forms of childlore. In the chapter in *The Singing Game* entitled

'Impersonations and Dance Routines', for example, the songs and performances included are all adaptations and transformations of older popular songs: 'She Wears Red Feathers' from 1952 (Opie and Opie 1985: 425); 'Sunny Side Up' from 1929 (Opie and Opie 1985: 429); The 'Tennessee WigWalk' from 1953 (Opie and Opie 1985: 432). Meanwhile, performances of the hits of the 1970s are omitted; though it is notable that the Opies found them worth recording and archiving.

Second, we conducted a two-year ethnographic study of two school playgrounds, one in London, one in Sheffield.[3] These studies, again, produced rich and varied data demonstrating how children integrate their playground and media cultures, one example of which will be explored in more detail in the second section of this chapter. The ethnographic study has in many ways extended the observation and recording of play to be found in the history of this field of study. It has recorded many instances of games, songs and rhymes recognizable as latter-day versions of the Opie 'canon', demonstrating continuity as well as change. Versions of many of the clapping games published in *The Singing Game* were found (Figure 4.1), as well as examples of counting-out rhymes, skipping games, chasing games and ball games. At the same time, it was clear that some genres had diminished: hopscotch, conkers and French skipping,[4] for example (though reports of hopscotch were documented on the Sheffield playground).

Figure 4.1 A clapping game at Monteney Primary School, Sheffield.

Meanwhile, the project found many new instances of play, documenting in particular a rich variety of play informed by children's media cultures (computer games, reality TV, pop songs, musicals and films), and pretend play scenarios which often intermingle domestic and fantasy settings: families, superheroes, fairies, witches and zombies. The studies also conducted surveys of the children in the two schools, partly to get a sense of the favourite games of all the children (rather than just the ones who are filmed or interviewed); and partly to get a picture of the media cultures that lie beyond the playground, in children's media consumption at home. The forms of play particular to the bedroom, and not possible on the playground, are those involving the technologies of new media: DVD players, MP3 players, PCs and game consoles.

Third, we made a documentary film of the playground games, charting the range of types and genres, and the social contexts in which they occurred, and interviewing children about them. The 50-minute documentary film *Ipidipidation, My Generation* (Mitchell, forthcoming) draws on ethnographic and observational methods and provides a detailed overview of playground culture and the diversity and variety of forms of play in the two primary school playgrounds in London and Sheffield. In doing so it follows in the tradition of filming and photographing children's games, such as *The Dusty Bluebells*, the 1971 film of Belfast children's street games by David Hammond.

The documentary film, like the rest of our project, updates the current scholarship, showing how children draw both on the long historical tradition of games passed from child to child, generation to generation and from adult to child; and also on the resources of their own contemporary media cultures. Like the website and the playground research, the film aims to give children's voices the dominant role in describing and interpreting their play.

Fourth, we developed a prototype for a computer game adaptation, the 'Game-Catcher'. This adapts the motion sensitive videogame controllers of the Nintendo Wii and Microsoft Kinect to create an application which allows the recording, playback, archiving and analysis of playground games in 3D.

This had two main aims. One was to develop a proof of concept of a system which would provide researchers in the arts and humanities with new and improved ways of archiving and analysing movement-based activities. The archiving of playground games currently relies upon video, or previously, as in the Opie and Damian Webb collections, upon audio recording supplemented by still photographs (see description of the Damian Webb collection below). These provide an incomplete record – even video only records the events from a single viewpoint and can therefore leave details obscured or off-screen. The Game-Catcher avoids these shortcomings by recording the position in 3D space of every joint. By recording the raw data, the movement can then be viewed from any angle and any distance and other alternative forms of visualization – for instance tracing the path taken by the hands throughout the entire game – also become possible.

In parallel with this, the Game-Catcher had a second aim, which was to develop a new and innovative type of computer game. This exercise is partly intended as a form of cultural intervention. We have become too used to cordoning off these 'traditional' games and songs as if they represent some purer folkloric form of play, untainted by the commercial interests of the media, and placing them in opposition to electronic or computer games, which embody a more modern and more sedentary form. These polarized popular views relate to historic constructions of idealized childhood and their opposite, childhood as uncivilized or as in a state of original sin (James *et al.* 1998; Buckingham 2000). By developing a computer game version of a playground clapping game, we were able to explore the tensions between these fields, as well as the areas for overlap and both actual and potential synergies (clapping games were chosen as they contain fast movement within a constrained physical space, thereby offering a suitable level of technical challenge).

Finally, we developed a website at the British Library: 'Playtimes: a century of children's playground games and rhymes'.[5] This was intended to display selections from the Opie archive alongside samples of play video-recorded during the ethnographic studies. In this way, we intended to represent the historical changes and continuities evident across the Opie collection and today's playgrounds. In fact, we have discovered new material during the project which has significantly enhanced the content of the website. Most importantly, we have collaborated with the Bodleian Library in Oxford, to whom the Opies donated their manuscript archive; and the Pitt Rivers Museum, also in Oxford, which holds an important collection of the folklorist and photographer Father Damian Webb.[6] The Bodleian collection provided valuable examples of written accounts of games sent by children and teachers to the Opies; while the Damian Webb collection provided examples of high-quality audio recordings from the mid-twentieth century, as well as strikingly beautiful black-and-white photographs of children at play (Figure 4.2).

The organization of the Playtimes website content proved to be a valuable part of the research collaboration in its own right. Two examples will make this point effectively. One is the process by which the collection of material was categorized. The project team was well aware of earlier taxonomies, both in the work of the Opies themselves, and in later publications (e.g. Bishop and Curtis 2001). However, a series of categories appropriate for the combination of historical and contemporary material represented on the website needed to be developed, and the project team and children's panels negotiated these categories over several months (Figure 4.3). The categories are not dissimilar from those used by earlier scholars: the main difference is the children's influence on the terminology, so that adult terms such as the Opies' category of 'Buffoonery' (Opie and Opie 1985: 391ff.) are avoided. The eventual list was:

- Clapping Games
- Skipping Games
- Ball Games
- Games with Things
- Running Around
- Pretend Play
- Singing and Dancing
- Jokes and Rude Rhymes
- Counting-out Rhymes

Figure 4.2 Boys playing marbles, Leyland, Lancashire, UK. Photo by Fr Damian Webb, 1967. Courtesy Pitt Rivers Museum, University of Oxford [2003.88.2626].

Figure 4.3 The homepage of the Playtimes website at the British Library, showing the categories of play around which the site is organized.

A second example of negotiation, this time between researchers, is the process which produced the to-camera pieces spoken by the poet and children's author Michael Rosen, who kindly agreed to act as presenter for these introductions to the categories of play on the route through the site intended mainly for adults. The script for these pieces was contributed to by members of the research team, then edited in collaboration with Rosen and with Steve Roud, the historian of folklore (Roud 2010).

Studies of childlore have tended to be *about* children rather than *with* them, but this project differed by trying to actively involve children in curating the online presence. The design of the website has been an innovative form of library exhibition, in terms of the extensive consultation carried out with children in our partner schools. We have held workshops with the panels of children in the schools (essentially the school councils, representing all classes), and have involved them in three ways: as researchers, designers and curators. They have contributed significantly to the research and collection of their own games. They have contributed concept drawings for the visual design and navigational structure of the website. They have produced animations which introduce the nine categories of play in the children's route through the site, serving as a form of curatorial interpretation (see Potter (2009) on children's curatorial practices). Children's culture is commonly observed, collected, interpreted, curated and archived by adults: these animations, along with other elements of the project such as the involvement of children in the videoing of playground games, was an attempt to redress this imbalance. The animations incorporate historical information gathered by the children through interviews with Steve Roud; and with their own parents, as well as spoken comments on, and visual representations of, the contemporary forms of play they have found on their own playgrounds.

This, then, provides the 'big picture', and hopefully gives some sense of the scope of the Children's Playground Games project. A further point to make, perhaps, is its inter-disciplinarity. Childlore has been studied from a range of different angles in the past: psychology, linguistics, sociology, folklore studies and music. The team in this project represented media and cultural studies, computer science, musico-ethnology, folklore studies and the sociology of childhood. This brings together different methods and theoretical frameworks in ways that can be uncomfortable; though my own experience of it has been an extremely productive sense of scholarly exchange, useful challenge to old preconceptions and settled conventions, and generally a rounder sense of what we have in front of us and how we might interpret it. With this in view, the next section will look at an example of a play episode that occurred during a lunch break in the London school.

Wildcats, sailors, Egyptians and Michael Jackson: improvization, composition and cultural provenance

This episode was filmed by the London ethnographer, Chris Richards. One of Chris's approaches was to film very long takes, aiming to capture more of the context of the games and other practices than would be the case if the recording was confined to the few minutes of a particular game, as most of the Opie recordings are. In this case, the boundaries of the form of play involved run for the full length of the half-hour lunch break.

In the foreground of the film, we see three Year 3 (7–8 years) girls, Diella, Rachel and Alia,[7] working out a dance routine. The sequence seems instantly recognizable as a cheerleader routine, partly because the girls are using cheerleading pompoms, one of the play resources available on this playground; and partly because the movements of the routine resemble, at first glance, generic moves of cheerleading.

It is also obvious that the development of the routine is happening partly by experiment, repetition and incremental addition of new moves; and partly by the direction of one of the girls, Diella, who seems to be in a lead role, even a kind of peer teaching role.

There is a strong sense of commitment. The girls stick at the routine for the whole lunchbreak, unconcerned by the (extremely loud) noise around them, by a wide range of other kinds of play also visible in the frame, and by the occasional disruption of a boy charging through their space.

Meanwhile, among the other play activities happening around them, in the background of the video record can be seen a succession of young girls playing clapping games. This genre is a well-documented form of game, strongly represented in *The Singing Game*, one of the forms growing in popularity in the recent history of playground culture (Roud 2010), and well-represented in our collection of games from these two playgrounds (Bishop 2010). The words and tune can just be heard over the noise of the playground, even though they are further from the camera than the cheerleaders. It is the well-known clapping game, 'A Sailor Went to Sea, Sea, Sea' (Opie and Opie 1985; Curtis 2004).

At first glance, then, it seems that the dual subject of our enquiry, the 'traditional' games of the playground and those derived from children's media cultures, are entirely separate here. Towards the end of the lunch break, however, the cheerleaders move to a different spot, and their routine changes into 'A Sailor Went to Sea', but still with the cheerleading pompoms. It appears to be a brief hybridizing of forms, perhaps as a kind of performative joke – there is a good deal of laughter and exaggeratedly raucous delivery of the tune and words. However, it represents two of the ways in which Bishop *et al.* propose that children employ references to media sources: by *synthesizing* them with established games, and by *parody* (Bishop *et al.* 2006).

As we studied the video sequence, our first concern was where the cheerleading sequence had come from. This was the first question in a follow-up interview, and the girls confirmed that the sequence was informed by the Wildcats chorus from *High School Musical* (2006), one of the most popular film choices indicated by girls in the survey.

It might seem, then, to a casual adult observer, that this sequence is no more or less than a form of straightforward imitation: three girls copying a routine from their favourite film. We checked the video of their performance against the Wildcats chorus in the film of *High School Musical*. The style, tempo and rhythm of the piece were very similar. To see exactly how similar, we extracted the audio-track from the film sequence and laid it under the video of the girls' performance. It fitted exactly, both in rhythm and tempo. Clearly, then, these elements (and possibly the words and tune, which they might have been singing), were derived from the film. However, none of the movements resembled those performed by the girls. What, then, was their origin? Were they just 'made up'?

In a later interview, the girls offer some clues. Rachel tells the interviewer that they had just been doing dance in PE (which is where Dance in the English National Curriculum is located):

Rachel: I think we might have had PE just in front of it so we did some dancing or something, so it might have got us into . . .

Researcher: Started you thinking about kind of moving in a certain way.

Diella: Yeah. We got started like we were trying to do something then we got . . . started dancing then we came up with the idea.

Two of the girls, Diella and Rachel, say they like dancing in their own time. The third, Alia, doesn't. Diella is particularly enthusiastic:

Diella: I dance anywhere

       . . .

Diella: I dance in discos anywhere. I'm not really shy.

Rachel: Last year when we were in our Year 2 well one of our teachers let us stay in and put some Abba music on and some people just stayed up there and did dancing to loads of different music and things.

Diella: We took off our shoes.

Researcher: Do you do that on the playground sometimes too? Make up . . .

Diella: Yeah yeah.

Diella is regarded by the other two as an expert, a leader, even a teacher in this field:

Rachel: Remember a few days ago that they were teaching

Diella: Yeah they were trying to learn a Michael Jackson song.

Rachel: . . . yeah she's trying to teach us some dancing.

Researcher: Who was?

Diella: Me.

Researcher: You were trying . . . to dance like Michael Jackson?

Diella: And the song yeah because they wanted to know 'Billie Jean'.

Alia: So she started teaching us then.

Her interest in Michael Jackson continues as a theme of the interview, which provides some idea of the provenance of these songs and dance routines:

Diella: I know all of the song of 'You Are Not Alone'.

Researcher: 'Billie Jean?'

Diella: No, 'You Are Not Alone'.

Voices:	'You Are Not Alone'.
Diella:	All of it.
Researcher:	Is that a Michael Jackson song?
Diella:	Yeah. I know nearly all of the songs of him.
Researcher:	Where did you?
Diella:	Sometimes . . . I just learned them, I don't know. I hear them in everywhere.
Researcher:	Do you watch MTV, is that how you see his dance moves as well?
Diella:	No . . .
Researcher:	YouTube?
Diella:	No me and my cousins we go on the computer because our favourite singer like Michael Jackson from the moment. So we've seen lots of videos and we just get the moves.
Researcher:	And then you teach them to Alia and Rachel?
Diella:	Yeah because they want to know.
Researcher:	Can you do Moon Walking and everything?
Diella:	Yeah.

It is notable here that Diella feels that she learns this material rather mysteriously, in a way which recalls the cumulative processes of accretion through which oral tradition works: 'I don't know, I just learned them. I hear them in everywhere'. At the same time, she is also able to give the example of watching online videos with her cousins to 'get the moves'. We might see this as a difference between the age of new media and the 1970s media cultures of the Opies' respondents. Song and dance routines learned from television could not be constantly revisited and called up on demand in the way that Diella and her cousins are able to do online, for example. However, in many ways both eras display a migration of popular cultural repertoires from the commercial media of radio and television (and then the internet) to the improvisatory bricolage of oral transmission and its equivalent in choreographed movement.

We also discover from the interview that the girls had been learning about Egypt recently, which also seems to have inspired some of the moves in the routine. At one point in the sequence, Diella introduces the 'Walk Like an Egyptian' movement. However, it is also worth noting that the moves of the dance, popularized in the Bangles' hit record of 1986, are also employed by Michael Jackson in his 1992 song and video, 'Remember the Time', and it seems quite possible, given her viewing of Jackson videos online, that Diella may have seen this.

We also learn that, while they are all fans of *High School Musical*, Rachel has actually been a cheerleader: 'We had loads and loads of cheers and my uniform was blue and white and my team was called the Marlins.'

In general, then, it seems to be the case that the girls' dance routine consists of specific features from a range of different sources: the tempo and rhythm of the Wildcats chorus; moves from their PE lesson; Michael Jackson moves; 'Walk Like an Egyptian'. This assemblage of source material, re-worked and integrated by Diella and taught to the other two, challenges the casual assumption that the girls are simply copying a routine from their favourite musical. Rather, they are making something new out of fragments: a choreographic equivalent of the process of composition-in-performance attributed in language and music to the oral-formulaic tradition, and applied to the musical aspects of children's singing games by Marsh (2008).

Developed originally to explain and analyse the Homeric epics, oral-formulaic theory proposed that certain formulaic structures enabled the poet to compose in performance (Parry 1930). It was later applied to Serbo-Croatian narrative poems (Lord 1960). Later adaptations of its use are relevant to our project. Finnegan, in particular in her 1977 book *Oral Poetry*, connects the textual theory of the oral-formulaic to a sociological emphasis on social context. In this view, the composition and performance of oral poetry only makes full sense in relation to the social conditions in which they occur.

Furthermore, Finnegan asserts the diversity and heterogeneity of oral poetry and narrative, arguing that genres, structures and cultural influences overlap, infiltrate and hybridize (1977: 15). Again, this is clearly a feature of our project, where it has proved it impossible, indeed undesirable, to police distinctions between supposedly folkloric forms and contemporary media forms. As the Opies demonstrated, once material from popular media has been absorbed into children's repertoires, it is subject to oral transmission just as folkloric material is transmitted. Everything becomes assimilated to this process, so that the apparently clear distinctions between folk culture for folklorists, and popular culture for sociologists, becomes not only fuzzy but barely tenable.

Finnegan's account is particularly instructive for our study. The social contexts of play have emerged as all-important, identifying the very particular sets of circumstances in which a child's memories of a particular text, or her learned repertoire of moves, or the hoop, pompom or wooden plank to hand, have converged with a moment of boredom, or of excited creative impulse, or of friendship through play, or of transgressive fantasy, to produce a unique event, albeit one that is dense with history and cultural reference. In Diella's dance routine, similarly, there is a concatenation of different social moments: watching Michael Jackson with her cousins; dancing in PE; making stuff up with her friends; performing for the boys. In some respects, it resembles the oral-formulaic process: particular formulaic memes are shuffled around and adapted, easy to recall, re-make and perform, both for teacher and learner, performer and audience. In other ways, though, it resembles an informal version of the choreographer, patiently assembling an expert repertoire for teaching through demonstration to pupils. And, of course, it resembles the work of the media fan, emulating the routines of the star performer.

More generally in our project, we have seen similar transformative processes deploying resources as diverse as fairytales and horror films, musicals and shoot-em-up computer games, texts as wildly different as Kurosawa's film *Seven Samurai* (1954) and the first-person shooter videogame *Call of Duty: Modern Warfare 2* (2009), scenarios that yoke together fantasy families and fantasy superheroes, zombies and ghosts, Harry Potter and Tig. In all of this, while particular cultural sources carry with them particular styles and structures of play, it is the heterogeneity that Finnegan emphasizes which is so striking. And, while it is often a vague and unhelpful meta-phor, the image of the bricoleur which Bishop *et al.* invoke is inescapable. But the bricolage is more substantially multimodal than the research has hitherto recognized: to address it, we need to move beyond the familiar territory of language and music, and look at the improvisatory grammars of dance, gesture, movement, and the elusive cultural histories that lie behind them, questions which the next section will address.

Multimodal performance

Multimodal theory (Kress and van Leeuwen 2001) proposes that contemporary acts of communication typically use a range of semiotic modes and material media, which integrate in complex ways to form the specific kinds of representation and interac-tion the sign-maker wishes to convey. In relation to children's playground games, this highlights the fact that, in the history of collecting, transcription, analysis and anthologizing that has conserved and interpreted these cultural forms, some modes have been privileged. The Opies' work, for example, began with written notation, focusing mainly on the linguistic features of the games, and it is these features that are interrogated in most detail in their historical analyses of change and continuity over, in some cases, centuries of play. The reason for this is simple: that the changing linguistic forms are relatively well-documented. The Opies also notated the music, though they relied on a colleague for the transcriptions. By the time of *The Singing Game*, they were using analogue tapes, both reel-to-reel and cassette. This, as we have discovered in our exploration of the archive, captured a far greater range of musical variation than was ever transcribed or published. More recently, the study of linguistic features of the games has continued (e.g. Widdowson 2001), as has study of the musi-cal features (Marsh 2008; Bishop 2010).

When it comes to physical movement, the picture looks considerably more sparse. The Opies noted with care the clapping routines, identifying the three-way clap that often, interestingly, accompanies songs in duple time. Other commentators have explored this in more detail since and found that children's musical play is consider-ably more complex rhythmically than conventional models of music education imag-ine (e.g. Marsh 2008; Arleo 2001).

Beyond the clapping repertories, however, there lies a greater range of movement, gesture, dramatic action, mimicry, dance, and embodied expression generally than studies so far have been able to analyse. This is partly because of the lack of conven-tional frameworks of notation, transcription and analysis of the kind that language and music can, to some degree, take for granted. To analyse this and other sequences, then, we experimented in our project with the frameworks of multimodal analysis suggested by the work of, among others, Kress and van Leeuwen (2001), Finnegan (2002), and Burn and Parker (2003). The analytical grid used here is adapted from the work of Roberta Taylor (cf. Taylor 2006). Its function is to identify specific modes in play at each moment of the sequence. The modes represented are: speech, action/gesture, gaze, facial expression, proxemics and music. Table 4.1 shows an extract of four minutes from the grid used to analyse the cheerleaders' sequence.

Table 4.1 Multimodal analysis grid of four minutes of the cheerleaders' sequence. (G1: Diella, G2: Rachel, G3: Alia)

Time	Vocalization/ speech	Action/gesture	Gaze	Facial expression	Proxemics	Music
00.10–00.19	(inaudible) singing of the Wildcats chorus	Girl 1 – r-hand in, l-hand in, both hands above head, jump up, touch ground Girl 2 out of shot Girls 3 – waving pompom with r-hand – jumping	G1 at Girl 2. G3 at other 2.	G1 – serious, intent G3 smiling.	G1 and 2 facing each other – dyad – G3 behind/at the side.	4/4 rhythm of the Wildcats chorus
00.20–00.45		G1 repeats the routine. Then improvises – alternate arms, and high leg kicks. G2 out of shot. G3 beginning to imitate the alternating r and l hands.	G1 at G2. G3 at other 2.	G1 serious at first, then smiling as she improvises. G3 smiling.	As above.	
00.45–00.57		G1 – shaking pompoms down; jump up. Kick both legs out.			Dyad	
1.35–1.42		G1 – r-hand in, l-hand in; cross arms, both hands down, shake to l, shake to r, jump up legs apart.			Dyad	
1.43–1.55		G1 and G2 face each other, arms above head, ready to try something.	G1 and 2 at each other. G3 at them. Then all 3 at each other.		Dyad – then G1 and 2 turn to include G3 in a triad.	
1.55 –		G1 crouches, pushing the other two's pompoms up – trying something new? G2 jumps up – all 3 put arms/pompoms in the middle to begin the routine – do	All 3 at each other. All 3 at each other.		Triad Triad	

Table 4.1 Continued

Time	Vocalization/ speech	Action/gesture	Gaze	Facial expression	Proxemics	Music
		alternate hands in to the middle – boy jumps in the middle, interrupts.				
2.29		G1 & 2 do shake-down to l and r, jump/legs apart, point at each other, G2 crossed hands.	G1 and 2 at each other		Revert to G1 & 2 dyad.	
3.00		Repeating the shake-down movement. G1 tries the 'Egyptian', jokily.	At each other.	G1 laughing.	Move to another part of the space; still moving between dyad and triad.	
		Routine firms up – r-hand, l-hand, shake-down l and r, jump up/legs apart, now Egyptian incorporated. G2 following closely; G3 increasingly imitating the movements.	At each other.		Still moving between dyad and triad.	
4.00		2 boys appear and seem interested. G1 does demo of routine so far, with extra elements improvised. G2 & 3 join in.	Girl 1 at boys. Boys at G1.		G1 facing the boys; other 2 girls join in. Girls move to face 'outward'	

We have already discussed the choreographed moves led by Diella, and can see here some of the detail. Though we do not have the additional information to match the moves to Michael Jackson videos, or the girls' PE lesson, or other sources, this information in principle would allow us to do that, and trace the provenance of the movements in that way.

The speech and music columns are mostly blank, because we were unable, amid the noise of the playground, to hear their singing of the Wildcats chorus; though again the interview helps us to fill in some of the missing information. If we add in the music from *High School Musical*, we can say something about the form of the movement, the tempo and the rhythm. But what can we say about the meaning?

Van Leeuwen's account of the social semiotics of sound and music (1999), gives the example of how, in the mediaeval church, the papal authorities prohibited the use of measured time, whether duple or triple, which represented the secular, and permitted only unmeasured time (as in plainchant), which represented the infinite nature of the sacred. These apparently formal qualities of music are never simply aesthetic categories, but express particular social meanings.

What, then, might the tempo and rhythm of the cheerleaders' routine signify? In general terms, the 4/4 march time typical of cheerleading, and found in these girls' routines, has quasi-military associations, in keeping with the uniforms, group formations and team support values of cheerleaders in American football. However, in films such as *High School Musical*, it is made to carry other meanings: of desirable teenage female identity, for example, attractive to the tween audiences who aspire to older identities and cultural properties (Willett 2009).

Meanwhile, these meanings, as we have seen, are combined with others. The appeal of a cult pop star such as Michael Jackson, various moves from PE and disco, and the humorous incorporation of the Egyptian dance, may all subtly change the social meanings bound up in this improvisatory process.

The other columns in the grid serve to alert us to the work of other modes employed by the girls. *Proxemics* refers to the disposition of bodies in space: how they relate to each other, what degrees of proximity, and so on. Two patterns are evident here. One is an oscillation between dyad and triad, showing how the third girl, Alia, is at times distanced from the action: not exactly excluded, but briefly separate, and then moving in, or invited in, to become part of the threesome. There is a kind of hierarchy here, in which the relationship between Diella as choreographer and teacher with the other two as loyal supporters, students, fellow-dancers, is the important function.

The *Proxemics* column also identified the movement of the girls between an inward-facing circle and an outward-facing line. The former is not at all typical of cheerleading, which is always performed in outward-facing lines. It is typical, however, of other playground games, especially clapping games, where any kind of performance is for the group itself, not for an external audience. It is also, arguably, indicative of the compositional process here, where the girls have to see each other in order to repeat moves demonstrated by Diella, and to keep together, evaluate, iterate. It is not clear that they ever really intend it for an external audience, in fact. In the interview they say they might have shown it to the class, but never got that far:

Alia:	Yeah, maybe to show the class or something.
Researcher:	Did you ever show the class?
All:	No.
Researcher:	Did you do this again?
Voices:	Well-la
Alia:	We said we were going to but then it turned out we didn't actually . . .
Diella:	Well we did it a little bit the next day but we didn't know what to do any-more because it became a bit boring.

However, on the playground, there seems to be a fluid movement between the inward-facing game-rehearsal circle and the outward-facing line, which seems to move towards a presentational formation, with passing boys as a provisional audience. The *Gaze* column reinforces this physical disposition of the girls. Their gaze is directed at each other when in the circle, and outwards or at the boys when they re-form in a line. Other than this, it provides evidence of their concentration, which barely wavers throughout the half-hour episode.

Finally, the *Facial expression* column displays an oscillation between serious facial expressions, which seem to express the concentration of composition, and laughter or smiling which accompanies performance, and pleasure in the humorous coupling of the clapping game and the pompoms at the end of the episode.

Conclusion: the absorptive power of childlore

To return to our main question, what have we learned, across the whole project, about the relation between children's cultural heritage of play, game and song, and their media cultures; and what in particular can we say on the basis of this example of the Wildcat Sailors (my own name for the girls' routine)?

Bishop *et al.* (2006) proposed four kinds of ways in which children's play and games might draw on their media culture: allusion, synthesis, mimicry and parody. In many ways, the Wildcat Sailors episode bears out these categories; but the analysis of movement here adds to them. In terms of allusion, first, Bishop *et al.* give several examples of linguistic allusion: names of media characters or stars, phrases from media texts, and so on. They also propose that allusion can be made through musical quotation. We had several examples in the project, and in the Opie archive, such as a version of 'When Susie was a Baby' which used the theme tune of the 1960s TV series, *The Saint*. In the Wildcat Sailors episode, the children seem to be singing some of the Wildcat chorus, and so allusion is made to *High School Musical* in word and tune. However, Bishop *et al.* begin to probe how physical movement can also form specific allusions: they give examples of characteristic gestures, such as those accompanying catchphrases.

Here, however, something more sustained is going on. The dance moves are more deeply intertwined in the structure of the whole piece, rather than supplementary. They make allusion, as we have seen, to choreographed movements in popular cultural texts such as Michael Jackson's dance moves. They are not, however, simply 'lifted' but, rather, creatively adapted. Bishop *et al.* give several examples of dance routines emulated by children in their 'mimicry' category, as well as citing the Opies' discussions of dance routines based on pop stars. Again, however, the Wildcat Sailors routine is clearly not an emulation of a single routine, but rather an original composition incorporating many different sources, identifiable to a greater or lesser extent.

As for Bishop *et al.*'s final category, parody, this does not seem to appear here until the final section, when the routine is hybridized with 'A Sailor Went to Sea'. It seems to be this, the traditional clapping game, which is the subject of parody, as they exaggerate the moves and scream out the song, perhaps suggesting that this is a routine for younger girls that they have outgrown.

Overall, then, this sequence appears to exemplify the four processes Bishop *et al.* propose: it makes passing allusion to media texts, it synthesizes such material with a traditional game, it mimics specific routines of pop and film stars, and it parodies. However, it seems to go further. Bishop *et al.* debate whether such processes are, in the end, transformative: they settle in the end for the lesser claim of re-contextualization. Here, by contrast, the compositional work of Diella, Rachel and Alia is clearly transformative: cultural sources and influences are significantly re-worked, re-combined and made into something new, not as a huge, high status cultural event, but as an almost casual, experimental improvisation, easy enough to discard.

What exactly is this transformative process, then? And is it legitimate to call it creative, a word which Bishop *et al.* use at times, despite their qualified judgement about the transformations? Since we have described such play as multimodal, it follows that transformation and creativity can occur in any or all of the semiotic modes in play, or across them. In this case, there is some evidence of transformation in the words: the girls say in the interview that they are spelling out their names in word and gesture. There is no evidence of transformation in some aspects of the movement: tempo and gesture. As we have seen, these are completely faithful to the original Wildcats chorus. But it is in other aspects of the choreography, the dance movements themselves, that the real creativity and transformation happen.

In this example, as is the case with all the data produced in our project, there is a critical intersection of the synchronic purposes to which these resources are put at this moment, in this social context, and the diachronic processes out of which the resources and their associated cultural practices emerge. There are complex histories behind Diella's improvisatory choreography: the sedimented practices of hand-clapping games and of cheerleading routines; the cultural history of Michael Jackson; the historic constructions of dance in the school curriculum; the life-histories of these girls and their fandoms, creative skills, friendships and school lives.

Finally, there is an elusive interplay between the durable and the ephemeral, a marked pattern throughout our project. It is the very ephemerality of childlore which makes it, like other forms of intangible cultural heritage, so challenging to preserve, research or exhibit. Between 2009 and 2011 we have seen games, routines and songs virtually identical to those the Opies collected 30 or more years ago, but with minor variations which may continue or may disappear after a week's experimentation. We have seen play based on computer game franchises which may last only as long as the franchise is popular (though that may last for decades). And these routines of the Wildcat Sailors incorporate moves which have decades of history with ones which may have a much shorter provenance. The patterns of continuity and change testify both to the robustness of childlore and to its persistently protean nature. It works in the service of these children, in this playground, at this moment: but the echoes of earlier moments, voices, movements and tunes ripple through its fabric, perhaps unseen and forgotten by these children, but potent nevertheless, absorbed into the play of game, skill and identity which inevitably lives in an eternal present, forgetful of its own history. This kind of persistent amnesia which children routinely express, insisting that they 'just made it up', is repeatedly noted by researchers. For this reason, the need to observe, collect, archive and curate the residual legacy of the secret cultures of the playground is particularly important. If children can take an active part in these activities, gaining some explicit understanding of their own play, then the ethnographic process of the interpretation of culture need not be left entirely to adults as it has been in the past.

Notes

1 The project 'Children's Playground Games and Songs in the Age of New Media' was funded by the UK's Arts and Humanities Research Council. It was a large project within a wider programme entitled 'Beyond Text'.
2 'The Opie Collection of Children's Games and Songs' is a collection of recordings originally held on 88 open reel and cassette tapes deposited with the British Library in 1998. A practical core element of our project, then, was to digitize the collection, making it available as an online resource for scholars worldwide. Collection details can be accessed at the Sound Archive Catalogue (collection number 'C898'). The entire collection is also available worldwide as streamed audio and as downloads to UK HEI researchers at the Archival Sound Recordings website.
3 Monteney Primary School in Sheffield and Christopher Hatton Primary School in London. The Sheffield school is located in a large housing estate serving a primarily white, working-class community. The London school is on the edge of Clerkenwell, close to the British Library, serving a multiethnic community.
4 Conkers is the UK children's game which uses horse chestnuts threaded on a string, with children taking turns to try to crack the opponent's conker. 'Elastics', also known as French skipping, is a form of long rope skipping using elastic ropes or loops.
5 Accessible at www.bl.uk/playtimes.
6 Details of the Webb photographic collection, prints, contact sheets and related manuscripts, can be found at http://www.prm.ox.ac.uk/manuscripts/webbpapers.html. The entire photographic collection of 8,265 photographs is viewable online at http://databases.prm.ox.ac.uk/fmi/iwp/cgi?-db=Photos_PRM&-loadframes.
7 Pseudonyms have been used for all participants.

References

Arleo, A. (2001) 'The Saga of Susie: The Dynamics of an International Handclapping Game', in Bishop, J. and Curtis, M. (eds) *Play Today in the Primary School Playground*, Buckingham: Open University Press.
Bishop, J.C. (2010) 'Eeny-Meeny Dessameeny: Continuity and Change in the "Backstory" of a

Children's Playground Rhyme', paper presented at Children's Playground Games and Songs in the New Media Age, Interim Conference, London Knowledge Lab, February 2010.

Bishop, J. and Curtis, M. (eds) (2001) *Play Today in the Primary School Playground*, Buckingham: Open University Press.

Bishop, J. and Curtis, M. with Woolley, H., Armitage, M. and Ginsborg, J. (2006) 'Participation, Popular Culture and Playgrounds: Children's Uses of Media Elements in Peer Play at School', Paper Presented at the Folklore Society Conference, Folklore, Film and Television: Convergences in Traditional Cultures and Popular Media, 31 March–1 April 2006, London.

Buckingham, D. (2000) *After the Death of Childhood: Growing Up in the Age of Electronic Media*, Cambridge: Polity.

Burn, A. and Parker, D. (2003) *Analysing Media Texts*, London: Continuum.

Curtis, M. (2004) 'A Sailor Went to Sea: Theme and Variations', *Folk Music Journal*, 8(4): 421–37.

Finnegan, R. (1977) *Oral Poetry: Its Nature, Significance and Social Context*, Bloomington: Indiana University Press.

Finnegan, R. (2002) *Communicating: The Multiple Modes of Human Interconnection*, London: Routledge.

James, A., Jenks, C. and Prout, A. (1998) *Theorizing Childhood*, Cambridge: Polity Press.

Jopson, L. (2010) 'The Opie Recordings: What's Left To Be Heard?', paper presented at Children's Playground Games and Songs in the New Media Age, Interim Conference, London Knowledge Lab, February 2010.

Kress, G. and van Leeuwen, T. (2001) *Multimodal Discourses: The Modes and Media of Contemporary Communication*, London: Arnold.

Lord, A.B. (1960) *The Singer of Tales*, Cambridge, MA: Harvard University Press.

Marsh, K. (2008) *The Musical Playground*, Oxford: Oxford University Press.

Mitchell, G. (forthcoming) 'Children on Camera: Video-Documenting Play and Games', in Burn, A. (ed.) *Children's Games in the New Media Age: Childlore, Media and the Playground*, Farnham: Ashgate.

Opie, I. and Opie, P. (1959) *The Lore and Language of School Children*, Oxford: Oxford University Press.

Opie, I. and Opie, P. (1985) *The Singing Game*, Oxford: Oxford University Press.

Parry, M. (1930) 'Studies in the Epic Technique of Oral Verse-Making. I: Homer and Homeric Style', *Harvard Studies in Classical Philology*, 41: 73–143.

Potter, J. (2009) *Curating the Self: Media Literacy and Identity in Digital Video Production by Young Learners*, London: Institute of Education, University of London.

Roud, S. (2010) *The Lore of the Playground*, London: Random House.

Taylor, R. (2006) 'Actions Speak as Loud as Words: A Multimodal Analysis of Boys' Talk in the Classroom', *English in Education* 40(3): 66–82.

van Leeuwen, T. (1999) *Speech, Music, Sound*, London: Macmillan.

Widdowson, J.D.A. (2001) 'Rhythm, Repetition and Rhetoric: Learning Language in the School Playground', in Bishop, J. and Curtis, M. (eds) (2001) *Play Today in the Primary School Playground*, Buckingham: Open University Press.

Willett, R. (2009) 'Parodic Practices: Amateur Spoofs on Video-Sharing Sites', in Buckingham, D. and Willet, R. (eds) (2009) *Video Cultures: Media Technology and Everyday Creativity*, Basingstoke: Palgrave Macmillan.

Chapter 5

The hidden heritage of mothers and teachers in the making of Japan's superior students

Mark A. Jones

For the families of modern Japan, the ideal child was (and still is) a striving student, a boy or girl spending days and nights studying at a desk in order to attain superior grades and examination scores. That being said, the pursuit of this cultural ideal has often yielded a less than ideal experience of childhood for many Japanese children. In contemporary Japan, popular terms such as *shiken jigoku* (examination hell) and *monsutaa parento* (monster parent), not to mention the persistence of stress-induced diseases such as high blood pressure among children, capture the unhealthy intensity of childhood striving and the familial obsession with educational success (see Field 1995).

Yet the popular understanding of how the Japanese child became a striving student often overemphasizes the role of the state and underemphasizes the role of the family in the making of this modern childhood ideal. In cultural heritage sites such as Matsumoto's famous Kaichi Gakkō and Matsuzaki's Iwashina Gakkō (both Western-style elementary schools founded in the 1870s that now serve as museums of Japan's educational history and have been designated by the government as 'important cultural properties' (*jūyō bunkazai*)) and Kyoto's Municipal Museum of School History, what is presented to the public, often in myopic detail, is the educational world of the school as created by the Ministry of Education, local government officials, and school administrators from Japan's Meiji era (1868–1912) through to today. For example, a visitor to Kyoto's Municipal Museum of School History encounters a series of exhibitions that furnish a historical overview of Japan's modern educational history through an analysis of national and local educational policies, the display of textbooks, and the presentation of photographs of school buildings and classrooms. Such an approach imputes a central role to the state in the making of children into students and largely ignores when, how, and why the importance of education took root within the lives of families. In other words, the representation of Japanese children's educational past through heritage sites has overlooked important aspects of the historical development of this ideal of childhood.

Nonetheless, if the custodians of public memory are expanded to include the mass media – namely film, television, and print culture – then the image of the child as striving student has a more established presence. As early as Ozu Yasujirō's 1953 film *Tōkyō monogatari* (Tokyo Story) and continuing with Morita Yoshimitsu's 1983 film *Kazoku geemu* (Family Game), children and families have been depicted as singularly concerned with educational success. Best-selling books such as Ibuka Masaru's *Yōchien de wa ososugiru* (Kindergarten is Too Late, 1971) and *Zerosai kara no hahoya sakusen* (Maternal Strategies for Starting Education at Age Zero, 1979), along with popular television such as the 1988 mini-series 'Kaiware zoku no tatakai' (The Battle of the Sprout Brothers), have further contributed to the acceptance and popularity of the image of the child as striving student. Yet even these renderings of the Japanese child-student evince a distinct lack of historical consciousness, for they do not grapple with the origins of the 'striving student' ideal.

This chapter, by examining two actors – mothers and school teachers – who helped to give birth to this new ideal of childhood in the opening decades of the twentieth century, seeks to add new dimensions to the popular understanding of Japanese childhood.[1] The first is to broaden it by moving beyond a state-centred view of childhood's creation and to introduce the family as a central institution to the making of modern Japanese childhood; the second is to deepen it, in a historical sense, by seeking the originary moment of the striving student ideal, namely, the 1910s and 1920s.[2]

The emergence of the educationally obsessed mother

The 1910s and 1920s in urban Japan was an era of *netsu* and *nan*, fever and frustration, difficulty and determination. Populations, prices, and pressures in the cities were rising. Manual labourers and education seekers streamed into cities from the countryside, increasing the number of people scrambling for a limited number of factory jobs, higher education openings, and corporate and bureaucratic positions. Furthermore, the post-First World War Rice Riots marked the beginning of a difficult-to-shake macroeconomic downturn that deepened the financially strapped lives that more and more Japanese, urban and rural, working class and middle class, were forced to endure. That being said, those who dissected what were called *seikatsunan*, or difficulties in livelihood, often attributed their cause to more than high prices. 'Today's difficulties in livelihood are caused by more than rising prices. Our desires too are swelling year by year in length and breadth', concluded a contributor to the women's magazine, *Fujin no tomo* (The Lady's Companion), in 1912 (Horie 1991: 57). Although an era of diminished expectations, Taishō-era Japan (1912–26) was not an era of diminished desires, especially among a stratum of urban families with modest incomes and high aspirations. Led by a new and ambitious generation of educated mothers, these families worked in alliance with elementary school teachers and principals to reorient the school's mission (and the child's daily life) to train elementary school children to become what was fast becoming a new social ideal – the child as *yūtōsei*, or superior student. The goal of these families was to realize the modern dream of meritocratic mobility and their means was the child's step-by-step navigation through the educational hierarchy and up the social ladder.

In the 1910s and 1920s, the primary obstacle to educational achievement was the entrance examination to middle school or girls' higher school, the two most important gateways to future positions of success and lives of modest comfort.[3] Applications to middle schools and girls' higher schools were skyrocketing; at the same time, new public and private middle schools and girls' higher schools were being built in major metropolises, prefectural capitals, and provincial towns, albeit not quickly enough to keep up with the demand. Therefore, instituting an entrance examination system, where the examination score was the sole determinant of admission, became the widely accepted solution among schools anxious to cope with an overabundance of applicants. Acceptance rates at top schools in Tokyo were reported to be as low as 10 per cent, whereas less competitive schools in Tokyo and elsewhere admitted only one in three applicants. Within this type of viciously competitive educational system, a group of upwardly mobile mothers committed themselves to becoming the child's partner in the quest for educational success.

By the end of the Taishō era in 1926, the parent most closely and often singularly associated with the child's school education was the mother. 'The family's housewife . . . must possess the awareness and responsibility of being the educator within the family from dusk to dawn', stated one elementary school teacher (Takizawa 1926: 37–8). These types of mothers were part of a new generation of early twentieth-century highly educated women, often graduates of girls' higher school, who were keen to pass on their desire for educational success and social ascent to their children. To ensure their child's success at elementary school, these mothers welcomed the school – all it taught and all it represented – into the home. From building the child a study room, to quizzing the child after dinner on the lessons of the day, to putting the child's grades on the altar for the family's deceased members (*kamidana*), mothers shaped the spaces and rhythms of the family's daily life to encourage academic achievement. Above all else, these mothers built their identity as practitioners par excellence of *fukushū*, or the child's review at home of the materials learned at school. *Fukushū* became an important daily event, supervised by the mother and performed by the child at various points throughout the day, including before breakfast, during breakfast, after the child's return from school, at the dinner table, after dinner, and/or before bedtime. For the mother, it was a time to measure the child's progress, to impart education's importance to the child, and to display her twin commitment to educational success and social betterment. As suggested by the title of a parenting guidebook of the day – *Katei kyōshi to shite no haha* (The Mother as Private Tutor, 1905) – mothers became private tutors to their own children. These women were the pre-war version of what came to be known in the postwar years as the *kyōiku mama*, or education mother.

Yet educational achievement was such a prized commodity to these families that education mothers took further control of their children's education by visiting the elementary schools themselves. Therefore, in addition to making the school a part of the home, the education mother made the home a part of the school. In particular, she worked to reorient the school's mission away from the cultivation of nationalism and toward the preparation of the child for the entrance examination to secondary school. This type of aggressive mother imagined the school to be an extension of the home – a 'second home' (*bessō*) or 'one's own property', in the words of one observant elementary school teacher – and integrated the school into her everyday routine (Katō 1921: 79, 101). One Tokyo school teacher noted how mothers 'wearing aprons' regularly 'stopped into school after errands like shopping at the market' ('Yūtōsei ni suru yoshū fukushū no sasekata', 1930: 94). Such women visited the child's elementary school at least once a month, sometimes once a week, and at times once a day. The education mother saw it as entirely natural for 'the home to stimulate the school' and for the mother to prevent 'the teacher from slipping into carelessness and slapdash behaviour' by 'asking the teacher countless questions' and monitoring classroom teaching (Hani 1914: 57; Hahaoya kondankai 1929: 62). The child's success and the family's future, it was widely believed, depended upon such efforts. Thus both the home and the school were important sites for the construction of the striving student ideal, and the relationship between the two was more interdependent and symbiotic than current representations of Japanese educational history make clear.

The education mother took advantage of every opportunity to strengthen the family's connection with the school and to acquaint herself with the child's learning environment. Formal parental involvement in the child's schooling began with the *nyūgakushiki*, the ceremony marking the start of the child's formal elementary education. For the family headed by these women, the *nyūgakushiki* marked less the encroachment of school into the family's daily life and more the beginning of a six-year active and dynamic relationship between home and school. In the eyes of the education mother, school teachers, principals, and mothers needed to begin to work together from the moment of the *nyūgakushiki*. Mothers pushed to the front of these crowded events and revealed their obsessive determination to make the child succeed. What interested the education mother was the child's teacher, the quality of his or her educational training, and the teacher's openness to cooperative endeavours. One mother named Sadako from Kanagawa (outside Tokyo) expressed frustration with the bureaucratic quality of the *nyūgakushiki*. 'At the *nyūgakushiki*, they performed what is called an individual evaluation. They ask about things like the child's name and age, the family's situation, the father's name and occupation, the mother's name. They examine things like . . . the child's appearance, even whether or not the child's nose is runny. Are these types of things really that useful? Couldn't they perform them on a school holiday?' she intemperately wondered. After finishing the ceremony's irritating formalities, Sadako rushed to meet her child's teacher. 'I told the teacher that I wanted to cooperate with him; I pleaded time and time again to teach my child according to his individual personality [*kosei*]. . . . I also stated my hope that this experienced teacher would be assigned to my child's classroom all the way through the sixth year of elementary school' (Sadako 1919: 44).

Clearly, the meeting of parents and teachers was a time not only for the school to make its plans known, but also for the parents to voice their concerns and to learn how to improve the child's academic performance. Other formal opportunities allowed the deepening of this budding relationship between school and family. Parent–teacher meetings, regularly held twice or three times a year, included speeches by school principals, school doctors and teachers, in addition to parents' visits to classrooms, individual and group conferences with teachers, and a question-and-answer session. In these meetings, parents actively looked to the school in utilitarian terms, hoping to shape the relationship between school and family in ways that promoted the child's educational achievement. The two most regularly asked questions at elementary school parent–teacher meetings were how to achieve entrance into middle school or girls' higher school and how to make the child review at home. At a 1911 meeting at an elementary school in the provincial city of Nagano, for example, parents asked the school principal, 'During preparation for the entrance examination, on what areas is it important to focus the child's efforts?' (Shinshū daigaku kyōiku gakubu fuzoku Nagano shōgakkō hyakunenshi henshū iinkai, ed. 1986: 320–1).

Whereas the formal connection between family and school occurred only a few times a year, enthusiastic mothers also practised the school visit (*gakkō sankan*) on a more regular, informal basis in order to learn the secrets of educational success by observing child and teacher. Mothers went to schools once a month, once a week, or, in the case of a mother of a boy named Ichirō, every day. Ichirō's mother recounted in 1919 how she was able to ascertain 'the cause of her child's bad grades' through visiting the school every day and ultimately to turn him into 'the top student in the class'. During her first visits to the school, she immediately noticed how 'the top student named H- *kun*' hated it when other students bettered him in class performance. He regularly bullied his classmates into submission and ostracized those students who refused to submit to his regime. Despite being a bright boy, Ichirō, a fourth-year elementary student, fell under H- *kun*'s rule and decided to 'get bad grades in order to be able to play with the children'. Ichirō's mother, fighting back tears, explained to her son the ill effects of 'wasting one's period of study' and the struggles he would face 'after stepping out into a world' characterized by 'the survival of the fittest'. Ichirō's mother did more than simply offer dire warnings; she also took concrete steps to ensure her child's academic improvement. She moved the family house closer to the school in order to be able to visit Ichirō's classroom 'without fail once a day and, on occasion, three times a day'. She 'observed her child's activities' by pretending to play with her youngest child during the school's recess yet 'never taking her eyes from the location of her eldest son Ichirō'. She even talked to the principal about the tactics of H- *kun*. In addition to taking such measures at school, Ichirō's mother worked hard to review the day's lessons with Ichirō at home. The results were astounding. Ichirō became the class *yūtōsei* by year's end. Ichirō's mother concluded her account by praising the positive effects of the school visit and finished with a call to other mothers. 'Even if your child's grades are not bad, visit the school regularly for the benefit of the child. I personally know of five or six children whose grades have rapidly improved as a result of the mother's school visit' (Ichirō no haha 1919: 20–3).

For reasons as varied as determining the cause of a child's bad grades to observing a teacher's pedagogical methods to comparing a child to its classmates, a certain type of mother became a regular presence in elementary schools throughout urban Japan. Although the ambitious mother has appeared in recent popular cultural representations, her absence from official educational histories communicated by museums and other heritage sites today leaves unclear the significant impact of domestic influences on the past – and indeed present – lives of Japanese children as students. The ultimate goal of a maternal presence in the elementary school, as the story of Ichirō's mother makes clear, was (and still is) to improve the child's grades and to make the child into a superior student. However, to increase the odds of her achieving this goal, this type of mother needed a partner within the school willing to work toward the same goal. She found such a person in the figure of the elementary school teacher.

Teachers as allies of education mothers

While historians and heritage professionals have represented the pre-war education system in Japan as an institutional network crucial to the extension of state influence, few have looked beyond state-led nation-building to explain the power of the elementary school within family life. The pre-war Japanese elementary school, however, was not merely an instrument of the state and its principals and teachers were far from submissive pawns. Indeed, they jockeyed successfully for positions of influence in the new urban society. That influence had long been denied the poorly paid figure of the elementary school teacher. Teachers had laboured from the end of the Meiji era (1868–1912) under the guidance and shadow of nationally known child experts, including normal school professors, child psychologists and Ministry of Education bureaucrats. Indeed, the voice of the elementary school teacher was rarely heard in the public debate on childhood in the late Meiji-era print media. That was not the case in Taishō-era Japan. The elementary school teacher and principal rocketed to stardom, fuelled by the clamorous calls of education mothers for help in the quest for educational success. The school teacher possessed the knowledge of proper study habits, school textbooks, and entrance examinations considered crucial to the child's attainment of educational advancement. As a result, a select group became national celebrities and the darlings of a blossoming mass media, while a greater number became local celebrities, people whose advice and counsel was sought by parents eager to jumpstart or further their social ascent by making their children into *yūtōsei*. Whether in print or in person, nationally or locally, the Taishō-era elementary school educator fomented and furthered the dream of upward mobility among aspirational families of urban Japan. Understanding their role is thus crucial to building a fuller picture of the historical underpinning, or the cultural heritage, of Japanese children as students in subsequent decades.

The new attention from education mothers turned principals and teachers into highly regarded and eagerly sought figures, bringing these educators both newfound opportunities and travails. For example, elementary schools came to be publicly evaluated according to their ability to prepare students to pass the entrance examination; as a result, according to one elementary school teacher, the spring of every year – the annual moment of the entrance examination – became 'a time of headaches among elementary school principals . . . because there is now the tendency to evaluate elementary schools according to examination results' (Harusame [pseud.] 1919: 45). Teachers also suffered under these new expectations. Parents often placed heavy demands on teachers and monitored their efforts closely. A teacher at Tokyo's Seishi Elementary School described the situation in the following vignette:

Because it was a school with only mothers of children who wanted to go to secondary school, they stuck to the walls like house lizards and watched me teach the [examination] preparatory courses [after school]. When it became dark to the point of no longer being able to see one's feet, the mothers finally went home with their children.

(Shozawa and Kimura 1988: 341)

At the same time, many elementary schools embraced their new role and improved their public reputation in the process. Elementary schools increasingly and deliberately staked their reputation on the ability to make their children into *yūtōsei*. 'If the percentage of children who proceed to secondary school declines, the number of the children at that elementary school declines. . . . As a result, elementary schools put much effort into examination preparation in order to make the school prosper', admitted one Tokyo middle school teacher ('Fukushū no sasekata', 1927: 17–18).

The dynamic relationship between school and home was forged therefore as much by the eager outreach of the school as of the home. Keen to capitalize on their new role, elementary school teachers and principals invited parents into the school and welcomed parental dependency on the teacher's expertise. Ishiguchi Gitarō, a teacher at Tokyo's Seishi Elementary School, encouraged the practice of parental school visits. He argued that the school was not 'a sightseeing location' and added how parents coming to school 'dressed up in their best clothes left him feeling strange' ('Yūtōsei ni suru yoshū fukushū no sasekata', 1930: 94). Indeed, mothers of children at Seishi Elementary School were such regular practitioners of the school visit that they earned themselves the nickname 'hallway sparrows' (*rōka suzume*) (Shozawa and Kimura 1988: 345). In forging new relationships with these parents, elementary school teachers and principals actively responded to the demands of the education mother and quietly disobeyed the directives of the Ministry of Education, earning the bureaucrats' ire and the mothers' allegiance.

To give an extended example of this new relationship between school and family, consider the case of Seishi Elementary School, once called 'The Number One Elementary School in Japan'. The school's reputation was earned through a combination of relentless parental calls for examination preparation and the school's active response. Beginning in the 1910s, the school established research divisions for each academic subject. Teachers like Futatsugi Shōji invented an 'arithmetic card' to help Seishi's students learn how to do addition, subtraction, multiplication and division more rapidly. Morning and night, in the hours before and after school, teachers conducted examination preparation courses in which school-made practice problem sheets were distributed to students. (The school's rotary press was said to run continually throughout the day.) The school's administration even made covert curricular changes such as decreasing the amount of time allocated to physical education in order to devote more time to the subjects that appeared on entrance examinations. Parents demanded such measures and regularly monitored both the child's and the school's efforts. Mothers attended classes during the day and, when a child was sick, sometimes even took the place of the child in the classroom. The attendance rate at the parent–teacher association meetings was said to be over 90 per cent. In the case of Seishi and other well-known public elementary schools, the result of such efforts by child, parent and school was undeniable success as measured by students' admission to top middle schools and girls' higher schools (Shozawa and Kimura 1988: 331–51).

The reorientation of the school to serve education mothers did not pass unnoticed. The trend toward *junbi kyōiku* (preparatory education) within the elementary school became a node of anxiety in Taishō Japan. From the perspective of the municipal and national educational bureaucracy, these developments portended the failure of the elementary school to serve the nation. Decreasing the amount of time devoted to physical education, for example, not to mention draining students of energy by keeping them in school from sun up to sun down, was producing a generation of weak, nervous little citizens. Scientists and others also joined the chorus of criticism, proclaiming *junbi kyōiku* to be 'in total disagreement with the child's psychology', an unnatural suppression of the child's 'rich, active nature' and an undeniable social problem (Ogawa sei 1925: 28). (Similar criticisms persist in twenty-first-century Japan, indicating how persistent this viewpoint has been.) Mounting evidence of *junbi kyōiku*'s widespread practice and harm prompted the pre-war Ministry of Education to discourage preparatory education. For example, in 1929 the chief of the Ministry's School Affairs Bureau issued a declaration prohibiting the following five practices, all considered to be widespread in elementary schools that prepared boys and girls for entrance examinations: teaching the child outside of daily school hours or on Sundays or holidays; changing class hours to favour subjects tested on the examination; changing the speed at which materials were taught; teaching children at a private residence; allowing the child to take practice tests or attend a private cram school. Despite its efforts, the Ministry reported in 1934 of hearing of a trend toward violating such prohibitions. Teachers and principals were not cowed by these bureaucratic mandates.

Their defiant entrepreneurialism yielded teachers and principals a variety of benefits, though their deleterious effects on students must also be remembered. In the most visible cases, some became mass media celebrities with nationally influential voices. Publishing houses recruited elementary school teachers and principals from well-known schools (and, often, from lesser known schools in minor metropolises and prefectural towns) as insider experts able to impart to their growing readership the secrets to success on the entrance examination. Publishers and editors actively enlisted these men to write education guidebooks, and these books went through multiple printings, bringing profit to both author and publisher. The principal of Tokyo's Taimei Elementary School, Kobayashi Saburō, authored a thorough guide on review at home entitled *Wagako no jishū fukushū* (My Child's Self-Learning and Review, 1927), and publishing giant Jitsugyō no Nihonsha issued a series of best-selling books – *Katei no fukushū no hōhō* (How To Review At Home, 1921), *Aiji no gakuryoku o susumuru kufū* (Tricks to Promote the Beloved Child's Scholastic Ability, 1922), and *Aiji nyūgakumae no yōi, nyūgakugo fukei no yōi* (Being Prepared Before and After One's Beloved Child Enters Elementary School, 1921) – by the prolific elementary school teacher Katō Suekichi. In addition, mass market magazines such as

Shufu no tomo (The Housewife's Companion, 1917–today) and *Fujin no tomo* (The Lady's Companion, 1908–today) sought the opinions of principals and teachers from Seishi, Banchō, Akasaka, and other famous elementary schools, solicited articles on topics ranging from the best way to build vocabulary and sharpen maths skills to the best type of meal to eat the night before the entrance examination, and printed roundtable discussions such as 'How to Make the Child Into a Superior Student Through Review and Preparation', 'How to Make Your Child Love Maths', and 'Getting Into the Best Middle Schools and Girls' Higher Schools'. Finally, Shōgakukan and other publishers of grade-targeted children's magazines regularly recruited elementary school teachers to write countless examination review exercises and to serve on the magazines' advisory boards.

Throughout these different venues, the message of the elementary school teacher was clear and consistent: hard work and thorough preparation lead to success. According to Suzuki Tomesaburō, a teacher at the respected Nanzan Elementary School in the Azabu district of Tokyo, nothing could replace the child's 'repeating again and again the same problem, reviewing the material daily, and moving on to the next level only when satisfied that understanding has occurred' (Suzuki 1930: 78). Teachers not only furthered but also profited from the idea that ceaseless preparation was the key to the child's becoming a *yūtōsei*. For elementary educators, marketing such dreams of meritocratic mobility was a way of marketing themselves. After all, student effort needed to be coupled with skilled guidance, and that guidance came from no one other than the elementary school teacher. In a world where educational advancement was increasingly perceived as the surest means of social ascent, the elementary school teacher positioned himself as the key holder to the gates of middle schools and girls' higher schools across the nation. The result, for a select few, was nationwide renown and influence.

Yet for every teacher who basked in the spotlight of the national media, there was a greater number of teachers and principals who received attention of a more modest sort. These teachers were local celebrities, and numerous parents, eager to see their children advance to secondary education, sought to curry their favour. During the Taishō era, school teachers in cities, towns, and villages across Japan received increased attention, respect, and even gifts from parents. Of particular interest to parents were the teachers of the fifth and sixth grades, in addition to the teachers who taught special examination preparation courses before and after school. As the recipients of such increased regard, these educators cashed in on parents' dreams of meritocratic mobility. The elementary school teacher employed his knowledge and skills not simply for social recognition but also for financial remuneration. Newspapers of the 1910s and 1920s reported regular instances of teachers being feted at parties after the announcement of the entrance examination results, or receiving gifts throughout the school year. These types of practices were not limited to Tokyo. A local newspaper in Miyagi Prefecture reported on an elementary school where 'examination preparation teachers' were given five yen by each parent whose child gained admittance to middle school or girls' higher school (Miyagiken kyōiku iinkai, ed. 1977: 106–7). Other teachers sought and found part-time work as private tutors (*katei kyōshi*) to supplement their own family's income. Still other teachers put their expertise up for sale by holding private lessons (often on weekends) at their homes for groups of students and for a price. In sum, for the elementary educator, there was much fame and fortune to be gained by catering to upward-climbing families. The result of their efforts, in combination with those of the pre-war education mother, transformed the elementary school into a modern factory of dreams, where thoughts of entrance examination questions, educational ascent, and social climbing danced in the heads of child, parent and teacher at the beginning of the twentieth century.

The ideal of the Japanese child as striving student was by no means imposed from above by an all-powerful state, but rather generated by the enthusiasms and energies of families in the early twentieth century striving to capitalize on what seemed the new opportunity of meritocratic advancement offered by the modern world. Understanding the mother's and teacher's role in creating the ideal of the child-student helps to explain the persistence of this version of modern Japanese childhood into the twenty-first century, where such understandings about childhood are strongly embedded in the culture of everyday life. After all, even as parents and others today bemoan the state of contemporary childhood and claim that childhood (defined as a time full of play and free from excessive psychological and physical stress) is disappearing, it is these same parents who also send their children to *juku* (cram school) on weekdays and weekends, sentencing their children to days and nights of ceaseless study. The role of the state – through educational policies, school architecture or changing curricula – is clearly an important element in the construction of the striving student ideal. But a focus solely on bureaucratic policies fails to explain the striking tenacity of this cultural ideal. A fuller understanding of Japanese students' cultural heritage requires a closer historical study of the actors most implicated in the child's daily life: the mother and teacher.

Finally, while we must acknowledge the need for children to be protected from the stresses and strains of the adult world, we must move away from seeing childhood as an enclave within human existence. That way of thinking makes childhood into a mere respite of privilege before the onset of adulthood. Instead, it is the symbiosis, not the separation, of the worlds of the child and adult that must become the focus of thinking about not only childhood's past but also its future. Laborious competition and strain-filled striving have been as much a part of the modern child's world as the modern adult's world. And how could it be any other way? The two worlds were born in tandem at the turn of the twentieth century. Childhood in Japan and elsewhere will become a more humane state only when adulthood does. Examination hell will disappear only when death by overwork (*karōshi*), a disease afflicting more than a handful of Japanese salarymen, disappears. The dream of upward mobility will stop structuring the child's world only after it stops structuring the world of the adult. Rethinking childhood is part of a larger project to rethink human existence and to remake daily life for the benefit of both child and adult. Just as the histories of child and adult are intertwined in Japan as elsewhere, the future destiny of child and adult will be shared.

Notes

1 This chapter's content builds upon Chapter 4 of my recent book Jones, M. (2010) *Children as Treasures: Childhood and the Middle Class in Early Twentieth Century Japan*, Cambridge, MA: Harvard University Asia Center.
2 Although the voices heard in the present essay belong to adults, not children, the absence of the child's voice does not imply that the child, past or present, has no part in shaping its environment. It does suggest, however, the difficulty of recovering the child's contribution. Recent work by children's historians has attempted to recover the child's agency in the construction of childhood and to recognize children as 'social actors, not beings in the process of becoming such.' See E. West and P. Petrik (eds.) (1992) *Small Worlds: Children and Adolescents in America, 1850–1950*, Lawrence, KS: University of Kansas Press.
3 Middle school (for boys) and girls' higher school (for girls) were five-year secondary educational institutions for children aged 13 through 18. Approximately 10 per cent of elementary school graduates advanced to these institutions by the end of the Taishō era. Graduation from middle school meant the prospect of white-collar employment for young men, and graduation from girls' higher school meant, for young women, marriage to one of the new male members of the white-collar class, dubbed the salaryman in early twentieth-century Japan.

References

Field, N. (1995) 'The Child as Laborer and Consumer: The Disappearance of Childhood in Contemporary Japan', in S. Stephens (ed.) *Children and the Politics of Culture*, Princeton, NJ: Princeton University Press.

'Fukushū no sasekata' (1927) *Fujin no tomo*, 21.3: 12–23.

Hahaoya kondankai. (1929) 'Kodomo o shōgakkō ni okuru junbi to chūi', *Fujin no tomo*, 23.3: 57–67.

Hani, M. (1914) 'Fukushū no sasekata', *Fujin no tomo*, 8.5: 53–58.

Harusame [pseud.] (1919) 'Seikō shita nyūgaku shiken no junbi kyōju', *Fujin no tomo*, 13.3: 45–47, March.

Horie, S. (1991) 'Meiji makki kara Taishō shoki no "kindai kazokuzō": fujin zasshi kara mita "Yamanote seikatsu" no kenkyū', *Nihon minzokugaku*, 186: 39–73.

Ichirō no haha. (1919) 'Rakudaiten to natta chōnan o shuseki to nasu made no kushin to doryoku', *Shufu no tomo*: 20–23, March.

Katō, S. (1921) *Aiji nyūgakumae no yōi, nyūgakugo fukei no yōi*, Tokyo: Jitsugyō no Nihonsha.

Miyagiken kyōiku iinkai. (ed.) (1977) *Miyagiken kyōiku hyakunenshi*, Vol. 3, Tokyo: Teikoku chihō gyōsei gakkai.

Ogawa sei (Fukui). (1925) 'Hito kyōin no mita hisan na shiken junbi', *Fujin no tomo*, 19.2: 28, February.

Sadako (Kanagawa). (1919) 'Onna no ko no shōgakkō nyūgaku no shitaku to hiyō', *Fujin no tomo*, 13.3: 43–44, March.

Shinshū daigaku kyōiku gakubu fuzoku Nagano shōgakkō hyakunenshi henshū iinkai (ed.) (1986) Shinshū daigaku kyōiku gakubu fuzoku Nagano shōgakkō hyakunenshi, Nagano: Shinshū Daigaku kyōikugakubu fuzoku Nagano shōgakkō hyakunenshi henshū iinkai.

Shozawa, J. and Kimura, H. (1988) 'Nihon no kindai shōgakkō to chūtō gakkō shingaku: Tōkyōshi kōritsu shingakkō no henka no jitsurei ni soku shite', *Tōkyō Daigaku kyōikugakubu kiyō*, 27: 331–351.

Suzuki, T. (1930) 'Seiseki furyō no kodomo o yūtōsei ni suru hiketsu', *Shufu no tomo*: 74–78, May.

Takizawa, M. (1926) *Wagako no nyūgaku*, Tokyo: Bunka seikatsu kenkyūkai.

'Yūtōsei ni suru yoshū fukushū no sasekata' (1930) *Shufu no tomo*: 86–95, April.

Chapter 6

Playing the author

Children's creative writing, paracosms and the construction of family magazines

Christine Alexander

Imitation of print culture is one of the earliest activities of many children. For them, writing is play, and the resulting stories, poems, dramas and magazines that I term 'literary juvenilia' are a vital part of the material cultural heritage of children.[1] Even more significant are the intangible elements of these works – the style, organization and shape of their content, and what they tell us about the creative imagination of children. Since Philippe Ariès' landmark study of the 1960s (Ariès 1962), historians of childhood have shown how radically attitudes to the child and the lives of children have changed over the centuries. Yet children have long been fascinated by the written word, not least for the sense of identity and control it bestows on those who wield the pen. Powerless, in the way that legal minors are, children have little or no agency in the 'grown-up' world; creative writing bestows agency. In the examples discussed in this chapter, children engage with the literary scene, reorganize and reimagine it as their own, and pass their enthusiasms and practices on to the next generation. Their practice of book making is a distinctive feature of literary play, a physical and intellectual activity that is part of the imaginative development of children, in particular those who become adult writers.

The recovery of literary juvenilia – youthful writing composed before the age of about twenty – is still in its infancy. Only a handful of scholars have worked in this field, chiefly because of the pejorative associations of the word 'juvenilia' itself and the difficulty of obtaining source material (see contributors to Alexander and McMaster 2005).[2] The writing of children, by its nature inchoate, imitative, and often unsophisticated, was until recently either ignored or denigrated in the academy along with the study of children's cultural heritage in general. The collection policies of museums and libraries understandably privileged the later, 'mature' writing that is responsible for the writer's fame; there has been little interest in where or how that writing originated. This chapter seeks to demonstrate the value of exploring this neglected body of writing as evidence of both early writing experience and the creative imagination of children.

Museums generally display miniature or picture books written *for* children rather than manuscripts *by* children themselves, unless the museum is celebrating a particular writer or writers as in the case of the Brontë Parsonage Museum. Libraries, however, have for many years displayed iconic juvenilia, like Jane Austen's Notebooks, as curiosities of the famous author. The surviving juvenilia are generally those of the upper- or middle-class child who had the privilege of education and whose early attempts at authorship are most likely to have survived. Locating their manuscripts, however, is often like looking for a needle in a haystack. Juvenilia are seldom catalogued in libraries or they are subsumed under general headings such as 'fragmentary works' or 'other writings'. Much of the juvenilia I have located still remain in private hands, considered variously as worthless, as personal and private, or even as financial investments. As a recent Sotheby's sale has dramatically demonstrated, the value of a single childhood manuscript by a famous author like Charlotte Brontë has risen exponentially: it is to be hoped that the sum of £690,850 paid for the miniature nineteen-page booklet, a sum considerably more than twice the pre-sale estimate,[3] represents a growing general interest in juvenilia and the cultural heritage of children.

Over the last thirty years, a number of studies have documented the early writings of individual children, chiefly those who have become famous as adults, such as Jane Austen, Lord Byron, the Brontës, John Ruskin, Virginia Woolf, Philip Larkin and Margaret Atwood, but also those of children whose early writing itself is celebrated: Marjory Fleming, who died when she was only eight but who appears in the *Dictionary of National Biography* and the *Oxford Dictionary of Quotations*; Daisy Ashford, who wrote her acclaimed novel *The Young Visiters* [*sic*] at nine years and lived to see dozens of reprints and adaptations for stage and screen; or Iris Vaughan and Opal Whiteley, whose remarkable diaries made them national icons of childhood in South Africa and Canada, respectively. Editions of English-language juvenilia are becoming more numerous and the range is extending to less-known writers like Mary Grant Bruce and Ethel Turner in Australia and Hope Hook in Canada. Dinah Birch has praised 'the quiet work of the Juvenilia Press, established in 1994', a pedagogic and research enterprise dedicated to the recovery and dissemination of juvenilia from all historical periods (2006).[4] Their editions range from poetry by the seventeenth-century British teenager Sarah Fyge Egerton to writings by modern Canadian adolescents such as Margaret Laurence and Carol Shields.

Through such efforts of recovery and analysis we can now more confidently study literary play and its formative place in cultural production and its heritage. In particular, the incorporative process of appropriation by which child writers learn the art of narration and the skill of bookmaking can be demonstrated in a variety of works by different authors. Such writings illustrate the way children learn to tell stories that represent their view of reality, their personal and social histories, and the way they learn to edit, to review and to design family magazines – activities that are as valid a contribution to civilization as any adult literary production.

Magazine and book making

Young writers who become particularly successful in later life have often developed what might be described as a fetish for the book that encompasses the need to imitate, reproduce and create. Charles Dickens referred to this as 'assumption' – the making up of games related to his reading or to the theatre, retelling tales he read, and creating his own stories about real people and places modelled on genres with which he was familiar (DeVries 1976: 14). He told his friend and biographer Forster that he entertained himself and the other boys at the infamous Warrens Blacking Factory by retelling stories he had earlier read and elaborated (Forster 1928: 16). Like David Copperfield, the twelve-year-old Dickens pretended to be Roderick Random or Tom Jones, or conceived of himself as 'the perfect realization of Captain Somebody, of the Royal British Navy, in danger of being beset by savages, and resolved to sell his life at a great price' (*David Copperfield*, chapter 4). He recalled later in life the profound joy of this creative imitation that he practised from childhood:

> Assumption has charms for me – I hardly know for how many wild reasons – so delightful, that I feel a loss of, oh! I can't say what exquisite foolery, where I lose a chance of being someone in voice, etc. not at all like myself.[5]

Assumption (we might call it 'appropriation' where the borrowing is remade as one's own) is responsible for Dickens' later memorable scenes and characters – people like the indomitably cheerful Mr Pickwick and Wemmick with his pillar-box mouth; they are all 'realities in which the commonplace, the comic, the pathetic, and the grotesque are inseparably blended' (Johnson 1952: 1, 22).

Dickens' experience is a graphic example of the way imaginative flights are stimulated by imitation and then reorganized in a new but still coherent pattern for a different audience. For highly creative children this is not simply intellectual acquisitiveness and conformist copying, the equivalent of school exercises. Educational psychologists talk about 'divergers', children who prefer to revise the known as Dickens clearly did. 'They prefer the novel and speculative, and are further characterized by openness, risk-taking, intellectual inventiveness, and innovation' (Getzels and Jackson 1962: 13–14; see also Hudson 1966: 36). For most youthful writers this assumption and recreation of the familiar constitutes the play element in their literary culture, which might be either collaborative or personal and secretive, or both.

'I shall write here in the loft and hide my book in the old box with straw where no one can see it. Every one should have a diery. Becos life is too hard with the things one must say to be perlite and the things one must not say to lie' (Alexander and Midgley 2004, rev. 2010: 1), reasons Iris Vaughan at the age of seven in her diary when she discovers the contradictions of the adult world and determines to record her own secret version of reality. Nine-year-old Daisy Ashford penned a very public version of her views on courtship and gender in *The Young Visiters*: 'Oh Bernard she sighed fervently I certainly love you madly you are to me like a Heathen god' (Ashford 1919: 57). The fifteen-year-old Jane Austen created, in her own words, 'a partial, prejudiced, & ignorant' *History of England*, reflecting her fierce partisanship of the Stuarts. She rails against 'that disgrace to humanity, that pest of society, Elizabeth' who scandalously beheaded the 'entirely innocent' Mary Queen of Scots; and her rewriting of Goldsmith's history book is matched by her sister Cassandra's recreation of pictorial images of the monarchs in the likenesses of family members, mischievously extending their revision of history into a private joke between sisters (see introduction to

Alexander and Upfal 2009). At a similar age, Lady Mary Pierrepont (later, the author Wortley Montagu) defied the reality of her gender and lack of choice in marriage and, in *The Adventurer*, imagined an 'enchanting' allegorical isle of love in which women are empowered (Grundy and others 2000: i–ii). Assuming the role of a male narrator, she charts in prose and poetry his romantic travels towards disillusionment, expertly drawing on the seventeenth-century tradition of allegorical typography gleaned from her female models Aphra Behn and Madame de Scudéry.

Such youthful writers not only reimagine and critique their contemporary social and political worlds but also engage with the literary scene, incorporating in their 'publications' the paratextual elements of books and journals (dedication, table of contents, title page, publication information, preface, advertisements and the like). Thus they engage with the literary world, adopt its bibliographical conventions and confidently identify themselves as authors. 'I have long been employed in writing a history of the Jews', writes twelve-year-old Emily Shore. 'It has more than two hundred pages, and is in the printing character. Moreover, it has a frontispiece, title page, vignette, preface, table of contents, and index' (Alexander and McMaster 2005: 4). Even her first booklet, written four years earlier, displays a title page clearly modelled on her favourite genre: 'Natural History, by Emily Shore, being an Account of Reptiles, Birds, and Quadrupeds, Potton, Biggleswade, Brook House, 1828, June 15th. Price 1 shilling.'

As a teenager, twentieth-century British poet laureate Philip Larkin acted out the editing and publication of many of his works, sewing together his latest poems into little pamphlets and then commenting on them, mostly disparagingly, in accompanying prefaces. Playing the role of critic he comments: 'The emotion is trite, the verse sloppy', 'pseudo-Keats babble', 'unforgettably bad', 'slobber', 'sentimentality', 'silly, private, careless or just ordinarily bad'. The best that he can find to say is that his poems are 'of interest to the psychologist, if not to the literary critic' (Tolley 2005). At twelve, H.G. Wells also played the critic, writing his own rave reviews of his novel *The Desert Daisy*. Half serious, half mocking, he cites the *Daily News*: 'Beats Paradise Lost into eternal smash' (Braybrooke 1989: 23).

Lady Mary Pierrepont made a fair copy of her writings in a large vellum-bound volume during her mid-teens and equipped it with a handsomely lettered title page:

Poems Novells Letters Songs &c.
Dedicated to the Fair Hands of the Beauteous
Hermensilda
By her Most
Obedient
Strephon.
made at the age of 14.
Anno Domini, 1704.

On the reverse she wrote a 'Preface':

I Question not but here is very manny faults but if any reasonable Person considers 3 thing[s] they wou'd forgive them,

1   I am a Woman,
2   without any advantage of Education,
3   all these was writ at the age of 14.

As Isobel Grundy points out (1994: ii), the young writer has succinctly encapsulated many a female preface of the period, with its protest of inequality thinly veiled
in a conventionally feminine plea for indulgence.

A precocious knowledge of the publishing world is most clearly documented
in youthful manuscript magazines. In most cases the organization and writing of
such juvenilia seems to have been collaborative, produced and 'published' among
family and friends. In this sense such productions can be seen as children's
'public' texts, considered as performances to entertain and impress their readers.
Many children, such as Virginia Woolf and her siblings, sought out an adult audience for encouragement and approval, while others, like Charles Lutwidge Dodgson,
before he became Lewis Carroll, organized family members until he grew tired of
wielding the stick and took over the entire production himself. The thirteen-year-
old Carroll castigates family members in an editorial titled 'Rust': 'We opened our
Editor's box this morning, expecting of course to find it overflowing with contributions, but found it – our pen shudders and our ink blushes as we write – empty!'
(Sanders and O'Reilly 2008: 38). He concludes his editorial diatribe with a witty
cartoon of a bovine-faced figure titled 'Ox-eyed', a homonym for the 'oxide' used
against his rusty contributors in the article itself (see Figure 6.1). And, like the
Mad Hatter at the Tea Party, he teases his recalcitrant contributors who are also
his readers by inserting in the magazine a series of puzzling 'Answers to Cor-
respondents' for which there are no questions, the contributors having failed to
write any.

With ten siblings, however, Carroll had a ready-made audience if not a team of
willing journalists. As eldest son, he organized family play, including a series of
magazines he edited between 1845 (when he was thirteen) and 1862 (when he was a
talented Oxford undergraduate in his early twenties). Four of the eight family magazines survive: *Useful and Instructive Poetry*, *The Rectory Magazine*, *The Rectory Umbrella*, and
Mischmasch;[6] and although they were addressed especially to the young members of
the Croft Rectory, they also included an adult audience who occasionally contributed.
He made a neat fair copy of contributions and took particular care to emulate the title
pages of printed books. In 'Reasonings on Rubbish', the thirteen-year-old Carroll's
editorial for the first issue of *The Rectory Magazine*, he thanks his contributors for their
efforts but adds that 'these are, with small exception, decidedly of a juvenile cast,
and we would observe that this Magazine is far from being exclusively intended for
Juvenile Readers. We have therefore been compelled, with considerable pain, to reject
many of them' (Sanders and O'Reilly 2008: 10). We can hear in the pseudo-pomposity
of this youthful editorial the amused child appropriating while ridiculing the exasper-
ated adult attitude to unruly children.

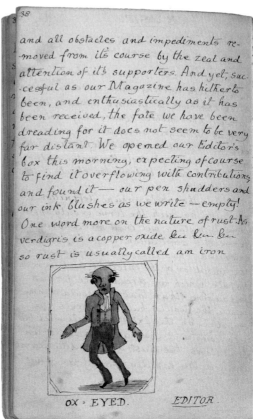

Figure 6.1 *The Rectory Magazine*, 'edited' by the thirteen-year-old Charles Lut-widge Dodgson (Lewis Carroll): title page and editorial page on 'Rust', with his punning 'Ox-eyed' illustration; by permission of the Ransom Humanities Research Center.

Useful and Instructive Poetry, written entirely by Carroll at thirteen for the amuse-ment of a younger brother and sister, subverts parental advice. His article 'Rules and Regulations', for example, turns adult moralizing on its head, advising the young to 'Believe in fairies' and 'Be rude to strangers', suggesting already his 'new, unpietistic handling of childhood' (Hudson 1954: 13). His dubious advice on handling sisters, entitled 'Brother and Sister', probably has some foundation in experience in a rectory of eleven children where the oldest siblings had to help entertain and organize the youngest; but his cannibalistic solution is as much a parody of himself and his identi-fication with the adult world as a tirade against naughty sisters.

'Sister, sister, go to bed,
Go and rest your weary head,'
Thus the prudent brother said.

'Do you want a battered hide
Or scratches to your face applied?'
Thus the sister calm replied.

'Sister! do not rouse my wrath,
I'd make you into mutton broth
As easily as kill a moth.'

The sister raised her beaming eye,
And looked on him indignantly,
And sternly answered 'Only try!'

Off to the cook he quickly ran,
'Dear cook, pray lend a frying pan
To me, as quickly as you can.'

'And wherefore should I give it you?'
'The reason, cook, is plain to view,
I wish to make an Irish stew.'

'What meat is in that stew to go?'
'My sister'll be the contents.' 'Oh!'
'Will you lend the pan, cook?' 'No!'

Moral: 'Never stew your sister.'
                (Hudson 1954: 28–9)

The freedom to play at ignoring adult injunctions, or to both explore the absurdity of one's own responses to the adult world and yet remain firmly within its parameters, is never clearer than in these juvenile magazines. Carroll's fluid imagination and linguistic play demonstrate what Carl Rogers speaks of in his theory of creativity when he describes the ability of such children 'to play spontaneously with ideas, colors, shapes, relationships – to juggle elements into impossible juxtapositions, to shape wild hypotheses, to make the given problematic, to express the ridiculous, to translate from one form to another, to transform into improbable equivalents' (Rogers 1959: 76).

The imaginative mix of self-parody and ridicule of adult behaviour leads directly to Carroll's own adult productions, to his composition of *Alice's Adventures Under Ground* (1863) for the entertainment of Alice Liddell and her sisters, the prototype of that masterpiece for adult children, *Alice's Adventures in Wonderland* (1865). Sibling rivalry and the cook reappear in *Alice*, Humpty Dumpty is anticipated in the poem 'Naught heeded he of their advice', and 'A Tale of a Tail' – which the young artist exuberantly illustrates in a series of spirals – points the way to the Mouse's 'long and sad tale' in *Alice*. While still writing for the last of his family magazines, he was already contributing to professional periodicals. The pieces he contributed – parodies on popular poems,[7] the first version of the text read by the White Rabbit at the Knave of Hearts' trial, and 'Hints for Etiquette' – are remarkably similar to the early versions found in his first magazines. 'Stanza from Anglo-Saxon Poetry' from his last magazine *Mischmasch* appeared even later in *Through the Looking Glass*, as the first stanza of 'Jabberwocky', exactly as it stands. Carroll made few concessions to his new audience, seeing his youthful literary play not simply as his apprenticeship but as the source and model for his later work.

Like Carroll, Amy Levy also honed her skills as a 'New Woman' journalist and novelist by organizing a series of journals amongst her 'Harum-Scarum Band of Scribblers', a group of middle-class London Jewish children, practising not only her editorial skills but also her advocacy of female social and sexual emancipation.[8] For Louisa May Alcott, too, the indulgence in 'gorgeous fantasies' in the family magazine, *The Pickwick Portfolio*, clearly inspired by Dickens, provided an apprenticeship for her later journalistic career. At the age of fifteen Dick Doyle, who was to become the popular *Punch* cartoonist Richard Doyle, known to Victorian audiences throughout the British Empire for his comic histories, social panoramas and satirical portraits of prominent figures, achieved his first publication of a comic series of paintings satirizing the 'medieval' tournament held by the Earl of Eglinton at Eglinton Castle in Ayrshire, Scotland, on 30 August 1839 (McMaster 2006: 88). His richly illustrated journal for the year 1840 records the progress of his painting and duplicates his works in miniature sketches, providing a valuable record of the growth of his imaginative powers. Page four of the journal records the completion of his series and his hope of its publication, together with a comic sketch of Lord Eglinton posing as a medieval knight (see Figure 6.2). Scholars detect hints of T.S. Eliot's 'later poetic and satiric technique in the *Fireside* magazine he edited and wrote himself in 1899 at the age of 10 years' (Soldo 1982: 25). *The Pistol Troop Magazine*, edited and typed with a carbon copy by nine-year-old Evelyn Waugh in 1912, marked the beginning of his writing career. Rosa Praed, novelist and spiritualist in late Victorian London, began her literary career at fifteen as 'editor' of a family journal, *The Marroon Magazine* (1866–8), on a remote sheep-station in Queensland, Australia. Remarkably, she had been inspired by the example of the young Brontës' magazines that she had read about in Elizabeth Gaskell's *Life of Charlotte Brontë* (1857).

Imaginary kingdoms

The Brontës illustrate a particular ontology of play in literary culture, one that is pre-eminent in childhood: namely, the creation of imaginary kingdoms or paracosms as distinctive representations of the experience of children. Paracosm is a sociological term, coined in 1976 in a British survey on imaginary worlds.[9] The survey showed that

but I must get the Tournament finished before I begin anything else as there is some chance of its being published, if it does, that day will be a very extraordinary one in my life. The sketches are nearly finished.

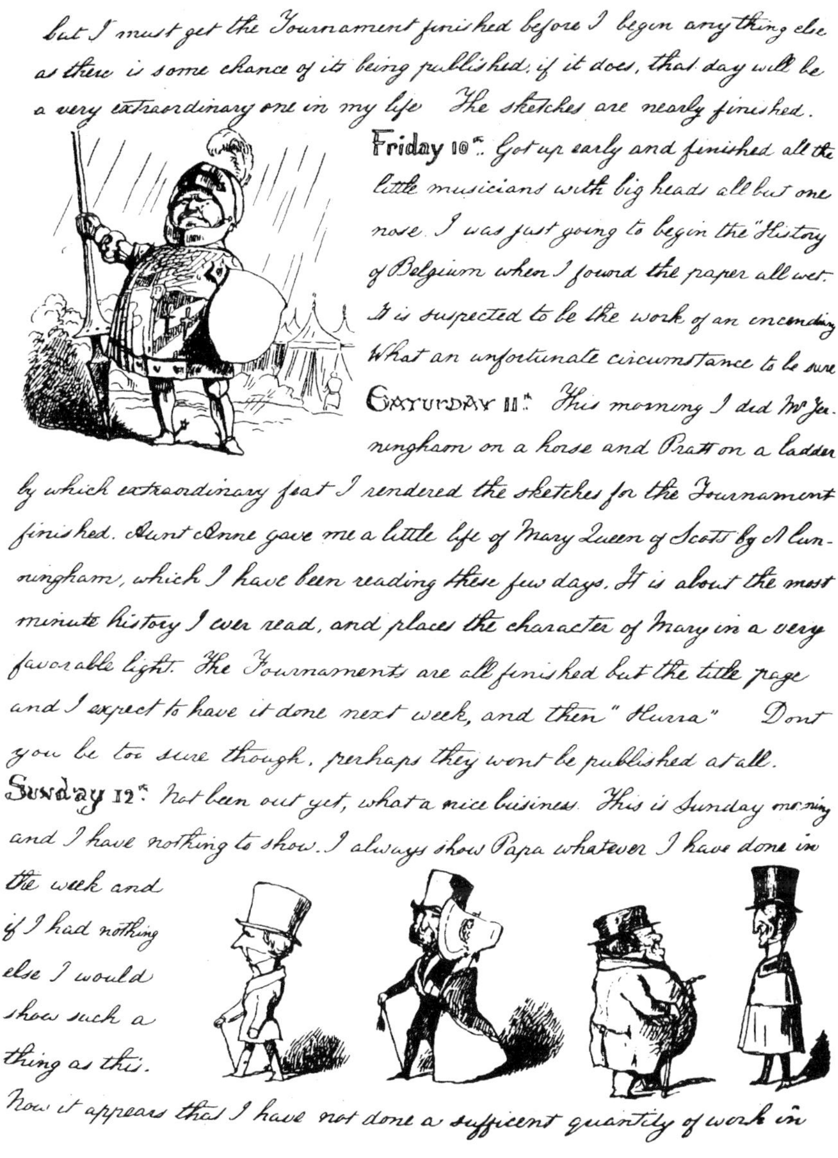

Friday 10th. Got up early and finished all the little musicians with big heads all but one nose. I was just going to begin the "History of Belgium" when I found the paper all wet. It is suspected to be the work of an incendiary. What an unfortunate circumstance to be sure. SATURDAY 11th. This morning I did Mr Cunningham on a horse and Pratt on a ladder by which extraordinary feat I rendered the sketches for the Tournament finished. Aunt Anne gave me a little life of Mary Queen of Scots by Alcunningham, which I have been reading these few days. It is about the most minute history I ever read, and places the character of Mary in a very favorable light. The Tournaments are all finished but the title page and I expect to have it done next week, and then "Hurra" Dont you be too sure though, perhaps they wont be published at all.

Sunday 12th. Not been out yet, what a nice business. This is Sunday morning and I have nothing to show. I always show Papa whatever I have done in the week and

if I had nothing else I would show such a thing as this.

Now it appears that I have not done a sufficient quantity of work in

Figure 6.2 A page from *Dick Doyle's Journal*, 1840, compiled at fifteen, by the later *Punch* artist Richard Doyle; from a manuscript facsimile published by Smith, Elder, & Co., 1885.

paracosms bear the imprint (often in satirical form) of their time and place, confirming that children's imaginations do not work in a vacuum. Imaginary kingdoms are alternative universes in miniature of the real literary, social and political world but also spaces for interpreting and playing out events and ideas circulating in the contemporary consciousness.

Robert Silvey and Stephen MacKeith identify five recurring themes within the paracosms: worlds centred on animals and toys; worlds that are countries or political states; fantasies about schools; 'technological' worlds (including scientific discoveries that clearly reflect their historical period); and worlds grouped around theatres. David Cohen, who later worked with MacKeith, noted that: 'The very fact that the 'worlds' fall easily into such categories is interesting because it seems to reflect the different influences on children' (Cohen and MacKeith 1991: 22). C.S. Lewis's imaginary world, for example, reflects his early passions for anthropomorphized animals, Norse myths and tales of chivalric adventure coupled with a child's-eye view of the adult world of politics discussed by his father and his friends; whereas Charlotte and Branwell Brontës' paracosm reflects their fascination for the military, political and romantic exploits of great men such as the Duke of Wellington and Napoleon Bonaparte, geographical exploration and colonial expansion, and the energetic rivalry amongst authors, editors, booksellers and publishers that they encountered in the literary world of early Victorian Britain.

Boxen, or Animal-Land, was invented by Clive Staple Lewis (or 'Jack' as he was then called) around the age of seven and recorded in notebooks. Based initially on the smartly dressed toy animals he played with in his attic room, he wrote about brave mice and rabbits who marched forth in chivalric armour to do battle with ferocious cats. When his brother Warren returned from boarding school in the holidays, medieval Animal-Land became modern to accommodate 'Warnie's' interests in trains, steamships and modern India. Lewis was left with the tasks of accounting for the change from medieval to modern times and of geographically reconciling his brother's India with Animal-Land: 'This led me from romancing to historiography; I set about writing a full history of Animal-Land' (Hooper 1985: 8), explained C.S. Lewis, the later creator of the fabulous *Chronicles of Narnia* for other children. Until he entered Malvern College in 1913, aged fifteen, he drew maps, made drawings and wrote chronicles often in archaic language, indulging in an endless invention. Animal-Land and India were united into the single state of Boxen. A series of consistent characters threaded their way through documents titled *The King's Ring*, *Manx Against Manx*, *The Relief of Murry*, and on into later 'novels' with titles like *Boxen: On Scenes from Boxonian City Life* and *The History of Mouse-Land from Stone-Age to Bublish I*.

Paracosms reflect an imaginative project perpetually in process; they adapt with their authors to suit their needs and their growing knowledge and interaction with the real world. C.S. Lewis's 'novels' offer a shrewd and often witty glimpse of an adolescent satirically playing with social and political behaviour. In *The Locked Door*, written when Lewis was about 14 years old, the self-important Lord John Big (a frog) witnesses a play lampooning him and exclaims,

Ah there's a libel action in every line. I won't stand it . . . It may be very funny Benjamin but no playwright should bring scorn and discredit on those who ought to be looked on as the pillars of the state.

(Hooper 1985: 111)

If passages like this anticipate Lewis's later social and political satire, others anticipate his measured natural description: 'The sea was calm and of a pale grey color. The sky was cloudless and almost colorless, and countless gulls were wheeling overhead with loud and raucous screeches' (124).

There are many examples of similar private worlds, elaborated and maintained throughout childhood, ranging from Hartley Coleridge's Ejuxria to Jack Kerouac's methodical world of baseball games. Cohen and MacKeith were particularly fascinated by fantasies dominated by making up a country and then organizing it. They found this kind of systematic imagination 'psychologically very curious': 'On the one hand, children are playing, fantasizing, imagining; on the other hand, the fantasy is very logical. Events in their world have to follow rules' (Cohen and MacKeith 1991: 53). Joetta Harty has made a valuable study of four such paracosms,[10] exploring their conception through their geography and relating it to concurrent cartographic ideology. She found that nineteenth-century children who could not physically venture into the British Empire engaged with it through literary projects.

The most famous example of a consistently organized imaginary world developed in childhood and extending into adult life is the literary project explored in the Brontë juvenilia.[11] Like Dickens and Lewis Carroll, however, the young Brontës' imaginative life was far from sedentary and their paracosms extended far into adulthood. They began their creative life by assuming and acting out characters and events from Scott's historical romances, Bunyan's *Pilgrim's Progress* and their father's Tory magazines and newspapers. Records survive of Emily Brontë breaking the branch of her father's favourite cherry tree while pretending to be Prince Charles escaping from the Roundheads. Her early fascination for civil war and royalty became central to her imaginative Gondal saga that survived in poems and diary papers throughout her life and beyond *Wuthering Heights*. She was still writing about civil war in her Pacific island of Gondal when she died.

For both Emily and Charlotte Brontë, heroic models from the pages of Scott, Byron and *Blackwood's Edinburgh Magazine* echo through their early writing and on to Rochester, Heathcliff, and Lucy Snowe. Their 'plays' as they called them, based on the art, literature, history and politics they read about from their earliest days, were documented as soon as they could write; yet, as in the case of Lewis, 'toy' objects provided the catalyst for their imaginations. When their brother Branwell received his now-famous set of twelve wooden toy soldiers it was natural that as soon as they had been given identities they should be provided with books to both entertain them and to record their progress. And so we have 'The History of the Year', 'Young Men's Magazine' and 'The History of the Young Men' – documents that began the elaborate *literary* plays that morphed first into the Glass Town saga and then, in later teenage years, into the kingdoms of Angria and Gondal.

The surviving manuscripts record every aspect of the apprentice writer. The earliest are characterized by their miniature size and minuscule script (see Figure 6.3), written in imitation of newspaper print and sewn into little booklets proportional to the size of the toy soldiers or 'Young Men' as they were initially called. Many manuscripts are no larger than a postage stamp yet contain over 100 words per page. With paper expensive and scarce, the children used found objects for the covers of their books: scraps of wallpaper, fragments of book advertisements, even a used Epsom salts bag. Poor spelling and often non-existent punctuation is as much a feature of these texts as their complex intertextuality and rich allusiveness. Later novelettes of Charlotte and Branwell, many of which contain at least 40,000 words, are written on larger loose sheets of paper but still in the same minuscule script used by all four children. Their output was prolific: Charlotte's manuscripts alone exceed in volume all her later novels combined, and Branwell's output exceeds that of Charlotte. None of Emily and Anne Brontës' Glass Town writings survive but their extant Gondal poems, like the writings of Charlotte and Branwell, are now available in scholarly editions.

Figure 6.3 The earliest miniature hand-sewn books of the Brontës, each measuring approximately 5.3 × 3.3 cm; by permission of the Brontë Parsonage Museum.

The title page to Branwell's *History of the Young Men* (Figure 6.4) illustrates the children's enthusiastic response to the print culture of their time and the way this helped them to begin to construct an identity of authorship. Branwell in particular reproduced scrupulously the bibliographical details from printed books, including the title pages of contemporary history books, with their customary long explanatory titles and the credentials of their authors, in this case the Glass Town historian, Captain John Bud (one of Branwell's pseudonyms). He includes the requisite quotation: 'To explore

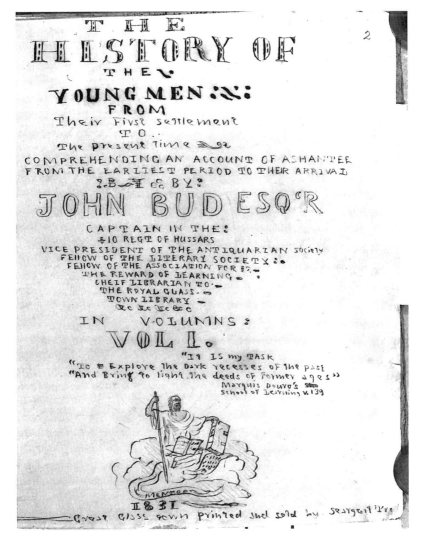

Figure 6.4 Branwell Brontë's title page to *The History of the Young Men*, a hand-sewn booklet of eighteen pages, 15.8 × 19 cm; by permission of the British Library.

the Dark recesses of the past/And bring to light the deeds of former ages', and a colophon of the learned 'Mentor'.[12] This Greek god-like figure riding on the clouds represents the Chief Genii Brannii Lightning, God of Thunder (Branwell had recently learned from his Classics lessons that 'Bronte' means 'thunder' in Greek). In the early days of the Glass Town saga, the Brontë children saw themselves as four Chief Genii (modelled on the *Arabian Nights* and the Greek gods). They participated in their own stories as genii and formed one of the many levels of narration in the saga. They were the all-controlling narrative powers that decided the fate of the Young Men.

'This is the Duke of Wellington! It shall be mine!' shouted Charlotte as she snatched up her toy soldier and named it after her father's revered hero. The real Duke, his family and friends, became her fictional equivalents in the children's plays, and when his character proved too restricting Charlotte replaced her chief hero by imaginary recreations of his two sons: Arthur, Marquis of Douro (later Duke of Zamorna and King of Angria) and Lord Charles Wellesley (later Charles Townshend). Branwell chose Wellington's adversary Napoleon, before creating his hero Alexander Percy ('Rogue', later Lord Ellrington and Earl of Northangerland); and Emily and Anne nominated soldiers who later grew into Parry and Ross, venerated kings of the Glass Town saga, named after famous Arctic explorers. The sheer delight and authority of Charlotte's claim of the Duke of Wellington characterizes the enthusiastic naming and recording of characters, institutions and landscape in imitation of the adult world. Charlotte and Branwell immediately documented their play as 'History' in language charged with excitement, drew up maps and tables, and over the following year reworked the advent of their Glass Town saga in fictional form.

Like the young paracosmists Hartley Coleridge, Thomas Malkin and Thomas De Quincey, the Brontës appropriated nineteenth-century imperialist ideology. They were colonizers, imaginatively imitating and then reconfiguring the British political and social world they encountered in their extensive reading. Throughout the 1820s and 1830s, *Blackwood's* carried articles on British exploration and emigration in Africa, on the Ashantee Wars and customs, and advocated settlement on the West African Coast, in the Gulf of New Guinea; and the Brontës' well-used *Grammar of General Geography* by Rev. J. Goldsmith reinforced European attitudes to territorial expansion and the need to civilize the 'many blank spaces on the earth' as Joseph Conrad's Marlow puts it in *Heart of Darkness*. Charlotte's 'A Romantic Tale' (also called 'The Twelve Adventurers') tells, in the form of a popular travel narrative, the story of the Young Men's voyage to the west coast of Africa, their settlement after warfare and negotiation with the indigenous Ashantee tribes, their election of Arthur Wellesley, Duke of Wellington as their leader, and the founding of Great Glass Town at the delta of the river Niger. Branwell's 'History of the Young Men', mentioned previously, documents the same events in exhaustive detail and provides a map of the new kingdoms. This fictitious world, however, bears little resemblance to Africa itself apart from occasional place names, incursions by Ashantee tribes and exotic scenery that owes as much to fairytale and the *Arabian Nights* as it does to geographical descriptions of what was known as 'the dark continent'.

From the ages of about ten and eleven until their twenties and even later,

Charlotte and Branwell, with the help of their younger sisters Emily and Anne (before they broke away to form their own world of Gondal), chronicled through prose, poetry and drama, the life of their fictional British colony in Africa with its recurring cast of characters and shifting geographical boundaries and allegiances within a federation of kingdoms ruled by each of the children. They not only wrote about their characters (their literary, political, military, and sexual exploits), but also illustrated them in accomplished pencil, ink, and watercolour drawings. Their fictitious world centred first on the Glass Town Federation, its capital Verdopolis (originally The Great Glass Town), and the society established by the first 'chief' men (the original toy soldiers who, although broken or lost, survived as literary incarnations); then moved to the new kingdom of Angria following the exploits of the next generation and their new concerns that reflected the Brontës' own maturing interests and anxieties. Charlotte's last Angrian novelettes, for example, focus on the fate of women associated with the Duke of Zamorna, King of Angria: his third wife, the haughty Mary Percy who becomes a pawn in her husband's complex relationship with his sometime mentor and rival her father Lord Northangerland; Mina Laury, the most loyal of his mistresses; the adolescent Caroline Vernon, illegitimate daughter of Northangerland and ward of Zamorna, whose seduction by her guardian we witness; and Elizabeth Hastings, who is a prototype for the later small, plain but self-reliant heroine of *Jane Eyre*.

Johan Huizinga pointed out in his seminal study on the anthropology of play, that in playing the child is free to be creative and to use the whole personality without fear of censure (Huizinga 1955: 4). One may cut off heads at random like Branwell in his bloodthirsty battles or, like his sisters, 'make alive' again so that characters can continue into the next Glass Town manuscript. The young authors may create and experience vicariously a world of sexual and political intrigue beyond the range of their years or parsonage upbringing. Charlotte's passionate involvement with her 'bright darling dream' is vividly demonstrated in her Roe Head Journal, a mix of autobiographical protest against 'this world's desolate & boundless deluge' (Alexander 2010: 158) and the comforting sustenance of her Angrian visions. When she records the violent interruption of the intense realization of her favourite hero, we witness the extent to which her imaginative world has become, for her, as real as the real world:

> Never shall I, Charlotte Brontë, forget what a voice of wild & wailing music now came thrillingly to my mind's – almost to my body's – ear; nor how distinctly I, sitting in the schoolroom at Roe Head, saw the Duke of Zamorna leaning against that obelisk, with the mute marble Victory above him, the fern waving at his feet, his black horse turned loose grazing among the heather, the moonlight so mild & so exquisitely tranquil, sleeping upon that vast & vacant road, & the African sky quivering & shaking with stars expanded above all. I was quite gone. I had really utterly forgot where I was and all the gloom & cheerlessness of my situation. I felt myself breathing quick and short as I beheld the Duke lifting up his sable crest, which undulated as the plume of a hearse waves to the wind, & knew that music which seems as mournfully triumphant as the scriptural verse

> 'Oh Grave where is thy sting;
> Oh Death where is thy victory'[13]

was exciting him & quickening his ever rapid pulse.

'Miss Brontë, what are you thinking about?' said a voice that dissipated all the charm, & Miss Lister thrust her little, rough black head into my face! 'Sic transit' &c.

(Alexander 2010: 157)

The Brontë juvenilia, however, are seldom written in the first person like this. Imitating the journalism of *Blackwood's*, the siblings invent a variety of personalities, write under their pseudonyms and practise a type of verbal pugilism. Under the guise of these fictitious poets, historians, and politicians, they jockey for the Glass Town public's attention by writing slanderous reviews on each other's work. In the process the young writers are not only playing with their material but with the process of narration itself. In one article the lawyer and bookseller Sergeant Bud (Branwell's voice) scorns Charlotte's degenerate editorial policy;[14] in the next, Lord Charles Wellesley (Charlotte's voice) satirizes Emily's 'Parry's land' with its Yorkshire puddings and dull landscapes.[15] The young writers carry on a continual verbal battle in editorial notes, prefaces, afterwords, and the actual texts of their stories – emulating while parodying their model of literary culture found in *Blackwood's*.

Referring to themselves as 'scribblemanics', they wove a highly sophisticated mix of satire, literary criticism, editorials, journalistic reports, reviews, poetry, plays, and short stories. In the process these young writers not only represent, misrepresent, and critique the adult world they appropriate but also parody their own paracosm, sending up Charlotte's romantic inclinations or Branwell's warmongering and poetic pretensions. In the play 'The Poetaster', for example, Captain Tree (Charlotte's pseudonym) issues the following lament upon reading the hackneyed verse of the aspiring poet, Henry Rhymer:

> Oh, how that noble profession is dishonoured! . . . Alas, alas, that those days would come again, when no one had even a transitory dream of putting pen to paper except a few choice spirits set apart from and revered by all the rest of the world; but it cannot be hoped for, it cannot be hoped for. And some years hence, perhaps, these eyes will see, through the mists of age, every child that walks along the streets, bearing its manuscripts in its hand, going to the printers for publication.

Captain Tree mocks the ambitions of the talentless Rhymer (alias Branwell), yet the play also satirizes the pompous and reactionary sentiments of the prose writer Tree himself. 'The Poetaster' is actually written by Lord Charles Wellesley (Charlotte's favourite pseudonym and Tree's rival) who in this speech is ridiculing Tree's attitude to him as a young writer by ascribing to Tree the ridiculous fear of a city overrun with hyper-literate children. At the same time, Charlotte is self-reflexively mocking the

Brontës' literary enterprise itself, since Wellesley's act of ridicule and her own play fulfil Tree's prophecy. Thus 'The Poetaster' is a sophisticated satire on literary types and a parody of the writing practised by the Brontës themselves.

Conclusion

The Brontë juvenilia provide the richest record we have of youthful literary activity; only rivalled by Jane Austen's brilliantly ironic juvenilia, which are neither as voluminous nor as revealing of the inner life of its author. But they were characteristic of many other child writers in producing an uncensored imaginary world that functions for the young author as a safe 'free' space, privately maintained and 'published' only among siblings, a place where they felt liberated to experiment with adult behaviour and to assume a power they were denied as children or young women in real life. All children experience this 'potential space between the individual and the environment' where the child psychologist Donald Winnicott locates an exciting interweave of subjectivity and objective observation (Winnicott 1971: 65). But not all children use this space to define their lives as writers, to create physical books, to practise writing skills, to assume roles in the publishing world, and to develop themes that are continued in their later works.

The children mentioned in this chapter have created a writing self, a personality or personalities that empower them not simply to engage with the adult world but to reimagine and re-engage, often through parody, in such a way as to mature and develop their own authorial voices. The creative manifestations of this process of play and appropriation become a comment not only on the child but also on adult reality itself and, as such, are part of our culture. Whether the voice of the child is autobiographical, disguised as a fictive character or as an omniscient narrator, juvenilia constitute a rich area of children's cultural heritage. It is vital to preserve the products of children's literary play for future generations wishing to understand imaginative worlds of children in the past.

Notes

1 The following discussion assumes that the words 'child' and 'children' refer to a young person up to the age of at least sixteen and often beyond. This spans the formative years, although exactly when any one individual can be considered 'adult' in terms of authorship is debatable. The Juvenilia Press, with which I am associated, arbitrarily selects the age of twenty as the chronological boundary. The United Nations Convention on the Rights of the Child (http://www2.ohchr.org/english/law/crc.htm) defines a child as 'a human being below the age of 18 years unless under the law applicable to the child, majority is attained earlier'.
2 This edited collection was hailed as 'nothing less than the definition of a new genre within the literary academy' (Birch 2006: 3).
3 *The Young Men's Magazine, Number 2*, sold at Sotheby's on 15 December 2011; reported in *The Telegraph*, 28 April 2012.
4 For information on the Juvenilia Press, see http://www.arts.unsw.edu.au/juvenilia/.
5 Charles Dickens to Bulwer-Lytton, 1851 (DeVries 1976: 16–17).

6 These are the first two and last two of the Dodgson family magazines; little is known of *The Comet*, *The Rosebud*, *The Star* or *The Will-o'-the-Wisp*, which were not edited by Carroll.

7 For example, 'The Three Voices' appeared in *The Train*, November 1856.

8 Unless otherwise indicated, the information on Levy and other young writers in this paragraph can be found in Alexander and McMaster (2005).

9 The survey, conducted by journalist Robert Silvey, former head of the BBC's Audience Research, and analysed in partnership with psychiatrist Dr Stephen MacKeith, is discussed in Cohen and MacKeith (1992: 11–14).

10 Hartley Coleridge's Ejuxria, Thomas Malkin's Allestone, the De Quincey brothers' Tigrosylvania and Gombroon, and the Brontës' Glass Town, Angria, and Gondal (Harty 2007).

11 The following information on the Brontës' juvenilia is derived from my research over many years. Interested readers may consult Alexander (1983, 1987 and 1991) and Alexander and Smith (2003).

12 The title page with 'Mentor' is illustrated in Alexander and Sellars (1995: 299), together with colophons from Branwell's various title pages.

13 Corinthians 15: 55. Charlotte Brontë's writing is redolent with biblical allusion, often used profanely but always aptly.

14 'Lines spoken by a lawyer on the occasion of the transfer of this magazine', in Neufeldt (1997: 73).

15 'A Day at Parry's Palace', in Alexander (1987: 229–33).

References

Alexander, C. (1983) *The Early Writings of Charlotte Brontë*, Oxford: Basil Blackwell.

—— (ed.) (1987, 1991) *An Edition of the Early Writings of Charlotte Brontë*, vol. 1: The Glass Town Saga 1826–1832; vol. 2: The Rise of Angria 1833–1835, Oxford: Basil Blackwell.

—— (ed.) (2010) *Tales of Glass Town, Angria, and Gondal: Selected Writings of the Brontës*, Oxford: Oxford University Press.

—— and McMaster, J. (2005) *The Child Writer from Austen to Woolf*, Cambridge: Cambridge University Press.

—— and Sellars, J. (1995) *The Art of the Brontës*, Cambridge: Cambridge University Press.

—— and Smith, M. (2003) *The Oxford Companion to the Brontës*, Oxford: Oxford University Press.

—— and Upfal, A. (eds) (2009) *Jane Austen's The History of England and Cassandra's Portraits*, Sydney: Juvenilia Press.

Alexander, P.F. and Midgley, P. (eds) (2004) *The Diary of Iris Vaughan*, Sydney: Juvenilia Press.

Ariès, P. (1962) *Centuries of Childhood: A Social History of Family Life*, trans. Robert Baldick, New York: Knopf.

Ashford, D. (1919) *The Young Visiters Or Mr Salteena's Plan*, with a Preface by J.M. Barrie, London: Chatto & Windus.

Birch, D. (2006) 'Eager to Please: Make Sure to Read the Children – But Sceptically', *Times Literary Supplement*, 10 February 2006: 3.

Braybrooke, N. (1989) *Seeds in the Wind: Twentieth Century Juvenilia from W.B. Yeats to Ted Hughes*, London: Hutchinson.

Cohen, D. and MacKeith, S. (1991) *The Development of Imagination: The Private Worlds of Childhood*, New York: Routledge.

DeVries, D. (1976) *Dickens's Apprentice Years: The Making of a Novelist*, New York: The Harvester Press Ltd, Barnes & Noble Books.

Forster, J. (1928) *The Life of Charles Dickens*. Edited and annotated with an introduction by J.W.T. Ley, author of 'The Dickens Circle', London & Tonbridge: Whitefriars Press Ltd.

Getzels, J.W. and Jackson, P.W. (1962) *Creativity and Intelligence: Explorations with Gifted Students*, London and New York: John Wiley & Sons.

Grundy, I. with Susan Hillabold (eds) (1994) *Indamora to Lindamira*, by Lady Mary Pierrepont, Edmonton: Juvenilia Press.

—— and others (eds) (2000) *The Adventurer*, by Lady Mary Pierrepont, Edmonton: Juvenilia Press.

Harty, J. (2007) 'The Islanders: Mapping Paracosms in the Early Writing of Hartley Coleridge, Thomas Malkin, Thomas De Quincey, and the Brontës', PhD Jacob W. Dissertation, George Washington University.

Hooper, W. (ed.) (1985) *Boxen: The Imaginary World of the Young C.S. Lewis*, London: Harcourt Brace Jovanovich.

Hudson, D. (ed.) (1954) *Useful and Instructive Poetry*, by Lewis Carroll, London: Geoffrey Bles.

Hudson, L. (1966) *Contrary Imaginations: A Psychological Study of the Young Student*, New York: Schocken Books.

Huizinga, J. (1955) *Homo Ludens: A Study of the Play-element in Culture*, transl. from 1944 German edition; London: Beacon Paperback.

Johnson, E. (1952) *Charles Dickens: His Tragedy and Triumph*, New York: Simon and Schuster.

McMaster, J. *et al.* (eds) (2006) *Dick Doyle's Journal for 1840*, Sydney: Juvenilia Press.

—— (1997) *The Young Visiters*, by Daisy Ashford, Edmonton: Juvenilia Press.

Neufeldt, V. (ed.) (1997, 1999), *The Works of Patrick Branwell Brontë: An Edition*, 3 vols, New York: Garland.

Rogers, C.R. (1959) 'Towards a Theory of Creativity', in H.H. Anderson (ed.) *Creativity and its Cultivation: Addresses Presented at the Interdisciplinary Symposia on Creativity*, Michigan State University, East Lansing, Michigan; New York: Harper and Brothers.

Sanders, V. and O'Reilly, E. (eds) (2008) *The Rectory Magazine*, by Lewis Carroll, Sydney: Juvenilia Press.

Soldo, J.J. (1982) 'Jovial Juvenilia: T.S. Eliot's First Magazine', in *Biography*, vol. 5, no. 1, Winter: 25–37.

Tolley, A.T. (ed.) (2005) *Early Poems and Juvenilia*, by Philip Larkin, London: Faber.

Winnicott, D.W. (1971) *Playing and Reality*, London and New York: Routledge.

Part II

Sites and places

The spatial heritage and commemoration of children

Taking the children

Children, childhood and heritage making

Laurajane Smith

Variations on 'taking the children', or 'for the educational benefit of the children', are frequently cited reasons chosen by survey respondents for visiting museums and other heritage sites (Falk and Dierking 1992: 15; Smith 2006: 139, 216). 'Family' is also often identified as an important aspect in heritage engagement (Rosenzweig and Thelen 1998; Ashton and Hamilton 2010). However, what does 'taking the children' mean? This chapter draws on interviews with visitors to a range of museums and heritage sites in both England and Australia. The data are part of an ongoing international project concerned with identifying the memory and identity work that visitors undertake when they visit sites and museums. Children were not the primary focus of the interviews; however, they are represented in four ways within this body of data. First, by parents who identified that their reason for visiting such places was 'taking the children'. Second, by the way visitors, both with and without children, invoked the image of 'the child' in relation to the heritage site or museum. Third, by the way that some visitors saw themselves as 'visiting', remembering and reflecting on their own childhoods in certain museums or sites and, finally, by the small number of children interviewed in the course of the survey work. The chapter argues that the agency of the child, both as a person and as an imagined ideal sustained by parents and other visitors, is as significant as it is political.

Interest by historians in the history of children and childhood is relatively recent, and a great deal had been assumed about the universal nature of both childhood and children's experiences (Jenkins 1998; Pascoe 2010). Historians stressed the importance of distinguishing between the histories and ideas of children and childhood (Cunningham 1995), and that childhood and children's experiences are not only historically and culturally bounded but intensely ideological (Pascoe 2010). The Western twentieth/twenty-first-century myth of childhood innocence has obscured the political power of ideas of childhood, and also robbed children themselves of their political and cultural agency (Jenkins 1998). Despite the fact that children are a significant heritage audience there has been little direct research on children (Hooper-Greenhill 1994: 237) or recognition that concepts of childhood are integral to the reminiscing and other memory work that visitors to heritage sites are believed to undertake. The focus has been on exploring and developing educational strategies and/or assessing how children or families learn (Hooper-Greenhill 1991; Falk and Dierking 2000; Jensen 1994;

although see Golding (2009) for a more developed analysis). While heritage studies as a whole have tended to focus on technical issues of management, education and interpretation, there is a widening literature that has begun to redefine heritage as an area of cultural production and communication (Kirshenblatt-Gimblett 1995, 1998; Dicks 2000; Smith 2006; Byrne 2009; Bendix 2009). This chapter aims to identify some of the themes of childhood and children's experiences of heritage that take heritage studies beyond a concern with children's education, and explore the acts of meaning making and communication that occur around the intertwined themes of children and childhood.

Heritage, children and childhood

The concept of heritage that frames this work recognizes that heritage is not simply a concern with materiality, but rather a discourse that frames a set of cultural practices that centre on the negotiation of cultural and social change and dissonance (see Smith (2006) for further development). Heritage is a performance in which individual and collective remembering and commemoration are central, and in which historical narratives and social and cultural values are continually re/created, arbitrated, affirmed or rejected. This process occurs in the choices made to preserve, or not, certain artefacts or places, in the ways exhibitions are developed and the ways sites are interpreted for the public. It is also found in the way visitors engage or disengage with museum exhibitions or heritage sites. Heritage making, the creation and recreation of historical and cultural meaning and identity, is done by both institutions and their visitors. Moreover, how visitors engage with exhibitions or sites, and the experiences and meanings that are thus created, do not necessarily conform to the intentions of curatorial or interpretive staff (Falk 2005: 266; Smith 2010a, 2012). If heritage is a negotiated experience, so too is the concept of childhood and the experiences it frames. As Cunningham (1995: 190) has argued, children, adults and social institutions are involved in constant negotiations over what childhood and adulthood mean. Western societies stress the romantic idea of childhood as a 'special' time; however, it is a constructed concept that families are continually negotiating (Pascoe 2010), partly with the various relevant state agencies that provide families with a range of resources to help socialize children (Cunningham 1995; Kline 1998). Heritage, as illustrated below, is not only part of the cultural tools that are used to socialize and acculturate children, amongst other groups, but it is also a resource in familial negotiation of the meaning of childhood and the values and understandings that parents wish to instil in their children.

Memory, or more critically remembering and forgetting, plays an important role in the cultural performance of heritage making. Remembering is an active and informed selection of images and ideas to form or recreate a memory that endeavours to complete various social and political goals (Misztal 2010). It is, in short, a 'mediated action' in which collectively or individually the past is reinterpreted through both the experiences and social and political needs of the present (Wertsch 2002: 8). Within the heritage literature, heritage and memory are often linked to concepts of nostalgia – to an ideal of a golden time when it was better back then (see Hewison 1987; Lowenthal

1996, 2011 for critique of this). However, these conceptualizations of nostalgia often misunderstand the political work that remembering is doing. Nostalgia is a form of remembering, and as such is part of the process of heritage making and of reinforcing or remaking social and cultural values. Thus, how childhood is remembered, either nostalgically or otherwise, is an integral part of heritage making, and the concepts of childhood so constructed have implications not only for the person doing the remembering, but for how that may then inform their interactions and negotiations with their own or another's children.

Methodology

The data for this chapter are drawn from visitor interviews in England undertaken at six country houses (454 interviews) and three social history museums (273 interviews) during 2004; and eight exhibitions marking the 2007 bicentenary of Britain's abolition of its slave trade undertaken in 2007 (1,498 interviews).[1] The Australia data represent 541 interviews from two museums, a house museum and two heritage sites collected during 2010–2011.[2] The interviews consisted of a number of demographic questions to determine, among other measures, age, gender, occupation and ethnicity (for fuller account see Smith (2006, 2010a)). These were followed by a number of open-ended questions depending on the site in question; however, 12 of these were common to all sites. Responses to the open-ended questions were either recorded or detailed notes were taken. The interview schedule was administered to individuals or family groups at the end of an exhibition or as they were about to leave the venue. All interviews were transcribed and read through to identify themes. Each question was then coded according to the themes that had emerged in the read through. These codes were used to facilitate cross referencing of themes with demographic variables. It is important to note, for the purposes of this chapter, that children were *not* targeted, and the material discussed here needs to be understood in that context. When children were interviewed it was done with the permission of parents, and occurred as part of a family group interview or because, on a few occasions, the child approached the interviewer and asked to be interviewed.

Taking it all for granted: parents and their children

In the overall sample from both countries, 7 per cent[3] identified their overall reason for visiting as 'taking the children'. Their motivation for doing so was significantly uniform across countries, different ethnic and class backgrounds and the different types of museums and sites included in the survey. All parents and grandparents accompanied by children reported that they wanted to foster in their children an understanding of how different the past was from the present:

> Mainly just show them that um . . . what it was, the way of life and how they actually lived and didn't know any better than that and kids today just don't . . . to explain things to the kids today and look at their faces, it's amazing. That's basi-

cally why we sort of wanted to do it.

(LR110: Stockman's Hall of Fame, 2010)

However, this was often accompanied by a strong desire that their children should appreciate how hard it was and how lucky they, as children, are now:

> It's just basically to show the children their heritage, the way of life, the way things were and to compare, because it's too easy now for the kids, it's just way too easy and to see how we struggled through the land.
>
> (NMA012: National Museum of Australia, 2010)

> Um, well I think it's important especially for the kids to know what's happened before instead of taking things for granted that they do.
>
> (OMG047: Old Melbourne Gaol, 2010)

> I hope the children learn how hard it was for children their age. They were shocked that children their age worked in mines.
>
> (NCM85: National Coal Mining Museum, England, 2004)

For some this desire was based on a concern with 'sharing [the past] with my children' (OMG068, 2010), and for others the museum or heritage site became a place useful for intergenerational communication:

> Ah yeah, I mean these type of places are so important for our children and our grandchildren to have to show them what it was like because they just live in such a different world these days, you know, I mean . . . it staggers me, I went into Longreach [town] today and I went to an internet place, a computer place, to say 'can I use your computer' and he said, 'ah no, we don't do internet anymore because most people travel with laptops now' [. . .] that just shows you how much our world changes, it's just uh . . . it's an amazing, amazing thing.
>
> (LR07: Stockman's Hall of Fame, 2010)

For some parents, museums and heritage sites presented a hands-on opportunity to show their children history and culture because it was object based:

> I guess it makes, especially for the kids, it makes it easier to understand a bit about our history, our background so we can read it, we can see it rather than, I guess, trying to find it in a thousand books and all that sort of thing.
>
> (LR126: Stockman's Hall of Fame, 2010)

However, for many 'taking the children' was important, as visiting the site represents important cultural values. For those parents and grandparents who were concerned that children took the past for granted, or that their children 'had it easy', there was often an implied message that they were concerned that their children took the parent for granted, and they wanted to engender respect for themselves from their child. Others were concerned about other values; for instance, this self-identified Anglo-Celtic Australian parent at the exhibition 'First Australians' at the National Museum of Australia talks about the opportunities the exhibition presented for children to learn about racism, opportunities that he did not have as a child:

> Um . . . I think it's good to remember that, you know, that things happen for a particular reason and that you know, by remembering what happened in the past hopefully it's a way forward in um, sort of getting past people's somewhat immature, or whatever ideals that they have, and if you can bring your children here, they're going to learn something from a younger age um, whereas as a child maybe I didn't, I had different sort of perspectives and points of view put across to me that maybe weren't that positive, so yeah.
>
> (NMA034: National Museum of Australia, 2010)

Other parents, and indeed their children, also report using museums and heritage sites quite explicitly for passing on cultural and familial knowledge, which was also noted by Rosenzweig and Thelen in the US, particularly amongst Indigenous Americans and other marginalized groups (1998: 60–1, 162f.). One Indigenous Australian visitor to the 'First Australian' exhibition, accompanied by his two children, noted:

> Oh well I hope my kids take away that they've learned something, you know, so I try and bring them here as much as I can to learn about their culture and um, you know, about Australia and how we live and yeah, about their heritage.
>
> (NMA050: National Museum of Australia, 2010)

In the next example, a visitor to the Immigration Museum in Melbourne, who identified as Italian-Australian, was using his visit to demonstrate to two generations not only what the migrant experience was like for him, but also that he was responsible for the family's future now being enjoyed as Australian citizens:

> Well I want to prove to my grandchildren and my children and this is the beginning, they can see those photos and I was one of them, I'm not in there but I was 21 years old, blah blah blah and that's where we started our future.
>
> (IMM099: Immigration Museum Melbourne, 2010)

However, the heritage moments that children produce are not well understood, nor can we assume that what a child sees as heritage is at all commensurate with what an adult may see. As part of research into the meaning and use of heritage by people in the deindustrialized town of Castleford, West Yorkshire, I asked residents to list their favourite heritage sites in the town. While most adults listed industrial sites or archaeological ruins, two 17-year-old males nominated the modern Xscape complex, which is defined as the 'Ultimate Entertainment Destination'. This was a place, they explained, where they could be themselves. As one museum visitor noted, the importance of heritage sites was giving 'kids a sense of the past and their own identity' (NCM41, 2004). If heritage is linked to identity, then a place where you can 'be yourself' must certainly be defined as heritage.

An important part of appreciating the past, especially for middle-class parents, was that children were learning *how* to visit. At one of the museums in the study, a staff member undertaking observational work of visitors noted that many younger people did not 'know how to visit', rushing from display to display, a process often curtailed, she noted approvingly, by attentive parents teaching their children to behave correctly in the museum. Learning the museum or heritage performance is a statement of identity. Museums and heritage sites are often places where visitors expect to see people like themselves – a point that emerges again and again in interviews. As one parent noted, the English historic house she had taken her children to made her feel 'safe here with the kids, as the same sort of people visit here' (CH58, 2004). This performance becomes almost ritualistic, with some visitors, particularly to country/historic houses, noting that they obsessively visit such places, but cannot explain why they do so (Smith 2006: 136). As one country house visitor explained to me heritage for him was 'historic identity, country houses and Englishness. Coming here with my Mum and Dad when I was a kid' (CH118: English country house, 2004).

This tradition or heritage of visiting was something, he informed me, he was introducing his own children to, as visiting was part of his heritage. For one parent, visiting was about maintaining rituals that allowed a connection with their children: 'And we've lost so much of our rituals and our connection with the children and I think it's very important to try and get some of that back' (RH011: Rouse Hill historic house, 2011). Here visitors recall their own childhood visits:

> My father when I was a child used to take me to a cultural site every Sunday and that interest has always stayed with me [I have] been to over 100 houses, [I] visit one a week.
> (CH328: English country house, 2004)

> Things carry on, reminds you of past visits as children.
> (CH436: English country house, 2004)

> [M]y mum used to often take me to historical houses, like she's been down to Elizabeth Farm and things like that, Rippon Lea in Melbourne, we used to do a lot of that with my parents but I haven't really done that with the children so I want to start taking them to things like this cos I think it's great for them to realize how people used to live.
> (RH08: Rouse Hill historic house, 2011)

Visiting with children is a form of acculturation in which, it is hoped, children learn a certain appreciation of the past and certain values and, for some parents, it is also about performing, or embodying, a certain sense of identity through the visit. Heritage sites and museums are part of the suite of cultural tools that families and societies use to socialize children; the aim is not only to teach them historical or cultural 'facts', but more importantly how to 'be' and how to value themselves and their parents/grandparents.

Ignorant or naive: the political use of the innocent child

Henry Jenkins (1998) has noted that the myth of childhood innocence carries political rhetorical force in Western societies. He argues that images of childhood innocence have been utilized in almost every major political battle of the twentieth century, and that invoking such images not only provides rhetorical and emotional force to pronouncements, but also shields the speaker from criticism (1998: 2–3). These images, he reveals, are not confined to particular political values, but are equally used on both the left and the right (1998: 4–14).

Heritage sites and museum exhibitions are utilized in wider heritage negotiations over historical and social values and meanings, and represent, as I have argued elsewhere, a political performance that has implications for how groups and nations both perceive themselves, and are themselves perceived (Smith 2006, 2007, 2010b). Not only are children being asked to embrace particular values, adults are, through their visit, often reaffirming their own ideological positions (Smith 2006, 2012). In these contexts, images of children and childhood frequently come into play to underline the importance of the point being made by a speaker, but also infuse a sense of the 'commonsense' of the position they are taking. These images play a similar role to what have been called self-sufficient arguments within political and social debates over racial and ethnic difference, i.e. clinching or 'commonsense' statements that are seen as rational, justified and above critique (Augoustinos and Every 2010). The innocent child motif and its rhetorical power can be seen as a type of self-sufficient argument, or commonsense statement, which also may come into play to support particular ideological positions. The idea of the 'innocent', or more often 'ignorant', child tended to come into play in response to the question 'Does the [site being visited] have any meaning for contemporary Australia/Britain?' Here, the idea of the ignorant child was used to lament the fact that the values the site represented were perceived by the speaker to be passing away or not given enough credence in contemporary society. The following examples come from the Stockman's Hall of Fame, where a particular sense of Australian identity was being celebrated by many visitors. This identity pulls on images and values of Australian nationalism that are linked to a particular and contested reading of aspects of Australian history, which privileges rural experiences of hardship and perseverance, and often obscures Indigenous and multicultural[4] histories:

> It [the Hall] probably hasn't enough meaning [to modern Australia] because we were talking to a gentleman only last night in Winton and having a beer and a meal in the RSL Club and he said, he was talking about some the early explorers and he said, 'there's not enough people know enough about them' and I don't

think we do know enough about them. There are names on [the exhibition] even me, at 67 years – 66 years of age doesn't know some of them. I do know of some but I don't know enough. I think our kids still should, there should be a little bit more of that Australian history, real stuff, so that they realize what a wonderful country it is, because of these people.

(LR113: Stockman's Hall of Fame, 2010)

Ah I think it should . . . by rights, I don't think there should be a child that shouldn't come through here and have a good look at what's here.

(LR057: Stockman's Hall of Fame, 2010)

I think it almost should be compulsory for today's youth of Australia, they need places like this to wake up themselves a bit. . . . The kids, the modern generation, have got no idea how tough it was for people back in the 1800s and the early 1900s and you know, I think if they knew a bit more about that and realized how tough it was, they might pull their selves together a bit, some of the young people, I really do think they get it too easy.

(LR076: Stockman's Hall of Fame, 2010)

In these extracts children are framed as being ignorant – almost wilfully so – and there is an element of contempt in the voices of some speakers. The need to educate children and youths is used as a shorthand to say 'my values need respect', and they are so important that 'children must be educated in them'. It is both a lament and a self-sufficient statement of legitimacy. Below is an example where the idea that 'this is something children should see' negates the dissonant heritage of Empire:

[It's] Important that children come to these places as it's part of their nation's heritage. Even though [the British] Empire exploited people we did so many good things with the money they got – improving the arts and so on.

(CH123: English country house, 2004)

Another visitor to an English country house used the idea that the house of a leading aristocratic family was part of a generic 'children's heritage'; to underline the importance of the elite and nationalizing history it represented, she stated that the house was 'our children's heritage and we should remember it and value it' (CH119: English country house, 2004).

While the examples used above are being used to reinforce reactionary politics, the need to educate the 'innocent' child was also used by visitors espousing ideologies that were more progressive. The need to educate children about multiculturalism, working-class history and Indigenous Australians was also used to underline the importance of these histories. Children, however, were more often characterized in these contexts as naive, or lacking the opportunities to be exposed to certain knowledge, rather than ignorant.

Memories of childhood

The links between heritage and nostalgia have been extensively commented on, and often heavily criticized (Wright 1985; Hewison 1987; Lowenthal 1985, 1996). Nostalgia tends to be defined within the heritage literature as those longing, lingering glances back to a past perceived to be, in many respects, 'better' than the present. It is associated with reactionary understandings of a present that paint the past as more attractive than it probably ever was. Childhood, too, is often painted with similar rosy or sentimental hues (Cunningham 1995; Pascoe 2010). Thus, it is not surprising that the cultural production of heritage, and the romance of childhood mythologies, will be extensively intertwined. As Raphael Samuel (1994: 93) argued 'the middle-class cult of childhood, with its celebration of the time-warped and its sentimentalization of the nursery' can be glimpsed in the way, for instance, National Trust properties in England are presented. As he observes, National Trust gift shops tend to privilege Beatrix Potter and other nursery favourites who tend to receive 'far more attention, as a writer, than Shakespeare, Dickens and Scott, or as illustrator, than Hogarth or Blake' in these contexts (Samuel 1994: 93). This infantilization of certain heritage places and the memories that they attempt to jog or recreate is part of the authorized heritage discourse that, among other things, defines heritage as 'good' and comforting (Smith 2006). This is a commingling of the imagined or mythical innocence of childhood, with the certitude that heritage sites, such as house museums, will have universal cultural and historical relevance. The innocent child motif is again underlying or speaking to the assumed and unquestioned relevance and cultural importance of the heritage on display.

Remembering childhood was a theme that emerged at those museums and heritage sites that dealt with aspects of social history. People responded to items on display that evoked for them memories of 'when they were a child':

> [I am remembering my] childhood through the exhibition. Granny made me a dress like the one in the exhibition.
>
> (CH446: English county house, 2004)

> The ranges in the kitchen, as I used to clean them as a lad. There are so many things that relate to my childhood.
>
> (CH336: English county house, 2004)

> Part of our childhood and seeing how life has changed from when we were children.
>
> (NCM09: National Coal Mining Museum, 2004)

> When places like this were on the go I was a child and brings back memories of the sound of the clogs as the miners went to work.
>
> (NCM07: National Coal Mining Museum, 2004)

It's good to see people having nice family days out – it reminds me of my childhood.

(CH126: English county house, 2004)

Here people are connecting to particular artefacts (dresses, kitchen ranges) or the exhibition in general, or as in the last case, the act of visiting. For some people this was nostalgia:

Uh, a bit nostalgic. I think a lot's been lost over the years because everything's become so modernized . . . and a little bit sorry that our children will never know and remember some of the things in the exhibits that we've seen today so I think it's important to have all this recorded.

(LR114: Stockman's Hall of Fame, 2010)

Although nostalgia is a feeling associated with loss, loss is not always perceived as a bad thing, and visitors often used the term 'nostalgia' interchangeably with reminiscing (Smith 2006: 219). Nostalgic remembering could be either a longing for better times, or simply a recognition that the past is gone and that this is not necessarily bad, and that the past was not necessarily 'better' than the present, but just gone. Thus, nostalgic remembering is not *always* about myths of idealized pasts or childhood, but simply memories that invoke emotions:

Interviewer: How does it make you feel to visit this place?
Oh, like a kid again! [*laughs*] Ah no it's just so interesting to see how tough things were for the people then and I mean, the old hut here and my grandparents when they lived, they cooked on an open fire. You know they had pots, Australia Cross, and I can remember that as plain as day. They didn't have a stove, they had no electricity, no running water, they had tank water outside, you know, just that sort of thing and it was just normal, it was natural, you know.

(LR076: Stockman's Hall of Fame, 2010)

I see things in here that I can relate to my childhood and I look at things and I think 'ah, this is wonderful' and 'we had this when we were kids' and one lady just said a while ago, she said 'I was alive when that happened' and I said, 'yep, so was I' so I think that's really great to see that this is all being preserved and you can feel part of you growing up.

(LR084: Stockman's Hall of Fame, 2010)

In these last two extracts, the speakers talk about feeling like a kid again, or feeling themselves once again growing up as they move through the exhibitions. These emotions can, however, be used in different ways. For LR076, his emotional response to feeling like a kid again reaffirmed for him the importance of the history displayed at the Stockman's Hall of Fame. His childhood rural experiences and memories were reinforced for him, and he defines the history represented at the Stockman's Hall of Fame as part of his own heritage. He goes further, however, and asserts that this history should be seen as part of the entire country's heritage, as he went on to say, this history 'should be almost compulsory to the history lessons in schools for kids, that's my opinion' and that youths 'need places like this to wake up themselves a bit'. However, in the following exchange between a mother (aged over 65) and her daughter (in her 30s), the mother's feelings of sentimentality about childhood experiences of immigration are used in much more politically and emotionally complex ways. Sentimentality or nostalgia is actively used in the way the two women renegotiate the meaning of the mother's childhood, the pride the mother takes in both her own experiences and that of migrants generally, and in the way they both negotiate the daughter's recognition of the importance of migrant experiences and history:

Interviewer:	*How does it make you feel to visit this exhibition?*
IMM030 [mother]:	I'm actually very proud of the people who did it, of my own people, and I very much admire the people who came from those very troubled backgrounds. Very proud. It makes me a bit sentimental really.
IMM029 [daughter]:	I think it just reinforces the ideas I always had about it, it just confirms, you know . . .
IMM030:	[interrupting] But you don't feel sentimental about it?
IMM029:	No, I was worried how mum would feel.
IMM030:	I do feel a bit sentimental.
IMM029:	I thought she might feel a bit depressed about it because you know, missing her homeland or I don't know, something about her childhood.
IMM030:	A little bit, I feel sentimental. I mean we all miss our childhood.
IMM029:	She arrived on her tenth birthday and it wasn't necessarily a wondrous experience was it?
IMM030:	For me it was, yes. For me it was yes, wonderful. Saw how the other half lived.
IMM029:	Not depressing at all?
IMM030:	No, no, no, total freedom. My mother was confined to a cabin with total sea sickness and I don't think I found my father or brother until we nearly docked.
IMM029:	You mean the voyage itself, what about the experience?
IMM030:	The experience, well there was a bit of a rejection of immigrants when we came, that was in '51, so there was a great hurry to lose my accent but yes, it was a wonderful experience really.
[. . .]	
IMM030:	It's sort of pleasing to see [in this museum] that the immigrants are recognized and the contribution they've made, that is pleasing.

IMM029:	Yes, they're really very much represented as the founders of our society at a much greater contribution than you would have anticipated, to the very base of our society.
IMM030:	We are, and I think it's we, we are everything.
[...]	
Interviewer:	*Are there any messages about the heritage or history of Australia that you take away from this exhibition?*
IMM029:	Well for me, that was the thing that I learnt that I wasn't aware of. I thought I kind of knew a bit about it because of mum's background but not so much about people from other countries, I didn't think about that so much and the contribution they've made. I think they've added to our cultural diversity and interest and multiculturalism but I wasn't aware that they were really not just an addition but that they are actually the backbone and . . .

The daughter is worried that her mother will feel depressed by remembering what the daughter sees as a childhood of discrimination and loss of homeland. While the mother acknowledges the discrimination she experienced (she lost her accent fast, she notes), she is taking pride in the fact that the museum is acknowledging her childhood and adult experiences, and of the contributions migrants have made to Australian society. This is a message the daughter picks up, but not at first. The daughter initially notes, that her existing ideas are simply being reinforced; her mother interrupts at this point asking the daughter if she feels 'sentimental', as the mother herself is feeling. This assertion of sentimentality is important, as it sparks the renegotiation of the feelings invoked by the mother's childhood. The daughter then acknowledges the contribution of migrants to Australian society is 'greater . . . than you [that is, she] would have anticipated' and finally notes it was something that she has indeed learned by being at the museum. The mother, in response to her daughter's first articulation of the desired message, asserts, with pride, 'we are . . . we are everything'. While 'we all miss our childhood', the mother can now be sentimental about her past because her experiences of both hardship and triumph as a migrant are, in some ways, being recognized. The mother has negotiated the daughter's recognition, not simply of the complexities of migrant history, but of herself.

Remembering childhood will almost inevitably invoke a sense of loss in most adults, as we cannot return to this aspect of our lives – it is gone. However, nostalgia is not always about regretting that loss. Childhood memories, like other memories invoked during heritage making, can raise a range of emotions that are utilized in any number of ways to reinforce or renegotiate both reactionary and progressive ideologies and values. This negotiation can occur around the meanings of national narratives or familial ones, or both, as the mother and daughter above illustrate. The emotions of nostalgia and sentimentality have multifaceted consequences, and cannot always be dismissed as expressions of simple mawkishness. The concepts of childhood, and the emotions around this, are continually remade in the way childhood is remembered and forgotten in the heritage moment. Memories of childhood are constructed to serve the needs of the present, whether that is a simple reaffirmation of self, or a chance to connect with other family members, or even to affirm national identity.

Children's own visit

As Jensen (1994: 269) notes, 'the experiences of adults in museums are qualitatively different from those of children', but this is also true of heritage sites generally, particularly as children are not always in control of whether or not to visit. Children tend also not to be in control of *how* to visit heritage sites. Children's experiences at museums and heritage sites are not well researched, and tend to be limited to issues of education. How children engage with heritage and the cultural meanings they construct for themselves (rather than 'learn') is not well documented. This section looks at the way older children engaged with the exhibitions they were visiting.

The year 2007 marked the bicentenary of Britain's abolition of its slave trade, and saw the opening of the International Slavery Museum in Liverpool. Two 14-year-old children, friends from school, had successfully asked their parents if they could have the day off school to see the new museum during its opening week. As one of them noted, they had come because they 'like to celebrate how cultures can overcome like obstacles, and today's society is still moving forward, and the abolishment of slavery obviously'. They noted that they liked the video displays the best, but thought that in the section of the exhibition that showed the achievements of contemporary descendants of the African diaspora they should show more figures that young people would recognize 'beside Nelson Mandela and Oprah', and nominated Naomi Campbell, 'who was the first black woman to appear on the front cover of *Vogue*'. The exhibition made them feel:

LA57(91):   Quite bad, I feel bad but I don't know why, I didn't do anything, it's really touching and it's really sad.

LA58(92):   Yeah, the same.

Interviewer: Are there any messages about the heritage or the history of Britain that you will take away from this exhibition?

LA57(91):   Any what? I knew it already to not be racist but this just like adds to it, why you shouldn't be racist and what they've done to come all this way from being slaves and treated really awfully, so . . .

LA58(92):   They're like an everyday part of society now, like black people.

Interviewer: What meaning does an exhibition like this have for modern England?

LA57(91):   Yeah. So people know like what's happened so they don't just have to read it so kids can come as well, because they don't really read, and they can see how they travelled and how awful it was.

LA58(92):   Yeah, I think it's very useful for young people because it's interactive like those buttons you can press, I know it sounds interesting but they can get involved and see what they want to see.

Interviewer: *Does this exhibition have personal importance or meaning for you?*

LA58(92):   The Anthony Walker part, because he was from like our area, he was from Liverpool and we're from Liverpool as well.

[. . .]

Interviewer: *Is there anything you've seen today that has changed your views on the past?*

LA58(92):   I think it's added to it like erm how shameful it would be to support slavery I think it's really added to that.

LA57(91):   Same.

For the opening, the museum had installed a large blackboard on which visitors could chalk in their comments. Before the interview they had written on this board 'we all rawk [*sic*] so don't treat anyone nasty cause rasism [*sic*] sucks RIP Anthony Walker' and '[their names] respect the bravery and spirit of all races xoxo let's keep movin [*sic*] forward'. Both children self-identified as white British, and they were making active attempts to understand and engage with the distressing history they were visiting at the museum. Indeed, the exhibition made them feel bad. Rather than rejecting the bad feelings, however, they both offer considered and thoughtful discussions about racism. During the interview, one of them asked me if the museum was dedicated to Anthony Walker, and I explained that the education centre attached to the museum was named for Walker. When I asked them if they felt that they were part of the history represented in the museum, one responded 'well, we're from Liverpool'. Walker, an 18-year-old African-British student from Liverpool, was murdered in 2005, a victim of race hatred. As the interview material and their writing on the board showed, Walker, as a local, was a figure of importance to them, his widely discussed murder having occurred when they were 12 years old. These two appear to have been using the museum visit to work through their concerns about Walker's murder, and what that then meant to them growing up and coming 'from Liverpool'.

The following is a response of a 16-year-old student, who identified herself as African-British, to the exhibition 'Breaking the Chains' held at the British Commonwealth and Empire Museum, Bristol:

Interviewer: *What for you is this exhibition about?*

BA58(59):   It's about what slavery was and the past in general and how America and England came about and how the people in slavery reacted towards the slavers.

Interviewer: *Whose history are you visiting here?*

BA58(59):   Um, I think it's, it's more English, European history than it is African, because the Europeans took the Africans for the benefits of their economies.

[. . .]

Interviewer: *How does it make you feel to visit this exhibition?*

BA58(59):   It makes me feel very proud that we have overcome slavery: I know it's still going on now but it makes me proud that we've overcome slavery in Africa.

Interviewer: *Are there any messages about the heritage or history of Britain that you will take away from this exhibition?*

BA58(59):   Any messages? (pause) Erm, not really. Not really. But I think that [the] English should consider about other affairs rather than theirs, because true with slavery they were doing things for their benefit only, and it was not only England.

Interviewer: *What meaning does an exhibition like this have for modern England/Britain?*

BA58(59):   It has lots of meanings, it means you have to stop slavery, it means you have to stop discrimination, because right now there is terrorism, and discrimination is terrorising, and I think it sends a message across to stop the discrimination and stereotyping.

Interviewer: *Does this exhibition have personal importance or meaning for you?*

BA58(59):   Yeah, to a certain extent because I am African and this happened in my heritage so yeah that's how.

Here, again, sophisticated and thoughtful responses are made about the exhibition and the history it was portraying. She is proud about what her ancestors had achieved in overcoming the legacies of slavery, and offers insight into the self-interest of the English nation, despite the media and governmental emphasis that 2007 should be about celebrating abolition (see Waterton (2010, 2011) and Agbetu (2011) for critique of this popular stress). Moreover, she draws considered and politicized observations about the links between discrimination and terrorism.

What is also interesting in this interview, as with the two Liverpudlians, is that they offer much more thoughtful responses to the exhibition than many adults did. As I have discussed in detail elsewhere (Smith 2010a, 2011), the dominant response of white British adults was one that aimed to distance the visitor from negative feelings, and a rethinking of what it meant to be British, as what had been a hidden history was revealed and discussed in the museum exhibitions they were visiting.[5] Of course, many adults did offer insightful responses to these exhibitions, but the most frequent response was one of distancing or insulating themselves from negative emotions. It is also important to note that many of the children we interviewed as part of the 2007 bicentennial study gave us quite bland, unconsidered and not particularly thoughtful responses as well. Indeed, many gave quite similar responses to the adult sample, though overall we only interviewed 25 (out of 1,498) people who identified as under 16 years of age. While this number is small, the profile of themes in interview responses was broadly similar to the adult sample (although it should be noted that many children were interviewed with their parents at hand). However, age offered no statistically significant correlation against any of the interview themes, with one exception. The exception was that younger people (those under 24) and older people (those over 55) tended to be less aware of the legacies of the history of enslavement, such as racism and multiculturalism, than other age groups (Smith 2010a: 200). This tendency emphasizes that the interviews I selected above are quite remarkable for the consideration they give these issues; however, they also illustrate three important points: that children have agency, they can be self-consciously political and they can construct their own meanings. These children were not simply 'learning', but engaged in active heritage making. Indeed, they were working out not only their own political positions, but their own identities as African, as British and as being 'from Liverpool'. Further, they were exploring the complex network of emotions that underpinned these identities. As Jenkins (1998: 4) states, 'Children, no less than adults, are active participants in that process of defining their identities, though they join those inter- actions from positions of unequal power'. Negotiations of this kind are inevitably political, in the sense that children are not only capable of, but do, engage with politi- cal issues, but also because their engagement tends to come from a point where their cultural and political agency is misrecognized or unacknowledged.

Conclusion

This chapter has explored four intertwined themes centred on the way heritage relates to children and childhood, and has illustrated that both 'the child' and 'childhood' are politicized phenomena within heritage making. Parents and grandparents actively use museums and heritage sites as cultural tools in the process of enculturating and social- izing their children. However, while there is a clear desire to instil an understanding of history and time depth, visits may also be part of familial negotiations over parental respect. In addition, the visit itself is part of what is being learned, and children are being taught to not only embody or perform a respect for the past, their parents' or grandparents' roles in it, but also an appreciation of the visit itself and what that means to their familial identity.

However, children are not passive in this process, and while there is a tendency for 'children to make themselves into whatever is expected of them' (Calverk 1998: 80), children create their own meanings. Children, despite their age and their tendency to view the world a-historically, are engaged in heritage making as much as adults are. The tendency to assume that children visit, or are taken to heritage sites, to learn, misunderstands or obscures the agency of children. This does not mean to say that learning is not going on, but that is not all that is happening.

The idea of children as heritage makers is something that is obscured by autho- rized accounts of heritage as a thing that you 'have', rather than something contin- ually recreated or produced. However, it is also obscured by the way childhood is often remembered or conceived as a concept. The innocent child motif is frequently invoked by heritage visitors to underline the legitimacy of the values and ideologies they are espousing, however, it is predicated not only on ideas of innocence (or igno- rance), but also on the idea that children not only do, but *should*, lack cultural and political agency.

Memories and concepts of childhood are revealed to have significant consequences, not only for framing the experiences of children in relation to heritage visiting and all that entails, but also in the way these concepts work to legitimize or delegitimize adult social and political values. Moreover, childhood memories and the emotions that they invoke, are used in a number of ways to negotiate not only familial, but also wider social understandings of the past, and what that means for present values and the identities they underpin. Overall, heritage is a process of negotiating a range of values and meanings, and is a process in which the experiences and values of children, childhood and adulthood are negotiated and re/created. The relationship between heritage and childhood, and the role of children in this relationship, need rethinking. The political consequences of the concepts of childhood, and the agency of children in heritage making, are issues that need further investigation within heritage studies.

Acknowledgements

The data used in this chapter were collected with funding from the British Academy (2003–04), the Arts and Humanities Research Council (UK) Knowledge Transfer Fellowship (2007–09) and the Australian Research Council Future Fellowship (2010–14). My thanks to the heritage agencies, museums and heritage sites that allowed me to interview their visitors.

Notes

1 The country houses were Harewood House, Nostell Priory, Waddesdon Manor, Audley End, Brodsworth Hall and Belsay Hall. The social history museums were National Coal Mining Museum in Wakefield (NCMM), West Yorkshire; the Tolpuddle Martyrs Museum in Dorset; and the colliery village exhibit within the North of England Open Air Museum, Beamish, Co. Durham. A general discussion of the findings of these interviews occurs in Smith (2006). The exhibitions on the British slave trade were: the British Museum; National Maritime Museum; British Empire and Commonwealth Museum; International Slavery Museum, Liverpool; Birmingham Museum and Art Gallery; Museum in Docklands; Wilberforce House, Hull; Harewood House. Further discussions of the findings of these interviews can be found in Smith (2010a, 2011).
2 The Australian data came from the Immigration Museum, Melbourne; the National Museum of Australia, Canberra; Rouse Hill Estate (historic house); Old Melbourne Gaol (Victorian National Trust property); and The Stockman's Hall of Fame and Outback Heritage Centre.
3 Selection of this reason varied across museums/heritage sites; at some historic houses, 31 per cent gave this reason for visiting, while other locations recorded this as low as 1 per cent. Of the 1,498 people interviewed at the exhibitions on slavery, only 4 per cent nominated this reason. The low percentage at some sites may represent the dissonant nature of some exhibitions and that interview times were not confined to weekends.
4 See Smith (2012) for further details and Gill (2005) for a critique of this image of Australian identity.
5 For a discussion of the degree to which this history may be defined as 'hidden', see Kowaleski Wallace (2006) and Oldfield (2007).

References

Agbetu, T. (2011) 'Restoring the Pan African perspective: reversing the institutionalisation of Maafa denial', in L. Smith, G. Cubitt, R. Wilson and K. Fouseki (eds) *Representing Enslavement and Abolition in Museums: Ambiguous Engagements*, New York: Routledge.
Ashton, P. and Hamilton, P. (2010) *History at the Crossroad: Australians and the Past*, Ultimo: Halstead Press.

Augoustinos, M. and Every, D. (2010) 'Accusations and denials of racism: managing moral accountability in public discourse', *Discourse and Society*, 21(3): 251–56.

Bendix, R. (2009) 'Heritage between economy and politics: an assessment from the perspective of cultural anthropology', in L. Smith and N. Akagawa (eds) *Intangible Heritage*, London: Routledge.

Byrne, D. (2009) 'A critique of unfeeling heritage', in L. Smith and N. Akagawa (eds) *Intangible Heritage*, London: Routledge.

Calverk, K. (1998) 'Children in the house: the material culture of early childhood', in H. Jenkins (ed.) *The Children's Culture Reader*, New York: New York University Press.

Cunningham, H. (1995) *Children and Childhood in Western Society since 1500*, London: Longman.

Dicks, B. (2000) *Heritage, Place and Community*, Cardiff: University of Wales Press.

Falk, J.H. (2005) 'Free-choice environmental learning: framing the discussion', *Environmental Education Research*, 11(3): 265–80.

—— and Dierking, L.D. (1992) *The Museum Experience*, Washington, DC: Whalesback Books.

—— (2000) *Learning from Museums: Visitor Experiences and the Making of Meaning*, Walnut Creek: AltaMira Press.

Gill, N. (2005) 'Life and death in Australian "heartlands": pastoralism, ecology and rethinking the outback', *Journal of Rural Studies*, 21: 39–53.

Golding, V. (2009) *Learning at the Museum Frontiers*, Farnham: Ashgate.

Hewison, R. (1987) *The Heritage Industry: Britain in a Climate of Decline*, London: Methuen London Ltd.

Hooper-Greenhill, E. (1991) *Museum and Gallery Education*, Leicester: Leicester University Press.

—— (1994) 'Museum education', in E. Hooper-Greenhill (ed.) *The Educational Role of the Museum*, London: Routledge.

Jenkins, H. (1998) 'Childhood innocence and other modern myths', in H. Jenkins (ed.) *The Children's Culture Reader*, New York: New York University Press.

Jensen, N. (1994) 'Children, teenagers and adults in museums: a developmental perspective', in E. Hooper-Greenhill (ed.) *The Educational Role of the Museum*, London: Routledge.

Kirshenblatt-Gimblett, B. (1995) 'Theorizing heritage', *Ethnomusicology*, 39(3): 367–30.

—— (1998) *Destination Culture: Tourism, Museums and Heritage*, Berkeley: University of California Press.

Kline, S. (1998) 'The making of children's culture', in H. Jenkins (ed.) *The Children's Culture Reader*, New York: New York University Press.

Kowaleski Wallace, E. (2006) *The British Slave Trade and Public Memory*, New York: Colombia University Press.

Lowenthal, D. (1985) *The Past is a Foreign Country*, Cambridge: Cambridge University Press.

—— (1996) *The Heritage Crusade and the Spoils of History*, Cambridge: Cambridge University Press.

—— (2011) 'From the tower of Babel to the ivory tower', in H. Anheier and Y.R. Isar (eds) *Heritage, Memory and Identity*, Los Angeles: Sage.

Misztal, B.A. (2010) 'Collective memory in a global age: learning how and what to remember', *Current Sociology*, 58(1): 24–44.

Oldfield, J.R. (2007) *'Chords of Freedom': Commemoration, Ritual and British Transatlantic Slavery*, Manchester: Manchester University Press.

Pascoe, C. (2010) 'The history of children in Australia: an inter-disciplinary historiography', *History Compass*, 8(10): 1142–64.

Rosenzweig, R. and Thelen, D. (1998) *The Presence of the Past: Popular Uses of History in American Life*, New York: Columbia University Press.

Samuel, R. (1994) *Theatres of Memory. Volume 1: Past and Present in Contemporary Culture*, London: Verso.

Smith, L. (2006) *Uses of Heritage*, London: Routledge.

—— (2010a) '"Man's inhumanity to man" and other platitudes of avoidance and misrecognition: an analysis of visitor responses to exhibitions marking the 1807 bicentenary', *Museum and Society*, 8(3): 193–214.

—— (2010b) 'Ethics or social justice? Heritage and the politics of recognition', *Australian Aboriginal Studies*, 2010/2: 60–8.

—— (2011) 'Affect and registers of engagement: navigating emotional responses to dissonant heritage', in L. Smith, G. Cubitt, R. Wilson and K. Fouseki (eds) *Representing Enslavement and Abolition in Museums: Ambiguous Engagements*, New York: Routledge.

—— (2012) 'The cultural "work" of tourism', in L. Smith, E. Waterton and S. Watson (eds) *The Cultural Moment of Tourism*, London: Routledge.

Waterton, E. (2010) 'Humiliated silence: multiculturalism, blame and the trope of "moving on"', *Museum and Society*, 8(3): 128–42.

—— (2011) 'The burden of knowing versus the privilege of unknowing', in L. Smith, G. Cubitt, R. Wilson and K. Fouseki (eds) *Representing Enslavement and Abolition in Museums: Ambiguous Engagements*, New York: Routledge.

Wertsch, J.V. (2002) *Voices of Collective Remembering*, Cambridge: Cambridge University Press.

Wright, P. (1985) *On Living in an Old Country*, London: Verso.

Chapter 8

'Let children be children'

The place of child workers in museum exhibitions and the landscapes of the past

Simon Sleight

Waiting on an underground platform at London's King's Cross station in March 2010, my attention was drawn towards a striking advertisement. Situated both literally and figuratively on the wrong side of the tracks, a photograph depicted a young boy standing over a whirring lathe. 'Shumon, just 13, works 7 hours a day in a factory', the poster announced, beneath a large and unequivocal statement – 'LOST: ONE CHILDHOOD'. In this image, created for a UNICEF fundraising campaign, the message is clear: children who labour for a living are denied a childhood, and children who work do so indoors, in dark workshops. The boy in the poster, whose story the charity elaborated online (UNICEF 2010), conforms almost precisely to the description of 'the "model" NGO-child' suggested by Olga Nieuwenhuys (2007: 156–7).[1] Identified by his first name only, commuters viewing the advertisement are invited to infer that young Shumon's activities are representative of a type of upbringing long outlawed in the West, though still endemic elsewhere. How can we sustain a global childhood of protected innocence, this image asks, if children continue to work? We must 'put it right' by donating, urges the poster's small print.

At the (UK) National Trust's Museum of Childhood at Sudbury Hall in Derbyshire, visitors encounter lost childhood through another tunnel. Just beyond the museum foyer, a forbidding passageway – reminiscent of the interior of a mine – opens out into the 'Work Gallery'.[2] When I first walked through the installation, a young visitor, looking around with his family, was prompted to inquire: 'Mummy, why is it dark?' The displays beyond the black passageway set out to answer this question, telling a story of successive Acts of Parliament intended to improve working conditions for British children in the nineteenth and twentieth centuries. A quotation from *David Copperfield* on the struggles of youth also features, alongside an image of a boy pushing a coal truck and various other artefacts from the period, including labour and indenture certificates. The displays acknowledge that children's work in Britain during the Victorian era also encompassed rural tasks such as gathering the harvest, and note that some children found time for play amidst the working day. But the inclusion in the exhibition of a climbable chimney for apprentice chimney sweeps reinforces the overall impression that Victorian child labour was unremittingly bleak, damaging and wrong, and that the employment of working-class children prevented them from accessing the delights of the 'Toys', 'School' and 'Stories and Imagination' galleries that lay beyond, enjoyed by today's young visitors. The overall experience of visiting the Museum of Childhood is one of reassurance. Moving through the installations, it is easy to conclude that British children have largely transcended the exploitation of the past and moved towards a 'proper' childhood.

If only society could just 'let children be children' – as the title of an exhibition at the Brooklyn Historical Society declared memorably in 2003 – wouldn't they all be (and have been) better off?[3] This chapter examines a number of approaches to tackling the history of children's work at museums and heritage sites in three countries: Britain, the United States and Australia.[4] Though they have different traditions of child employment (Humphries 2010; King 1995; Robinson 2007; Bowden and Penrose 2006), each of these post-industrial societies has witnessed a recent expansion in the representation of children's lives within the museum sector (Roberts 2006), a growth inspired by studies of childhood (as an idea) and later of children (as agents of history) since the 1960s. Despite these developments, the history of children's work is usually accorded little space within the walls of museums. Instead the spotlight most often falls on children at leisure or at school, with once-loved toys and ink-splattered desks used to evoke a sense of the past. Children have always played and have long been offered an education in Western nations, but for the working classes these activities have competed historically with the common experience of labour.[5] For those less affluent, the nineteenth-century middle-class ideal of childhood as a sheltered period of dependency and instruction was often impractical. Factors of class – as well as gender and ethnicity – differentiated the experience of growing up, emphasizing the now standard historical understanding that 'childhood' is a temporally specific concept. While Britain, the United States and Australia all witnessed efforts to regulate and reduce children's labours from the second half of the nineteenth century, the decline in the number of working children is a relatively recent phenomenon. The socially unacceptable nature of children's work in these three countries today need not obscure its long heritage.

Where the histories of working childhoods have been presented to the public, three approaches have been employed: the traditional walk-through installation of objects and explanatory text; the photographic exhibition; and the heritage site experience. Eight examples of these different representational modes are examined here, drawn from the last decade and often, it should be noted, from small-scale and/or temporary exhibitions that underscore the marginal place afforded to displays on children's work.[6] Some of these exhibitions can be seen to demonstrate a greater awareness of the historical reasons for, experiences of, and variations within children's work than others. While many curators have allowed present-day views on what constitutes a 'normal' childhood to influence exhibition content, others show an appreciation of the contingent and constructed nature of childhood as a concept and consider the potential perils of juvenile work alongside the possibilities for youthful autonomy that some pursuits offered. As the Brooklyn exhibition declared, we do indeed need to 'let children be children', but this, I argue here, entails a greater emphasis on historical context, an acknowledgement of the shortcomings of relevant source material, a broadening of focus to consider the 'hidden' work of girls and young women (Todd

2005) and, above all, an approach which imbues children with agency rather than mere victimhood. In addressing these issues, the chapter considers a pressing issue for curators reliant on objects, rather than just words, to fashion an accessible narrative. How, in short, can children's labours be displayed when so often this work leaves behind relatively little that is palpable?

To Western sensibilities in the early twenty-first century, the very idea of child labour can seem incongruous: a product of a backward past, an index of 'underdevelopment' or proof of bad parenting. These views have currency within popular culture (*Suffer the Little Children*, 2010)[7] and historians have not been immune from issuing moral pronouncements on the subject. As Clark Nardinelli has summarized (1990: 34), the scholarship on children's employment 'may well be the most emotional of all the writings on the industrial revolution', and – one might add – capitalism more generally. For E.P. Thompson, writing in the 1960s on the early industrial period in England, 'the exploitation of little children, on this scale and with this intensity, was one of the most shameful events in our history' (1991: 384). More recently, Michael Lavalette has attacked the cultural relativism of 'liberationist' scholars who challenge the 'commonsense picture of childhood' as 'protected from the cares and concerns of the adult world' and in so doing make it seem 'inappropriate' to condemn 'sending young children up chimneys' or, he continues, racism, female circumcision or paedophilia (1999: 6, 16, 18, 21, 35). Such provocative writing, laden with value judgements about past activities and current scholarship, is common in this field, and is illustrated by even the briefest search of library catalogues using the lightning-rod terms 'child labour' or 'child labor', as distinct from the less emotive terms 'child worker', 'working childhood' or 'industrious childhood' (Bekele and Myers 1995; Fyfe 1985; de Coninck Smith *et al.* 1997). Writers in this mode frequently equate 'child labo(u)r' with 'industrial violence' (Schmidt 2010), efforts aimed at reduction of a practice perceived as self-evidently harmful, and the denial of liberty; the use of other terms, by and large, portends less one-sided views. In this chapter I avoid the term 'child labour', regarding it as essentializing, and freighted with too many negative connotations to be useful.

Just as concern to rescue from posterity the silenced experiences of past lives informed the classic 1960s social history of E.P. Thompson, so too a later phase of writing emerging in the 1990s is arguably influenced by the spirit of the times, namely the new policy agendas that have witnessed the establishment of bodies including the International Labour Organization's International Programme for the Elimination of Child Labour (active since 1992) and the 1999 convention on the Worst Forms of Child Labour (Nieuwenhuys 2007: 154, 156; Morrow 2010: 435–6). Popular histories reinforce the negative views of children's work promoted by these bodies, with recent publications including *The Worst Children's Jobs in History* (Robinson 2006), the *Horrible Histories* series of books for children (from 1993) and the discussions of child work in the television series *The Worst Jobs in History* (circa 2009). The recent revival of interest in Dickensian characters including Oliver Twist, Smike and Jo the crossing sweeper also feeds into a popular conception about the hardships of times past. It is indeed easy, then, as Anna Davin notes, to accept uncritically what we were all taught at school: in the bad old days there was child labour, but through heroic campaigning by humane and far-sighted leaders like Lord Shaftesbury, successive reforms during the course of the 19th century eliminated this barbarism and civilized ideas came to the prevail.

(1982: 650)

A select number of counter-arguments have emerged to challenge the dominant view of brutal child exploitation: Nardinelli's work on industrial England (1990) is cited frequently, and, intriguingly, some of the scholars included in Lavalette's edited collection (1999) disagreed with the book's overall tone, arguing that so far as contemporary children's work is concerned 'For the vast majority . . . no significant health, safety or welfare issues are raised by what they do' and that adult policy makers (and by implication historians) should listen to children for their opinions rather than simply assuming they know what represents their best interests (Whitney 1999: 247; Leonard 1999: 191–2). One recent example where researchers did just this – interviewing 100 child traders aged between 6 and 16 in the Peruvian city of Cusco – found grounds for cautious optimism (Bromley and Mackie 2009). On the one hand, the young traders risked physical abuse by the police, theft of their wares and a relative lack of time for play compared with children who did not work; on the other hand, the positives of street trading were 'substantial': pocket money allowed access to the internet, parks and treats including sweets; confidence and self-esteem grew through trading; foreign language skills were gained in exchanges with tourists; and most children stated that they enjoyed their work, fitting it in around their schooling and combining work and play through their trading activities (141–58).

Such research builds upon the 'right *to* work' arguments advocated by Viviana Zelizer (1994: 208–9, 219–21) and earlier by Colin Ward (1978: 138–42, 149). Davin has also suggested that in the nineteenth century children might well be 'pleased and proud' to contribute to the family coffers, especially where an adult male breadwinner was absent or incapacitated (1982: 647). Then as now, the *type* of work involved and individual circumstance appear crucial in determining children's experiences. Most recently, a major study of children's work in England during the Second World War (Mayall and Morrow 2011) has challenged the conception of children as passive victims of bombing or merely emotionally priceless objects, evacuated for their own sake from England's industrial heartlands. Instead the authors show that the transition of children from earners to learners was far from complete by 1939, and that after the outbreak of conflict children performed all manner of socially useful activities from salvage collecting to gardening and even rescuing people from bombed houses. Though they did not always enjoy this work, many children gained a new sense of self-worth through their activities, standing in – indeed being expected by adults to act – as a 'reserve army' of labour when their country was in crisis (Mayall and Morrow 2011: 24).

While few people would argue that dangerous work down mineshafts, up chimneys or in factory sweatshops benefits children, analyses that focus on cases of extreme exploitation offer only limited insights. Historically, 'the archetypal model of child labour in large factories and mines was never . . . predominant' (Kirby 2003: 132), with a greater proportion of children located in the service sector of the economy. Similarly, in contemporary times in countries such as Peru it is the part-time child worker who is in the majority, rather than the homeless and desperate 'street child' of popular imagination (Bromley and Mackie 2009: 143). The trend since the 1860s for child factory workers or miners to be increasingly excluded from these pursuits has since accelerated, with jobs such as running messages and domestic service gaining in significance, and in some cases being dominated by the young (Rahikainen 2004: 154–5; Cunningham 2000: 412–13). These types of jobs may offer less emotive images and narratives for curators to attract visitors to museums, but they are more representative of past experience.

Amidst bookshelves groaning under the weight of righteous indignation about children's work, more balanced introductions to the history of the subject in the West are becoming available (Kirby 2003; Rahikainen 2004; Mintz 2004; Mayall and Morrow 2011)[8] and there is now general agreement on certain aspects of the topic, including the steady 'adulting' of the labour market in the nineteenth century, the consistent underestimation by earlier scholars of the significance of agrarian and domestic labour, the fact that working children often earned more than their mothers, and the slow rise to prominence of one cultural ideal – 'the protected childhood' – over another, 'the useful childhood' (Cunningham 2000: 410, 420; Kirby 2003: 55–60, 68–9; Davin 1982: 644–5; Mintz 2004: 152–3). Nonetheless, scholarly debate remains fierce on the causes of the decline in the numbers of children working, the extent of the dangers faced by those so doing, the reliability of evidence produced by reform-minded middle-class observers and the validity of comparisons between working childhood today and in the past (Cunningham 2000: 413–19).

Given the evident complexity of children's work as a topic, one would expect exhibitions on the theme both to reflect a plurality of views and acknowledge uncertainty. Yet such equivocation is seldom evident. The *Children at Work* exhibition, held at the Victoria and Albert Museum of Childhood between December 2004 and October 2005, is a case in point. Commencing in the year 1800, the display told a story of past dangers, reforming initiatives and ongoing exploitation in the form of under-age working and child trafficking. An introductory text panel sets the scene, stating that in the nineteenth century 'children . . . sometimes under 5 years of age, would work alongside adults. Working days were long – 16 hours or more. Jobs were often dangerous with many children seriously injured or killed'.[9] While less fortunate children, the panel continued, were employed to fit through gaps in factory machinery or squeeze up chimneys, others were 'lucky' and gained an apprenticeship and hence the skills for a secure living. Leaving aside questionable assertions concerning the job prospects and working conditions of apprentices, the exhibition (aiming, remember, to give visitors an overview of two centuries of children's work) concentrated on urban-industrial work, predominantly in factories. As outlined above, this focus is not representative. 'Did you know?' text panels amplified the gloomy tone, introducing visitors to 'phossy jaw' and 'chimney sweeps' cancer' – diseases caused through contact with toxic chemicals – and outlining the plight of camel racers in the Middle East, 'snatched as young as 3-years-old from families and sold into slavery'.[10] Together with an overview of current British law relating to the employment of children, and further information on child trafficking and the pressures faced by child actors including Judy Garland, the curatorial narration of *Children at Work* left little room for exploring more complex aspects of the theme.

If the textual component of this exhibition can be described as narrow in its interpretation, the accompanying exhibits nonetheless lent a greater sense of depth and diversity to the display. Five objects in particular stood out for their direct relevance to the theme, and several others illustrated the type of lateral thinking that can serve to evoke historical associations where no obvious artefact is available. First, a rare fishergirl's garment (circa 1900) spoke to the lives of teenage girls in Scotland, cleaning and gutting fish and working in an industry underwritten by geographical factors. Two official documents – a 1914 child's labour certificate and an apprentice weaver's indenture from 1810 – pointed to the start of a regularized working life for two 13-year-old children in different centuries and the procedures necessary for this transition to occur within a legal framework. Nearby, a group of nineteenth-century postcards produced by Dr Barnardo's charity illustrated the emphasis given by Barnardo to training young people in similar manufacturing pursuits. These cards highlight the tensions within 'child rescue' bodies identified by Rebecca Bates and others: turn-of-the-century philanthropists, in stressing the benefits of youthful labour (and indeed emigration to seek work), were 'at odds' with the larger cultural trend towards a childhood without work (Bates 2009: 145). Finally, the persistence and diversity of children's labours were brought home to visitors through a 1982 photograph depicting a Sikh boy delivering an evening newspaper in Leeds. Work and education are commitments long balanced by children (Davin 1982: 643); despite the intimations of the exhibition's text panels, one pursuit does not always occur at the expense of the other.

Also inducing a sense of historical immediacy, other artefacts featured in *Children at Work* included 1920s matchboxes and dressmaking coursework, silk fabric from Spitalfields and an 1890 'sweep doll', with the miniature coal sack serving as a pin cushion (and hence facilitating potential labours beside, rather than inside, the fireplace). Comparing the fascinating stories suggested by these objects with the supporting written material, museum visitors may well have wondered why the text information boards at the exhibition offered such a simplistic view.

In another recent English exhibition about children's work, the 2010 *Childhoods Past* exhibition at Winchester Discovery Centre offered a broader interpretation of the theme, placing local histories in wider perspectives and employing well-chosen photographs and objects to open windows to the past. The exhibition approached the history of childhood from three angles, promising 'a family friendly exhibition about the way children played, learned and worked over 100 years ago'.[11] Certainly the installation offered plenty to see and do for all ages: as well as text information boards to read, objects to observe and a photography wall offering nearly 120 perspectives on the local history of children, visitors could play with old toys including a diabolo, dress up in costumes of the past, complete a scavenger hunt and sample the smells of bygone children's treats including pear drops and toffee apples. In addition to proving a fun way of keeping different family members engaged, the introduction of a playful element is entirely apt for this subject, for contrary to popular perception even working children found time for play in the workplace. The comments book captured a high level of praise for the curators: one young visitor wrote 'Very fun and facts everywhere!'; another added 'A lovely exhibition – Mummy enjoyed it just as much as me!! William x'.[12] Older visitors were also impressed: Valerie Standfield noted that 'Holly and Daisy had lots of fun & took interest in the photograph exhibition. Nice for Grandma to have a sit down. We will come again'; Mrs Brooks concurred, adding 'Brilliant exhibitions here. Love this child themed one as it has entertained my daughter . . . and given me greater knowledge of local history'.[13]

In terms of content specific to the theme of children's work, *Childhoods Past* managed with limited space to explore local varieties of juvenile labour and place these examples within the *longue durée*, hence accounting for change across time.[14] 'Childhood has not always been as long as it is now', a panel noted in introduction, before pointing out the division between the types of work undertaken in rural and urban areas and noting the existence since medieval times of apprenticeships for 'those whose parents could afford it or [in cases where] a charitable benefactor came forward'.[15] Supporting photographic evidence depicted servants outside a local rectory stables in 1869, another group of servants at Stratton Park three years later, children and women gleaning in a field during harvest time and two 'butcher's boys' ready to make basket deliveries from the town of Bishop Waltham in 1905. To these insightful images, curators added detailed information on two local tailor's apprentices, Ada Head and Maud Simmonds. Surrounded by exhibits including a picking wheel and cloth-cutting scissors, these case studies lent considerable immediacy. Visitors learned, for example, that Maud was nominated for an apprenticeship in 1897 (when she was aged 13) and that her father had died in 1892. Living in a house with four siblings and her mother, the landlady of a lodging house, the opportunity to acquire a trade would likely have been regarded as an essential opportunity to contribute to the family's coffers. That the transition to full-time work occurred earlier for Maud than would be the case in Winchester today was a point the exhibition underscored by including an extract from the 1871 census indicating the ages of boys also earning a living.

Childhoods Past, then, managed to convey a considerable amount of historical information on working childhoods within a setting that visitors evidently enjoyed. The exhibition revealed a rare interest in exploring girls' work,[16] and, given Winchester's pastoral surroundings, it acknowledged the significance of farm-related labours. Tantalizingly, the exhibition also featured an unlabelled photograph depicting two boys hauling a laden cart through Victorian streets. This image is potentially significant, offering a glimpse of the more informal outdoor work that occupied many children at this time. Were these children making a delivery, assisting family or neighbours as part of a 'local economy of favours' (Davin 1982: 648–9) or dragging home collected items as part of a semi-legal supply chain to dealers in second-hand goods? No exhibition I have yet seen has probed this particular area of children's work, though historical scholarship has attempted to reveal its hidden intricacies (Kirby 2003: 68–70; Sleight

2008: 86–90). Some aspects of children's work are easier to represent than others, and for museum curators reliant on objects the relative dearth of artefacts connected to the informal economy is problematic. Acknowledging absences in any collection is important, but thinly occupied display cases are unlikely to draw in the public.

Across the Atlantic, a number of exhibitions have concentrated on photographs to explore the issue of children's work. A conspicuous sense of moral outrage can be seen to inform several of these displays, mirroring a trend in much of the literature on this subject. Indeed, the moral aspect is exhibited more overtly than is evident at Sudbury Hall or the Victoria and Albert Museum, as the titles to two of the three exhibitions I wish to discuss here – *Before Their Time: Child labor through the lens of Lewis Hine* and *Let Children be Children: Lewis Wickes Hine's crusade against child labor* – suggest.[17] The third exhibition, held at the Virginia Historical Society,[18] also drew upon the extensive and unique Lewis Hine archive, necessitating a brief discussion of his career by way of introduction to the displays.

Born in 1874, Hine is perhaps best known by the public for his captivating photographs of construction workers on the Empire State Building in the early 1930s. Here men enjoy their lunch while sitting, without harnesses, on girders hundreds of metres in the air or else fabricate the giant structure by hand, again at great personal risk. Hine's earlier training as a sociologist and work as a teacher can be seen to inform his work, most particularly the many thousands of photographs he took while employed by America's National Child Labor Committee (NCLC) from 1906. The NCLC aimed to pressure politicians to regulate children's working conditions by pricking the public conscience with lectures and campaigning literature. As Hine himself put it, in a quotation featured prominently at the Virginia exhibition, 'we promise to make you and the whole country so sick and tired of the whole business that when the time comes, child labor pictures will be records of the past'.[19] Digitized collections of Hine's evocative portraits of children engaged in all manner of employment across America are now freely available,[20] and have given rise to a substantial body of scholarship (Goldberg 1999; Sampsell-Willmann 2009; Gutman 1967). Despite Hine's stated aim to 'pluck you by the sleeve' in revealing working conditions through his photography,[21] no federal legislation to regulate children's work was passed in the US until 1938 – indicating, one might argue, the failure of Hine's images as campaigning tools.[22] Hine died in poverty in 1940, the value of his photographs as social documents by then neglected.

When a selection of Lewis Hine's photographs arrived in New York for an exhibition of his work in 1977 (purportedly the first of its kind since his death), exhibition curator Walter Rosenblum appeared on the NBC's 'Today Show'. The subsequent interview is notable for two moments: the host's reference to Hine's stated intention 'to show things that had to be corrected, and to show things as well that should be appreciated'; and Rosenblum's opinion that Hine's reforming photographs reveal an 'inner strength and dignity' within his subjects.[23] A little over 25 years later, when Hine's work returned to Brooklyn for the *Let Children be Children* exhibition, such sensitivity to Hine's *oeuvre* appeared to have been lost. With a quasi-religious emphasis on Hine's 'crusade' to limit child labour, the exhibition portrayed the issue as a battle between good and evil and 'revealed the appalling circumstances that poor, working-class children endured until legislation against child labor prevailed'.[24] Some two dozen photographs of children at work in New York – in factories, at home and shining shoes and selling newspapers on the streets – featured as supporting evidence. In New Hampshire, the *Before Their Time* exhibition adopted a similar line, with 56 of Hine's photographs displayed. As the title of each exhibition indicates, little attempt was made to interrogate the concept of childhood as transitional; had this occurred the implied 'norm' of a sheltered and non-working childhood could have been shown as anomalous for most children of the working classes during the period covered by Hine's images.

Moreover, regardless of how the photographs of working children were located within curatorial narratives, the photographs themselves are often open to interpretation. Several of those displayed in Brooklyn, New Hampshire and at the Virginia Historical Society exhibition do not seem to speak of children's work as an evident evil but rather of the stoicism, and sometimes joy, of children in and around the workplace. I refer in particular to images available online as a legacy of these exhibitions, namely the portrait of Fred Normandin and friends in 1909 (see Figure 8.1),[25] the image of Western Union messenger boys in 1911,[26] and the group portrait, also composed in 1911, of child workers outside the Old Dominion Glass Company.[27] Could it be, as the Rosenblum interview elaborates, that Hine found things to appreciate as well as to condemn? What would this mean for historical interpretation of his work? And why did the Brooklyn and New Hampshire exhibitions in particular seem to ignore this possibility in favour of a 'crusade' narrative when some of the very photos on the display appear to allude to a more varied experience of working children? Recent work by Jane Lydon on 'looking relations' has asserted that photographs often escape the intentions of their makers. Agency persists, it is argued, even where the intended outcome of a photographic project would seem to deny its existence (Lydon 2005: 1–32, 242–3). This contention, inspired by analysing photographs of Indigenous adult subjects, also holds relevance for photographs of children. Hence whether forgetting (or unconsciously ignoring) his NCLC commission as child workers appeared before the lens, Lewis Hine clearly possessed a more complicated relationship with his subjects than these exhibitions allow.

Putting photographs on museum walls and looking at objects in glass cases are two approaches to representing the history of children's labours; another is to offer a taste of those labours to today's children in the very place where the work once occurred. Such is the experience available at Quarry Bank Mill near Manchester, operated by the National Trust.[28] Here visitors can tour an industrial relic of the cotton boom, see working machinery including a huge spinning mule and explore the Apprentice House where pauper children resided in the late eighteenth and early nineteenth centuries. This heritage package is clearly popular: around 130,000 people visit Quarry Bank Mill each year, of which 29,000 are school children.[29] To immerse visitors in their surroundings, tours of the property are led by costumed interpreters, promising 'theatre-in-education' experiences including a day in the life of an apprentice child worker.[30] As well as taking in the sleeping, eating and schooling arrangements

Figure 8.1 Lewis Hine, Boy with bare arms, Fred Normandin (employee at Mill no. 1, Amoskeag Manufacturing Company, Manchester, New Hampshire, May 1909). Photograph courtesy of The Photography Collections, University of Maryland, Baltimore County.

for apprentices, young visitors also learn about often dangerous mill jobs including the role of the 'piecer' (who was required to walk alongside the moving mule and tie together any broken threads of cotton) and the 'scavenger' (who crawled underneath the moving machine to sweep up pieces of cotton fluff in an effort to prevent fires). Visitors can also dress in replica nineteenth-century clothing and try their hand at weaving, as photographs from a recent field trip by 10- and 11-year-old students at Westholme School illustrate (see Figure 8.2).[31] The educational experience does not end there, either: after leaving the mill, visitors can read about the life of apprentice Esther Price in a Quarry Bank booklet and take away an education pack that offers further insights from primary source documents into children's working conditions at the mill and poses essay questions to older students including 'Assess how far it is true to say that the terms and conditions of work in Quarry Bank were at least no worse than in many other mills' and 'What evidence can you find to support the case for factory reform by 1850?' (Robinson 1994).[32]

By any measure Quarry Bank Mill offers a rich experience. It tells a story of why young children were employed in the factory from 1790 to 1847 (when the pauper apprentice system was abolished), explains the jobs they performed, explores their living conditions and asks why some children would want to run away while others saw themselves as better off in the mill than in the workhouse. The site would be regarded

Figure 8.2 Schoolchildren from Westholme School visiting Quarry Bank Mill, January 2010. Photograph courtesy Mrs Carol Laverick, Headteacher, Westholme Girls' Junior School. Photograph by Mr John Whittaker.

as pioneering by many of the museum curators, heritage practitioners and teachers who have contributed to the steadily growing body of literature on how children relate to museums and how those museums could offer more (Coelho Studart 2000; Museums Etc. 2009; McRainey and Russick 2010; Cave 2010). In fostering a sense of empathy, together with a sense of place and an understanding of causation (Spock 2010: 126–3; Filene 2010: 180–5),[33] Quarry Bank Mill does much to live up to these ideals through concentrating, as one would entirely expect, on the experiences of children working in the cotton industry. Yet there are dangers to this exclusivity of focus. There is a risk that confining the experience to an institution in effect institutionalizes the history of children. This is a problem affecting not just heritage sites but written histories of children more generally (Sleight 2008: 46–7). Institutions are attractive to historians as they often yield discrete bodies of evidence for analysis. Subsequent histories of places such as reformatory schools and mills usually then reveal evidence of abuses by adults but only fleeting examples of the agency of children, fighting the system. Such narratives can create the impression that childhood must have been miserable, particularly for children of the working classes. That the vast majority of children had minimal or no contact with places like prisons, workhouses or mills is all too easily forgotten.

Encompassing not simply a single site, but rather the streets of an entire city, *Melbourne's Newsboys*, the final exhibition I wish to discuss here, ran at the City Gallery in

Melbourne from May to July 2005.[34] Like most of the other displays discussed above, this installation was modest in size, occupying just one room in the city's Town Hall. Yet it offered a variety of fresh perspectives. In telling the stories of some of the estimated 15,000 newsboys who have traded in the streets from the mid-nineteenth century, *Melbourne's Newsboys* assessed one of the most popular, yet least exhibited, modes of child work in the modern city. It further illustrated an awareness of the potential benefits, as well as the costs, for children selling newspapers, highlighted the biases informing historical discussions of the activity and demonstrated that the phenomenon was not static across time but instead linked to shifting conceptualizations of childhood. Crucially, the exhibition also offered a sense of these newsboys as individual actors, able to make their own choices within the context of their times. Numerous references to newsboys' lusty 'street cries' – their principal means of advertising their wares – together with an audio clip of Kelvin Moore's own twentieth-century call reinforced this impression. Newsboys (and less regularly newsgirls) were a fixture of Melbourne's thoroughfares and train stations from the gold rush years of the 1850s right through to the mid-twentieth century, by which time regulation (especially from 1925) and the rise of news kiosks had limited the trade. *Melbourne's Newsboys* attempted to re-imagine a once commonplace encounter between adult consumer and child trader.

Unlike in the exhibitions inspired by Lewis Hine, here children's work was not something to be condemned out of hand, but a facet of life that might even be missed (see Figure 8.3). As the catalogue (produced in the form of a miniature newspaper) asserted, the exhibition 'evokes a sense of loss', for 'Melbourne salutes its vanished newsboys!'[35] In part a 'celebration', then, of a lost street calling, *Melbourne's Newsboys* was also careful to recognize that modernity had 'in very many respects improved the lot of the city's youth'.[36] The exhibition was able to make these assessments with authority because it weighed *representations* of newsboys with *experiences* of street trading, placing both within the context of a regulatory framework that tightened over time in response to middle-class adult concerns about the purpose of public space and the 'right' activities for children. To illustrate its narrative, *Melbourne's Newsboys* drew on multiple sources: articles from the very newspapers once sold on the streets; letters of complaint to civic authorities; cartoons; photographs; recollections of the Secretary of the City Newsboys' Society; and the words of newsboys themselves. Considered juxtaposition of materials such as a written objection to newsboys as 'eyesores' with period photographs of beaming newsboys in smart attire left visitors to draw their own conclusions about the contrasting prejudices of a city ratepayer and the Newsboys' Society in producing these documents. Glass cabinets featured – this was not a 'hands-on' exhibition aimed purely at children – but in displaying text in the form of large sheets from a newspaper and incorporating cartoon-like representations of pint-size newsboys and street furniture the installation aimed to engage young and old alike.

If Quarry Bank Mill shows what might be achieved with an industrial site, *Melbourne's Newsboys* does likewise for a museum gallery. Absent were assumptions regarding the supposed inevitability of a non-working childhood. Instead visitors encountered

Figure 8.3 Melbourne's Newsboys exhibition (City Gallery, Melbourne Town Hall, 3 May–24 July 2005). Photograph courtesy City of Melbourne Art and Heritage Collection.

newsboys as active agents, plying a trade out of economic necessity and carving out their own space in the city. In this exhibition, popular conceptions of working children as mere victims were thoroughly contested.

Letting 'children be children' is, to conclude, precisely what museums and heritage sites can aim to achieve where histories of children's work are concerned. This does not, however, imply promoting moral judgements about the social practices of the past, but instead suggests adopting a more sensitive approach that takes historical context into account and explores the experience of working children on their own terms. In some of the most evocative exhibitions analysed here, today's young visitors were allowed to indulge in a sense of childish playfulness within the exhibition space, trying their hands at yesterday's labours and hence establishing empathy with their historical counterparts. Where traditionally there has been a difference between exhibitions *for* children and exhibitions *about* children (Coelho Studart 2000: 32–3) – the former tending to feature in children's museums; the latter in museums (including museums of childhood) or heritage sites aimed at informing the public more generally – this division is now breaking down. Children's museums are taking a stronger interest in children's history and history exhibits are becoming more welcoming to children. Old-fashioned boundaries between academic history and museum curatorship are also weakening, with historians increasingly appreciating how to engage the wider community and curators designing displays that historicize the assumptions of the present. Most auspiciously, some newer exhibitions leave open interpretative possibilities, encouraging evaluation of the sources and artefacts displayed. Together these developments promise a more wide-ranging past for visitors to encounter, one where both the pitfalls and the possibilities of children's work are encompassed.

Notes

I wish to acknowledge my joint affiliations in the writing of this chapter, namely with the Department of History at King's College London (as Rydon Fellow with the Menzies Centre for Australian Studies) and as adjunct research associate with the School of History at Monash University. All web pages referenced in this chapter last accessed 27 August 2012.

1 This child, states the author, 'is preferably sufficiently small in size to appear much younger, has a heart-rending story of extreme abuse that refracts negatively on both his or her society and parents, has the determination and intelligence of an autonomous adult yet nourishes only one dream: be restored to a lost childhood'.
2 After a major refurbishment, the museum reopened in March 2008.
3 *Let Children be Children: Lewis Wickes Hine's crusade against child labour*, Brooklyn Historical Society, New York, 13 December 2003 to 7 March 2004. See <www.brooklynhistory.org/exhibitions/lewis_hine.html> for an introduction.
4 Defining 'childhood' is, of course, problematic. The life phase is historically contingent, thoroughly entwined with factors of class, gender and ethnicity, and further subject to internal age-dependent definition. In the exhibitions discussed here, the upper age limit for 'children' appears to be 16 years, though this is not explicit.
5 Statistics pertaining to the historical prevalence of working children are notoriously sketchy, but some calculations have been attempted. Peter N. Stearns (2009: 42) notes that in the United States in 1910, 2 million children under 15 (18 per cent of the total) were employed, even aside from farm labour. This represented a high point. By 1920, only 8 per cent of children similarly aged worked, and by 1940 just 1 per cent. On the complicated and contentious picture in Britain, see Kirby (2003) and Humphries (2010). For Australia, see Sleight (2008: 90–3), where census analysis reveals that between 1871 and 1901 between one-fifth and a quarter of 'boys' aged under 20 worked in various capacities and between 10 and 15 per cent of 'girls' similarly aged were also employed. These figures are likely to underestimate the prevalence of child work. It would not always be considered wise for adults to report truthfully to census enumerators, with domestic 'help' by children also falling outside the survey.
6 This marginalization is arguably characteristic of a broader underrepresentation of children's history within museums generally. Despite advances associated with the new social histories of children, Inloes (2011, n.p.) and Roberts (2006: 155–6) maintain that there has been a distinct lag in translating this impetus into exhibitions, particularly so for children of the working classes. Many mainstream museums offer only simplistic depictions of past childhoods (if they address the subject at all), and even in specialist museums of childhood all too often nostalgia acts as a 'regulatory influence' (Roberts 2006: 157).
7 The programme (part of the *Do-Gooders* series) followed the efforts of well-known individuals including Lord Shaftesbury to enact labour legislation and give – in the words of the BBC's website – 'youngsters a proper childhood'. See <www.bbc.co.uk/programmes/b00wmpc0>.
8 For younger readers, Belinda Hollyer (2007) is a good introduction, using source excerpts from social surveys by Henry Mayhew and others to assess both the joys and sorrows of working childhoods in the British capital.
9 For a similar interpretation see the *Improving Lives* exhibition at the Museum of London and the companion 'Pocket History' guide, 'Children in Victorian London'. The latter is

available online: see <www.museumoflondon.org.uk/NR/rdonlyres/15CE7040-8AD6-4F6B-A45F-E6D9DDA86246/0/WhatwaslifeforchildreninVictorianLondon.pdf>.

10 Supporting web material – incorporating some of the text from the exhibition together with additional information – is available: see <www.vam.ac.uk/moc/childrens_lives/work/>.
11 Quotation taken from a promotional flyer for the exhibition.
12 *Childhoods Past* comments book, entries dated 3 August 2010 and 10 August 2010.
13 Ibid., entries dated 4 September 2010 and 24 September 2010.
14 Another successful example of this regional approach is the *Industrial Revolutionaries* exhibition held in 2010 at the Harris Museum and Art Gallery in Preston, Lancashire. The exhibition, curated by Laura Briggs, blended industrial artefacts, period images, supporting text and, significantly, the recorded voices of female 'half-timers' interviewed about their experiences in Preston's cotton mills.
15 The exhibition noted that in Winchester apprenticeships had been offered since at least 1566, when Sir Thomas White left a substantial sum for young men to be taken on. The text panels also acknowledged (unlike in the V&A exhibition discussed above) that securing an apprenticeship could be a mixed blessing. A trade would be acquired, but 'many [apprentices] were also treated as cheap labour by their masters'.
16 A theme also explored in *Industrial Revolutionaries* through a focus on 12-year-old Annie Hill, a Preston cotton weaver who posed for a remarkable portrait in 1906. For discussion, see Briggs (2011). Copy kindly provided by the author.
17 *Before Their Time* ran at the Museum of New Hampshire History from February 2000 to November 2001. Information on the exhibition can be found at <www.nhhistory.org/hineexhibit.html>. *Let Children be Children* ran from December 2003 to March 2004 at the Brooklyn Historical Society. See <www.brooklynhistory.org/exhibitions/lewis_hine.html> for information.
18 The exhibition – *Child Labor in Virginia* – ran from October 2001 to March 2002. Information, together with an online sampler, is available. See <www.vahistorical.org/exhibits/hine_intro.htm>.
19 The quotation is included in the digital exhibition: <www.vahistorical.org/exhibits/hine01.htm>.
20 See for example: <http://www.historyplace.com/unitedstates/childlabor/index.html>, the Hine collection at the University of Maryland <http://contentdm.ad.umbc.edu/hine.php>, the selection available via the George Eastman House archive: <www.geh.org/ar/letchild/letchil_sld00001.html>, and the Library of Congress collection: <www.loc.gov/pictures/collection/nclc/>.
21 Quotation drawn from online forum 'Using Lewis Hine's Child Labour Photographs'. See <www.jgape.org/ node/90>.
22 Various local and state labour laws were enacted before this date, however.
23 For a transcript see <http://icue.nbcunifiles.com/icue/files/icue/site/pdf/663.pdf>.
24 See <www.brooklynhistory.org/exhibitions/lewis_hine.html>.
25 See <www.nhhistory.org/museumexhibits/hine/hine4.html>.
26 See <www.vahistorical.org/exhibits/hine_photographs04.htm>.
27 See <www.vahistorical.org/exhibits/hine_photographs10.htm>.
28 See <www.nationaltrust.org.uk/main/w-quarrybankmillandstyalestate> for an introduction to the site.
29 Information from <www.nationaltrust.org.uk/main/qbm_preliminary_informatiion_single_doc-2.pdf>. (Note misspelling of 'information' in web address.)
30 A taste of this experience, led by Mill employee Malcolm Cooper, can be viewed online. See: <www.youtube.com/watch?v=YxB_QaVv408>.
31 See: <www.westholmeschool.com/index.php/news/59/274/>. A similar taste of past labours is on offer in Boston at the USS Constitution Museum. In the exhibition *A Sailor's Life for Me?*, young visitors are invited to 'Get on your knees and scrub!' to replicate the

task of scrubbing the decks. This exhibition is discussed in D. Lynn McRainey (2010: 164). For images see: <www.ussconstitutionmuseum.org/images/press_kit/exhibit_newsletter. pdf>, p. 4. For an enthusiastic review by mother-of-two Katherine Whitney, see <www. exhibitfiles.org/all_hands_on_deck>.

32 For essay questions, see <www.nationaltrust.org.uk/main/gcse_pdf_for_qbm.pdf-GCSE pack>.

33 Also see Coelho Studart (2000: 83–4) for discussion of the theory of museum 'flow experi- ence', applicable to the mill site.

34 The exhibition was curated by Andrew May. Photographs of some of the exhibits and information boards, together with a copy of the exhibition catalogue, are available online. See: <www.melbourne.vic.gov.au/citygallery/Exhibitions/Pages/MelbournesNewsboys. aspx>.

35 See: <www.melbourne.vic.gov.au/citygallery/Exhibitions/Documents/Newsboys_ Catalogue.pdf>, p. 1.

36 Ibid.

References

Bates, R.J. (2009) 'Building imperial youth? Reflections on labour and the construction of working-class childhood in late Victorian England', *Paedagogica Historica*, 45, 1–2: 143–56.

Bekele, A. and Myers, W. (1995) *First Things First in Child Labour: Eliminating Work Detrimental to Children*, Geneva: United Nations Children's Fund: International Labour Office.

Bowden, B. and Penrose, B. (2006) 'The origins of child labour in Australia, 1880–1907: a health and safety perspective', *Journal of Occupational Health and Safety*, 22, 2: 127–35.

Briggs, L. (2011) 'Balancing biographies: exhibiting people's stories in *Industrial Revolutionar- ies*', paper presented at 'Peopling the past: private lives, public histories and the museum', National Maritime Museum, Greenwich, 22 July 2011.

Bromley, R.D.F. and Mackie, P.K. (2009) 'Child experiences as street traders in Peru: contrib uting to a reappraisal for working children', *Children's Geographies*, 7, 9: 141–58.

Cave, V. (2010) 'Planning for young children and families in museums', in *The New Museum Community: Audiences, Challenges, Benefits: A Collection of Essays*, Edinburgh: Museums Etc.

Coelho Studart, D. (2000) 'The Perceptions and Behaviour of Children and their Families in Child-Orientated Museum Exhibitions', PhD thesis, University College London.

Cunningham, H. (2000) 'The decline of child labour: labour markets and family economies in Europe and North America since 1830', *Economic History Review*, 53, 3: 409–28.

Davin, A. (1982) 'Child labour, the working-class family, and domestic ideology in 19th century Britain', *Development and Change*, 13, 4: 633–52.

De Coninck Smith, N., Bengt, S. and Schrumpf, E. (eds) (1997) *Industrious Children: Work and Childhood in the Nordic Countries 1850–1990*, Odense: Odense University Press.

Filene, B. (2010) 'Are we there yet? Children, history, and the power of place', in McRainey, D. L. and Russick, J. (eds), *Connecting Kids to History with Museum Exhibitions*, Walnut Creek, California: Left Coast Press.

Fyfe, A. (1985) *All Work and No Play: Child Labour Today*, London: TUC.

Goldberg, V. (1999) *Lewis W. Hine: Children at Work*, Munich and London: Prestel.

Gutman, J.M. (1967) *Lewis W. Hine and the American Social Conscience*, New York: Walker.

Hollyer, B. (2007) *Coster Girls and Mudlarks: Street Voices from Victorian London*, London: Scholas- tic Children's Books.

Humphries, J. (2010) *Childhood and Child Labour in the British Industrial Revolution*, Cambridge: Cambridge University Press.

Inloes, T. (2011) 'One size fits all? The representation of children's history in California museums', paper presented at Society for the History of Children and Youth conference, New York, 24 June 2011.

King, W. (1995) *Stolen Childhood: Slave Youth in Nineteenth-Century America*, Bloomington: Indiana University Press.

Kirby, P. (2003) *Child Labour in Britain, 1750–1870*, Basingstoke: Palgrave Macmillan.

Lavalette, M. (ed.) (1999) *A Thing of the Past? Child Labour in Britain in the Nineteenth and Twentieth Centuries*, Liverpool: Liverpool University Press.

Leonard, M. (1999) 'Child work in the UK 1970–1998', in Lavalette, M. (ed.), *A Thing of the Past? Child Labour in Britain in the Nineteenth and Twentieth Centuries*, Liverpool: Liverpool University Press.

Liebel, M. (2004) *A Will of Their Own: Cross-cultural Perspectives on Working Children*, London: Zed Books.

Lydon, J. (2005) *Eye Contact: Photographing Indigenous Australians*, Durham and London: Duke University Press.

Mayall, B. and Morrow, V. (2011) *You Can Help Your Country: English Children's Work during the Second World War*, London: Institute of Education.

McRainey, D.L. (2010) 'A sense of the past', in McRainey, D. L. and Russick, J. (eds), *Connecting Kids to History with Museum Exhibitions*, Walnut Creek, California: Left Coast Press.

McRainey, D. L. and Russick, J. (eds) (2010) *Connecting Kids to History with Museum Exhibitions*, Walnut Creek, California: Left Coast Press.

Mintz, S. (2004) *Huck's Raft: A History of American Childhood*, Cambridge, MA and London: Harvard University Press.

Morrow, V. (2010) 'Should the world really be free of "child labour"? Some reflections', *Childhood*, 17, 4: 435–40.

Museums Etc. (2009) *Rethinking Learning: Museums and Young People: A Collection of Essays*, Edinburgh: Museums Etc.

Nardinelli, C. (1990) *Child Labor and the Industrial Revolution*, Bloomington and Indianapolis: Indiana University Press.

Nieuwenhuys, O. (2007) 'Embedding the global womb: global child labour and the new policy agenda', *Children's Geographies*, 5, 1–3: 149–63.

Rahikainen, M. (2004) *Centuries of Child Labour: European Experiences from the Seventeenth to the Twentieth Century*, Aldershot: Ashgate.

Roberts, S. (2006) 'Minor concerns: representations of children and childhood in British museums', *Museum & Society*, 4, 3: 152–65.

Robinson, K. (1994) *Esther Price: Life Story of an Apprentice at Quarry Bank Mill*, Manchester: Quarry Bank Mill Trust.

Robinson, S. (2007) *Something Like Slavery? Queensland's Aboriginal Child Workers*, Melbourne: Australian Scholarly Publishing.

Robinson, T. (2006) *The Worst Children's Jobs in History*, London: Macmillan Children's Books.

Sampsell-Willmann, K. (2009) *Lewis Hine as Social Critic*, Jackson: University Press of Mississippi.

Schmidt, J.D. (2010) *Industrial Violence and the Legal Origins of Child Labor*, New York: Cambridge University Press.

Sleight, S. (2008) 'The Territories of Youth: Young People and Public Space in Melbourne, *c.*1870–1901', PhD thesis, Monash University.

Spock, D. (2010) 'Imagination: a child's gateway to engagement with the past', in McRainey, D. L.

and Russick, J. (eds), *Connecting Kids to History with Museum Exhibitions*, Walnut Creek, California: Left Coast Press.

Stearns, P.N. (2009) 'Child labor in the industrial revolution', in *The World of Child Labor: An Historical and Regional Survey*, Armonk, NY and London: M.E. Sharpe.

Suffer the Little Children (2010) dir. Helena Braun, narrated Ian Hislop, BBC documentary.

Thompson, E.P. (1991, originally 1963) *The Making of the English Working Class*, London: Penguin.

Todd, S. (2005) *Young Women, Work, and Family in England, 1918–1950*, Oxford: Oxford University Press.

Townsend, L. (2011) 'Seen but not heard? Collecting the history of childhood in museums', paper presented at Society for the History of Children and Youth conference, New York, 24 June 2011.

Ward, C. (1978) *The Child in the City*, London: Architectural Press.

Whitney, B. (1999) 'Unenforced or unenforceable? A view from the professions', in Lavalette, M. (ed.), *A Thing of the Past? Child Labour in Britain in the Nineteenth and Twentieth Centuries*, Liverpool: Liverpool University Press.

The Worst Jobs in History (c.2009) Channel 4 documentary series.

Zelizer, V.A. (1994, originally 1985) *Pricing the Priceless Child: The Changing Social Value of Children*, Princeton, NJ: Princeton University Press.

Web resources

http://contentdm.ad.umbc.edu/hine.php
http://icue.nbcunifiles.com/icue/files/icue/site/pdf/663.pdf
http://www.bbc.co.uk/programmes/b00wmpc0
http://www.brooklynhistory.org/exhibitions/lewis_hine.html
http://www.channel4.com/programmes/the-worst-jobs-in-history/episode-guide
http://www.exhibitfiles.org/all_hands_on_deck
http://www.geh.org/ar/letchild/letchil_sld00001.html
http://www.historyplace.com/unitedstates/childlabor/index.html
http://www.jgape.org/node/90
http://www.loc.gov/pictures/collection/nclc/
http://www.melbourne.vic.gov.au/citygallery/PastExhibitions/Documents/Newsboys_Catalogue.pdf
http://www.melbourne.vic.gov.au/citygallery/PastExhibitions/Pages/MelbournesNewsboys.aspx?i=7&s=12&n=22&FontSize=1
www.museumoflondon.org.uk/NR/rdonlyres/15CE7040-8AD6-4F6B-A45F-E6D9DDA86246/0/WhatwaslifeforchildreninVictorianLondon.pdf
http://www.nationaltrust.org.uk/main/w-quarrybankmillandstylestate
http://www.nhhistory.org/hineexhibit.html
http://www.nhhistory.org/museumexhibits/hine/hine4.html
http://www.vahistorical.org/exhibits/hine_intro.htm
http://www.vahistorical.org/exhibits/hine_photographs04.htm
http://www.vahistorical.org/exhibits/hine_photographs10.htm
http://www.vahistorical.org/exhibits/hine01.htm
http://www.westholmeschool.com/index.php/news/59/274/
http://www.youtube.com/watch?v=YxB_QaVv408
UNICEF (2010) <http://www.unicef.org.uk/Latest/Photo-stories/Shumons-Story/

Chapter 9

Roman children and childhood and the perception of heritage

Mary Harlow

Two funerary inscriptions for three children from ancient Rome read:

> Sacred to the departed spirit of Q. Sulpicius Maximus, son of Quintus and of the
> Claudian tribe, a native of Rome. He lived for 11 years, 5 months and 12 days.
> He performed at the third celebration of the Competition, amongst 52 Greek
> poets, and the favour which he attracted through his young age was turned to
> admiration by his talent: he acquitted himself with honour. His extempore verses
> are inscribed above, to show that his parents have not been carried away in their
> affection. Q. Sulpicius Eugramus and Licinia Ianuaria, his desolate parents, have
> set this up for their devoted son and for themselves and their successors
>
> (*CIL* 6. 33976, end of first century AD)[1]

In two parallel columns (see Figure 9.2):

> To the departed spirits of
> Nico, her sweet son, who lived 11 months and 8 days; and
> Eutyches, her home-born slave, who lived for 1 year, 5 months and 10 days;
> Publicia Glypte made this
>
> (*CIL* 6. 22972, early second century AD)

To the modern eye such memorials are very moving. The recording of exact age
suggests the sadness of parents at the untimely death of their offspring. These are
just two examples of the many monuments to children that have survived from
the Roman world. In their own time they served as commemorative memorials to
the child and the parents' grief, and to the Roman viewer they conveyed a series of
additional messages about the status of the deceased and the dedicators. Today they
serve as artefacts of the cultural heritage of the classical world, and provide a variety of data for historians about Roman death, commemoration, memory and childhood. Using these inscriptions as a starting point, this chapter will look at the ways
ideas of Roman children and childhood are perceived by modern society, how our
view of cultural heritage is coloured accordingly and how ideas about Roman childhood today are filtered through contemporary understandings of children. Finally, it

Figure 9.1 Funerary altar for Q. Sulpicius Maximus, dating to late first century AD, now in Palazzo dei Conservatori, Rome. Photo: German Archaeological Institute, Rome, 71. 1694.

briefly examines how we engage twenty-first-century children in the cultural history of childhood.

The city of Rome is in itself an outstanding resource for the heritage and tourism industries, but it is also highly problematic in terms of whose history is privileged and for what ends. In many early archaeological excavations post-Roman material was stripped away in order to access the remains of the classical past since that was perceived as Rome's most important and influential period. At its peak the Roman Empire reached from the modern near east, south into the Egyptian deserts, north to Hadrian's Wall and west to the Rhine and the Danube and lasted for over seven hundred years. Almost since the fall of Rome in the fifth century AD every new

Figure 9.2 Funerary altar for the infant son and *verna* of Publicia Glypte, dating from the early second century AD, now at Villa Albani, Rome. Photo: German Archaeological Institute, Rome, EA 4553.

generation has re-invented an idea of Rome to suit its own political and cultural agenda. For instance, during the Renaissance various popes engaged in building pro- grammes that linked the monuments that expressed the greatness of Rome's imperial past to the power of the Church. In the twenty-first century the idea of Rome and its empire is so embedded in Western culture that we all think we 'know' something about it. Ancient Rome is a popular setting for film and television dramas, and for modern novels of all genres. Film and television have given us a visual landscape with all the iconic elements we have learned to expect: colonnaded squares, statues on podiums, temples, amphitheatres, cobbled streets. Scriptwriters and novelists have peopled this cityscape with characters who speak with current linguistic forms and idioms and use a body language that a modern audience can recognize and empathize with. But the danger here is that an audience slips easily into thinking the ancient Romans were much like 'us'.

The idea of ancient Rome is such a pervasive element of Western cultural baggage that it is easy to use it as a background to narratives of all kinds. This is not a new concept, as Roman history has been a magnet for story tellers since ancient times. We need only think of the story of Antony and Cleopatra, re-told across time from the Greek, Plutarch, in the second century AD; to Shakespeare in sixteenth-century London, to Cecil B. DeMille's twentieth-century Hollywood extravaganza, to the 2011 film version starring Angelina Jolie. This entertaining and attractive ancient Rome of popular culture is seductive and exists, for the most part happily, alongside the historical version. The symbiosis of popular cultural Rome and the Rome of academic research has produced some fortunate results: the reception of Rome in modern media has become a new discipline developing its own methodologies and critical toolbox; for universities it has attracted renewed student interest; and in the heritage sector the Rome of popular culture has brought new consumers of tourist sites, including monuments such as the Coliseum, museums and archaeological sites both in Rome and elsewhere. In Italy well known sites like Pompeii and Herculaneum are suffering from the high numbers of tourists; in France (Roman Gaul) Roman heritage is also exploited, from small local museums like that at Civaux, to major monuments like the Pont du Gard; while in the UK attractions range from some of the rugged parts of Hadrian's Wall to the reconstructed Roman villa at Fishbourne. Where children and the history of childhood stand in this mix is not always clear. However, there is certainly an interest within museums such as Bath and Corinium (Roman Cirencester) in the UK to exploit both the perceived emotive nature of children's history (to a twenty-first-century adult audience) and to encourage the interest of children as a distinct audience through displays of 'childhood' alongside interactive exhibitions and activities.

Examining the history of children and childhood in any period is a complex process. The evidence for Roman childhood comes in many forms: literary (including documentary material such as laws and census returns, poetry, letters and history writing), iconography, epigraphy, material culture and archaeology. Each of these areas produces particular images of children and childhood, but arguably none of them allows children themselves a voice. Literary, iconographic and epigraphic evidence is reflected through the prism of Roman adult ideas of childhood, and the adults tend to be male, and frequently, but not always, from the upper echelons of society. Even within an apparently homogeneous social group such as the Roman upper classes attitudes to children are not universal.

The spectrum of attitudes towards today's children that a viewer/reader might experience in a cursory glance at modern media is salutary: images of cute infants in advertising for baby accessories; the sweet children of celebrities; whole television channels devoted to children's programmes; horror stories of child labour; children in disaster areas; the physical and sexual abuse of children; child soldiers; and children as criminals. Such images produce a response in the reader/viewer which is predicated on their own particular social and cultural context and, arguably, their own experience of childhood. In ancient Rome, attitudes towards children were as equally varied across a continuum that ranged from affectionate, proud and indulgent parents at one end, to the slavery and sexual abuse of small children at the other. Lucretius can write of 'sweet children' who run to be kissed and 'move your heart with unspoken pleasure' (*On the Nature of Things* 3. 894–901) while a letter from an absent husband to a wife can state about the imminent birth of their child: 'raise it if it's a boy, put it out if it's a girl (*POxy.*iv.744). Meanwhile the imperial biographer Suetonius reports that the emperor Tiberius kept little boys to perform oral sex on him while in the swimming pool (*Tiberius* 44). Depending on which selection of evidence is examined a positive or negative view of childhood experiences can be constructed. There was no single normative childhood in the Roman world, any more than there is today. Then, as now, social and cultural norms dictated the assumptions and expectations of the relationship between parents and children, and with the wider society.

This also begs the question of the definition of childhood in the Roman period. This chapter has started with a presumption that the idea of childhood as a separate and specific stage of life is an uncontested notion. This is not the case: in the 1960s Philippe Ariès brought the idea of childhood as a normal stage of life into stark focus by asserting that the concept of childhood, as a state distinct from adulthood, was a relatively recent development (Ariès 1962: 125). A so-called 'darker side' of childhood was stereotyped by Lloyd deMause (1974) who stressed the idea of infant exposure and abandonment and general indifference or even cruelty in Roman child care practices. The arguments of Ariès and deMause have since been complicated and lent greater nuance by historians, and we now have a far more balanced view of how far the evidence can take us in assessing Roman childhood(s) (see, for example, Rawson (2003), Dixon (1992) and papers in Dixon (2001), Bradley (1991a), Néraudau (1984), Harlow *et al.* (2007: 5–6) and Laes (2011); on abandonment and exposure see most recently Vuolanto (2011) and Evans Grubbs (2010, 2011); and on approaches to childhood in the past more generally Crawford and Lewis (2008: 5–16)).

Any definition of Roman childhood would not map neatly onto twenty-first-century Western ideas. Rome was a pre-industrial society in which the patterns of life and ways of living, even in urban contexts, are mainly alien to the modern developed world. This was a world with limited sanitation, despite the Roman passion for baths, and high levels of disease and mortality. Infant mortality was high. The children and childhoods we know most about are those from the wealthier urban households. Those who study ancient demography engage with a combination of evidence from inscriptions and census returns, to the use of Model Life Tables. Given the geographical expanse of the Roman Empire and its long duration it is hard to get more than an overall impression, but there is agreement that up to 35 per cent of new-borns would not survive the first month of life and that only 50 per cent of those who did so would survive to the age of 10. Such high child mortality means that simply in order to ensure the continuation of a family, a woman would, on average, have to give birth five times (this assumes the non-survival of some of the children and miscarriages), and that the loss of a child in the family, or among friends and relations, would not have been uncommon (Parkin 1992, 2010; Scheidel 1996, 2009; Saller 1994).

In the households where parents may have been part of the relatively homogenizing Greco-Roman upper-class culture, children may have experienced a period of time when they were indulged, allowed to play, had freedom from some social constraints, and were not required to engage with the activities of the adult world. However, within these households there would have been slave children who presumably would have laboured in some way. In working urban households or peasant communities the period of childhood might have been shorter or restricted only by physical ability and manual dexterity – once a child could play a part in providing income for the household, however small, they became (even if only part-time) workers or perhaps carers for younger siblings (Larsson Lovén and Strömberg 2010). The extent to which an individual child enjoyed a period free from responsibility, room to play rather than work, and had expectations of the provision of basic care, were dependent on their own gender and the economic and social status of their parents. Some children might enjoy a childhood, others might be abandoned at birth, still others, especially slaves, might find themselves working as soon as they were able. Childhood as a particular stage of life was not a normalized condition across Roman society.

Rome was a hierarchical, patriarchal and slave owning society: all aspects which impose particular dynamics on family structure and the relationships within that grouping. It is not possible here to discuss all the nuances of Roman family life, but to avoid the seductive notion that the Romans were much like 'us' I will make just two points, the first to do with legal definitions, the second to do with gender. In legal terms, the Roman *familia* meant all those in the power of the eldest male ascendant (the *paterfamilias*). This group included his children, the children of his sons, slaves and sometimes ex-slaves and retainers. In this sense *familia*, although it is the word from which the modern word family is derived, is more accurately translated and conceptually understood as a household. The father controlled all economic resources until his death, and this meant that even an adult male son aged in his twenties could still legally be in the position of a child when it came to ownership of property or dealing in business. In early Roman history the wife would also be in the power of her husband or his father (if alive), but by the first century BC, a woman remained under the control of her father even if she married. This meant that in legal terms a mother was not in the same *familia* as her children. Social behaviour and living conditions, not to mention ideals of family life, militated against this legal framework, but it does serve to highlight the fact that we need to be aware that Roman family structure was in many ways alien to modern assumptions about family relationships. That said, children were an expected and desired part of family life. Aside from any affective and emotional role, a Roman father wanted children to continue his family name into the future, to remember the past deeds of the family and to maintain the patrimony for subsequent generations. For those with less to bequeath, children were expected to contribute to family income and to repay their parents by looking after them in their old age. For all groups, children were expected to maintain the family cult, which would keep the gods onside.

Rome was also a society which privileged the male citizen and males generally. Women and girls were not perceived as part of the public world of civic life and politics so their lives are to a large extent hidden from us. Like the children with whom they shared the domestic realm, what we do know about women comes largely from the writings of men. Women who had possession of economic resources and/or were of high social status could control their own lives to a certain degree, but still historians struggle with the tension between the idealized representation of women (and children) in Roman life and social reality. For girls in upper-class families, childhood ended with marriage, which could legally occur as young as twelve. Studies of age at first marriage have, however, shown that outside the high elite marriage did not usually take place until the late teens, when a girl would traditionally marry a man about eight years her senior, and with a much wider experience of life among adults (on age at marriage see Saller and Shaw (1984) and Shaw (1987); for differential life courses see Harlow and Laurence (2002)). We know very little of the lives of girls before they entered the social world of adults once they were married (see Hemelrijk 1999 on the education of girls); and for girls of the lower classes the canvas is practically blank (Rawson 1966, 2003).

One of the methodological problems we face in dealing with Roman childhood is not only that the sources we have available are seen through the eyes of Roman parents (mostly fathers), but that these diverse sources reflect contemporary attitudes. The inscriptions from the first century AD which opened this chapter are a case in point. These are monuments which show the public face of grief and, as memorials, fit the Roman iconographic language of death. However, there is also a personal and private aspect to the relationships expressed there: for example, the pride of Sulpicius Maximus's parents in his extempore verse, which is inscribed on the monument, or Publicia Glypte's joint memorial to her baby son and an infant home-born slave. Both these inscriptions are products of a commemorative practice current in late first/early second-century Rome, and while the parents must have chosen the style, design and text of the inscription there is still much here that is formulaic and part of the cultural language of memorials at this time (Huskinson 1996, 2005). However these memorials do tell much larger individual stories.

One of the reasons I selected the memorial to Q. Sulpicius Maximus is because it features as a key element around which eminent academics have introduced or situated wider historical discussions of Roman childhood, society and cultural memory. Indeed, this memorial is beginning, by virtue of the academic attention it has attracted, to serve as an icon in itself (Rawson 2003; Coleman 2010). It is also very much part of the modern heritage landscape of Rome. In its own time the monument was placed conspicuously on the Via Salaria where it would have been seen, if not read, by those using this main thoroughfare, and it was still complete in the third century when it became part of the Porta Salaria (the gateway) in the new wall built by the Emperor Aurelian. The original has now been moved to the Capitoline Montemartine Museum in Rome, but there are two copies: one can be seen on the Via Salaria in the Piazza Fiume near to where it was originally situated, the other is in the Museo della Civiltà Romana in EUR. The copy in Piazza Fiume stands on a podium near to the Porta Salaria and on a very busy main road. The copy is eye-catching because its whiteness stands out against the brick of the monumental walls behind it. While the original would have stood among a number of other memorials – as the Romans did not bury their dead within the city, the roads into Rome were lined with funerary monuments – its position so close to the boundary gives it a special place. It would also of course have been painted, rather than the clean white marble we now assume is characteristic of classical monuments. This could have played up aspects such as the facial features and costume detail, which are lost to us today. The inscription in the Piazza Fiume replica is hard to read (even if one is conversant with Greek and Latin) due to the height of the monument. Sulpicius is also remembered in the civic topography of Rome by having a street named after him, the Via Sulpicio Massimo, the sign for which also remembers him as 'giovanetto romano, poeta e oratore del 1 sec'. The modern city of Rome authorities have thus made him conspicuous in a number of ways, the most obvious of which are the fact that he was a child and accomplished at composing and reciting poetry.

The monument is an altar and remarkably survives intact. The statue in the central niche faces forward and depicts a young boy wearing a toga, standing in an orator's pose, with his left hand extended and holding a scroll. On either side of the figure are inscribed extracts from the Greek poem young Sulpicius composed for the competition. Beneath the figure, in Latin, is the commemorative epitaph quoted at the start of the chapter. The context and content of this memorial reflects multiple messages about Roman culture in the late first century AD. The statue shows a young citizen, Sulpicius, presumably wearing the purple bordered toga *praetexta* worn by boys (and girls) although the purple, probably painted on, is now lost. His citizenship is also shown by his three names (*tria nomina*) and designation to a tribe. The stress on his education and his ability to versify in Greek is clear, as is his parents' pride in his achievement. The monument presents us with the grief of Sulpicius's parents at the untimely loss of their son, but also the sub-texts of parental investment, both emotional and financial, and the loss of Sulpicius's potential to be a great orator. The monument expresses the hopes and aspirations of Sulpicius's parents for their son; it also reflects their role as 'good' parents in creating such an exemplary offspring. This is not to deny their grief, but to recognize that the setting up of such an elaborate monument in such a public place (by the Porta Salaria on one of the main routes into Rome) also reflects positively on the parents' status. In Roman culture the use of elaborate funerary monuments was part of the shaping of family identities. Sulpicius's memorial is as much about his parents as it is about him, perhaps more so as we have no understanding of his own opinions of his life. Education in Greek and Latin oratory was a fundamental part of the Roman system, especially for boys of the upper classes, or aspiring lower classes (Laes 2010a). Poetic competitions were also part of the system and this one was part of the Capitoline festival held in the third year of the reign of Domitian (AD 94). School masters, however, often get a bad press (Booth 1981; Laes 2011) and we cannot tell how much Sulpicius enjoyed or feared this competition, or how hard he had to work to achieve his success. Expressions of grief are, however, like expression of any emotion, culturally specific and need to be taken as such.

Sad though it is to imagine the short life of Sulpicius, if we take the sentiments of the memorial at one level it is a life which reflects a parent's view of a 'good' childhood by current Western definitions: here is a child who had two parents who loved him and were inconsolable at his death, were happy to invest in his education and so proud of his achievements that this is what they chose to record on his monument. Sulpicius's monument has resonance for twenty-first-century parents who might identify with its expression of unfulfilled potential and untimely loss rather than his bilingual poetic achievements, but the monument might also say something about parental aspirations: were Sulpicius's mother and father Roman versions of today's 'pushy parents'? It is difficult to judge how a twenty-first-century 11-year-old would respond to the memorial. Its power as an encapsulation of a set of cultural values is apparent in the way it is exploited today in Rome, both in the preservation of the monument and the street name, and also in the work of historians of the ancient world. In 2003 Beryl Rawson used the monument as the opening quotation and scene-setter in the first chapter of *Children and Childhood in Roman Italy* (17–20); more recently, in 2010, Kathleen Coleman, giving the prestigious Jerome lecture series at the American Academy at Rome, used it as a springboard for five lectures.[2]

Not all Roman childhoods had the potential to be so happy, if we believe the implication of Sulpicius's memorial. One has to ask questions about what lies behind the other memorial inscription cited at the start of this chapter, recognizing the death of the two one-year-olds. The fact that Rome was a slave society had many ramifications for social dynamics within the household and the family. In practical day-to-day terms, upper-class Roman children were often raised more by slave wet nurses, nurses and carers than their parents and, despite the potential for affectionate relationships between those who cared for them, the master's children presumably unconsciously assimilated their superior status position in respect of slave members of the household (Bradley 1986, 1991b, 1991c; Joshel 1986). Slaves, too, could have families, but such relationships could only exist at the whim of their owners; a slave had no legal persona and could not form a legitimate marriage. Children born to slave women took on their mother's status and their fate was outside their birth parents' control. A master or mistress was within his/her rights to expose the child, sell or send it away to be raised elsewhere. In some cases these 'home-grown' slaves (*vernae*) are recorded as holding special places in the affections of their master and/or mistress, occasionally acting as substitute or foster children, or close companions to the children of their owners, such as Eutyches, memorialized by his owner, Publicia Glypte. Above the inscription are two figures, which are clearly little boys but not as young as one year. They are depicted wearing togas and carrying tiny scrolls – both attributes that in reality they are far too young for. Many issues surround such an image and its accompanying dedication: for the slave child the toga (worn traditionally only by free citizens) was a sign that he had been freed before his death or that Publicia Glypte intended to free him. Like Sulpicius, the scroll was a mark of the aspirations of Publicia to educate them both. A fine monument such as this suggests she at least had the resources to pay for it. Rawson, who has written extensively on this altar, also posits that the boys may have been nurslings together, an idea encouraged by the image in the pediment which would remind the Roman viewer of the story of Telephus who was nursed by a hind. It was not uncommon in the Roman world to use wet nurses, and it may be that Eutyches was the child of the nurse, or of another slave in the household (Rawson 2003: 259–61). The monument and dedication do suggest that Eutyches may have been fortunate enough to hold a special place in the affections of his mistress and the family (see also Laes 2011: 197–200).

Other slave children were not so fortunate. There is a group known as *delicia/deliciae* (loosely translated as 'delights'). The position and fate of such children is difficult to quantify and brings a modern audience up against an uncomfortable set of presuppositions. These children were often kept as 'pets' for their cuteness: some appear to have been much loved and stood in the role of foster children, while others were doubtless used for sexual purposes (Laes 2003, 2010b, 2010c; McKeown 2007a). The term is ambiguous and hides both genuine surrogate parental relations and what we would now term gross abuse. Evidence certainly suggests that there was a market for such children, but they could also be born in the household. The first century AD poet Statius wrote a series of verses which commemorated the early deaths of children who were very close to their masters – or perhaps, as we have no idea how the children felt, it would be better to say children who their masters felt very strongly towards. As the verses are somewhat formulaic, it is difficult to discern whether Statius is addressing genuinely close affection between childless masters who have taken up home-born slave infants as foster children, or putting a gloss on pederasty (Laes 2010b). *Deliciae* are not an easy issue for modern readers to deal with. Comparative images spring to mind, from the 'designer' adoptions of children by celebrities, to grimmer forms of paedophilia; however, both these types deny the complex social and cultural world of Roman society. The social milieu that indulged such 'pets' was hierarchical, and the slave status of such children would have put them lower in the social hierarchy than legitimate and non-slave children. It may not, of course, have put the childen known as *delicia/deliciae* lower in the emotional hierarchy of their master, but that is almost impossible to judge now. We should also not discount the genuine desire on the part of some childless individuals to have children to love and be loved by, although again, this is difficult to discern confidently in the surviving evidence.

The case studies above have been about the relationship between parents and children, and are examples in which the children themselves have no voice. Recent research has made inroads into attributing agency to children in the past and attempting to relocate them within the archaeology of childhood, and one of the ways of doing this might be through material culture associated with children (papers in Moore and Scott 1997; Sofaer Deverenski 2000). This approach is also not without its problems. Museum exhibits which focus on childhood as a stage of life are often full of objects that the modern viewer might associate with contemporary views of childhood, such as feeding bottles, miniature objects and figurines and jointed figures – some of which may be identified as toys. The current small exhibition case in the British Museum labelled 'Childhood', which is part of a series of cases covering Greek and Roman life and which has not been updated in many years, reflects a very traditional view of childhood with an emphasis on play and education. The display includes Greek vases which show images of children playing with balls and small animals. Little jointed terracotta figures from one girl's grave dating to *c*.420 BC are assumed to be 'dolls'. A series of miniature items are exhibited: a figure on a throne, a model of tiny booted feet; a model of a little jointed female figure; a miniature thigh guard used in wool preparation; and a miniature *gamikos* (bowl used in the marriage ceremony). There is also a rattle in the shape of a pig, a spinning top and other miniature items such as small lead figurines of a camel, a horse and chariot and a soldier on horseback. The associated text in the display case makes it clear that placing a secure definition on many of these artefacts is not possible, but in placing them in a display case labelled 'Childhood' the implication is that children in the classical world had much in common with the modern world in terms of play and the use of small items made for small hands.

In reality the material culture of childhood is harder to define, as it is not easy to separate artefacts into categories of 'child' or 'adult' in the archaeological record. Even the interpretation of finds such as miniature objects or 'dolls' found in children's graves as 'toys' is problematic. We rarely know if an object has ritual significance, is an heirloom, or really is simply a toy (or any combination of these categories). There is also a difference between an item which a child might play with and something that is made by an adult specifically for a child – a toy. As the British Museum display on 'Childhood' shows, there is of course evidence that children played with nuts, spinning tops, dolls, toy soldiers and other types of toys, but to simply confine these objects to childhood is a misconception. And to give the impression that play was a major part of childhood denies the fact that for most children in the Roman world life was short and cruel. Current work aiming to attribute agency to children in the past and the growing awareness of tracking children in the archaeological record can only improve both our understanding of childhood in the past and the material culture associated with it (see, for example: Baxter 2005; Wileman 2005; Sánchez Romero 2008; Sofaer Derevenski 2000). The archaeological evidence will, however, remain fragmentary and we should refrain from attempting to create from it a narrative that looks like modern versions of childhood.

There is another side to the implications for cultural heritage. In the twenty-first century the heritage industry has recognized the potential for children (with or without their parents) as a distinct market segment and audience. In contrast to its more traditional display case mentioned above, children aged between 8 and 15 can now have a sleepover at the British Museum with structured craft activities, a tour of the museum by night, and bedding in the Egyptian and Assyrian galleries. As this demonstrates, the (imagined) realities of living in the past and attempts to make the past 'come alive' by experiential or other means have become the focus of museum exhibits and activities, at least in the UK. At the recently re-vamped Corinium Museum at Cirencester, which is dedicated to the original Roman town and its environs, the emphasis is on the interaction and engagement of visitors. The Corinium Museum has successfully managed to engage visitors of all ages in its exhibits with interactive computer screens, dressing up, re-enactors and an impressive spatial layout, but there is a clear focus on the younger visitor. The displays are a mix of traditional reconstruction and state of the art museum technology. Their website is full of activities and downloadable projects for children to complete, and is part of the new initiative, 'Kids in Museums'.[3] This is an independent charity founded in 2012 which aims to make museums 'family friendly'.

In 2007, to cite another example, the Museum of London took part in a Roman Household Weekend where artefacts from the collection were used to show children how diet and health in the past can be determined from surviving teeth. The Museum of London has also recently developed a specialized downloadable computer application called *StreetMuseum* which allows the viewer to conjure up Roman Londinium as they walk through the modern city.[4] This re-enactment and reconstruction experience can be aimed at different age groups, and encourages children to question how an activity might be done with the tools of the past, to appreciate the differences between the past and the present and to develop an enquiring mind in a way that is very different in practice to more passive museum displays.

But how is Roman childhood portrayed to the twenty-first-century child? Film, television and children's fiction writers have also seen the attraction Rome has for their target audience. Caroline Lawrence's *Roman Mysteries* series, first published in 2002 and centred around a group of children in the Roman city of Ostia, has been a phenomenal success. The first books have been serialized by the BBC, and there is also an associated website.[5] The central characters are all aged around twelve, and constitute Flavia, the main protagonist whose mother died in childbirth, Jonathan, a Jewish refugee, Nubia, a slave from Africa and Lupus, an orphaned Greek mute. The diverse cultural and social backgrounds of the children would not have been unknown in a Roman port town of the first century AD, but the plots and relationships are probably more reminiscent of twenty-first-century ideas of social interaction. The lack of controlling parents is the mainstay of plots for children's fiction, but also not far from the realities of the Roman world: slave children might not know their parents; many children would have lost mothers through childbirth. Novels such as these and the many books there are for children on the Roman world now often stress the fate of slaves alongside the seemingly more glamorous icons of Roman history such as gladiators.

The examples used in this chapter are selective, and are not intended to be an exhaustive coverage of the many ways Roman childhood can be defined in different contexts, or how the idea of Roman childhood has become part of our present-day cultural heritage. My stress has been on how contemporary preoccupations and anxieties have influenced (whether consciously or not) our interpretations of childhood in the past. For museums, monuments and archaeological sites, this is an obvious point of visitor access, through gripping the public imagination and feeding into relevant cultural, social and political agendas. The danger is that the tension between being too verbose or providing over simplified museum captions can result in the original contexts being missed. For instance, in an ideal world historical representations such as exhibitions would acknowledge that there are many childhoods in Rome.

Interestingly, in relation to childhoods in other historical periods there has been a shift over the past decade in the focus of popular media and heritage interpretation away from more privileged childhoods to the lives of those who were not so lucky: those who were abandoned or died young or lived in slavery. This reflects a contemporary concern voiced by the United Nations Children's Fund (UNICEF) and other charities over practices such as child abandonment and the trafficking of children, which implies sold, stolen or abandoned children. In London, the opening of the Foundling Museum in 1998 put a particular focus on the histories of child abandonment. This museum preserves the records of over 27,000 children who passed through the Foundling Hospital between 1739 and 1954. In a series of moving exhibits ranging from the tokens left with babies by their mothers to the oral histories of more recent residents, the aims of the original founders (Thomas Coram, William Hogarth and George Frideric Handel) and the experiences of children are carefully recorded. Arguably these children who grew up in the Foundling Hospital were the lucky ones (http://www.foundlingmuseum.org.uk/). Their historical story directs attention away from the upper classes to focus on the poor and other groups that traditionally have found little voice either at the time or since. In the academic world of ancient history and archaeology the focus has likewise shifted away from the social elite, with many recent publications concentrating on precisely these 'muted groups' (Joshel 1992, 2010; McKeown 2007b; Bradley 1994). This growing academic interest in the under classes of Roman society is now finding its way into the more popular histories and exhibits of Roman life, and abandoned and enslaved children who left little in the written or archaeological record are at least now being remembered as a part of the cultural history of Roman childhood.

Acknowledgements

I would like to thank both the editors, Kate Darian-Smith and Carla Pascoe, and John Hunter, for their comments on earlier drafts of this chapter. It is undoubtedly a better piece of work as a result and any errors and omissions are down to me.

Notes

1 *CIL* stands for *Corpus Inscriptionum Latinarum* (Corpus of Latin Inscriptions).
2 http://sofaarome.wordpress.com/2010/02/21/for-2010-jerome-lectures-at-aar-harvard-classicist-kathleen-coleman-explores-world-of-roman-child-poet/ (January 2012).
3 For Corinium Museum see: http://coriniummuseum.cotswold.gov.uk/. For the manifesto of 'Kids in Museums' see: http://www.kidsinmuseums.org.uk/.
4 Museum of London: www.museumoflondon.org.uk/Streetmuseum.htm.
5 http://www.romanmysteries.com/ (accessed February 2012).

References

Ariès, P. (1962) *Centuries of Childhood: A Social History of Family Life*, London: Penguin Books.

Baxter, E. (2005) *The Archaeology of Childhood: Children, Gender and Material Culture*, Walnut Creek: Alta Mira Press.

Booth, A. (1981) 'Some suspect schoolmasters', *Florilegium*, 3: 1–20.

Bradley, K. (1986) 'Wet nursing at Rome: a study in social relations', in B. Rawson (ed.) *The Family in Ancient Rome, New Perspectives*, London; Sydney: Croom Helm.

—— (1991a) *Discovering the Roman Family*, Oxford: Oxford University Press.

—— (1991b) 'The social role of the nurse in the Roman world', in *Discovering the Roman Family*, Oxford: Oxford University Press.

—— (1991c) 'Child care at Rome: the role of men', in *Discovering the Roman Family*, Oxford: Oxford University Press.

—— (1994) *Slavery and Society at Rome*, Cambridge: Cambridge University Press.

Coleman, K. (2010) 'Q. Sulpicius Maximus, Poet, Eleven Years Old', Jerome Lectures at the American Academy at Rome (unpublished) http://sofaarome.wordpress.com/2010/02/21/for-2010-jerome-lectures-at-aar-harvard-classicist-kathleen-coleman-explores-world-of-roman-child-poet/ (accessed January 2012).

Crawford, S. and Lewis, C. (2008) 'Childhood Studies and the Society for the Study of Children in the Past', *Childhood in the Past*, 1: 5–16.

deMause, L. (1974) 'The evolution of childhood', in L. deMause (ed.) *History of Childhood*, New York: Psychohistory Press.

Dixon, S. (ed.) (2011) *Childhood, Class and Kin in the Roman World*, London and New York: Routledge.

—— (1992) *The Roman Family*, Baltimore, MD and London: Johns Hopkins.

Evans Grubbs, J. (2010) 'Hidden in plain sight: expositi in the community', in V. Dasen and T. Spath (eds) *Children, Memory and Family Identity in Roman Culture*, Oxford: Oxford University Press.

—— (2011) 'The dynamics of infant abandonment: motives, attitudes and (unintended) consequences', in C. Laes and K. Mustakallio (eds) *The Dark Side of Childhood in Antiquity and the Middle Ages*, Oxford: Oxbow Books.

Harlow, M. and Laurence, R. (2002) *Growing Up and Growing Old in Ancient Rome: A Life Course Approach*, London: Routledge.

Harlow, M., Laurence, R. and Vuolanto, V. (2007) 'Past, present and future: the study of Roman childhood', in S. Crawford and G. Shepherd (eds) *Children, Childhood and Society*, Oxford: BAR Int. Series 1696.

Hemelrijk, E. (1999) *Matrona Docta: Educated Women in the Roman Elite from Cornelia to Julia Domna*, London and New York: Routledge.

Huskinson, J. (1996) *Roman Children's Sarcophagi: Their Decoration and its Social Significance*, Oxford: Clarendon Press.

—— (2005) 'Disappearing children? Children in Roman funerary art of the first to the fourth centuries AD', in K. Mustakallio, K. Hanska, J. Sainio and V. Vuolanto (eds) *Hoping for Continuity: Childhood, Education and Death in Antiquity and the Middle Ages*, Rome: Institutum Romanum Finlandiae.

Joshel, S. (1986) 'Nurturing the master's child: slavery and the Roman child-nurse', *Signs*, 12: 5–22.

—— (1992) *Work, Identity and Legal Status at Rome: A Study of Occupational Inscriptions*, Norman: University of Oklahoma Press.

—— (2010) *Slavery in the Ancient World*, Cambridge: Cambridge University Press.

Laes, C. (2003) 'Desperately different? *Delicia* children in the Roman household', in D. Balch and C. Osiek (eds) *Early Christian Families in Context: An Interdisciplinary Approach*, Grand Rapids, MI: Eerdmans Publishing.

—— (2010a) 'Education', in M. Harlow and R. Laurence (eds) *A Cultural History of Childhood and the Family, vol. 1: Antiquity*, Oxford and New York: Berg.

—— (2010b) 'When classicists need to speak up: antiquity and present day pedophilia', in H.F. Horstmanshoff (ed.) *Hippocrates and Medical Education. Selected papers read at the XIIth International Hippocrates Colloquium, Universiteit Leiden, 24–26 August 2005*. Leiden.

—— (2010c) '*Delicia* children revisited: the evidence of Statius' *Silvae*', in V. Dasen and T. Spath (eds) *Children, Memory and Family Identity in Roman Culture*, Oxford: Oxford University Press.

—— (2011) *Children in the Roman Empire, Outsiders Within*, Cambridge: Cambridge University Press.

Larsson Lovén, L. and Strömberg, A. (2010) 'Economy', in M. Harlow and R. Laurence (eds) *A Cultural History of Childhood and the Family, vol. 1: Antiquity*, Oxford and New York: Berg.

McKeown, N. (2007a) 'Had they no shame? Martial, Statius and Roman sexual attitudes towards their slave children', in S. Crawford and G. Shepherd (eds) *Children, Childhood and Society*, Oxford: Oxford: BAR Int. Series 1696.

—— (2007b) *The Invention of Ancient Slavery*, London: Duckworth.

Moore, J. and Scott, E. (eds) (1997) *Invisible People and Processes: Writing Gender and Childhood into European Archaeology*, Leicester: Leicester University Press.

Néraudau, J-P. (1984) *Être Enfant à Rome*, Paris: Les Belles Lettres.

Parkin, T. (1992) *Demography and Roman Society*, Baltimore, MD and London: Johns Hopkins.

—— (2010) 'Life Cycle', in M. Harlow and R. Laurence (eds) *A Cultural History of Childhood and the Family, vol. 1: Antiquity*, Oxford and New York: Berg.

Rawson, B. (1966) 'Family life among the lower classes at Rome in the first two centuries of the empire', *Classical Philology*, 61: 71–83.

—— (2003) *Children and Childhood in Roman Italy*, Oxford: Oxford University Press.

Saller, R. (1994) *Patriarchy, Property and Death in the Roman Family*, Cambridge: Cambridge University Press.

Saller, R.P. and Shaw, B. (1984) 'Tombstones and Roman family relations in the Principate: civilians, soldiers and slaves', *Journal of Roman Studies*, 74: 124–56.

Sánchez Romero, M. (2008) 'Childhood and the construction of gender identities through material culture', *Childhood in the Past*, 1: 17–37.

Scheidel, W. (1996) *Measuring Sex, Age and Death in the Roman Empire: Explorations in Ancient Demography*, Ann Arbor, MI: Journal of Roman Archaeology Supplementary Studies.

—— (2009) 'The demographic background', in S. Huebner and D.M. Ratzen (eds) *Growing Up Fatherless in Antiquity*, Cambridge: Cambridge University Press.

Shaw, B. (1987) 'The age of Roman girls at marriage: some reconsiderations', *Journal of Roman Studies*, 77: 30–46.

Sofaer Deverenski, J. (ed.) (2000) *Children and Material Culture*, London: Routledge.

Vuolanto, V. (2011) 'Infant abandonment and the Christianization of Medieval Europe', in C. Laes and K. Mustakallio (eds) *The Dark Side of Childhood in Antiquity and the Middle Ages*, Oxford: Oxbow Books.

Wileman, J. (2005) *Hide and Seek: The Archaeology of Childhood*, Stroud: Tempus.

Chapter 10

Children, colonialism and commemoration

Kate Darian-Smith

The landscape of Australia today is resonant with memorials to the people and events of the colonial past in forms as varied as plaques, stone cairns, statues, commemorative buildings, heritage sites and monuments. The majority of these mark the historical presence of European men and their imperial contributions as explorers, entrepreneurs, judges, politicians, soldiers and social reformers, with the occasional writer or artist. War memorials to men who were killed or served in the First World War and subsequent conflicts are to be found in every Australian country town and city suburb, the 'sacred places' of imperial and national myth-making and modern Australian identity (Inglis 2008). The incidence of colonial white women in public memorials is comparatively muted. The notable exceptions are the numerous public statues of an imperial Queen Victoria, and a scattering of twentieth-century tributes in the form of monuments, fountains or gardens to the collective achievements of 'pioneer women'.

Memorials to the pre-settlement experiences of Indigenous peoples and the violence of the colonial frontier are rarer still.[1] From the mid-nineteenth century to the 1960s, the few public monuments that acknowledged the presence of Indigenous men and women portrayed them in limited ways: as 'treacherous natives', the 'last' survivor of a tribe or as the helpmeets of explorers and settlers (Batten 2004: 101–2). Since the last decades of the twentieth century, and especially after the Bicentenary of British settlement (or invasion) in 1988 sparked much debate and contestation about Australian history, there has been a growing desire by Aboriginal people to recognize their past, including resistance to colonialism, through public memorials.

However, until recently it is the cultural heritage and historical experiences of children – particularly Indigenous children – that has been most persistently omitted from Australia's memorial landscape. This is perhaps unsurprising, given that the historical lives of children have generally been subsumed within the broader adult world and the social unit of the family, and consequently there has been little commemorative recognition of children's distinct sufferings or achievements. Yet the experiences of children within a British colonial society such as Australia *were* distinctive from those of children in metropolitan Britain. The emerging historiography of children and childhood in Australia has highlighted that although white children were positioned as immigrants and colonizers, and Indigenous children were subjected to the destructive forces of colonization, *all* children in Australia had limited agency in comparison to adults. Moreover, children's experiences were dictated, in varying degrees and at different historical moments, by state policies and regulations in accordance with their class and, most importantly, their race.

Today, the histories of Australian children whose lives were shaped by the circumstances of British colonialism have, in a short period of time, become the subject of public knowledge, debate and memorialization. Since the late 1990s, the extent of state intervention into children's lives has been the subject of three major national inquiries in Australia: *Bringing Them Home: Report of the National Inquiry into the Separation of Aboriginal and Torres Strait Islander Children from Their Families* (1997); *Lost Innocents: Righting the Record on Child Migration* (2001); and *Forgotten Australians: A Report on Australians Who Experienced Institutional or Out-of-Home Care as Children* (2004). Each inquiry relied upon copious first-person testimonies to assess the impact of government practices that controlled the lives of these children from the early colonial period until the present.

In addressing the individual and national legacies of the respective policies pertaining to child removal, unaccompanied child migration and the institutional care of children, the three national reports acknowledged the importance of recognizing and redressing the past. Recommendations were made, if not always undertaken, 'in relation to archives, record-keeping and memorials, in order that the history not be forgotten' (Swain *et al.* 2012: 17). Further symbolic and political weight was given to the historical injustices experienced by children through a series of landmark national apologies. In 2008, Australian Prime Minister Kevin Rudd formally apologized in the Australian parliament to Indigenous Australians, acknowledging the pain of children who were removed from their families and have become widely known as the Stolen Generations. In 2009, Rudd made a second national apology to the Forgotten Australians, a term used to refer to children who experienced out-of-home institutionalized care, and Former Child Migrants. Then in 2010, British Prime Minister Gordon Brown apologized to the 150,000 children who were sent by the British government, often without the permission or knowledge of their parents, throughout the British Commonwealth and primarily to Canada and Australia.

This chapter provides an overview of how the histories and cultural heritage of children in Australia have been publicly commemorated, and how this has altered over time. It begins with an examination of the memorialization of the lives and deaths of white children in the colonial period. The public commemoration of the removal of Indigenous children from their families is then examined in a context where the Indigenous child has become central to the politicized and contested public histories of colonial dispossession of Indigenous lands and cultures. Finally, the chapter explores how the deprived and difficult childhoods of the many thousands of Australians who were institutionalized or sent as migrants from Britain have been recently acknowledged in monuments and exhibitions. While these are Australian case studies, the core issues that they address – first, the concepts of children's rights, Indigenous rights and human rights more generally; and second, the connections between such rights discourse and cultural heritage and its conservation and protection – are of global significance.

Colonial children

Within the white settler colonies of the British Empire, white children were seen to be symbolically, socially and economically tied to the success of the colonial project. European children shared with adults the privations and the privileges of colonization, and children's experiences were shaped by the realities of their class, gender and family circumstances within new worlds and on imperial frontiers. In colonial New South Wales, for example, when the First Fleet of convicts and British marines landed at Sydney Cove in 1788, among the arrivals were almost 50 children ranging from infants to those just under the legal adult age of 14 years. In addition, a small number of convicts were actually children when they were sentenced to be transported to the new penal colony (Holden 2000).

The sentencing and transportation of children, aged as young as nine, from Britain to Australia continued until the 1840s. These children were initially housed alongside adult prisoners, but gradually and in recognition of their distinct status as children they were accommodated in separate quarters. By the 1830s, the majority of boy convicts were moved to barracks at Point Puer, near the notorious Port Arthur Penitentiary in Tasmania (MacFie and Hargraves 1999). Point Puer was the first purpose-built reforming institution for juveniles within the British Empire, and its underpinning philosophy emphasized the potential of education, training and religious instruction in transforming young offenders into productive citizens. Today, a visit to the Port Arthur Historic Site, included in 2010 on the World Heritage list of Australian Convict Sites, includes a tour of the crumbling remains of Point Puer Boys' Prison, where 3,000 boy convicts lived until the reformatory was closed in 1849.[2]

Throughout the Australian colonies, as in other parts of the British Empire, settler children were an important source of labour, whether in the fledgling towns or in vast tracts of country that were 'opened up' for European agriculture and grazing. Initially, the proportion of children among the white population was significantly less than in Britain. This relative scarcity meant that children's mental and physical characteristics were monitored and noted by government authorities. With the increase of family-based 'free' immigration to Australia in the 1830s and 1840s, the numbers of children increased. By the 1860s, almost half the population of Sydney was children aged under 12 years (Kociumbas 1997: 77), a proportion similar to that of Britain. Poorer urban children lived in straightened circumstances, often within a one-parent family, and made a living by selling matches or flowers, or doing small jobs. Those who were destitute or abandoned were placed in state or charitable institutions, while the introduction of universal education acts from the 1870s meant that all Australian children, not only those of the middle class, attended schools.

In the expanding rural economy, it was well recognized by colonial officials that a family unit comprising several children, preferably boys, had a greater chance of success in the establishment of farming allotments. From a young age, colonial children assisted in tasks such as gathering firewood and feeding stock, and, for girls, undertaking household chores. As they grew older, they took on heavier work including the planting and harvesting of crops, the shepherding of sheep and the mustering of cattle.

Whether in the town or country, the life of the settler child was beset by danger. The newspapers of colonial Sydney and Melbourne were crammed with descriptions of children being harmed or killed through accidents: scalded by boiling water; falling from bullock drays; consuming opium, brandy or poisonous fruits; or receiving terrible burns in household fires. The most frequent cause of accidental child death was drowning (Torney 2005: 13). Combined with a high rate of infant and child mortality, especially in the hot summer months, and limited medical care and regular outbreaks of contagious diseases, around 20 per cent of white children did not live into adulthood. Although parents were aware of the physical vulnerability of children, historian Pat Jalland has commented that 'there is little evidence that parents in the nineteenth century invested less affection in their children and felt less distress than parents a century later' upon the death of a child (Jalland 2002: 73). While Christian beliefs may have provided consolation, the diaries and letters of bereft parents reveal a deep need to remember their children's brief lives through personal mementos. These included the preservation of a lock of hair or cherished item of clothing, or a photograph or sketch of the deceased child.

In public forms of memorialization, graves of settler infants and children are commonplace in urban and rural cemeteries throughout Australia. For middle- and upper-class children, these sometimes included elaborate headstones, especially in the case of the death of older children or to mark the sole grave of multiple siblings. The recognition of the experiences of the general or localized experiences of settler children (and settlers more generally) has also prompted latter-day community memorials, particularly from the 1980s when there was a growth of interest in local histories in Australia partly stimulated by national Bicentennial funding. These include monuments to the pioneer children in the frontier town of Kalbar in south-east Queensland or to unmarked children's graves at the Moonta cemetery in South Australia. A Pioneer Children's Monument, erected in 1983, marks the graves of five Robinson children who died in the 1890s of heat exhaustion and bad water in the outback opal-mining town of White Cliffs.[3]

In a distinctive Australian response to the colonial environment, there are also memorials to 'lost children' who wandered from parents and home and perished in the bush. While there were certainly documented cases of children becoming lost in the forests and prairies of other colonial societies, in North America, South Africa and New Zealand the predominate settler fear concerned the abduction and captivity of white children by Indigenous peoples. By the late eighteenth century, regular incidents of white captivity occurred on North American frontiers; by the nineteenth century hundreds of written accounts of captive and rescued white settlers, including children, were circulated throughout the broader British colonial world (Colley 2002). In Australia, however, Aboriginal people did not kidnap settlers but instead assisted escaped convicts or castaways who had been separated from white society (Darian-Smith 1996). In this context it was the natural environment, rather than its Indigenous owners, that was perceived by colonists to pose a threat to children.

Kim Torney's exhaustive study of the potency of the lost child in the Australian national imagination explores repeated and multiple forms of commemoration both at the time and subsequently through literature, art, school textbooks, films and memorials (Torney 2005; see also Pierce 1999). The two largest public memorials are located in the state of Victoria.[4] The first of these, near the town of Horsham, records how in 1864 Jane Duff, aged 9 years, cared for her two younger brothers until they were rescued after nine days alone in the bush. Jane Duff became a popular heroine, her story reinterpreted and re-commemorated for over a century. The Duff memorial was erected in 1935, funded by donations from school children; a headstone was placed on her grave in the 1940s; and in the 1980s the Jane Duff Highway Park was opened nearby (Torney 2005: 199–227).

The second memorial is to three young boys who disappeared in 1867 while playing in heavily forested land near Daylesford, in central Victoria. Their remains were found months later in a large hollow tree. The boys' funeral was attended by over a thousand mourners, and public subscriptions paid for a headstone and a single stone column engraved with their tragic story over a joint grave in the local cemetery. Other commemorations followed, including a scholarship to honour the boys at the Daylesford school, and the preservation of the hollow tree until the 1950s. In the 1980s, a Bicentennial history project established a stone cairn in The Three Lost Children Memorial Park.[5] A Lost Children walk of about 15 kilometres retraces the boys' wanderings, and culminates in a second cairn and memorial garden where their bodies were recovered, and now on the side of a secondary road cutting through open farming land. In 2009, bushfires in the area destroyed the community memorial, but it has been rebuilt and is now carefully tended, indicating the power of this colonial tragedy for the history and heritage of the local community.

Indigenous Children and the Stolen Generations

When on 13 February 2008, Prime Minister Kevin Rudd delivered a formal apology to Australia's Indigenous Peoples, his speech focused on 'the mistreatment' of the Stolen Generations removed from their families as children by government authorities. 'The time has now come,' Rudd stated, 'to turn a new page in Australia's history by righting the wrongs of the past' (Rudd 2008). These words were greeted by a hushed crowd of thousands of people, many Aboriginal, who had travelled to Canberra to witness the event. The apology came after more than two decades of lobbying and protest, and a change of federal government; conservative Prime Minister John Howard, in office from 1996–2007, strongly opposed any national apology for past injustices and denied that Indigenous child removal was a breach of human rights.

In accordance with official government policies on the protection and assimilation of Indigenous Australians, from the early 1900s until 1970 somewhere between 10 and 30 per cent of all Indigenous children were forcibly removed from their families and communities. The children were placed in state or charitable institutions, missions, or foster homes where they were not allowed to speak their traditional language or to refer to their own culture. The education offered was limited, with boys trained as labourers and girls as domestic servants (Haebich 2000). Now known as the Stolen Generations, many of these children were permanently separated from their parents and had little, if any, knowledge of their traditional lands and beliefs. By the 1970s and 1980s, there was a growing recognition within Indigenous and welfare bodies of the traumatic longer-term impacts of child removal on successive generations, and organizations were formed to support and reunite Indigenous children and parents.

In 1987, among the final recommendations of a Royal Commission into Aboriginal Deaths in Custody was the need to investigate the impact of cases of child removal on Aboriginal individuals and communities. As a result, the Human Rights and Equal Opportunity Commission undertook an Inquiry into the Separation of Aboriginal and Torres Strait Islander Children from Their Families. The Inquiry found the conditions of the missions and government institutions accommodating children were poor, with insufficient resources to keep children adequately fed, clothed, sheltered and educated. It also found that most Indigenous parents had not freely relinquished their children to the care of the state. Evidence was taken from over 500 Indigenous people around Australia, and these first-person accounts were included in the Inquiry's report, *Bringing Them Home* (HREOC 1997). Remarkably, after its release in 1997, the Report was a best-seller. The interviews by the Stolen Generations were received within the Australian community with considerable empathy, and puzzlement that the history of child removal appeared to be little known (see Haebich 2011). Several spin-off collections of testimony were published, and an oral history collection of Stolen Generation memoirs was compiled by the National Library of Australia (Bird 1998; Mellor and Haebich 2002).

The *Bringing Them Home Report* galvanized some within the white community to participate in a popular cross-racial reconciliation movement that had been gaining public and political traction from the late 1980s. Alongside this expanding public recognition of the legacies of Indigenous child removal, was ongoing political agitation for Indigenous self-determination and land rights. In 1992 the High Court of Australia passed the Mabo judgment, which overturned the legal doctrine of *terra nullius* by finding that at the time of European settlement Indigenous peoples had ongoing cultural ties to their land. This was followed, in 1993, by the Native Title Act which recognized the right to land by Indigenous people who had maintained their connection to that land. The issue of Indigenous cultural rights assumed a new national prominence, and was increasingly in the press (see Langfield 2010). Conservative mining and pastoral interests sought to contain Aboriginal claims to land and sovereignty. There were numerous public attacks on the 'truth' of Stolen Generations narratives, the reliance of the *Bringing Them Home Report* on oral history rather than archival government evidence, the degree of trauma experienced by separated parents and children, and any suggestion that there be compensation for the victims (for a range of views see Birch 2004; Attwood 2008; Haebich 2011; Kennedy 2011).

In these 'history wars', controversies arose over historical accounts, and museological representations, of settler massacres of Aboriginal people on colonial frontiers (Macintyre and Clark 2003). The application of the definition of 'genocide' to government policies of Indigenous child removal and assimilation was equally unsettling for mainstream Australia (see Moses 2008). The *Bringing Them Home Report* itself condemned child removal as cultural genocide in line with the definitions of the United Nations Genocide Convention of 1948, which was ratified by Australia in 1949.

It was in this context that the Council for Aboriginal Reconciliation, established by the federal government in 1991, encouraged widespread acknowledgement among the Australian community of the historical experiences of Indigenous peoples. The Council's high-profile initiatives included the Sydney Harbour Bridge Walk for Reconciliation undertaken by 250,000 people in 2000. Within local communities, many Sorry Books were produced. These tangible objects enabled many non-Indigenous Australians to express their personal apologies to Indigenous people – including to the children who were removed from their communities. The Sorry Books were circulated around Australia through schools, libraries, churches and community groups, and continue to be exhibited online.[6]

Among the outcomes of the *Bringing Them Home Report* was the initiation and acknowledgement of the Stolen Generations in forms of public commemoration. Numerous historical exhibitions, memoirs, performances, visual and literary works have addressed the removal of Indigenous children over the past two decades. A recent survey of historic sites and memorials related to Aboriginal Sydney, for instance, includes the listing of several commemorative formats whereby Indigenous communities have publicly told their own stories of child removal. These range from the Indigenous Australians exhibition at the state-run Australian Museum, to a community Riverside Walk in the outer suburb of Parramatta which portrays local Aboriginal history and the colonial removal of children through visual and aural means (Hinkson *et al.* 2010).

There are also a number of specific plaques and monuments to the Stolen Generations, mostly erected after the issuing of the *Bringing Them Home Report*. Some are located on the extant buildings and sites of former institutions. At Eden Hills on the suburban fringe of Adelaide, two statues evocatively called 'The Fountain of Tears' and the 'Grieving Mother' commemorate the former Colebrook Home in a memorial garden setting. The accompanying plaques make, in Peter Read's words, 'a majestic innovation' (2007: 104) to the pain of Indigenous parents and children:

> Let everyone who comes to this place know they are on Aboriginal land. The site of what was once Colebrook Training Home where between 1943 and 1972, some 350 Aboriginal children lived, isolated from their families and the beloved home of their ancestors.

And, in the words of a former inmate of Colebrook Home, another plaque reads:

> And every morning as the sun came up the whole family would wail. They did that for 32 years until they saw me again. Who can imagine what a mother went through? But you have to learn to forgive.[7]

Another example of how language powerfully evokes the loss of childhood is the Stolen Generation Memorial in Darwin's Botanical Gardens. Dedicated in 2005, it is inscribed with the words of a poem 'Broken Hearts':

Hearts broken
Mothers left with empty arms
Hearts broken, minds with no claims.
Children without an identity taken from their country.
For such was the policy a strong destructive force.
For the government's command 'Deny them access to culture and land'.
Tears fell in empty arms as they sat in silence waiting and hoping in vain for the
    child they could not claim.
They were silent victims,
Aboriginal mothers of yesterday.
So children of the stolen generation remember them today.[8]

More abstract forms of memorialization were evident in an open competition for an unrealized Memorial to the Stolen Generations, co-organized by Museum Victoria and the Indigenous agency Link-Up in 2001. Many of the 140 entries and short-listed designs departed from 'traditional memory modes' to re-tell the history of the Stolen Generations, relying on 'multiple participants for their effectiveness' through techniques of audience interaction and response (Ware 2004: 127).

However, it has been the national Stolen Generations Memorial in Canberra that has been the most prominent and controversial. In May 2000 Prime Minister Howard announced that a 'reconciliation square' would be constructed in Canberra as a symbol of the government's commitment to the ongoing reconciliation process. Located in the central parliamentary zone or Parliamentary Triangle in the heart of Australia's national capital, what was to become Reconciliation Place was officially opened in July 2002. Its design involves a central mound, pathways connecting the site with Lake Burley Griffin and major cultural institutions, and a number of 'slivers' or sculptural artworks that represent aspects of Indigenous culture both prior and after British colonization, as well as acknowledging the role of key individuals and events.[9]

From its inception, there were plans for a memorial that recognized Indigenous children. However, the initial design for the children's 'sliver', overseen by a committee and lacking any consultation with those who had experienced child removal, was met with protest by Indigenous organizations. They were angered by what they saw as a 'whitewash' of history, claiming that the design was not explicit enough about the past and its legacies within Indigenous communities (*Sydney Morning Herald*, 27 May 2002; see Read 2007). As a result, a new design was developed that included direct mention of the term 'Stolen Generations', and incorporated oral history to convey the immediate and long-term grief and loss caused by child removal policies.

Today at Reconciliation Place, two large memorials to the theme of 'Separation' stand side-by-side. The first, 'Artwork 3', is constructed of slumped glass and stainless steel, and features a large image of an Aboriginal boy, and an empty coolamon, a traditional vessel for carrying an infant. There are other images of children playing and the words in several Aboriginal languages for 'baby', 'child' or 'children'. The second, 'Artwork 4', is made of oxided concrete and inspired by the red soil of central Australia. On the northern face, small holes have been made where people can leave messages about their own experiences of child removal, or flowers or other mementos. Sixteen fragments of Stolen Generations testimony are inscribed on the monument, and a movement sensor triggers a recording of the narrative song 'Took the Children Away' by Indigenous performer Archie Roach.

The fraught political responses to the acknowledgement and commemoration of the Stolen Generations in Australia are indicative of the tense relationship between understandings of cultural heritage and human rights in postcolonial nations. As recipients of the cross-generational transfer of traditional forms of knowledge, language and belief, children are central to the continuation of Indigenous culture and identity, and the ongoing relationship with traditional lands. Article 25 of the United Nations Declaration on the Rights of Indigenous Peoples (2008) makes this explicit by stating that Indigenous people have the 'right to maintain or strengthen their distinctive spiritual relationship with traditionally owned or occupied lands, territories, waters and coastal seas and other resources and to *uphold their responsibilities to future generations* in this regard' (my italics).[10] However, for those Indigenous children who were stolen from their homes and dislocated from their people, their connections with land and culture have been severed, if not irrevocably damaged. It is the recognition of these historical consequences that is most powerfully conveyed in Stolen Generations memorialization.

Forgotten Australians and child migrants

On 16 November 2009, Australian Prime Minister Kevin Rudd made a second formal apology to address the historical wrongs inflicted on children by the state. The Apology to the Forgotten Australians and Former Child Migrants was addressed to 500,000 children who had been placed in institutional and out-of-home care in Australia, as well as around 10,000 child migrants sent unaccompanied from Britain during the twentieth century. Rudd, speaking on behalf of the nation, told them:

> Sorry – that as children you were taken from your families and placed in institutions where so often you were abused.
>
> Sorry – for the physical suffering, the emotional starvation and the cold absence of love, of tenderness, of care.
>
> Sorry – for the tragedy, the absolute tragedy, of childhoods lost, – childhoods spent instead in austere and authoritarian places, where names were replaced by numbers, spontaneous play by regimented routine, the joy of learning by the repetitive drudgery of menial work.
>
> (Rudd 2009)

This was followed in February 2010 by British Prime Minister Gordon Brown's apology to child migrants sent to Australia, Canada and elsewhere in the Commonwealth. Describing the Child Migration Scheme as 'shameful' and a 'deportation of innocents', Brown acknowledged child migrants were cruelly lied to, their childhoods 'robbed' and their 'cries for help not always heeded' (Brown 2010).

The Australian apology followed two national inquiries into the Lost Innocents or child migrants in 2001, and the Forgotten Australians in 2004, as well as an inquiry by the British House of Commons Health Committee on *The Welfare of Former British Child Migrants* undertaken in 1998, and which had collected evidence in Australia. In all of these, there were parallels with the Stolen Generations national inquiry of 1995 in the importance placed on the collection of first-person testimony as a corrective to the archival historical record. Moreover, the publicity attached to the *Bringing Them Home Report*, and its calls for compensation for the victims, spurred non-Indigenous Australians who had been institutionalized to increase their political lobbying for greater recognition of their history within the public sphere. It also increased government support for potential family reunion, health and ageing issues.

The experiences of child migrants and those children placed in institutionalized care converged in many ways, but also had discrete historic dimensions. Child migration from Britain to Australia dated back to the transportation of juvenile convicts in the colonial period, and longer within the British Empire: destitute children were first sent to the American colony of Virginia as labourers in the early seventeenth century. From the middle of the nineteenth century, British religious and charitable organizations sent thousands of children to Canada, Australia, Southern Africa and New Zealand. Some were as young as 3 years, with an average age of around 7 years. Child migration provided Britain with a solution to the need to house the poor and destitute in London and other industrial cities, and met the untapped labour demands of the colonies.

By the twentieth century, the British government provided assistance to private organizations who sent children to the British Dominions, primarily to Canada and Australia. After the Second World War, the Canadian government no longer accepted unaccompanied child migrants. Australia continued to do so, admitting somewhere between 7 and 10,000 British children from 1947 until the scheme was discontinued in 1967. Child migrants to Canada were generally sent to board with families on farming properties, and their experiences were dependent on the attitude and opportunity provided by their hosts. In Australia, a distinctive feature of child migration from the nineteenth century was that children were placed in residential institutions, run by church organizations and charitable bodies such as Barnardo's homes, and the Fairbridge Society. Many of these were geographically isolated and children were subjected to harsh regimes of discipline and work (see Gill 1998; Hill 2007).

Around half a million Australian children – comprising the Forgotten Australians – were placed in out-of-home care throughout the twentieth century, and were primarily accommodated in government, charitable and religious orphanages or homes. These children included state wards who had been removed by the government from their families, those whose parents were dead or unable to look after them for a variety of reasons, child migrants and Indigenous children. The *Forgotten Australians Report* concluded that many children had experienced physical, sexual and emotional abuse while in institutions, were often neglected and generally received inadequate food, medical care, education and vocational training. In the longer term, many children bore the ongoing traumas of physical and psychological damage, often suffering from ongoing health and emotional issues in adulthood (ASCARC 2004; see Penglase 2005).

Public commemoration of the lives of Australian children who were separated from their families and institutionalized has been one of the outcomes of the national inquiries and the apology. An oral history project at the National Library is now gathering the life stories of Forgotten Australians and Child Migrants. Plaques and memorials to child migrants, including a small number from Malta who came to Australia under the British scheme, have been erected in the last decade outside the National Maritime Museum in Sydney, the Migration Museum in Adelaide and at Victoria Quay in Fremantle, Western Australia.

There are also now prominent memorials dedicated to the Forgotten Australians in most state capital cities.[11] The earliest of these, the Historic Abuse Network Memorial, also known as Child Abuse Memorial, was erected in Brisbane in 2004. It consists of a bronze statue of a barefooted boy carrying a suitcase, and is dedicated to 'all the children who suffered and those who did not survive abuse' in Queensland institutions. In 2009, the New South Wales government unveiled an inscribed stone plinth to the Forgotten Australians in the Sydney Botanical Gardens during a 'healing service' attended by over 700 people who grew up in institutions.

In 2010, three state memorials to the Forgotten Australians were dedicated. The South Australian Memorial consists of four huge stainless steel daisies in different stages of opening, symbolizing hope. The Western Australian memorial is modelled on a child's fortune telling game of folded paper, and includes lines of testimony by Forgotten Australians. The inscription reads: 'There is a strong thread that links the way a child is raised with the person they become in adulthood. This memorial stands as a reminder of that thread to all who create policies that affect children.' The Victorian Memorial is located on Melbourne's Southbank Promenade, and its artwork reflects the constellations in the sky at the historic time and date that the national apology was delivered in 2009. However, the absence of a national memorial, similar to the Stolen Generations Memorial at Reconciliation Place in Canberra, is seen by some Forgotten Australian activists as a slight that needs to be addressed.

Finally, two recent exhibitions have highlighted the historical experiences of institutionalized children. In late 2011, the National Museum of Australia opened a small temporary exhibition, 'Inside: Life in Children's Homes and Institutions' which incorporated objects and oral histories of the Forgotten Australians.[12] More ambitiously, the 'On Their Own: Britain's Child Migrants' travelling exhibition was developed as a collaboration between the Australian National Maritime Museum and National Museums Liverpool in the UK.[13] It opened in Australia in Sydney in late 2010, touring to other Australian cities.

The 'On Their Own' exhibition draws upon historical materials such as letters, toys, photographs and film to situate the history of child migration within the broader context of British imperialism. It uses cases studies and oral histories to emphasize the personal impacts of the larger migration schemes, and the diversity of children's experiences – including, for some, enhanced opportunities. Viewers to the exhibition can follow an individual life story throughout the display, as in this example:

> Frederick Snow (1909–1994)
>
> In 1913, aged four, you are forcibly removed from your home by the Church of England Waifs and Strays Society. In 1925, at 15, you are given the choice of emigrating to Canada or Australia. Staying in England is not an option. You choose Canada because your friend is going there. You will never see your family again.

The 'On Their Own' exhibition has attracted among its audience many former child migrants, and their children and grandchildren, as they strive to understand their individual histories within broader policy decisions and experiences. The moving personal responses in the exhibition's Visitors Book and Message Board indicate the importance of recognizing and commemorating this difficult past, not only for those who were the victims but also within the wider Australian community.

Conclusion

The commemoration of the historical experiences of children in Australia has become increasingly prominent since the late twentieth century; indeed, the last two decades have seen an unprecedented number of plaques, monuments and other built and creative responses to mark the cultural heritage of distinct groups of children. This increase has been, in part, due to a growing interest from the 1980s in local and national histories of settlement and colonization in Australia, stimulated through various funding programmes for historical and community projects, and national discussions stressing the importance of Australian history, including Indigenous history, within the Australian school curriculum.

More significantly, however, has been the wider historical and political context framing the rights of children and what this means in terms of cultural heritage. Internationally, children's rights have received increasing recognition and protection since the adoption by the United Nations of the Universal Declaration of Human Rights in 1948. The international human rights framework includes specific human rights treaties that relate to children, such as the Convention on the Rights of the Child (1989), as well as more wide-ranging instruments where children are understood to be included: the protection of the rights of vulnerable minorities or Indigenous peoples, or the prevention and punishment of genocide, or the UNESCO World Heritage Convention (1972). The consequences of this international recognition of children's rights for children's cultural heritage are twofold. First, when children's rights have been grossly abused during circumstances of war or genocide, or as the result of policies that failed to care for and protect their interests, the subsequent public memorialization of this abuse may – despite detailed historical documentation of its occurrence – remain highly politicized and contested within communities. Second, the greater the protection accorded to cultural heritage at local, national and global levels, the more likely it is that the cultural heritage of children and childhood, whether this be natural and built heritage sites of significance or symbolic objects or the intangible heritage of oral testimonies, will be preserved and valued.

Although the discussion here has been concerned with Australia, the issues associated with the commemoration of difficult childhoods have wider international applications, including within other postcolonial nations. Canada, for instance, shares with Australia a history of receiving child migrants from Britain, and enforcing government policies of Indigenous child removal. However, the response of the Canadian government to its past is somewhat different from that of Australia. While Canada declared 2010 to be the year of the British Home Child to commemorate the thousands of children who arrived between 1869 and 1948, there has been no state apology to former child migrants.

In 2008, however, Canadian Prime Minister Stephen Harper did issue a national apology for the suffering experienced by 150,000 Indigenous children forced into residential schools under a policy notoriously seeking 'to kill the Indian in the child'.[14] The compensation since offered to those affected has been accompanied by the establishment of the Truth and Reconciliation Commission, with the aim to provide Canadians with greater knowledge about the history of the residential schools as part of a national healing process (TRCC 2012: 1). Among the Truth and Reconciliation Commission's Recommendations in its interim report of February 2012 is the requirement that the lives of the Indigenous children who had suffered be publicly commemorated, including within school curriculum (TRCC 2012: 18–19). This recommendation illustrates how, as part of a wider trend towards confronting the often difficult and troubling histories of nationhood and colonization, the symbolic and practical recognition of children's past suffering can become a critical step towards cross-cultural reconciliation and a deeper social understanding of the cultural heritage and legacies of childhood.

Notes

1 Australia has two Indigenous peoples. The majority are Aboriginal peoples, whose traditional lands are on the Australian mainland and Tasmania. Torres Strait Islander peoples live in the small islands of the Torres Strait, in Australia's north and their cultures more closely resemble that of other Pacific island peoples.
2 Statistic from the Port Arthur Historic Sites website: http://www.portarthur.org.au/index.aspx?base=1923 (accessed 10 May 2012).
3 See the Monument Australia website for details of the Kalbar remembrance plaque: http://monumentaustralia.org.au/monument_display.php?id=91749&image=0; the Children's Memorial at the Moonta Cemetery: http://monumentaustralia.org.au/monument_display.php?id=51224&image=0; the White Cliffs Pioneer Children's Monument: http://monumentaustralia.org.au/monument_display.php?id=23768&image=0 (all accessed 1 May 2012).
4 http://monumentaustralia.org.au/monument_display.php?id=32646&image=0 (accessed 21 May 2012).

5 http://monumentaustralia.org.au/monument_display.php?id=30988&image=0 (accessed 21 May 2012).

6 AIATSIS, 'Sorry Books', Online exhibitions: http://www.aiatsis.gov.au/collections/exhibitions/sorrybooks/selections.html (accessed on 17 March 2010).

7 See the Monument Australia website for more information regarding the Colebrook Memorial 'Fountain of Tears': http://monumentaustralia.org.au/monument_display.php?id=50688&image=0 (accessed 12 March 2012).

8 http://monumentaustralia.org.au/monument_display.php?id=80187&image=0.

9 Australian Government. National Capital Authority. *Reconciliation Place*: http://www.nationalcapital.gov.au/index.php?view=article&catid=59%3Alinks-national-land-a-lake&id=82%3Areconciliation-place&tmpl=component&print=1&layout=default&page=&option=com_content&Itemid=300 (accessed 28 March 2012).

10 The UN Declaration on the Rights of Indigenous Peoples was initially opposed by Australia, Canada, the United States and New Zealand, all former British colonial nations with Indigenous minorities. All nations have subsequently ratified the Declaration: http://www.un.org/esa/socdev/unpfii/documents/DRIPS_en.pdf (accessed 12 May 2012).

11 Images and details of all the state monuments are to be found on the website of the Alliance for Forgotten Australians: http://www.forgottenaustralians.org.au/monuments.html (accessed 28 March 2012).

12 National Museum Australia. Inside: Life in Children's Homes and Institutions: http://www.nma.gov.au/exhibitions/inside_life_in_childrens_homes_and_institutions/home (accessed 8 April 2012).

13 See http://otoweb.cloudapp.net/ (accessed 2 May 2012).

14 Available online: http://www.pm.gc.ca/eng/media.asp?id=2149 (accessed 14 May 2012).

References

Attwood, B. (2008) 'In the age of testimony: The Stolen Generations Narrative, "Distance", and Public History', *Public Culture*, 20(1): 75–95.

ASCARC (Australian Senate Community Affairs Reference Committee) (2001) *Lost Innocents: Righting the Record on Child Migration*, Canberra, Australian Government Publisher.

ASCARC (2004) *Forgotten Australians: A Report on Australians Who Experienced Institutional or Out-of-Home Care as Children*, Canberra: Australian Senate Community Affairs References Committee. Available online: http://www.aph.gov.au/Senate/committee/clac_ctte/inst_care/report/report.pdf (accessed 13 May 2012).

Batten, B. (2004) 'Monuments, memorials and the presentation of Australia's Indigenous past', *Public History Review*, 11: 100–21.

Birch, T. (2004) '"The first white man born": contesting the "Stolen Generations" narrative in Australia', in J. Ryan and C. Wallace-Crabbe (eds) *Imagining Australia: Literature and Culture in the New World*, Cambridge, MA: Harvard University Committee on Australian Studies.

Bird, C. (1998) *The Stolen Children: Their Stories – including extracts from the Report of the National Inquiry into the separation of Aboriginal and Torres Strait Islander Children from their families*, Milsons Point: Random House.

Brown, G. (2010) 'Apology to Child Migrants', 24 February 2010, London: British Parliament, House of Commons. Hansard. Available online: http://www.parliament.uk/business/news/2010/02/prime-ministers-statement-child-migration/ (accessed 23 May 2012).

Colley, L. (2002) *Captives: Britain, Empire, and the World, 1600–1850*, London: Jonathan Cape.

Darian-Smith, K. (1996) '"Rescuing" Barbara Thompson and other white women: captivity narratives on Australian frontiers', in K. Darian-Smith, L. Gunner and S. Nuttall (eds) *Text,*

Theory, Space: Land, Literature and History in South Africa and Australia, London and New York: Routledge: 99–144.

Gill, A. (1998) *Orphans of the Empire: The Shocking Story of Child Migration to Australia*, Sydney: Random House.

Great Britain, House of Commons, Select Committee on Health (1998) *The Welfare of Former British Child Migrants*, London: House of Commons, British Parliament. Available online: http://www.publications.parliament.uk/pa/cm199798/cmselect/cmhealth/755/75502.htm (accessed 10 February 2012).

Haebich, A. (2000) *Broken Circles: Fragmenting Indigenous Families 1800–2000*, Fremantle: Fremantle Arts Centre Press.

Haebich, A. (2011) 'Forgetting Indigenous histories: cases from the history of Australia's Stolen Generations', *Journal of Social History*, Summer: 1033–46.

Hill, D. (2007) *The Forgotten Children: Fairbridge Farm School and its Betrayal of Australian Child Migrants*, Sydney: Random House.

Hinkson, M., Harris, A. and Australian Institute of Aboriginal and Torres Strait Islander Studies (2010) *Aboriginal Sydney: A Guide to Important Places of the Past and Present*, 2nd ed., Canberra: Aboriginal Studies Press.

Holden, R. (2000) *Orphans of History: The Forgotten Children of the First Fleet*, Melbourne: Text Publishing.

Human Rights and Equal Opportunity Commission (HREOC) (1997) *Bringing Them Home: Report of the National Inquiry into the Separation of Aboriginal and Torres Strait Islander Children from Families*, Sydney: Commonwealth of Australia. Available online: http://www.hreoc.gov.au/social_justice/bth_report/index.html (accessed on 13 May 2012).

Inglis, K.S. (2008) *Sacred Places: War Memorials in the Australian Landscape*, 3rd ed., Carlton, Victoria: Melbourne University Publishing.

Jalland, P. (2002) *Australian Ways of Death: A Social and Cultural History 1840–1918*, Oxford: Oxford University Press.

Kennedy, R. (2011) 'Australian trials of trauma: The Stolen Generations in human rights, law, and literature', *Comparative Literature Studies*, 48(3): 333–55.

Kociumbas, J. (1997) *Australian Childhood: A History*, St Leonard's, New South Wales: Allen & Unwin.

Langfield, M. (2010) '"Indigenous Peoples are not multicultural minorities": cultural diversity, heritage and Indigenous human rights in Australia', in M. Langfield, W. Logan and M. Nic Craith (eds) *Cultural Diversity, Heritage, and Human Rights: Intersections in Theory and Practice*, London: Routledge: 135–52.

MacFie, P. and Hargraves, N. (1999) 'The Empire's first Stolen Generation: the first intake at Point Puer, 1834–39', *Tasmanian Historical Studies*, 6: 129–54.

Macintyre, S. and Clarke, A. (2003) *The History Wars*, Melbourne: Melbourne University Press.

Mellor, D. and Haebich, A. (eds) (2002) *Many Voices: Reflections on Experiences of Indigenous Child Separation*, Canberra: National Library of Australia.

Moses, A.D. (ed.) (2008) *Empire, Colony, Genocide: Conquest, Occupation and Subaltern Resistance in World History*, New York and Oxford: Berghahn Books.

Penglase, J. (2005) *Orphans of the Living: Growing up in 'Care' in Twentieth-Century Australia*, Fremantle: Curtin University Books.

Pierce, P. (1999) *The Country of Lost Children: An Australian Anxiety*, Cambridge and Melbourne: Cambridge University Press.

Read, P. (2007) 'The truth which will set us all free: national reconciliation, oral history and the conspiracy of silence', *Oral History*, 35(1), Spring: 98–106.

Rudd, K. (2008) 'Apology to Australia's Indigenous Peoples', 13 February, Parliament House, House of Representatives, Canberra. Available online: http://www.aph.gov.au/Parliamentary_Business/Hansard/ (accessed 2 April 2012).

Rudd, K. (2009) 'Apology to the Forgotten Australians and Former Child Migrants', 16 November, Parliament House, House of Representatives, Canberra. Available online: http://www.aph.gov.au/Parliamentary_Business/Hansard/ (accessed 2 April 2012).

Swain, S., Sheedy, L. and O'Neill, C. (2012) 'Responding to the "Forgotten Australians": historians and the legacy of out-of-home "care"', *Journal of Australian Studies*, 36(1): 17–28.

Sydney Morning Herald (27 May 2002) 'Stolen generations fury at memorial "whitewash".'

Torney, K. (2005) *Babes in the Bush: The Making of an Australian Image*, Fremantle, WA: Curtin University Books.

TRCC (Truth and Reconciliation Commission of Canada) (2012) *Truth and Reconciliation Commission of Canada: Interim Report*, Winnipeg, Manitoba. Available online: http://www.cbc.ca/news/pdf/TRC_InterimReport_Feb2012.pdf (accessed 12 April 2012)

Ware, S.A. (2004) 'Contemporary anti-memorials and national identity in the Victorian landscape', *Journal of Australian Studies*, 28(81): 121–33.

Chapter 11

The last remnant of the Holocaust

The representation and reality of child survivors' lives

Beth B. Cohen

The public representation and memorialization of Holocaust children in museums and memorials shine a stark light on those most vulnerable victims who were subjected to horrific brutality on a path towards death. From the United States Holocaust Memorial Museum to Yad Vashem in Jerusalem, and from Israel to killing sites in Europe to sites around the world, including regional Holocaust museums in nearly every state in the United States, these institutions and memorials attempt to remember nearly 1.5 million children who were murdered. In doing so, they also frame our perception and collective memory of children's experiences during the Holocaust.

The creators of these memorial sites have approached the topic in a variety of ways, some symbolic and some literal, depending on the context and the viewer. A single child's shoe, which belonged to an anonymous young victim, for example, was one of the first examples of the memorialization of children at Yad Vashem, Israel's largest Holocaust memorial and the first major Holocaust museum created. Though the shoe was removed when this museum was redesigned in 2005, the idea to use a child's shoe as an artefact of memorialization prevailed in other places such as Chapman University's Samueli Holocaust Memorial Library (see Figure 11.1). Other major museums, such as the Auschwitz-Birkenau Museum and the United States Holocaust Memorial Museum exhibit piles of shoes from victims of all ages. But it is the single child's shoe, battered, empty and forever preserved, that has become a powerful cultural symbol for an entire generation of slaughtered children.

Following the 1987 publication of *I Never Saw Another Butterfly*, the collection of poems and art by children imprisoned in the Terezin ghetto (Volavkova 1994), butterflies have become a recurring motif to express lost childhoods, destroyed futures and stolen freedom. The entrance of Yad Layeled, the Children's Memorial at the Ghetto Fighters' House, Nahariya, Israel is one of many other memorials to children that uses this motif. With growing demands for making the history of the Holocaust accessible to increasingly younger audiences through various formats, including museum and memorial exhibitions, the theme of butterflies gives educators a vehicle to connect students to children during the Holocaust without featuring atrocity (Figure 11.2). The iconic photograph of the young boy from the Warsaw ghetto, hands up, being marched away by German soldiers is yet another visual image embedded in our collective memory of Holocaust children.

Figure 11.1 Child's shoe from Majdanek, Samueli Library, Chapman University.

Figure 11.2 Butterflies. Outdoor Memory Wall at the Heschel School, Northridge, California.

With the proliferation of Holocaust museums around the world from and during the 1980s, the interest in Holocaust exhibits deemed appropriate for a young audience also increased. One of the earliest in the United States was 'Remember the Children: Daniel's Story', which was originally developed and shown at the Capitol Children's Museum in Washington, DC and adapted for the United States Holocaust Memorial Museum where it became part of their permanent exhibits in 1993 (United States Holocaust Memorial Museum 2000). As the United States Holocaust Memorial Museum's website indicates, 'It presents the history of the Holocaust in ways that children can understand'.[1] The exhibit, recommended for children aged eight years and older, is told from the perspective of a composite character, Daniel. It follows the boy from his comfortable life in Germany through liberation, including time in the Lodz ghetto and Auschwitz-Birkenau. Another Holocaust exhibit aimed at younger audiences is the Children's Memorial at the Ghetto Fighter's House in Nahariyah, Israel, which highlights ghetto experiences, including an exhibit on Janusz Korczak and his orphanage in the Warsaw ghetto that features interactive sessions around Korczak's work with ghetto orphans. These are just a few examples that reflect how the public representation and commemoration of children who survived the Holocaust has largely been bracketed by the genocidal years and the concomitant range of experiences including imprisonment in ghettos, hiding with gentiles, death in concentration camps. Holocaust museums and memorials consistently display the cultural heritage of the Holocaust through images and artefacts associated with events from 1933–45, with little attention to what came after the destruction.

The loss of European Jewish children during the Holocaust was staggering. Only a small number of these children, estimated at around 150,000, were alive in 1945. It was these surviving children, however, rather than the lost generation who first entered the public eye immediately after the Second World War. From 1946, with stories of the first ship bringing children to the United States, images of child survivors began appearing in the media (for instance, *Herald-Tribune*, 1 October 1946). The representations of the child survivors differed markedly from the later accounts of Jewish children who had perished in the Holocaust. Indeed, the early accounts of surviving children rarely mentioned what they had experienced in Europe but focused on the promise of what lay ahead. Soon narratives of the young newcomers' successful new lives appeared, which belied the complex challenges facing child survivors' postwar experiences in the United States. Representations of child survivors that emphasized optimistic accounts and near seamless adjustments to life in America became popular narratives that were to define public perception of child survivors' postwar years, both at the time and in the historical record.

A November 1947 *Life Magazine* article entitled 'Orphans Clothed', for example, portrays Irene and Charles, two Jewish children who had survived the Holocaust (*Life Magazine* 17 Nov. 1947: 57–60). The photo essay was designed to highlight the efforts of Busy Buddies, the women's auxiliary of Rescue Children Inc., one organization committed to helping young Jewish victims of the war. The pictures capture the children's visit to New York and the shopping, eating, sightseeing and fundraising that was, according to the article, an unqualified success. The photographs of the children eagerly eyeing the plenty around them suggest the abundant possibilities of life in America but show little hint of their recent experiences: years in hiding and concentration camps, separation from and the death of their parents, their siblings, their friends and their childhoods.

These and other images of child survivors in the postwar media prompted me to ask about the paths of children like Irene and Charles: What brought them from Europe to America and the pages of *Life Magazine* and beyond? Which American Jewish organizations played a role in this process? How did the children's wartime years inform their postwar experience? My earlier research on adult survivors had revealed that children's experiences were vastly different from those of adults and worthy of a closer and more nuanced look (Cohen 2007). Drawing on oral histories, both those I conducted and those held in collections, and on archival documents (including case files of Jewish agencies that worked with child survivors), I scrutinized the lives of child survivors whose journeys took them to the United States. In the process, as this chapter explicates, I hope to expand our collective understanding of the difficult heritage of the Holocaust and the role that has been played by children in that narrative. This complex story begins in Europe as the Second World War ended, and world Jewry was confronted with the realization of both the enormity of the loss of the Holocaust and of challenges in reclaiming the children who had survived.

In 1946, American labour leader Emanual Patt visited Europe and wrote about what he discovered. 'Seven years ago there were one and a half million Jewish children in Europe. After the war the picture of horror unfolded before the eyes of the world', and 'only 150,000 children remained alive' (Patt 1947; Wulman 1948 estimates this figure at 180,000). This near total destruction of children prompted Patt to call this small group 'the greatest treasures of the Jewish people'. Other Jewish organizations, ranging from ultra-Orthodox to Zionist, were quick to affirm this claim. That the surviving remnant of Jewish children took on symbolic proportions in the eyes of the postwar Jewish world is no surprise. With 90 per cent of the children murdered, world Jewry saw the survival of the children as particularly miraculous. But adults also looked to the children to embody and perpetuate the cultural heritage that had so nearly been destroyed. It was these children who would rebuild Jewish religious institutions, raise families to carry on Jewish names and build a new Jewish state. They were emphatically tied to a future, salvaged from the ashes, for the Jewish people.

As news circulated about child survivors of the Holocaust, the Jewish world immediately sprang into action. All manner of responses to the children's situation reflected institutional and personal interest and agendas, as letters written to Jewish organizations from 1945 on illustrate. One inquiry to the Jewish Labor Committee asked:

> We are a young couple who live in Youngstown Ohio. We are writing to you in regards to adopting a baby. My husband and I have decided on a girl, if not a boy will be loved just as dearly . . . we want a baby, the younger the better. We would appreciate it if you would let us know immediately as to what steps we are to take in order to turn our cherished dream [into] a reality.[2]

May Bromberg, president of the Jewish Labor Committee's women's division wrote in response:

> Unfortunately it is at present not in our power to bring children from Europe to America for legal adoptions. We do, however, have a foster parent program whereby individuals or organizations maintain a child in Europe for a period of one or more years.[3]

These letters highlight several aspects of the postwar reality. One is the interest expressed by families in the adoption of Jewish children. However, given the restrictive quota system of the United States there were limited opportunities to do so. At first, Jewish organizations' efforts were generally channelled into fundraising. Popular campaigns included the Jewish Labor Committee and Rescue Children's Adopt-A-Child program whereby people pledged funds to support individual children in homes in Europe. But the numerous inquiries regarding adoption also reflect the deep lack of understanding of the demographics of these survivors. Couples expressed a preference for young children but there were few to be had. Leon Wulman explained in 1948 in the *American OSE Review* that this was due to 'the proportionately higher rate of children murdered as compared to adults, and by the very small number of five- to ten-year-old children, owing to the drop in births during the last years of the Hitler regime'. Of the surviving children, Wulman noted, 'nearly 20 per cent of them were orphans' (Wulman 1948: 4).

Despite the restrictive immigration quotas, adults usually had some autonomy over their eventual place of settlement after the Second World War. Individuals or agencies both in Europe and the United States, however, often determined children's destinations, especially those of orphans. Rescue Children, Inc. was one Orthodox American group whose name articulates its postwar mission. With the help of Rabbi Hertzog, Chief Rabbi of Palestine, representatives located Jewish children, largely in Poland, who had been hidden in monasteries, convents or with gentile families. The children were then placed in Rescue Children homes in France, Belgium, Sweden and Germany, which were financially supported by the organization's Adopt-a-Child campaign. Numerous stories appeared in the Jewish media, including one in the *Grossinger News* in September 1947 that reminded its readers that their donation to Rescue Children, Inc. served 'to guarantee at least one more happy, healthy, and secure member of a fast-dwindling European Jewish community'.[4]

Hebert Tenzer, chair of Barton's Candy and Rabbi William Novick were two Rescue Children, Inc. members who travelled from the United States to France after the war in order get a first-hand look at the homes they supported.[5] At one, Maison de Fublaines, they found Irene, the little girl featured in the previously mentioned *Life Magazine* article. What the article did not mention was that Irene was a twin and survivor of Auschwitz and Josef Mengele's horrific experiments on twin children and adults. Irene Gutman Hizme's postwar testimony of the period when she was brought to Fublaines as an eight-year-old and after illuminates the intersection of an organization, its ideology, and a young child survivor's life. She recalls:

I would listen as many of the children related their tales of what happened to them and how they got to be here, and many of them were hidden by Catholic or non-Jewish families. Some of them still had relatives and parents and were just waiting to be reunited. Some had hidden with the partisans in the woods . . . I was the only child with a number. In fact, I was the only child from a concentration camp. So, when I heard all the stories that were being told, I said, they're never going to believe where I was and I never spoke about it. I never spoke about it. Nobody asked me . . . But I was crying the whole time inside. I was so lonely. I just desperately wanted somebody just to hug me, just to hug me, and I didn't know how to go about getting somebody to do that.[6]

Irene developed a close relationship with one older girl, Miriam, who became in her words a 'surrogate mother'. Miriam was planning to go to Palestine and Irene wanted to go with her. Rescue Children, however, had other plans. One day she was informed that she was going to America. She remembers:

I didn't want to go to America. I wanted to go with Miriam. She was the only person who I felt close to and so this very nice gentleman said to me, well it will only be for a little bit and we'll bring you right back. I believed him. The next thing I knew was I was together with another little boy . . . from another orphanage. We were on this big airplane on the way to America . . . Then, it turned out there was a lot of commotion about us. Subsequently, I learned that we were chosen to raise money for the war orphans of Europe by this organization called Rescue Children, and I guess we were quite successful because they did raise quite a bit of money. We stayed at hotels and I saw white bread. I saw things that were totally magical to me . . . – I could not believe my eyes. They bought us things and they gave us things. It was unbelievable, unbelievable. But I have to be honest, I only wanted to go back and be with Miriam and go to Israel and all these extraneous things, the teddy bears, the dolls, the chocolate didn't mean anything to me . . . When it came time to ask well when am I going back, this very nice gentleman said to me, we're not sending you back.

Does she feel that she was exploited? Yes. Still, she hastened to add, they really didn't know any better (Hizme 2008). Rescue Children, Inc. was in contact with a family who had expressed interest in adopting Irene and shortly after her arrival in New York she was sent to spend the weekend in their home. This came to naught – the head of the family called Rabbi Novick and told him that Irene was too quiet for them, that no they did not wish to adopt her. Irene wasn't disappointed, however. She had started growing attached to the Rabbi and his wife and was hoping they would keep her. But shortly after the first failed attempt, the Rabbi told her she was going to yet another home. Irene recalls the drive there and being left with the family against her will. She remembers crying and running out of the house in the snow, chasing the car as the Rabbi and his wife drove off. Fortunately, the stay with her new family turned out differently and in Irene's words 'her [adopted] mother stood by her, adding "it was a blessing in disguise"'. Providentially, too, the *Life Magazine* article found its way to the family in Czechoslovakia where, unbeknown to Irene, her surviving twin Rene was living. Somehow the connection was made and a physician contacted Rescue Children. Irene's new family went to great lengths to bring Rene to America and adopt him, as well. At the age of 12, the twins were reunited.

Isaac Millman was one of the orphans who lived at another children's home in France. Isaac spoke in September 2008 about his experiences during the war and its aftermath that brought him to the Le Mans Children's Home. He recounted how, shortly before his mother's deportation in 1942, she paid a man to take Isaac to a neighbour in Paris who had agreed to hide him. Under the cover of darkness, the man followed his instructions and delivered Isaac to the woman's home. When presented with the boy, she changed her mind. The man abandoned eight-year-old Isaac on the street near his former apartment building. Unsure what to do, he stood waiting. A woman approached him and determined he was a Jew. Luckily, she was one as well. Moreover, she worked for the Oeuvre de Secours aux Enfants, Children's Aid Society (OSE), the French agency that went underground during the war and had contacts with families who were willing to hide Jewish children. She kept Isaac in her home until she found a family who agreed to take him. Isaac spent the remaining war years with two gentile families. He was 12 years old and an orphan when the war ended. His Jewish rescuer retrieved Isaac from the last gentile woman who had sheltered him and placed him in the Le Mans Home, run by a Jewish couple, Serge and Rachelle Pludermacher (Millman 2008). The home was organized through the Workmen's Circle in Paris and the director, Mr Pludermacher, was a son of Gershon Pludermacher, a Jewish educator who died in Vilna. As it turned out, Isaac's rescuer, who became his guardian, was an avowed Bundist and believed in the importance of Jewish culture and its heritage, which is why she brought the boy to Le Mans.

Isaac remembers being told that American Jews supported the home. There were approximately 35 boys and girls there. Not all were orphans. Some had surviving family members who periodically showed up to claim their offspring. 'Others, like me,' he remembered, 'didn't have anybody'. It was difficult 'seeing other children with family members leaving the home . . . there was some form of jealousy and also some anger'. In some ways Isaac's recollections of classes, holiday celebrations, games and skits echo the lively atmosphere Patt described. Mrs Pludermacher instructed the children in Jewish secular topics while Mr Pludermacher taught them about world literature and culture. In addition, the youngsters attended the local public school. Isaac noted that husband and wife were strong disciplinarians, especially Mr Pludermacher and this created tension at Le Mans. 'There were children who were six years old', he explained, 'so it was difficult to have those children behave as adults and I think in that respect they lacked that talent'. About his overall feelings and memories of that time, he remembered:

> when you're an orphan you start to withdraw within yourself. I think I learned to keep quiet. I learned to keep quiet, of course, during the war . . . I hid during the war and I also hid afterwards. And I was being careful not to be heard.

When kids don't belong to anybody and you don't really have anything . . . even though you're given something . . . it's not really yours. So, yes, there were some joyous moments: playing, having friends, going to the movies, forgetting things . . . there were those moments but at the same time thinking and waiting . . . for the parents.

After nearly three years in the home, his guardian told Isaac that an American family wanted to adopt him. Was he pleased with this turn of events? 'No', he stated emphatically. 'I wanted to stay in France or go to Israel. This was something that was forced upon me.' He could not follow his own wishes because his guardian felt otherwise. He reflected on this tension: 'you depend on someone's generosity . . . but still, a stranger who commands and is in charge of your life'. Isaac's first choice was Israel where an uncle lived. Here is where the Bundist and non-Zionist leanings of both the home and the woman who had saved him shaped the decision to place Isaac with a family in Brooklyn. Isaac arrived in New York in 1948. He was 15 years old and had never corresponded with or met his new family. Isaac's rocky beginning lasted several years during which time he struggled with depression. But his guardian's influence also had a deeply positive side. Isaac met her granddaughter after the war. They fell in love and in 1953 they were married in New York. Isaac became a well-known children's author. He writes often about children in the margins of society. While his relationship with his adoptive parents was not easy, the birth of his own two sons and the subsequent connection between the boys and their American grandparents, Isaac believes, is what transformed his own relationship with them for the better (Millman 2008).

Was the transition to life with a new family smoother for those who went to their American relatives? The files of the European Jewish Children's Aid (EJCA) shed some light on this question. The EJCA was part of the refugee organization, the United Service for New Americans (USNA), created in 1946 when the National Refugee Service and the National Council of Jewish Women's Service to the Foreign Born merged (Cohen 2007: 9). The EJCA itself was a postwar continuation of the German Jewish Children's Aid, which was established in 1936 to help German children. Dormant during the war, it resumed activity in 1946 as part of USNA after US President Truman issued a directive, which allowed 60,000 Displaced Persons (including 1,000 orphans) to enter the United States. The EJCA worked with the United States Committee for the Care of European Children, a federal agency that designated and approved the immigration of orphans from Europe to America. Once here, the US Committee monitored the EJCA's work placing children around the country with the help of local Jewish agencies (Cohen 2007: 95–6).

Mark and Phyllis B., for example, were twin 16-year-olds living in New York City. They were en route to Palestine when their American uncle persuaded them to come to New York where the twins had several relatives, none of whom they had met.[7] After arriving, however, the file indicated the teens had constant disagreements with their aunt and uncle. The twins were adamantly opposed to their relatives' wish to separate them. Both wanted to finish high school but their aunt and uncle would not provide them with funds, and the siblings felt they could not continue their studies without financial help. The tension was intolerable, and finally the aunt and uncle asked the twins to leave. When the social worker spoke to the aunt and uncle for clarification, she recorded that 'the uncle went into a veritable flood of complaints'. He insisted that the twins were a 'difficult and unruly lot'. The aunt also added, 'Those people that come across from the other side are not thankful, they are just trying to get the best of you'.[8]

The testimony of Leah W. and her sister offer another example of children who came to their relatives. Hidden in France in several homes and orphanages, the teenage girls arrived in 1946 at the New York home of their maternal aunt and uncle. It was not a warm welcome; they were forbidden to speak French to each other, use the refrigerator, or enter the living room. Leah commented she 'had gone from one hell to another' (LW 2002). In 1949 their aunt decided she no longer wanted to keep her nieces. The agency sent the girls to Texas, where they resided briefly in the Wolf Home, a Jewish orphanage, before finding work as maids in Jewish homes. While at the Wolf Home, Leah encountered three orphaned boys with similar stories. These examples are not atypical. Many child survivors were adolescents and their American relatives were not prepared or willing to tolerate what they viewed as wilful and ungrateful behaviour. In addition, orphans often recall their ongoing sense of loss for their parents that being in a nuclear family provoked. While social workers may have been somewhat sensitive to this dilemma, foster parents often were not. A 1949 study in the *Journal of Social Case Work* shows that of the 38 orphans who were sent to Detroit more than 50 per cent of foster placements were not successful (Zwerdling and Polansky 1949). The reason was simple: both parties expected too much from each other.

Fred M. was one orphan whose placement in foster care personalizes these statistics. Born in Germany, he and his brother, three years his senior, spent the war years together. At the ages of approximately three-and-a-half and seven years old, the boys were sent with the help of the Jewish community first to Belgium and then to France, where they spent the war years hiding in an orphanage in France (Fred M. 2010).[9] Fred recalls the period before 1943 as relatively pleasant, although he describes himself as an 'enfant terrible' often throwing tantrums and acting out, relying on his brother to protect him. After the Germans occupied Vichy, the situation for the boys became more dangerous. With the underground's help, they were smuggled over the Pyrenees and reached Barcelona and eventually Lisbon. Setting sail for the United States on Christmas Day, the two arrived in Philadelphia in January 1945 and soon reached their uncle in New York. Fred was nearly 10 years old. His uncle, a shipping clerk, had three children in a small apartment and was of limited means. He therefore enlisted the aid of the Jewish Child Care Association, which placed the boys in separate foster homes. Fred had never been separated from his brother. Being apart, he commented, was 'torture'. Never an easy child, he remembers that he began acting out. Between February and the summer, he lived in numerous places including a group home he described as 'almost a reformatory'. At the end of the summer, Fred went to live with a husband and wife, a garment worker and nurse. He subsequently learned that the couple had a deceased daughter and he was 'supposed to be a replacement'. This was not a successful match. Although Fred lived with them for four years, his foster family did not adopt him. Moreover, they were unsympathetic to his difficulties. Fred recalled that his foster mother beat him regularly and 'she threw me in the closet when I didn't behave'. In addition, he had to clean the toilets and the house. He stated, 'It wasn't a very nice environment for me but I didn't know what parents were like and I figured this is just part of what happens to you when you don't have your own family' (Fred M. 2010). Eventually Fred was removed and placed in another home where he bonded with another foster child.

For those who were reunited with parents, or in the majority of cases, one parent, the story was again not simple. Now 74 years old, Natalie G. credits her father Leon with saving her life (Gold 2009). Natalie explains that when she was an infant in the Warsaw ghetto her father heard rumours of deportations. Natalie's parents smuggled their baby out of the ghetto then left her in a box on the doorstep of an acquaintance, a well-off lawyer, with a cross around her neck and a note saying that she was a Polish orphan. They watched from a hiding spot while the man discovered the box and carried it to a nearby police station. Natalie's parents returned to the ghetto. Her father survived but her mother was deported to Treblinka extermination camp. According to Natalie's account, after the war Leon learned from the police that Catholic nuns had cared for Natalie. After months of fruitless searching, Leon finally found scrawny four-year-old Natalie whom he identified because of a distinguishing birthmark on her stomach. After paying the nuns a considerable sum, which Natalie believes her father received from the American Jewish Joint Distribution Committee, the nuns released the child to Leon and the pair returned to Poland.

They set up a general store that became a stopover for returning Jews searching for surviving relatives including a young woman, survivor of five Nazi camps, whose entire family had been murdered. She and Natalie's father married and soon had a baby. Natalie commented that her new stepbrother left her feeling like 'the fifth wheel'. She believed her stepmother resented Natalie since her presence was a constant reminder of Leon's first wife.

Furthermore, Natalie agonized, 'Am I really his [Leon's] daughter? For many, many years I wondered this,' she commented. But, she said, 'I felt reassured when I visited my mother's surviving sister in Israel' (Gold 2009). Why? Because her aunt burst into tears when Natalie buttoned her shirtsleeve in a particular way, claiming that Natalie's mother had made the very same gestures as a young girl. Natalie clung to this slim evidence, but the question gnawed at her and shadowed her adolescence and adulthood. In 1951, Natalie, her father, stepmother and half-brother were sponsored by relatives and migrated to Los Angeles. Natalie spoke of her complicated and ambivalent relationship with her family, her belief that her stepmother drove a wedge between father and daughter, and her ongoing feelings of displacement. Still, she maintains they were her parents; she looked after her stepmother when she became ill until her death and continued to care for her father until his recent death at the age of 101 years old (Gold 2009). Other child survivors speak similarly about fraught relationships with stepparents and half-siblings and the lingering and fundamental mystery of parents they never knew or those they did know but suspect were not really theirs.

While the postwar media showcased refugee youngsters who were models of good citizenship and academic achievement, the archives of social service agencies offer examples of those who struggled to adjust to a new life. The reports of Henry D. illustrate one instance of the tension between a young survivor, his family and an American Jewish communal agency. A few details of the war are recorded when Mr D., Henry's father, tells the social worker how all three members of the family miraculously survived in Poland: Mr D. in the underground, while peasants sheltered Henry and his mother. They were reunited after the war and arrived in Denver in 1949, sponsored by their American relatives. Their file recounts several years of interaction with the agency beginning in 1950 after 13-year-old Henry began running away, most recently to New York City. The parents resisted going for help but their social worker recorded:

> [W]hen he (Henry's father) found that I was sympathetic to the difficulty which he was having, he relaxed considerably and was able to express a great deal about the difficulty he has had in Europe and in adjusting in this country and was able to say that he was impatient with the boy because of his own nervousness and unhappiness.[10]

Henry's multiple disappearances appeared to be sparked by tension around his refusal to go to Hebrew school. The strict curfew Mr D. imposed, and pressure on Henry to attend synagogue, echoed other immigrant inter-generational conflicts. But added to this was the devastating impact of the family's wartime experiences, hinted at in Mr D.'s reference to his own unhappiness. The agency believed the family should work out their differences separately and referred Henry to Bellefaire, a home for troubled Jewish boys in Cleveland. Mr and Mrs D. are heartbroken but powerless to intervene. Once at Bellefaire, Henry revealed that he had younger siblings who had been murdered in a concentration camp. The authorities at Bellefaire wrote to the JFCS to verify Henry's statement. Yes, it is true Mrs D. admitted, but she thought Henry was too young to remember.[11] Henry struggled with the staff at Bellefaire for nearly three years before he returned to Denver in April 1953 at the age of 16. Towards the last entry in the file, the social worker notes, 'Neither he (Henry) nor his parents seem to indicate that they want any help from us in resolving their conflicts'.[12] That concluded the relationship between the D. family and the Jewish agency that believed it was doing its best to help Henry. Other instances of adolescents sent to institutions noted in both oral histories and archival records indicate that this may have been an infrequent but certainly not isolated occurrence.

Given the context of the times, is it unreasonable to expect agencies to have behaved differently? The response of the Jewish Family and Children Services in Boston argues most tellingly and persuasively for the possibility that the professionals, at least, could have done so and, in fact, some did. In 1946, the agency decided to experiment with placement strategies for refugee children who were beginning to arrive in the United States. One effort was a separate New American Unit at an already existing Jewish summer camp, Camp Kingswood, in Bridgton, Maine. Beatrice Carter, the JFCS director, delivered a paper to a national social work conference in which she stressed the therapeutic nature of this initiative. The New American Unit was intended to offer a supportive setting in which the youths 'are able to utilize many of the skills acquired in European experiences to master the rugged environment, which the new campsite offers' (Carter 1950). This unique programme began with seven children in 1946 and by 1949 had grown to include 19 orphans.

Leonard Serkess was a young social worker whose involvement with the New Americans began in 1947 at the summer camp. In 2002, he recalled the staff's response to the refugees' attitude toward food. 'One of the biggest problems we had was the kids would steal food and bring it back to the tents. And we tried to explain to them . . . that there would be plenty of food', he remembers. Still, 'they found it hard to believe. There was a perpetual hunger . . . [T]hey just never felt secure that there would be enough food for them' (Serkess 2002). The staff recognized the special significance of food for the young Displaced Persons and allowed for it. That understanding pervaded the camp. The youngsters spent some of their time learning English, but there were also opportunities for creative expression. This included an original play by the teens about their lives during the Holocaust. In a literary magazine of the campers' work, one boy wrote 'Why We Put the Play On', in which he describes the unusual production:

> One day Szmul came out with the idea of a play about concentration camp events, and, in talking, he had already acted out parts of the future play. At first we were stunned and resented to be overcome again by the flood of evil memories. Then we resolved to face once more the reality that had been. We only needed to pass out roles, never learned any parts and never twice said quite the same words during the life-like rehearsals. Within a week we were ready to perform in front of the entire camp. During that week we had little time for classes. We lived only partly in the present. Some of us sang the songs of the concentration camps; some, who were to act as Nazis, sang the songs which before we so often had heard and hated. Then the Friday night came. We were deeply steeped into the past and we played from our hearts . . . In some way we are freer now to live for the future.
>
> (Plow 1948)

In this environment the young people when encouraged spoke often and freely about their past, which was highly untypical for the times. And the JFCS's relationship with the newcomers did not end with the summer. The agency also created two small group homes for the adolescents once they returned to Boston. Responses such as these were rare among the Jewish communal organizations but they highlight that a more innovative and sensitive approach was possible, even given the context of the times.

The public has come to understand Holocaust children largely through representations and commemorative museum exhibits and memorials of their genocidal experiences from 1933–45. Long before these appeared, however, there were other glimpses. The first images of children in the aftermath of the Holocaust, in fact, were those who had survived. And their appearance in contemporary American media was depicted in terms of promise and optimism: young children surrounded by plenty, happy family reunions and successful adjustments (Figure 11.3). These accounts, however, contrasted sharply with the often brutal reality experienced by children who came to the United States. An examination of the historical records reveals that the ambivalent heritage of child survivors of the Holocaust is far from straightforward. This study shows that at times organizations designed to help the newcomers privileged their own agenda first and the individual child's expressed desires second. It also reveals the mismatched hopes of child survivors and relatives, which were exacerbated by a combination of factors such as the emotional turbulence of adolescence, the traumatic aftermath of Holocaust experiences and the high expectations of foster parents. Such delicate relations could be further complicated by interaction with the various American aid agencies that were often ill-prepared to assist either children or their biological and adoptive families. Furthermore, the reunion of children with one or both parents was often the beginning of a new and arduous family dynamic. The varied case studies here serve to highlight the range and complexity of the postwar experiences of children who were Holocaust survivors, which began in Europe but were to continue long after the children's arrival in the United States.

THEY'VE LEARNED TO LAUGH AGAIN: After years of homelessness, Mrs. Reuben Wasser and her 8-year old daughter, Anna, the first to occupy the shelter, show their joy in being able to begin a new life in America as they entertain their new friends.

Figure 11.3 'They've Learned to Laugh Again', *New Neighbors*, 1950.

The difficult accounts of the stories of child survivors *after* the Holocaust have been largely absent from heritage representations at museums and similar sites. Rather, the focus has been on the wartime years and the enormous loss of 1.5 million children with, at times, a depiction of the optimistic renewal of these youngsters in the war's immediate aftermath. Now, in the early twenty-first century, child survivors have become the last living link to the Holocaust. The time is ripe, urgently so, to create more nuanced understandings in both memorial sites and historical studies by capturing and representing the authentic and complex narratives and the individual and collective cultural heritage of those children who survived.

Notes

1 See http://www.ushmm.org/museum/exhibit/exhibit/.
2 Letter to May Bromberg, Director Women's Division, Jewish Labor Committee collection, I-377; Box 203, Taimiment Library, New York University.
3 Ibid.
4 Quick Notes in the *Grossinger News*, 13 September 1947, Rescue Children, Inc. Collection, Box 10, Yeshivah University Archives, New York, NY, Box 10.
5 Rescue Children, Inc. Collection, Box 1. Yeshiva University Archives.
6 RG-50.233*0056, United States Holocaust Memorial Museum.
7 RG 249, MKM 8.22–8.23, German Jewish Children's Aid (EJCA Case Files) YIVO Institute.
8 Ibid.
9 Most of Fred's pre-1942 memories are based on his brother's recollections. After that he stated that his own memories became very vivid.
10 JF and CS Denver, Case File, Box 13, File 424, Record Group 1–065, American Jewish Historical Society.
11 Ibid.
12 Ibid.

References

Archival records

Letter to May Bromberg, Director Women's Division. Jewish Labor Committee collection; I-377; Box 203, Taimiment Library, New York University.
JF and CS Denver, Case File, Box 13, File 424, Record Group 1–065, American Jewish Historical Society, New York and Boston.
Rescue Children, Inc. Collection. Boxes 1 & 10, Yeshiva University Archives, New York.
RG 249, MKM 8.22–8.23, German Jewish Children's Aid (EJCA Case Files), YIVO Institute for Jewish Research, New York.
*RG-50.233*0056*, United States Holocaust Memorial Museum, Washington DC.

Interviews

Irene G. Hizme, telephone conversation with the author, September 2008.
Isaac Millman, interview with the author, New York, September 2008.

LW, telephone interview with the author, 3 January 2002.
Fred M., telephone interview with the author, 30 July 2010.
Natalie Gold, interview with the author, Los Angeles, California, July 2009.
Leonard Serkess, interview with author, Newton, Massachusetts, 27 February 2002.

Published sources

'20 War Orphans among 945 on the Ernie Pyle', *Herald-Tribune*, 1 October 1946.
Carter, B. (1950) 'Social Case Work with the Adolescent in a Program of Social Case Work with Displaced Persons', paper presented at National Conference of Social Work, 1950, cited in Glantz, B. 'Factors in the Adjustment of New American Children in their First Year in the United States', unpublished thesis, Simmons College.
Cohen, B. (2007) *Case Closed: Holocaust Survivors in Postwar America*, New Brunswick: Rutgers University Press.
'Orphans Clothed', *Life Magazine*, 17 November 1947: 57–60.
Patt, E. (1947) *Jewish Children Return to Life*, New York: Jewish Labor Committee.
Plow, H. (1948) 'Why We Put the Play On', in J. Rosenberg (ed.) *Twice Born: Writings from the New American Unit, Camp Kingswood, Bridgton, ME*.
'Quick Notes', *Grossinger News*, 13 September 1947.
United States Holocaust Memorial Museum (2000) *Remember the Children, Daniel's Story: Teacher Guide*. Washington, DC: USHMM. Online. Available: http://www.ushmm.org/education/foreducators/resource/pdf/rtcteachguide.pdf.
Volavkova, H. (1994) *I Never Saw Another Butterfly*, New York: Schocken Books.
Wulman, L. (1948) 'European Jewish Children in the Post-war Period', paper presented at XIXth Yearly Conference of the Yiddish Scientific Institute, January 1948; printed in the *American OSE Review*, 5(1–2).
Zwerdling, E. and Polansky, G. (1949) 'Foster Home Placement of Refugee Children', *Journal of Social Case Work* 30 (July): 277–82.

Chapter 12

School buildings and the architectural heritage of childhood

Designing mid-twentieth-century schools in England

Elain Harwood

More so than any other public building, the school is a child's space, and marks the journey from childhood to maturity both educationally and in the development of communications with others. With the introduction of universal education acts from the late nineteenth century throughout the developed world, generations of children have commonly spent five days a week for up to thirteen years of their lives within the confines of educational environments. The experiences of schooling can be terrifying or highly enjoyable – or somewhere in-between – as is evident from the copious memoirs and oral histories of growing up that have been collected and published over the past century. Adults can often recall in very fine detail the physical environment of the classrooms, assembly halls, canteens and playgrounds of their schooldays, as well as many associated sensory experiences: the taste of school lunches, the smell of chalk or the sound of the school bell. School buildings and their grounds are one of the most omnipresent examples of the cultural heritage of children, and the architectural heritage of structures so closely associated with childhood. However, precisely because of their everyday presence schools are often a taken-for-granted feature of the built environment.

This chapter considers the design of mid-twentieth-century school buildings in England, as a means of exploring how the built heritage of children can be seen to reflect the social conditions, pedagogical theories and aesthetic preferences of its era (Harwood 2010). Indeed, during the postwar period, school architects in Britain adopted for the first time, and on a mass scale, a design approach that was 'child-centred' in provision of educational spaces that were highly conducive to children's learning and creativity. Such design innovations were introduced in response to the new ideologies and practices of teaching and curriculum reform that underpinned the expansion of the British educational system in the 1950s and 1960s. They were made possible through technological developments in building materials and construction methods. Alongside this analysis, the chapter examines why some buildings from this period have been recognized on the Heritage Register list for England as being of architectural and/or social significance, and the reasons why some examples fail to receive this protection.

Between 1945 and 1970, a total of 11,145 new schools were built in England and Wales during a boom in school building more intense than at any other time in British history, with the possible exception of the years following the Elementary Education Act of 1870. The figure represents about 48 per cent of the total number of schools that were in use by 1970 (Seaborne and Lowe 1977: 155–6). Two elements that drove this post-Second Word War provision of school buildings stand out as worthy of particular note: a changing pattern of education for younger children which emphasized a heightened awareness of children's needs, and a concern to reduce costs and construction times in the erection of school buildings by the use of prefabrication in construction methods.

Schools built in this period are generally modest buildings, with many designed anonymously by County Architect's departments who consulted closely with their respective education services. As a result, the buildings were not subjected to the public criticism of their architectural style directed against other educational structures, including many iconic buildings at British universities, designed in line with the Modern Movement and New Brutalism. Although many smaller, prefabricated schools were intended to have a life of around 40 years, they were consciously designed as 'permanent' structures by their architects (White 1965: 226) and remained in use into the 1980s and 1990s with few modifications or repairs. In 1992 and 1997, research undertaken by English Heritage, the government's statutory advisory body on the value and preservation of the historic environment, found a largely unaltered stock of school buildings dating from the postwar period. The buildings' modesty in design meant that an extensive selection process had to be employed to decide which specific schools would be designated as Listed Buildings of national heritage significance. Of the current English Heritage listing of 39 schools built in the postwar decades, more than half (22) were designated in March 1993, following the first of these thematic studies. Work on a second study, begun in 1997, was resumed in 2011 and is only now being completed. It will update our understanding of the heritage of schools which were constructed before 1990.

Since the 1990s, however, there have been rapid changes to the built fabric of postwar English schools. Initially buildings were remodelled, but subsequently many have been completely replaced. Primary schools serving a small geographical area, perhaps a single housing estate, have always been subject to the vagaries of demographics; today award-winning schools built by Hampshire County Council in the early 1980s, for instance, have been closed and sometimes demolished because their catchment area now has an elderly population. In 2004, a campaign for the provision of new secondary schools or academies, 'Building Schools for the Future', commenced in Britain and was soon followed by a capital works programme for primary schools. Some £8.2 billion were spent by the time the programme was curtailed in 2011, and in some English counties nearly every school building has been rebuilt or substantially remodelled.

While Victorian school buildings dating from the nineteenth century, and consequentially seen to have recognizable 'heritage' architecture, have generally been adapted to other institutional uses or sold as offices or housing, the fate of mid-twentieth-century school buildings has been radically different. Secondary schools of this period have, for the most part, simply been demolished, while primary schools may remain in use only after radical alterations.

There is a widespread belief among educational authorities today that schools built in the 1950s and 1960s offer poor facilities for modern teaching and learning practices, particularly in relation to secondary education. This has made it extremely difficult for English Heritage to designate further examples of mid-twentieth-century school buildings as having features of special architectural and/or social history heritage significance that require preservation from destruction or unsympathetic development. Since 2000 only ten schools from the period have been added to the National Heritage List. This includes just one state secondary school, Haggerston Girls' School in Hackney, built in 1964–7 by the noted émigré Hungarian architect Ernö Goldfinger; it consists of three linked blocks and is illustrative of his mature style. Following the ongoing research by English Heritage on schools erected from the late 1960s, two primary schools have been listed, both also in London. Other schools have been listed following individual requests from the public for 'spotlisting', usually because a school has been threatened by alteration or redevelopment.

Background: the postwar reconstruction of schools

Appreciation of the architectural and historical heritage values of postwar English schools requires some understanding of the social climate in which these buildings were constructed. England faced a severe shortage of schools at the end of the Second World War. Many had been damaged by bombing – in London only 50 of its 1,200 schools were undamaged and 290 were unusable – but other factors were equally important, including internal migration to new centres of employment and the suburbs. Such population movements had begun in the 1930s, continued during the war and accelerated with the development of suburban housing estates and 'new towns' after 1945.

The shortage of schools was also compounded by the raising of the school leaving age to 15 years, introduced by the government in 1947 after its postponement in September 1939 on the outbreak of war. The Education Act of 1944 (known as the Butler Act) drew on the spirit of optimism that dominated postwar planning in Britain more generally. The Act created a three-tier system of secondary education with grammar, technical grammar and 'modern' schools. The aim was to ensure greater opportunities in education across Britain for all children so that young people would be entering the workforce with improved qualifications. However, the rising birth rate in England after 1942 had not been anticipated. In late 1946, the government realized there was a 30 per cent growth in the number of four-year-old children ready to enter school, an increase in student numbers that was even more pronounced in areas settled by migrating Londoners, such as in Hertfordshire.

A shortage of school buildings was evident even before the Second World War, despite the fact that population figures in Britain were relatively static during the 1930s. In most areas, schools were made of brick and, with the exception of London, were usually only one storey high. Schools built in the late 1930s, as Britain recovered from the economic Depression, were often inspired by the work of Willem Dudok, the architect to the new town of Hilversum in the Netherlands. Only a handful of alternative designs existed, although in 1939 the Board of Education relaxed its strictures and admitted the erection of 'semi-permanent' structures with a 20-year life expectancy, for which it offered government loans. This reflected an existing shift towards lighter forms of construction. In West Sussex the County Architect, C.G. Stillman, adapted a light, cold-formed steel system developed locally for building caravans into a classroom unit that could be transported by lorry in sections. Designed to cope with families moving from the industrial north, lines of these classrooms were quickly and cheaply erected in Sidlesham, Rustington, North Lancing and Littlehampton.

More work on prefabrication was undertaken by Denis Clarke Hall for the Committee for the Industrial and Scientific Provision of Housing in Coventry. This was rapidly adapted for schools when in March 1943 the Board of Education invited both Hall and Stillman to join a committee chaired by Sir Robert Wood to consider standardized construction and to advise on the future planning and layout of school buildings. The Ministry of Education, as it became known in 1944, was better organized than most government departments for building after the Second World War, and had organized a team of architects during wartime to construct school canteens. This programme was followed by the Hutting Operation for Raising the School Leaving Age (HORSA), which aimed to physically accommodate adolescents now required stay on at school until they reached 15 years. By December 1948, 3,583 concrete-framed classrooms and 1,629 work rooms had been erected for this purpose, with local authorities paying an annual rent to the government (Dent 1954: 22–5).

In July 1945, Stillman became County Architect for Middlesex and introduced England's first extensive programme of prefabricated schools. The result, beginning at Hanwell, near Ealing, was an evolution of Stillman's work at West Sussex on a larger scale. Lines of single-storey, light steel classrooms were set off low corridors, usually with an assembly hall and kitchen of brick which could be added later. These schools provided accommodation for 10,000 children by 1950. A similar system was developed commercially by the Bristol Aeroplane Company, which had diversified into prefabricated housing after the war before discovering that the larger buildings required for schools were more financially profitable.

The Bristol Aeroplane Company commissioned standard classroom units, with corridors and lavatories, which could be arranged in lines (known as a bay system) similar to Stillman's work but using aluminium rather than steel. Bristol councillors were anxious that the prototype should be erected in their city and in 1948 offered a site in Lockleaze, a new estate with a high birth rate, for a junior school accommodating 480 pupils. By 1955 some 450 schools for 95 local government authorities had been built or extended using the 'Bristol' system, many in Scotland and Wales, and 600 units were exported to Australia (*The Builder* 1949: 338–9; *Architects' Journal* 1949: 405–10; Bristol Aeroplane Company 1955). The school building at Lockleaze had been predicated to last for 30 years, and in 1998 was much loved and in excellent condition. Yet in 2006 it was demolished, a fate that was typical for mid-century schools as funds for new buildings became briefly available in the 2000s.

Linear-planned schools, with their long lines or fingers of classrooms, were too expensive in materials to continue for long, especially in areas such as Middlesex where there were high land values. In Hertfordshire, the progressive Education Officer John Newsom predicted that the county's school population was set to increase by 6,000 a year, mainly through migration from London. Four of England's first 'new town' developments, and several London County Council overspill estates, were being rapidly constructed in the county. A new Deputy Architect, Stirrat Johnson-Marshall, set out in December 1945 to find a solution. Among a number of significant architects, he brought in David Medd, with whom he had worked in a wartime camouflage unit, and Mary Crowley crossed from the Hertfordshire Education Department (Saint 1987: 17–24, 60–4). These architects formed the nucleus of interest in the design of prefabricated schools in England throughout the 1950s and 1960s. In Hertfordshire they adapted a system developed for wartime hutting by Ernest Hinchliffe for a glazing firm, Hills and Company, using a steel frame with concrete cladding panels, into a three-dimensional kit of parts for building compact schools on any site. The kit allowed the whole school to be prefabricated, including the hall, which tended to become the centrepiece of the composition.

The Hertfordshire system was first used for primary schools at Cheshunt and Essendon in 1947. Ten more schools were completed in 1949, followed by 22 in 1950. Morgan's Walk School, opened in Hertford in 1949 to designs by Bruce Martin, exemplified their style. The hall was set centrally, with low spurs at each corner: one housed the school's administration, two the larger junior classrooms, and one contained a line of infants' classrooms with projecting bays for messy play that created a stepped profile. Strong colours were thought to stimulate the children, so a range of primary colours for the corridors with more muted shades for classrooms were developed. Johnson-Marshall took a personal interest in the development of child-sized lavatory equipment, beginning with the small, round 'Bean' sink. Care was also taken with the planting of vegetation around the schools.

Elsewhere, Newsom introduced a scheme to bring art into the schools, beginning with a sculpture 'Two Sisters' by Georg Ehrlich for the entrance hall at Essendon School. Some schools received murals, others appliqué curtains by Gerald Holtom, usually of figures. Yet despite their common ingredients, felicities in their overall form and interior finish gave some Hertfordshire schools a special finesse. The paramount example was Templewood School, built in Welwyn Garden City in 1949–50 under Cleeve Barr, where the careful detailing of all aspects of the building were aided by its woodland setting. Templewood School was completed just before cuts curtailed separate dining and entrance areas, which were enhanced by three murals by Pat Tew depicting Russian folk tales.

The Hertfordshire schools embodied the postwar aesthetic of simple spatial principles, without unnecessary embellishment, that extended to every component of school design in a quest to make a child-centred architecture. As the architects Richard Llewelyn Davies and John Weeks explained:

Figure 12.1 Templewood Primary School, Welwyn Garden City, built in 1950, an example of the prefabricated steel system developed by Hertford-shire County Council. The light frame and staggered plan allowed large amounts of light into the classrooms, considered important for children's eyesight. © James O. Davies, English Heritage.

> Most of the normal elements of architecture are missing. There is no recog-nisable formal element whatever, proportions seem almost accidental, spaces and places are divided in the most elementary manner . . . There is an utter and refreshing absence of conscious detailing.
>
> (Davies and Weeks 1952: 371)

Other local government authorities experimented with a mixture of traditional and prefabricated building. Prefabrication was further encouraged by Johnson-Marshall when in 1948 he and his assistants Maurice Lee, Mary Crowley and David Medd (Crowley and Medd marrying in 1949; Mary later used both her maiden and married names in her work) left Hertfordshire to form the nucleus of a Development Group at the Ministry of Education. Their first task was to disseminate the successful lessons of the Hertfordshire programme to other local government authorities through a series of reports or Building Bulletins. Their second was to push prefabrication to two or more storeys so that it could be used for large secondary schools. St Crispin's in Wokingham, designed in 1950–3 by the Medds with Michael Ventris, and Woodlands

Figure 12.2 Bousfield Primary School, Kensington. A one-off steel and aluminium-framed school by Chamberlin, Powell and Bon for the London County Council, 1952–6, with a dining room servery reduced to a child-sized scale. © James O. Davies, English Heritage.

School in Coventry both used Hills' system. These schools were followed in 1953–5 by a technical school at Durrington, near Worthing, built by Maurice Lee, Mary Medd and John Kitchin using a pre-cast, pre-stressed concrete frame patented as Intergrid and which failed in the 1990s. A simpler post-and-beam system, Laingspan, used at Arnold Grammar School, Nottinghamshire, was erected in 1957–9, continuing the experimentation with rapid construction techniques.

Nottinghamshire and CLASP

In all these post-Second World War school building schemes, the Ministry of Education worked with a friendly local government authority with the aim that this would encourage similar work by authorities on their own. One of Stirrat Johnson-Marshall's closest friends was Donald Gibson, City Architect for Coventry until 1955 and then County Architect for Nottinghamshire. Nottinghamshire had a rapidly growing population with a dearth of schools; indeed, in 1945 there were no state grammar schools in the populous industrial areas outside its major town, Mansfield (the city of Nottingham, where some schools were attended by children on academic scholarships, was outside the county's control). At Coventry, Gibson and his schools architects had experimented with a cold-rolled steel system supplied by John Brockhouse and Company, a technique developed by the Ministry of Education for The

Parks Secondary School at Belper, built in 1953–4. Brockhouse erected more schools with Essex County Council, and in 1955 Gibson suggested that Nottinghamshire work with the company.

Nottinghamshire is a county about the same size as Hertfordshire, and in the late 1940s had commenced a building programme to provide schools for expanding communities, many associated with the coalmining industry. By 1955, the annual school building programme was funded at £1 million. However, Gibson soon found that many schools were taking three years to complete, there was a severe shortage of bricklayers and plasterers, and large sums were being spent on deep foundations in abortive attempts to resist mining subsidence. By combining with other local government authorities with similar problems, the development costs of designing a new lightweight steel system that would allow rapid construction even on difficult sites, could be shared. As a result, the Consortium of Local Authorities Special Programme (CLASP) was formed.

In 1960 a CLASP primary school, with furniture also designed by the consortium's architects, was shown at the Milan Triennial Exhibition of Decorative Arts and Modern Architecture where it won the highest architectural award. This was seen as a triumph of exhibition design in its success in creating a completely child-sized environment, with the heights of chairs and tables, and fittings such as toilets and sinks, scaled to suit children. The consortium secured contracts in West Germany and Italy as a result, and Brockhouse marketed the system in France and elsewhere. After the limited success of earlier system-built housing and schools, CLASP's rapid take-up was remarkable, and other local authorities formed their own consortia, of which the largest was the Second Consortium of Local Authorities, SCOLA, founded by Shropshire and Cheshire councils in 1961.

Open planning

Already by the late 1950s, the Ministry of Education's Development Group (from 1965 renamed Department of Education and Science) was no longer primarily concerned with prefabrication in the construction of schools but rather with design innovations that encouraged new ways of teaching and learning. These were to prove influential, beginning in 1956–7 when a traditionally built junior school in Amersham made space for children to do more robust woodwork and science than was possible in a normal classroom. From 1959 schools were costed on the total area per pupil, which put a premium on circulation space, and this came to be incorporated into the ways that classrooms were configured for creative activities. The Ministry's *Handbook on Primary Education* encouraged an informal environment that could be used for groups either larger or smaller than the conventional class size.

The multi-functional classroom was traditional in small rural schools where children of different ages were taught together. Shortly after Amersham was completed, Mary and David Medd met Edith Moorhouse, Assistant Education Officer for primary education in Oxfordshire, who was anxious to bring Hertfordshire's progressive ideas on primary teaching and building to the county's one- or two-class schools.

The Medds designed a new school at Finmere in Oxfordshire, which educationalists considered 'set the course of primary school design for at least a generation' (Pearson 1972 quoted in Bennett *et al.* 1980: 21). Built in 1959 for just £10,000, Finmere was a simple brick shed with a broad timber roof. The Medds introduced folding screens around a central area that could be used separately for recreational purposes. The pitched roof gave this space sufficient height for gymnastic equipment. On either side the two classrooms had practical and study bays; that for the older children had a library, while the infants had a kitchen and a carpeted and wallpapered 'sitting room' for playing house or reading stories, called a 'kiva' from an old Pueblo term (*Architects' Journal* 1960: 1005–11.)

From being the poor relation of education, the village school, with the necessity for mixed-age and group teaching, become influential in shaping school design and pedagogical practice, particularly in the inner cities. The mixed-age groups encouraged children to learn from each other, while a 'home base' replaced the formal classroom. Such ideas had their origins in Maria Montessori's ideas of spontaneity and self-discovery, as evolved in England by Helen Parkhurst in the 1920s. This liberal curriculum was first adopted by education departments in Leicestershire, the West Riding, Bristol and Oxfordshire, and it was there that open planning was first given an architectural expression. In 1966 Oxfordshire built a school at Eynsham entirely based on vertically grouped classes of 4–9-year-olds.

In 1967, The Plowden Report, which reviewed primary schools in England, praised the current child-centred approach to education and brought the lessons of Finmere School to designated 'priority areas' in the inner cities. Another influential school design was that of Eveline Lowe School in Peckham, erected in 1964–6. Its architects, David Medd and John Kay, were struck by the range of activities in primary schools and explored the design implications of mixing age groups, group teaching and specialist classes. Each group of 40 children had a home base with tables for normal work and painting, a carpeted 'retreat' on a separate level for individual reading, writing and arithmetic, space for messy activities with a sink and work bench, and a covered verandah. Shelving, cupboards and screens divided this area as the teacher required. The older children had a library, while the younger ones had a stepped 'kiva'. Medd designed special furniture for nursery children, later marketed as the FORME range, which was to become an integral part of the material culture of British schools (*Architects' Journal* 1966; Medd 2004).

In Leicestershire there was a particularly close rapport between the architects, led by Tom Collins and then Thomas Locke, and the Director of Education, Stewart Mason. Appointed in 1947, Mason had previously worked with Henry Morris, the influential Director of Education for Cambridgeshire who pioneered the idea of village colleges to bring amenities to rural areas, and in 1937–8 commissioned Walter Gropius to build Impington Village College. Mason's experience convinced him of the value of community facilities in rural schools and of the importance of art and music in the school curriculum. These ideas were seen most dramatically in Leicestershire's secondary schools, but – as Mason emphasized – they began at the primary level in a programme that pushed architecture as an expression of educational reform.

Mason expanded places for quiet study, and libraries were symbolically placed in the heart of the building. Glenfield Frith School, built in 1966, was one of the first planned for team teaching, with semi-open-plan classrooms grouped in fours. Other Leicestershire plans were strongly geometric, such as Oadby Laude (1964), designed as a tessellation of hexagons (*The Builder* 1964). Most logical of all was Middlefield (now Richmond) Primary School in Hinckley, a near-circular building. Its wedge-shaped classrooms fanned out from a central library, with covered practical spaces around the exterior and a hall to one side. A small room for story-telling sat above the library, but otherwise it was single-storeyed and dependent on top-lighting (Mason 1970: 1–29; *Architecture East Midlands* 1969; *Building* 1970). Mason also commissioned private architects, including Ahrends, Burton and Koralek (ABK) who built Eastfield School, Thurmaston in 1966–8, with classrooms in pairs around a central courtyard and a library immediately beside the entrance door. Changes in level, under a stepped glazed roof that became an ABK trademark, and carefully placed cloakrooms and activity areas, gave clear separation to the open-plan building (*Architects' Journal* 1969; *Architecture d'Aujourd'hui* 1971). These Leicestershire schools marked a move away from prefabrication while remaining child-sized, with a design emphasis on encouraging creativity through their free planning, resource centres and inclusion of artistic works, most notably sculpture.

Secondary schools

So far this chapter has concentrated on primary schools as the place where postwar ideas on child-centred architecture, prefabrication and open planning came to the fore. The same ideas also appeared in secondary schools, but there the design brief was more complex and uncertain. This was particularly so in the third tier 'secondary modern' schools created under the 1944 Education Act where children were supposed to leave at the age of 15 without taking formal examinations, and for which there was for many years no established curriculum.

We have seen how the Ministry of Education explored prefabrication as a quick and economical means of building to three storeys in large schools. Multi-storey design and careful planning became still more important where, as in Coventry, very large schools were built as part of a programme of comprehensive education that rejected the Ministry's three-tier system and made no attempt to determine a child's future by selection at the age of 11. To have viable sixth form or final year classes, such schools had to have around 2,000 pupils. In these cases, an important element of their design was in the attempts to break down this large size into units that could be readily managed by teachers and gave the child a sense of a more contained identity. Coventry schools adopted a house system whereby pupils were given a house, with its own assembly room and kitchen, where the children started each day and ate their lunches.

Other cities, notably Birmingham and parts of London, preferred a year system whereby the school was divided into junior, middle and senior areas. Nottinghamshire built annexes for 11 to 13-year-olds that provided a friendly base for the transition between primary and secondary education, and were also an economic means of extending an existing school for use as a comprehensive one. These annexes, notably Lakeside at Chilwell Comprehensive School, also adopted elements of open planning, with study areas gathered round a central resource area (*Architects' Journal* 1980). Elsewhere, particularly in Leicestershire, arts and crafts facilities and some science laboratories were generally open plan to allow greater flexibility of use, particularly where they doubled as adult education centres in the evenings. The most notable example is Countesthorpe College, its name reflecting its debt to William Morris's original concept, built in 1969–71 on a pin-wheel plan around a resource centre and library.

The size and design muscularity of secondary schools was evident in the Brutalist aesthetic used in many prominent examples. Hunstanton Secondary School was built following a competition won in 1950 by Alison and Peter Smithson. Its plan resembles the symmetrical layouts of inter-war grammar schools like the King George V School, Southport, with a central hall set between two courtyards. However, it was among the first school design to set its classrooms in pairs on the upper floors, accessed not by corridors but by spindly staircases from ground-floor corridors that ran round most of the school. In contrast to the Smithsons' later emphasis in their writings on the personalization of space by its users, the school was photographed while it was empty, emphasizing the exposed steel ceilings and pipework, and its Braithwaite water tank (*Architectural Review* 1954; Smithson and Smithson 1979).

More schools, however, adopted the heavy concrete aesthetic first used by architectural firm Lyons Israel Ellis when in 1954 they won a competition for Trescobeas School, near Falmouth in Cornwall, built in 1956–7. The exposed concrete frame was a response to the stark Cornish landscape, and incorporated local china clay, sand and crushed granite, and was left rough with the imprint of the formwork still visible. The *Architects' Journal* asserted that 'the structure [of the school] . . . is virile, compatible with the bold topography' (*Architects' Journal* 1959; Forsyth and Gray 1988: 62). Lyons Israel Ellis, whose list of famous assistants included James Stirling and James Gowan, went on to design many schools in the Midlands and north of England. This marked a distinct change from the lightweight prefabrication, moving to a robust aesthetic, with a tough-looking environment built to withstand the wear-and-tear of school life that also appeared progressive and modern in these traditional communities.

In England, the architectural designs for secondary schools were never as successful as they were for primary schools. The briefs to architects were never as clear, partly because the educational trend to move from a system of secondary modern schools towards comprehensive schools made planning difficult. In addition, adolescents proved more unruly clients than small children and this meant buildings had to take a lot of hard knocks. However, an educational system was established in England in the years 1945–75 that gave every child access to a secondary education. If the buildings of secondary schools were often repetitive in design, nonetheless these spaces – and the activities that occurred within them – provided a valuable stepping stone to adult life, with science laboratories, libraries and specialized rooms for handicrafts, music and art seen to encourage lifelong skills and hobbies.

Conservation and re-use of postwar schools

The changes to the British education system brought about by the Education Act of 1944 resulted in a 'unique contact between the state and the citizen' (Saint 1987: 3) and offered an optimistic view of the future capacity and opportunities for all British children. This was realized through the construction of new primary and secondary schools which in design emphasized the educational and social needs of children. However, relatively few postwar English schools have been listed, and these are mainly examples of the better-known prefabricated systems across Hertfordshire, or works by major architects such as Denys Lasdun, Alison and Peter Smithson or Ernö Goldfinger. The Smithsons' school at Hunstanton is one of the few examples of a postwar school that is venerated as a work of art by those who work and study there, and where heritage listing and regular visits by architects and academics have aided its appreciation. The building's glass cladding panels were renewed around the time of its listing in 1993, with advice from English Heritage, and a careful programme of maintenance by committed on-site caretakers and experienced local contractors has since kept the building in good order. Lyons Israel Ellis's concrete-framed and rugged-looking schools at Oldbury Wells outside Bridgnorth and at Up Holland, Lancashire, also remain in good order and are admired by their users. In late 2012, Up Holland School was threatened by insensitive window replacement.

Figure 12.3 Oldbury Wells School, former Girls' School, 1959–60 by Lyons Israel Ellis. An example of a Brutalist aesthetic for older children. © James O. Davies, English Heritage.

One listed postwar school that has been very successfully refurbished for continued school use is the Lansbury Lawrence (formerly Susan Lawrence) Primary School built in 1949–50 by Yorke, Rosenberg and Mardall as part of the Festival of Britain's showcase 'Live Architecture' exhibition on the Lansbury Estate in East London. The long disused foyer, which featured golden-yellow tiles by the artist Peggy Angus, was reinstated as the school's main entrance and the school's circulation pattern returned to that originally planned by the architects.

Elsewhere, listing has ensured the retention and restoration of a key architectural feature, usually an assembly hall, while other parts of a school have been demolished. This is true of Two Saints School by Chamberlin, Powell and Bon and built in 1958–60 for 1,260 girls in south London. Although the school was listed as a building of special architectural interest in 1993, it was demolished in 2007 when the site was reorganized as the Globe Academy with hedge fund charity Absolute Return for Kids providing financial support. A new school was built to designs by Amanda Levete Architects, with only the original spectacular five-sided assembly hall, covered with a hyperbolic paraboloid roof and known as the Pentagon, preserved and restored. Another listed building, Rhodesway Secondary School in Bradford, designed by Scherrer and Hicks from 1957–9, is set to be demolished in 2013 when a new school alongside is completed. These schools are being demolished as they are thought to be too expensive to maintain and inappropriate for the modern needs of children's education. The belief of educational and government experts is that children and teachers respond better to a new school building, with a new name and management structure, and examination results have generally improved in these new environments. The idea of a cultural history of education and its impact on children and the broader experiences of childhood as conveyed through school buildings generally has no value to most educationalists.

A few schools no longer required for teaching older children have been adapted as nurseries for pre-school children. In Ilford, Greater London, the listed moderne-style domestic science block added to Uphall Elementary School by the Ilford Borough Council Architect's Department in 1937 was adapted as a nursery in 1999. The architects for the refurbishment, Tooley and Foster, dropped ceilings and added porthole windows at a child's eye level, their style in keeping with the ocean-liner imagery of the original.

Very few postwar schools have found other uses and most that have closed have been destroyed. A rare exception is at Harlow, where Latton Bush Comprehensive School closed in the 1980s due to falling enrolments. The local council sought a continued community use for the site, which was eventually adapted to workshops and business centre, with conference facilities and a local radio station. This building is still very recognizably a school, though playground areas have been adapted for parking and additional entrances made. At Lilian Baylis School in Lambeth, London, some 14 projects occupy the former school buildings of 1964, including sports, music and drama groups for young people. In 2012 it is proposed to convert the building into housing, and its London location and heavy aesthetic (with smaller areas of glazing than earlier schools) may mean this can be realized effectively.

Where attempts have been made to adapt other listed twentieth-century schools to residential use as an alternative to demolition, this has proved difficult. This is particularly true of lightweight, prefabricated and highly glazed school buildings, where the partition of larger spaces leads to a reduction in transparency and difficulties with insulation. A rare attempt at such building preservation is being made at Oaklands College, a college of further education built in 1960 by Hertfordshire County Council using a late variant of its prefabricated schools system. Here, the five listed buildings that make up the core of the original development are being converted to residential use by PRP and John Pardey Architects. However, there has been community concern at the loss of the Oaklands College buildings to the public realm, although not specifically their cultural and social value to children and young people. Permission to develop additional residential blocks in the landscaped grounds was granted after a public enquiry also permitted the loss of public use of the old assembly hall, which has been subdivided.

The future for the heritage conservation of mid-twentieth-century schools in England is thus a bleak one. Although recent government cuts have halted redevelopment of school buildings and sites for the moment, this has also meant that other investment in the preservation of schools is limited. With the exception of those school buildings that have the highest architectural profiles, such as in Hertfordshire and at Hunstanton, redevelopment remains a serious possibility with little safeguard in the form of the heritage listing process. Most mid-century schools are taken for granted as commonplace structures, and of no cultural value. Indeed, where the loss or conversion of these schools to other uses has been challenged, this has been on the grounds that a public asset is being removed from the community – rather than the resonance of the school with the past and present experiences of children and as a site of childhood.

The postwar period in Britain was uniquely optimistic in its expansion of educational facilities and a progressive curriculum for all children, so that they could fulfil their future capacities as engaged and productive citizens. This expansion of schools was realized by the introduction of responsive, lightweight buildings that could be quickly erected to cater for burgeoning numbers of children entering the school system. These buildings were notable for a new child-centred approach to school design, including specially scaled fittings, fixtures and furniture and spatial responses to pedagogical ideals and practices. Such schools, as the setting for modern twentieth-century ideas of education, have played enormously profound roles in the lives of the millions of students who were educated within their walls.

However, politicians, teachers and educational theorists, many of whom were educated in such buildings, rarely favour such buildings as suitable for teaching in the twenty-first century, largely because government capital works funding has been more generous than maintenance budgets. Mid-twentieth-century schools now appear old fashioned to younger teachers and their pupils, and the belief that a new school will give a child a better start in life predominates over the desire to protect the built heritage of schools to recognize the cultural and social significance of the school environment in the everyday past and present experiences of children. In this current context, postwar school buildings have therefore to be exceptional, in terms of their architectural form and educational rationale and pedagogical practice, in order to be protected from redevelopment. Yet, as is argued in this chapter, in the most progressive English educational authorities of the postwar period, including London, Hertfordshire and Leicestershire, a fervent desire for the cultural development of the child found a striking architectural expression well worthy of preservation.

References

Architects' Journal

Vol. 110, no. 2853, 13 October 1949, 405–10.
Vol. 129, no. 3339, 26 February 1959, 342.
Vol. 141, no. 7, 17 February 1966, 397–410.
Vol. 150, no. 18, 29 October 1969, 1081–92.
Vol. 172, no. 47, 19 November 1980, 985–95.

Architecture d'Aujourd'hui

No. 154, February–March 1971, 46–7.

Architectural Review

Vol. 116, no. 693, September 1954, 148–62.

Architecture East Midlands

No. 23, March–April 1969, 36–8.

Building

Vol. 219, no. 6635, 17 July 1970, 66–8.

The Builder

Vol. 176, no. 5535, 18 March 1949, 338–9
Vol. 207, no. 6326, 14 August 1964, 325.

Bennett, N., Andreae, J., Hergarty, P. and Wade, B. (1980) *Open Plan Schools*. Windsor: NFER/ Schools Council.
Bristol Aeroplane Company (1955) *Bristol Review*, Spring.
Davies, R.L. and Weeks, J. (1952) 'The Hertfordshire Achievement', *Architectural Review*, 111: 666.
Dent, H.C. (1954) *Growth in English Education 1946–1952*. London: Routledge and Kegan Paul.

Forsyth, A. and Gray, D. (eds) (1988) *Lyons Israel Ellis Gray*, London: Architectural Association.

Harwood, E. (2010) *England's Schools: History, Architecture and Adaptation*. London: English Heritage.

Mason, S.C. (1970) *In Our Experience*. London: Longman.

Medd, D. (2004) Conversation with David Medd, 17 October, Medd Archive, Institute of Education, University of London.

Pearson, E. (1972) *Trends in School Design*. London: Macmillan.

Saint, A. (1987) *Towards a Social Architecture*. London: Yale.

Seaborne, M. and Lowe, R. (1977) *The English School, its Architecture and Organization, vol. II, 1870–1970*. London: Routledge and Kegan Paul.

Smithson, A. and Smithson, P. (1979) *Signs of Occupancy*, Pidgeon Audio Visual, PAV 793.

'Two Village Schools', *Architects' Journal*, vol. 131, no. 3402, 30 June 1960: 1005–11.

White, R.B. (1965) *Prefabrication*. London: HMSO.

Part III

Objects and collections

The material culture of children

Putting away the things of childhood

Museum representations of children's cultural heritage

Carla Pascoe

When I was a child, I spoke and thought and reasoned as a child. But when I grew up, I put away childish things.

(1 Corinthians 13:11, New Living Translation 2007)

Introduction

In popular imagery, childhood is constructed as an age of joyful innocence and care-free play. It is hardly surprising then, that when we think of children's objects, what springs to mind are toys: those archetypal symbols of childhood. Museum collections and exhibitions relating to the history of children have tended to reflect and perpetuate this trend. And, as the passage from the Corinthians cited above suggests, by focusing on the playful material culture of children, museum representations of childhood have often implied that children's heritage is less serious and less important than that of adults. We 'put away' the things of childhood when we are ready to take on the roles and responsibilities of adults, as full members of society. In 'putting away' toys for preservation as representative of children's lives, museums can in many ways exacerbate this longstanding cultural trend to not take children seriously on their own terms.

Yet a complex issue clouds the role of museums in representing children's heritage. As Sharon Brookshaw explains 'the objects we most commonly associate with this group were not made or controlled directly by its members, but rather are imposed on it by another group: adults' (2009: 367). Identifying the material culture of children is therefore a vexed process as the objects used by children are often created or gifted by adults. Can we then argue that the teddy bear, cot and sandals used by children adequately represent children's cultural heritage? Or do these artefacts tell us much more about adult perceptions and expectations of children than those of children themselves?

This chapter considers the ways in which the history of children has been represented in museums, within a global context in which displays on the material culture of childhood have been steadily proliferating since about 1990 (Van Slyck 2004: 69). Drawing upon examples taken from the United Kingdom, the United States, Canada and New Zealand, we will explore several key issues: the trend towards nostalgic, sentimental representations of childhood; the difference between museums of childhood and museums of children; and the blurring of the distinction between museums of childhood and children's museums. Such issues are not purely of academic interest, I argue: they have significant ramifications. Our understandings of children in the present – as innocent, carefree, vulnerable and dependent – have profound implications for how we view children in the past, what we choose to preserve as representative of children's heritage and what, therefore, is kept for the future as explanatory and commemorative tools for interpreting children's history.

Sentimentalizing childhood

In the early twenty-first century, the concept that children are dependent, frail and innocent appears 'natural' or biologically determined. However, commencing with Philippe Ariès' *Centuries of Childhood* (English translation published 1962) several decades of historiography have revealed that concepts of childhood are historically specific and change with socio-cultural contexts (Ariès 1962; Cunningham 2005). Indeed in the pre-modern era Western children were seen as miniature adults capable of adult responsibilities, a concept strange to current sensibilities. But over time the view emerged that children possess an innate vulnerability, requiring the protection and guidance of adults. Some historians date this shift to between the eighteenth and nineteenth centuries (Calvert 1992; Reinier 1996; Wishy 1968) whilst others identify the transition as occurring much later (Stearns 2009). If the exact timing of this conceptual change is disputed, it has certainly been underscored by reductions in infant mortality and birth rates. As Western children increasingly moved from the domains of work to school, they became costs rather than assets to the family economy. While children were once valued for the contribution of their labour, they have become seen as 'economically "worthless" but emotionally "priceless"' (Zelizer 1985; Sánchez-Eppler 2005).

This view of children as both precious and carefree produces nostalgia about the supposedly halcyon days of youth that precede the adoption of adult responsibilities and anxieties. Much is at stake in historicizing childhood, whether at the level of the individual or society. Historian of childhood Paula Fass argues that adults are often deeply emotive about their recollections of growing up for important cultural reasons. Since the Enlightenment, the notion that the self is made up of the sum of one's memories – especially those of childhood – means that childhood has come to be understood as the foundation of identity. The nineteenth and twentieth centuries emphasized this trend, with childhood memories featuring as a major theme in Victorian literature and in the emergence of psycho-analysis and psychology (Fass 2010). Childhood memory is now understood as the bedrock of adult personality. Within this context, adult understandings of childhood have profound implications.

This strong cultural and individual impulse to sentimentalize childhood has often led, unsurprisingly, to nostalgic representations of children's material culture within museum displays. The origins of many museums of childhood in the antiquarian impulses of private collectors may partially explain why their collections so often portray sentimentalized understandings of childhood, as opposed to objects which raise more difficult and troubling questions about childhood experiences. For example, both the Strong Museum of Play and the Edinburgh Museum of Childhood developed from the passions of private collectors. Material culture scholar Thomas Schlereth hypothesizes that nostalgic impulses and the human delight in miniaturization motivate private collectors of childhood artefacts (Schlereth 1990: 90–1).

The Strong Museum grew from the private collection of Margaret Woodbury Strong, born in Rochester in 1897. After the death of her husband in the mid-1950s, Strong became devoted to collecting, amassing more than 27,000 objects by the late 1960s. Whilst her collections spanned a range of themes, the majority related to play, particularly her collections of dolls and toys. When Strong died in 1969, she left her collections and financial resources for the continuation of the museum. In 1982 the Margaret Woodbury Strong Museum opened to the public. The museum claims to have the world's largest and most historically significant collection of dolls and toys, with play-related material culture the focus of its collections rather than a wider scope which takes in objects relating to other aspects of children's lives.

The Edinburgh Museum of Childhood markets itself as the first museum in the world to have specialized in the history of childhood. Collector Patrick Murray (1908–81) founded the Edinburgh Museum in 1955, purportedly in response to discovering that two dolls once owned by Queen Victoria were being transferred to London as there was no place to display them in Scotland. Although a Town Councillor when he established the museum, in 1962 Murray left council to become the museum's full-time curator. In the museum's first guidebook Murray insisted that 'This is not a children's museum; it is a museum about them', and this emphasis upon children as subject matter rather than audience influences the museum to this day. Murray cultivated a comical reputation for disliking children, claiming to possess 'a rooted conviction that children are only tolerable after their baths and on their way to bed'. Nevertheless, upon his retirement in 1974 he reflected on his pride at offering adult visitors to the museum a reminder of beloved artefacts associated with their early years (Heyes *et al.* 1993: 1, 2). For Murray, satisfying the adult desire for nostalgic excursions to childhood was an important achievement of the museum.

Alongside sentimental museum depictions of children's history, however, a countervailing trend to vilify the past can be discerned. Sharon Brookshaw (née Roberts) argues that in Western society childhood is either envisaged as a protected period of freedom and joy or as a time of imprisonment in poverty, sadness and abuse (Roberts 2006: 156). In broad terms, the past is either idealized as a golden period prior to modern decline, or depicted as an age of cruel ignorance before the happier days of the present. Both tendencies frame museum representations of childhood. Most commonly, dedicated museums of childhood tend towards romanticization whilst displays about working or institutional childhoods emphasize the abusive aspects of the past (see Simon Sleight's chapter in this volume for discussion of how the latter view predominates in museum depictions of children's work). Historical studies of childhood have been framed in largely linear terms through one teleology or its counterpart: history is understood as either a story of progress from the bad old days to the idyllic present, or a steady decline from a golden age to modern ills, and this historiographical dichotomy has strongly influenced the ways in which museums represent childhood.

A question of sources: museums of childhood and museums of children

Issues of methodology and source material have also been critical influences in the development of a historiography of the child. Particularly in the early days of the discipline, historians largely relied upon adult-constructed sources about children. When studying children beyond the reach of living memory, it is far easier to find adult-authored texts on child-rearing advice or adult-made items of furniture for children than it is to find historical sources created by children themselves (Schlereth 1990: 103). For this reason, some scholars insist on the need to distinguish between histories of childhood – adult views of the nature of childhood – and histories of children – the opinions and experiences of children themselves.

This distinction applies as much to artefacts as it does to documents. As noted above, Brookshaw concluded that the basic principles of material culture analysis are difficult to apply to children's objects, given that most items are originally made by adults for children. For example, it is impossible to appreciate precisely what toys mean to the children who play with them. She argues that given this, scholars and museums should distinguish between the material culture of children and the material culture of childhood, with the former being objects manufactured or adapted by children and the latter those objects made by adults (Brookshaw 2009: 379–81). Extending this analysis to museums, one might argue that there is an important difference between museums of children and museums of childhood, with the second type predominating amongst cultural institutions.

The Edinburgh Museum of Childhood, for example, is very much a museum of childhood, which charts changing adult perceptions of childhood. Displays at Edinburgh are presented in traditional glass display cabinets and primarily relate to the history of childhood, organized into themes. Some of these relate to different phases or spheres in a child's life, such as 'Baby', 'Christening', 'Health and Hygiene', 'Food and Drink', 'Schooldays', or 'Children at Work'. Many others relate a history of toys rather than a history of childhood, including 'Push, Pull and Riding Toys', 'Sunday Toys', 'Musical Toys', 'Puppets', 'Dolls' Houses' and 'Teddy Bears'. There are also displays on 'Outdoor Games', 'Pastimes' and 'Children's Clothes'. With few interactive displays there is relatively little incidence of young visitors playing, though children can be observed riding a rocking horse, dressing up or reading. Higher numbers of adults reminiscing about their pasts can be observed here than at similar institutions such as the Victoria & Albert Museum of Childhood, and visitor engagement with displays is more often the hushed tones of adults reminding each other they used to play with certain toys or games.

There are also other museums with a wider representational scope whose exhibitions relating to childhood can both confirm and challenge traditional concepts of children's history. For years, many museums of childhood have survived, and indeed found popularity, by focusing upon nostalgic representations of childhood. But in recent years the very definition of a museum has become more complex. Museums have been democratized and decolonized, as diverse social groups have demanded that their history also be preserved and represented in museums. Less political pressure is exerted to bring children's history to the forefront of popular consciousness; children rarely agitate for themselves in the same way that adults might. Indeed, the added factor militating against a greater focus on childhood is that unlike the experiences of most social groups displayed in museums, childhood is an experience all adults have passed through and so implicitly adults feel they can speak on behalf of children (Shepherd 1996: 262). But one effect of changing academic and political discourses is that contemporary exhibitions have tended to be more nuanced. For example, displays have considered the ways in which class, race and gender create multiple experiences of childhood, rather than universalizing and idealizing a single version of childhood. This highlights another facet of the difference between museums of children and museums of childhood. Whilst childhood as an abstract notion might be a uniform and unified construct, experiences of children are always bound to be varied and multivalent. Traditionally museums of childhood have relied upon objects that depict a romanticized adult view of childhood. By contrast, recent exhibitions at the McCord Museum in Montreal and the Auckland Museum were more interested in the historical perspectives and experiences of children themselves, bringing them closer to the definition of a 'museum of children'.

From 2004 to 2008 the McCord Museum displayed an exhibition entitled 'Growing Up in Montreal' which engaged with new museology and emerging scholarship on children's history. Reflecting an increasing scholarly interest in geographies of childhood, 'Growing Up in Montreal' was organized around the spaces in which children live their lives: the home, the school, the street and health care centres. The exhibition invited visitors to engage with the history of Montreal's children through memories of the phenomenology of everyday life:

> At unexpected moments, we recall the smell of Sunday dessert simmering in the oven, the comforting softness of a tattered blanket or the scary-excited feeling of walking to school alone for the first time. There are darker memories too – earaches and chicken pox, sore tummies, casts and crutches, a menacing pinch from a big sister and the sound of parents arguing in another room.

And, as this quote from the exhibition website reveals, the display attempted to engage with all manner of childhood experiences: positive, negative and ambivalent. The exhibition focused also upon the ways in which medical and technological changes intersected with and impacted upon childhood experiences in the past. In particular, curators were explicitly attentive to shifting understandings of children's agency, insisting that 'Children are far from passive participants in an adult world. You will see how their needs, desires and actions have changed and shaped our city and our lives'.

Objects on display illustrated a vast range of themes. Hospital ID bracelets were used to talk about birth, whilst pasteurized milk bottle tops provided a point of entry for discussions of infant mortality. Toys were explored through collectible figures such as Smurfs, Trolls and Transformers, as well as displays of toys for learning that reflected theories of educational development. The gendering of children's clothing and toys were analysed, as well as the ways in which the many religions of Montreal influence different experiences of growing up. A reflex hammer and a certificate of vaccination were displayed in a section on children's health, while schoolbags and a report card were used to talk about school experiences.

Whilst these displays all tried to complicate exhibition narratives with issues of class, gender and religion, the video viewing area was perhaps the most effective tool to demonstrate that childhood has always been a varied experience. Here visitors could watch video excerpts dealing with a wide range of childhood memories and this section of the exhibit proved very popular. Visitors were also invited to contribute their own memories of childhood as they were leaving the exhibition through comments or drawings. Both of these strategies personalize specific stories of children as opposed to creating a generalized history of 'childhood' as an abstract concept.[1]

Exhibitions such as 'Growing Up in Montreal' demonstrate the ways in which museums have begun to interrogate how space has affected the histories of children and childhood, in line with trends within academic scholarship. On the other side of the world at Auckland Museum, the 'Wild Child' exhibition which opened in 2007 looks at the history of New Zealand children through three spaces: 'the twin citadels of control that were The Home and The Schoolhouse – and the Wild Space in between'.

Within the home section there are traditional museum themes such as a nineteenth-century nursery, but such pampered Victorian childhoods are implicitly destabilized by the inclusion of information on infant and mother mortality rates. Contributions of children to the domestic economy of the family are acknowledged through labels on household chores, collecting bottles and newspaper rounds. The rise of children's bedroom spaces is explored, including the suggestion that 'cyberkids' find freedom through online exploration.

The school section contains predictable items such as classroom photographs, but also surprising material culture such as the random contents of a small boy's pockets. Whilst the school is portrayed as a place of 'strictures and teacher controlled behaviour', a school locker is reproduced as a space of juvenile autonomy. Exhibition labels suggest that over the years the school has become a place where the state takes responsibility for child health and welfare through free milk and dental checks, whilst teachers increasingly sought to control schoolyard play through military drills and physical education.

Through the physical layout of the 'Wild Child' exhibit, curators contrast the regulated spaces of the home and school with the wild play spaces that children supposedly find for themselves. Curators explain that:

> This space 'in between' school and home is where children invented their own games and took up the endless opportunities afforded behind the bike sheds, by

the fields on the way to school, by the gullies, bush and beach off the path, and by the neighbour's overgrown section.

In the exhibition, the 'Wild Space' is represented by a huge tree containing a tree house. Toys made by children themselves are featured in this section, including knuckle bones, hoops, stilts, peashooters, spud guns and bows and arrows. The exhibition's focus upon children's own subculture of toys and customs complicates the picture presented in traditional museums of childhood, where the distinction between histories of childhood and histories of children is rarely questioned.[2]

Blurring boundaries: museums of childhood and children's museums

Continuing this taxonomy of museum types relating to children, while there is an important distinction to be made between museums of childhood and children's museums (also called discovery centres), in practice the distinction is often blurred. Both increased steadily in popularity over the twentieth century due to a rising interest in children: their history and their learning needs. Both are reflective of radical changes in how the institution of the museum is defined, in terms of subject matter and audience. Despite their similarities, however, the historical development of these two types reveals that their fundamental aims are born of different impulses.

Museums of childhood are essentially cultural institutions devoted to studying, preserving and representing the lives of children in the past through their material culture. As Anthony Burton's detailed history of the V&A Museum of Childhood at Bethnal Green elucidates, most museums of childhood originated as toy museums and only later incorporated other aspects of children's material culture (Burton 1997). The widening of their scope has in many ways reflected and influenced the maturing of a historiography of childhood.

Burton situates his history of the museum within a broader history of the study of toys. Children's games were first studied seriously by folklorists in the nineteenth century but there were few private or museum collections of children's toys at that time. A concerted interest in the history of toys emerged around 1900, linked to growing international interest in child development and innovations in toy making. At the same time, the pressures of industrialization were inspiring a trend towards romanticizing what was perceived as a simpler, pre-mechanized past. Due to its flourishing toy industry, France developed a collecting culture for toys in the early twentieth century. Interest in the history of toys similarly grew in Germany, where a strong toy trade and fascination for folk culture influenced the establishment of toy museums in the decades immediately preceding the First World War (Burton 1997).

Throughout Britain and France the study of toys continued to grow after the Second World War and the V&A Museum of Childhood mounted toy exhibitions under several themes through the 1950s and 1960s. Nevertheless, whilst acquisitions and exhibitions expanded, 'toy research in Britain remained in the hands of collector-enthusiasts'. Meanwhile in Edinburgh, the private toy collection of Patrick Murray had become the City of Edinburgh's Museum of Childhood in 1955. In 1968 Murray published *Toys*, an important testimony to the role of museum collections in contributing to research on the history of toys (Burton 1997).

From the 1980s and 1990s, museums with toy displays began to prove their popularity with visitors. Nevertheless, under political pressure to demonstrate the significance and worth of toy collections, the V&A Museum of Childhood tried to broaden its representation of the material culture of childhood beyond toys to include children's dress, furniture and publications (Burton 1997). With the passing of the welfare state and the rise of neo-liberal political theories, cultural institutions throughout the Western world have increasingly had to shift from demonstrating their social worth to their commercial value. Some museums of childhood have not survived the transition: the closure of the Edith Cowan University Museum of Childhood in Perth, Australia, is a notable example of the demise of a cultural institution that held what was arguably the most significant collection of children's material culture in the country (for more on this museum, see Shepherd 1996). Others have prospered by reinventing themselves as serving the interests of children, not just as subject matter, but as audience too.

Children's museums are essentially cultural institutions whose primary interest is in the creation of stimulating educational environments, often through hands-on learning. Whilst traditional museums prohibit visitors from interacting with objects, children's museums posit that one cannot truly understand objects without using and touching them (Lewin 1989: 52). Such an approach is typified by Philadelphia's famous Please Touch Museum, which explicitly markets itself in contrast to museums where visitors cannot touch material culture. This new way of understanding the interaction between visitors and displays first emerged in the United States, during a time in which considerable adult concern for children was also funnelled into movements to prohibit children's labour, shift children's play from streets to playgrounds, and improve juvenile health. Brooklyn Children's Museum was established in 1899, with the Boston Children's Museum following soon after. Between 1899 and 1930 approximately 50 children's museums were established in the United States, as well as children's rooms or galleries in traditional museums. The first European museum designed for a juvenile audience was the Museum for Education (Museum Voor Het Onderwijs) in the Hague, Holland in 1904. Conversely, there were almost no examples of children's museums in the UK until the 1980s, with the exception of the Children's Gallery, opened in the Science Museum, London in 1931 (Studart 2000).

During the 1960s children's museums experienced another period of growth, alongside the development of more interactive museum-style spaces such as science centres and discovery centres. This reinvigoration of children's museums was due largely to developments in educational psychology and to the movement to popularize museums. The appointment of Michael Spock as director of the Boston Children's Museum during this period saw the pioneering of new approaches using participatory exhibits that were 'discovery-based' and invited 'cross-generational learning' (Studart 2000). By 1984 the National Learning Centre in Washington DC had received 531 requests for information on how to start a children's museum from 47 US states and

40 countries overseas. By 1989 there were over 400 existing in the US alone (Lewin 1989). A strong children's museums movement developed in Europe from the early 1990s, and in Britain most museums now have interactive galleries for children and families. Ultimately, the rapid growth of children's museums and hands-on centres have influenced displays within traditional museums too, resulting in an overarching trend towards cultural institutions becoming 'active learning environments' (Studart 2000).

In addition to adapting display styles to suit children's learning preferences, children's museums have prided themselves on overturning the model of the traditional, elitist museum. Writing in 1978, Hodges called for the reform of traditional museums, which he saw as ignoring the needs of visitors. He praised instead the emergence of a new type of museum; connected to the rise of children's museums. In his description, this new museum was distinctive for decentralizing services and resources; allowing visitor interaction; affording minority groups greater voice; and acknowledging the needs of children (Hodges 1978).

Despite the contrasting foundations of museums of childhood and children's museums, over the last few decades the distinction between these types of institutions has become more difficult to discern. Many cultural institutions devoted to depicting children's history have decided to pitch their displays and activities squarely at children and their carers.

One of the world's most significant cultural institutions devoted to children's heritage, the V&A Museum of Childhood is a typical (and successful) example of this blurring of categories. In terms of identity, the museum maintains an interesting tension between different museum types. The Creativity Gallery is akin to a children's museum with its emphasis on play and developmental learning, divided into sections such as 'Make it happen', 'Explore', 'Be inspired' and 'Imagine'. The Moving Toys Gallery mimics some of the approaches of a science museum, categorizing toys in relation to laws of the physical world such as 'Pushes and Pulls', 'Springs and Cogs', 'Circuits and Motors' and 'Look See'. Temporary exhibits tend to be more like art galleries, focusing on artistic work by, for or about children. Recent examples include sketched portraits of children, a 'grotesque' interpretation of children's colouring books, nineteenth-century photographs of children and an installation by local schoolchildren and artists depicting a dark fairytale. By contrast the Childhood Galleries are more historical in the manner of a museum of childhood. The organization of this space around the themes of 'Who will I be?', 'What we wear', 'How we learn', 'Home', 'Families', 'Babies' and 'Good Times' results in predominantly sentimentalized messages about children throughout history.

In the past, the museum has tended to prioritize playful, feel-good aspects of childhood. In 1991, Ludmilla Jordanova criticized the V&A Museum of Childhood for failing to display the negative aspects of children's lives, such as child labour. She argued that by universalizing our perception of childhood, museums can restrict the complexity of our ways of thinking about children's history (Jordanova 1991). But in recent years, the museum has been moving towards more complex representations of children. Information on children's work and education is now included on its website (less nostalgic topics than toys and play) and more nuanced exhibitions dealing with topics from autism to the darker side of fairytales have been displayed. Current director Rhian Harris (see her chapter in this volume) is consciously seeking to engage adult visitors by including more 'serious' topics as befits a national museum of childhood, without alienating the families and school groups who have long enjoyed visits to the museum (Stephens 2009).

As institutions that both shape and mirror wider understandings of children's heritage, museums must pay some heed to visitor expectations. The fact that the Childhood Galleries are organized into rather nostalgic themes is presumably reflective of the museum's recognition that visitors expect to see largely positive and light-hearted themes conveyed in a museum dealing with the history of childhood. When Brian Shepherd (former director of the Edith Cowan Museum of Childhood) conducted a visitor survey at the V&A Museum of Childhood in 1994, he 'failed to elicit one response suggesting that the displays in that museum concentrate on children's toys at the expense of other important aspects of children's lives' (Shepherd 1996: 261). One might argue that museums that sentimentalize childhood are simply providing visitors with what they have come to see.

Given that a pure museum of childhood is in danger of becoming an economically unviable niche interest, and a children's museum might struggle to be more than an adventure playground, the V&A Museum of Childhood attempts to find a balance between these two identities. In catering to the needs of young visitors as a children's museum, the museum attempts to be educational and fun, through a learning centre, dedicated play spaces, and book-reading and other directed activities. This all takes place amongst more formal display cases curated historically or thematically, giving those (generally older) visitors interested in the history of childhood a chance to engage with such material.

Crossing the Atlantic, the Strong National Museum of Play in Rochester, New York, is a slightly different model of museum. Unlike the London or Edinburgh based museums of childhood, the Strong's location in upstate New York outside of a major capital city means that the museum has to work harder to attract visitors. The museum has achieved this by appealing to a range of visitor types including 'families, children, adults, students, teachers, scholars, collectors and others' by producing many different products and services, including exhibitions, a library, a butterfly garden, a carousel, a passenger train, shops and food court.[3] Teachers and students are catered for through educational programmes, school lessons and teacher development opportunities. Like many other cultural institutions of the twenty-first century, the Strong has attempted to transcend geographic distance and move interaction with the public beyond the old-fashioned visitor experience by providing access to its collections online and producing a blog.

Through its 'Play Partners', the museum has also widened its role beyond that of a traditional collecting institution. The Strong retains some of the traditional elements of museums of childhood such as a romanticization of play and a strong focus upon toys, as is evident in the National Museum of Play and the National Toy Hall of Fame. But the museum is engaged with more than just the past as it actively seeks to influence policy relating to contemporary children's play in the United States, for instance through the *American Journal of Play*. The museum also houses the Brian Sutton-Smith Library and Archives of Play, this collection from a renowned scholar of play affording it serious scholarly credentials as a research centre. The inclusion of the International Centre for the History of Electronic Games represents an acknowledgement of the fact that children's play today has largely moved away from the simpler technology of tops and skipping ropes.

On its website, the museum claims that it 'blends the best features of both history museums (extensive collections) and children's museums (high interactivity)'.[4] The museum has adopted an interesting strategy to marry these two types. Through its self-characterization as a 'museum of play', the Strong is arguably the first museum of childhood to explicitly acknowledge that its collections and exhibitions deal largely with this aspect of children's lives. This self-identify allows it to engage with the nexus between the play of children in the past and the present without presenting an image to the public that is a confusing hybrid of a museum of childhood and a children's museum.

Conclusion

This lightning tour of museum displays across the globe serves to illustrate both the limitations of nostalgic approaches to children's histories but also the diversity of ways in which children's history *can* potentially be preserved and represented in museums. Many museum exhibits have shifted from a reliance on oversimplified cultural tropes to more nuanced and complex representations. Such changes have occurred in response to changing social expectations of visitor experiences, as well as shifting understandings of childhood itself. Over the modern era the role of children in Western society has moved from capable workers to helpless dependants, though there is now an emerging sense in which children are viewed as independent consumers. Within museums children have shifted from subject matter to audience, as curators increasingly seek to design displays that reflect juvenile modes of learning and engagement.

Museums seeking to represent children's history are often in a difficult bind. They operate in environments of financial constraint and must be aware of political sensitivities. Given the vast range of views across any given population, museum curators walk a fine line between challenging and offending visitors. To some extent, museums must cater to what visitors desire and expect. In the case of museums of childhood, this appears to be largely nostalgic and sentimentalized views of children, as Shepherd's survey demonstrated (Shepherd 1996). Nevertheless, this is not the view of every visitor: writing in 1997, Burton related that visitors to the V&A Museum of Childhood were increasingly likely to comment that there were few poor children's toys on display (Burton 1997). In addition, contemporary museology increasingly stresses that museums have a social role to play in confronting stereotypes and ensuring that a varied range of experiences is represented within their walls.

Shepherd offers a potential way forward for museums of childhood facing this conundrum. Museums need to make the visitor feel comfortable and satisfied by going some way towards meeting their expectations, which might mean retaining the traditional symbols of the museum of childhood such as teddy bears, rocking horses and dolls houses. Indeed, nostalgia for childhood is a powerful and legitimate emotional experience. From this foundation, museums of childhood can seek to provoke and surprise their visitors, whether through making explicit the gendering of children's toys, confronting the reality of corporal punishment, or exploring the stories of children who have grown up in circumstances of war. Museums can harness the kinds of strong emotional responses that visitors experience in exhibitions about growing up whilst also complicating visitor understandings of historic childhoods. As Shepherd points out, it would be considered ridiculous to establish a museum of adulthood: we recognize immediately that the range of experiences is too vast to be summarized under one roof (Shepherd 1996). Children's experiences are just as varied. The most interesting contemporary museums engaging with histories of children and childhood are able to simultaneously satisfy visitor expectations while still managing to encapsulate and represent the dazzling diversity that comprises children's experiences in the past. Rather than merely 'putting away childish things' within glass cases, some museums are now managing to complicate and challenge our very definitions of what is children's cultural heritage.

Notes

1 For an online tour of the exhibition, see http://www.mccord-museum.qc.ca/expositions/expositionsXSL.php?lang=1&expoId=1&page=accueil.
2 For more on the 'Wild Child' exhibition see http://www.aucklandmuseum.com/296/wild-child.
3 See Strong Museum website at http://www.museumofplay.org/.
4 http://www.thestrong.org/about-us

References

Ariès, P. (1962) *Centuries of Childhood: A Social History of Family Life*, trans. Robert Baldick, New York: Knopf.
Brookshaw, S. (2009) 'The Material Culture of Children and Childhood: Understanding Childhood Objects in the Museum Context', *Journal of Material Culture*, 14(3): 365–83.
Burton, A. (1997) 'Design History and the History of Toys: Defining a Discipline for the Bethnal Green Museum of Childhood', *Journal of Design History*, 10(1): 1–21.
Calvert, K. (1992) *Children in the House: The Material Culture of Early Childhood, 1600–1900*, Boston, MA: Northeastern University Press.
Cunningham, H. (2005) *Children and Childhood in Western Society since 1500*, 2nd ed., Harlow: Pearson/Longman.
Fass, P. (2010) 'Childhood and Memory', *The Journal of the History of Childhood and Youth*, 3(2): 155–64.
Heyes, J. *et al.* (1993) *Museum of Childhood, Edinburgh*, 2nd ed., Edinburgh: City of Edinburgh Museums and Art Galleries.
Hodges, D.J. (1978) 'Museums, Anthropology, and Minorities: In Search of a New Relevance for Old Artifacts', *Anthropology & Education Quarterly*, 9(2): 148–57.

Jordanova, L. (1991) 'Objects of Knowledge: A Historical Perspective on Museums', in P. Vergo (ed.) *The New Museology*, London: Reaktion Books.

Lewin, A. (1989) 'Children's Museums', *Marriage & Family Review*, 13(3): 51–73.

Reinier, J.S. (1996) *From Virtue to Character: American Childhood 1775–1850*, New York: Twayne Publishers.

Roberts, S. (2006) 'Minor Concerns: Representations of Children and Childhood in British Museums', *Museum and Society*, 4(3): 152–65.

Sánchez-Eppler, K. (2005) *Dependent States: The Child's Part in Nineteenth-Century American Culture*, Chicago and London: The University of Chicago Press.

Schlereth, T.J. (1990) 'The Material Culture of Childhood: Research Problems and Possibilities', in T.J. Schlereth *Cultural History and Material Culture: Everyday Life, Landscapes, Museums*, Ann Arbor, MI: UMI Research Press.

Shepherd, B.W. (1996) 'Making Children's Histories', in G. Kavanagh (ed.) *Making Histories in Museums*, London and New York: Leicester University Press: 257–69.

Stearns, P.N. (2009) 'Analyzing the Role of Culture in Shaping American Childhood: A Twentieth-Century Case', *European Journal of Developmental Psychology*, 6(1): 34–52.

Stephens, S. (2009) 'Family Values', *Museums Journal*, January: 36–9.

Studart, D.C. (2000) 'The Perceptions and Behaviour of Children and their Families in Child-Orientated Museum Exhibitions', PhD in Museum Studies, University College London.

Van Slyck, A.A. (2004) 'Kid Size: The Material World of Childhood, An Exhibition Review', *Winterthur Portfolio*, 39(1): 69–77.

Wishy, B. (1968) *The Child and the Republic: The Dawn of Modern American Child Nurture*, Philadelphia: University of Pennsylvania Press.

Zelizer, V.A. (1985) *Pricing the Priceless Child: The Changing Social Value of Children*, New York: Basic Books.

Chapter 14

Museums and representations of childhood

Reflections on the Foundling Museum and the V&A Museum of Childhood

Rhian Harris

There has been an upsurge of serious interest in childhood in the last 15 years. That upsurge has been evident across public policy, academia, the arts and certainly in museums as well as throughout the general population. In the UK, New Labour initiatives have placed the child and the family firmly at the heart of public policy. Childhood Studies has emerged as a major academic discipline, whilst interest in family history has expanded significantly.

Museums have participated in this trend. New museums of childhood have been created, such as the Foundling Museum, which opened in 2004. Some established museums of childhood have received significant funds to revitalize themselves, including the V&A Museum of Childhood and the National Trust Museum of Childhood. Other museums have mounted major exhibitions relating to childhood. These include the Imperial War Museum's (London and regional branches) recent or current exhibitions 'The Children's War', 'A Family in Wartime' and 'Once Upon a Wartime', or Birmingham Museum and Art Gallery's exhibition on 'Children's Lives'.

During this exciting period it has been my privilege to lead two London-based museums that, in different ways, explore and represent aspects of childhood and children's history; as curator (1996–2001) and then Director (2001–8) of the Foundling Museum and as Director of the V&A Museum of Childhood (2008–present). In this chapter I draw on the contrasting and complementary experiences of directing these two institutions to reflect on aspects of museums' representations of childhood. I propose, first, briefly to consider some of the conceptual issues around the subject; second, to compare and contrast the two institutions to explore some of the principal factors influencing museums in this challenging area; and third, to outline some recent initiatives at the V&A Museum of Childhood that are intended to broaden and deepen aspects of that institution's representation of and engagement with childhood.

Some conceptual issues

What is meant by a museum of childhood? And is it conceptually different from any other kind of museum? In 1990, the Museums Association, which represents collecting institutions in the UK, agreed on the following definition:

Figure 14.1 V&A Museum of Childhood exterior.

> Museums enable people to explore collections for inspiration, learning and enjoyment. They are institutions that collect, safeguard and make accessible artefacts and specimens, which they hold in trust for society.
>
> (Museums Association 2010)

A museum of childhood is an institution that acquires, preserves and displays object-based collections that relate broadly to childhood and to children's history. Those collections will tend, therefore, to privilege the 'material culture of childhood' rather than the 'material culture of children', that is, objects made *for* children (generally with a dominant focus on toys), rather than objects made or adapted *by* children (Brookshaw 2009). Museums of childhood are collections-based. Collections will often be supported by additional material – text, audio-visual, interactive – to provide context, enhance accessibility and to encourage deeper exploration by visitors. Museums of childhood may, and the good ones almost invariably do, include interactive and experiential elements but this is in addition to the display and contextualization of the collections.

Such institutions differ from the American conception of a children's museum, where the emphasis is on the 'discovery' by children of the world around them. The US-based Association of Children's Museums offers the following definition:

> An institution committed to serving the needs and interests of children by providing exhibits and programs that stimulate curiosity and motivate learning. Children's museums vary greatly in style, size and content. Because of this creativity and diversity, the field is on a continuum of exciting change.
>
> (Association of American Museums)

Children's museums are generally experiential and activity-based and are *for* children, with children as their principal participants, rather than engaging, as museums of childhood do, *with* childhood and children's history. The Children's Museums movement is a major phenomenon in the US. The Brooklyn Children's Museum was established in 1899 and there are now approximately 300 children's museums across the US. There are few such institutions in the UK, perhaps reflecting a stronger tradition of children visiting mainstream object-based museums, castles and other historically significant locations with families and in school groups; and organizations such as the National Trust have been instrumental in these visitation patterns. Eureka! in Halifax, West Yorkshire, is perhaps the best known children's museum in the UK, and, as its name indicates, it associates itself with the idea of discovery. Opened in 1992, Eureka! calls itself 'The National Children's Museum'.

Although a museum of childhood is not structured exclusively *for* children, accessibility for children as part of the intended audience is always a crucial element in such factors as design, display and layout. And children, whose intellectual curiosity and excitement is always so wondrous to behold, are invariably a core audience for museums of childhood, whether visiting with family, or in school, community or other interest groups, such as youth clubs or the Scout and Guide movement.

Childhood – defined biologically or legally, if not culturally, in terms of a positive and unencumbered period of innocence – is arguably a universal experience. Thus museums of childhood have both a particular responsibility and a particular attraction to the communities they serve. Museums of childhood have a responsibility to represent the extraordinary breadth and depth of childhood and children's history, ranging from representations of the circumstances of innocence, freedom, imagination and learning to the problems of poverty, cruelty and neglect. Equally, visitors may have a stake in – or an emotional attachment to – the subject matter and collections of museums of childhood that may transcend their attachment to even the greatest museums of art, science, natural history or antiquity and their collections.

In these ways, museums of childhood do differ from other museums, and their specific role and collections do provide particular opportunities. One of the great joys of working within the museum of childhood sector is the opportunity to pursue intergenerational projects, which invariably yield enormous benefits for all participants across the age spectrum. Childhood is crucial to our development as human beings. It is crucial to the culture of any society and it deserves to be explored and represented in all its facets. Museums of childhood provide a vibrant, stimulating and accessible means of doing so.

The V&A Museum of Childhood, a branch of the Victoria and Albert Museum, is perhaps the largest museum of childhood in the world and is the UK's national museum of childhood. But it is far from alone. In the UK there are broadly conceived and dedicated museums of childhood in Edinburgh and at the National Trust's Sudbury Hall Museum, whilst smaller and more specifically focused museums include the Highland Museum of Childhood and the Foundling Museum in London. There are also important childhood collections and displays in other museums across the UK, notably National Museum Wales, Hampshire Museums Service and Birmingham Museums and Art Gallery. Increasingly, national and regional museums have also used the history of childhood as an accessible means of illustrating part of a larger story in exhibitions. The exploration of childhood in a particular context has enabled museums to encourage visits from a family audience attracted by the subject matter. The Imperial War Museum and Sheffield Museums are good examples of this approach. It should be noted, however, that for these museums the collection and display of objects related to childhood is a secondary activity, rather than their principal remit.

In seeking to fulfil its aim of representing the history and culture of childhood more broadly than any comparable institution in the world, the V&A Museum of Childhood organizes its 30,000 objects, of which approximately 12 per cent, or 3,600, are on display, into seven collections.

The V&A Museum of Childhood is organized around three principal galleries. The Childhood Galleries explore the social history of childhood, represented primarily through such objects as dolls' houses, games, puzzles, clothing, furniture and items associated with the early years. The Moving Toys Gallery showcases an extensive collection of moving and optical toys. The Creativity Gallery features a broad variety of toys, puppets, toy theatres and other objects relating to the development of children's imagination and creativity. Further material from the collections is often displayed in a series of temporary exhibitions, therefore widening the perspectives on the lives of children in the past.

Table 14.1 Collections at the V&A Museum of Childhood

Collection	Description
Archive	Areas of interest include – but are not restricted to – British toy manufacture, toy design, education and child development, theories of play, childhood experiences.
Children's clothing	The UK's premier public collection of children's clothing (0–18 years of age).
Dolls' houses and miniatures	One of the largest and highest quality public collections of dolls' houses in the world with around 80 houses, mostly from Britain and Europe, dating from the seventeenth to the early twenty-first century.
Ephemera	Includes greeting cards, official documents, letters and diaries.
Home and childcare	Comprises early years feeding, teething, hygiene, mobility and ritual objects dating from the 1730s and one of the best collections of children's furniture in the UK.
Play and learning	One of the largest and most significant collections of dolls in the world, with over 8,000 items. One of the finest collections of games and puzzles in the world, with approximately 3,000 items. The collection includes learning and development toys, puppets and toy theatres and soft, optical, mechanical, construction, figure and character toys.
Representations of childhood	31 paintings, mainly from the Dixon Bequest. Approximately 800 photographs dating from the 1860s documenting children's lives, including family photograph albums and posed studio portraits.

The Foundling Museum and the V&A Museum of Childhood: museums' representation of childhood

The two museums of childhood that I have directed are respectively shaped by their own histories, by the histories of the institutions they commemorate or have succeeded and by the political, social and intellectual impulses that attended their creation and continue to influence them. The Foundling Museum commemorates the Foundling Hospital, and its generations of abandoned children (a total of 27,000) from the mid-eighteenth to the mid-twentieth century as well as three inspirational figures from the era of the hospital's foundation: the campaigning philanthropist Thomas Coram, the painter and engraver William Hogarth and the composer George Frideric Handel.

The Foundling Hospital was established as the product of a specific set of historical circumstances. London's population doubled to almost one million during the eighteenth century, with the capital at the heart of the nation's expanding and transforming economy. This period saw the emergence of the British Empire and laid the foundations for Britain's Industrial Revolution. London was a city of economic dynamism and of contrasts and extremes: a city of social hierarchy and mobility, of wealth and poverty and of industriousness and criminality. In the early eighteenth century infant mortality approximated 75 per cent, whilst perhaps a thousand babies a year were abandoned on the streets or rubbish heaps of the city, almost invariably to die. Abandonment often befell infants born outside marriage or whose parents were unable or too poor to care for them.

Figure 14.2 A view of the Foundling Hospital, originally published in 1750. © Coram in the care of the Foundling Museum.

This was the London to which the retired sea captain, Thomas Coram, returned in 1719 after many years in the Americas. Coram was morally outraged at the widespread abandonment of infants but equally, having experienced the effect of labour shortages in America, he was also incensed at the waste of these potentially productive lives. With the economic and imperial expansion of Britain dependent on a growing population, these questions of morality and national economic imperatives were to coincide.

Coram was determined to petition the King to create a hospital to care for the abandoned children that would be supported by public donations and subscriptions. However, without access to the monarch and in the face of significant opposition, it took Coram almost 20 years before George II signed the Charter for the 'education and maintenance of exposed and deserted young children' on 17 October 1739. Coram's campaign had been advanced considerably by the new fashion among society ladies to support charity and benevolent causes, and by an increasingly sentimental interest in motherhood and childhood among the British upper classes.

The hospital opened its doors in temporary accommodation on 25 March 1741, before moving to its permanent site on Lamb's Conduit Fields in 1745. It was both London's first home for foundlings and the nation's first public art gallery, as the precursor to the Royal Academy of Arts which was established in 1768.

William Hogarth, himself childless, was an active founding governor of the hospital. In another example of enlightened self-interest, during what Hogarth called 'a golden age of English philanthropy', he persuaded contemporary British artists to donate paintings and sculptures to the hospital. Hogarth hoped to attract the wealthy and fashionable to the hospital by allowing British artists to exhibit in public for the first time. Those visitors who came to view the art were encouraged to give donations for the maintenance of the hospital. At the same time George Frideric Handel, who like Coram and Hogarth was childless, composed his Foundling Hospital Anthem. Handel also gave hugely successful benefit concerts, often performing his Messiah, in the hospital's chapel.

The hospital would persist, in the face of vicissitudes, especially around the policies of admitting children, for more than two centuries. In the twentieth century, the hospital was moved out of central London to Redhill and Berkhamstead before its closure in 1954. The hospital was succeeded by the childcare charity Thomas Coram Foundation, based at 40 Brunswick Square in London in a building constructed in 1937 near the site of the original hospital. The building contained several interiors preserved from the eighteenth-century hospital, including the Boys' Staircase, the Sub-Committee Room, the Picture Gallery and the magnificent Court Room. Both these interiors and the Foundling Hospital collections had become neglected by the end of the twentieth century.

In 1998, The Foundling Museum was established as a separate entity, with the intention of restoring, extending and redeveloping 40 Brunswick Square as a high specification environment in which to conserve and display the Foundling Hospital collections. Twelve million pounds were raised to undertake the capital project. This consisted of £6 million from private sources, £3 million from the National Heritage Memorial Fund to provide an endowment fund for the Foundling Museum, and a

Figure 14.3 Court Room at the Foundling Museum. © Foundling Museum.

further £3 million from the National Heritage Memorial Fund to allow the museum to acquire Hogarth's famous oil painting 'The March of the Guards to Finchley' from the Thomas Coram Foundation.

This brief history of the hospital and the establishment of the Foundling Museum illustrates a number of important features relating to the museum's exploration and representation of aspects of childhood and children's history, that contrast with the history and nature of the V&A Museum of Childhood. The Foundling Museum is unequivocally a museum of childhood, rather than a museum for children, even if it deals, for example, with extraordinarily difficult aspects of childhood and includes children's entry into the labour market – features that, under some definitions of 'childhood', might be excluded from such a museum (Roberts 2006: 154). The Foundling Museum also runs an impressive Learning Programme. Indeed, the area of education, with a particular emphasis on the educational experiences of children, was always conceived as being at the heart of the museum's activities. The museum also includes a number of interactive exhibits that engage younger visitors, although its displays and interpretation are principally oriented towards an adult audience.

Furthermore, the content of the museum is multi-stranded and complex, with collections falling into three main categories. First, the museum's social history collections relate to the generations of children who passed through the hospital, along with the preserved and restored interiors from the hospital. Second, the museum's art collection comprises the hospital's nationally important collection of paintings and other works that have been preserved intact since the eighteenth century. And third, the museum houses a major collection of material relating to Handel and his life and work.

The profoundly difficult nature of the experiences of a foundling childhood, and the history and context of the hospital and its activities, mean that the collections and exhibitions of the Founding Museum are varied and complex. The hospital consistently aspired to be progressive in its handling of the abandoned children and orphans in its care – for example, in terms of diet and healthcare – but its practices in relation to the welfare of children were inevitably defined and constrained by its era. So while the hospital accepted foundlings and ensured their survival, at times during its history many of those children who were presented at its doors were not accepted. Even on acceptance, infants were first sent from the hospital to be wet-nursed, only to face a second abandonment when they were aged 3–6 years and were removed from their wet nurses and returned to the hospital.

In addition, foundling children were educated and brought up in a disciplined, strictly Christian environment that emphasized duty. They were encouraged to entertain limited expectations for their future, with careers in domestic, agricultural, industrial or military service often ahead of them. Children left the hospital to work at the age of 10 or 11 years of age in the eighteenth century, rising to 14 or 15 years of age by the early twentieth century. Thus philanthropy, in combination with both societal requirements and self-interest, underpinned much of the early impetus for the hospital's existence and regime.

This history of the Foundling Hospital offers a narrative of moral complexity. It is neither inaccessible nor inappropriate for children, but it is certainly a narrative that requires careful presentation and mediation in its telling. Whilst much of what is on display at the Foundling Museum is oriented towards an adult audience, considerable amounts of this material are accessible to children, depending upon their age and especially so when they are accompanied by adults in either school or family groups. The strength, clarity, moral imperatives and emotion that underpin the history of abandoned children contribute to the hospital's compelling story, and are perhaps best encapsulated in the memorable and poignant tokens left by mothers with their infants on acceptance into the hospital.[1] These features also contribute to the museum's broader capacity to introduce and sensitize both adult and younger audiences to the historical and continuing issues around the vulnerability and importance of childhood.

A third feature that contrasts the Foundling Museum with the V&A Museum of Childhood is the specificity of the former institution. This has three principal aspects. First, despite the multi-stranded nature of its collections and the moral complexity surrounding the hospital's history, the Foundling Museum celebrates a single institution across approximately 200 years of its existence. Second, the Foundling Museum was established at a particular and recent moment in time with public and private funds raised to achieve a clearly articulated vision and outcome. And third, the Foundling Museum and its trustees are able autonomously to manage and assess the success of this private, medium-sized and very clearly defined museum, with visitor numbers currently around 46,000 per annum.

By contrast, the V&A Museum of Childhood, located in Bethnal Green in the East End of London, arguably occupies a more privileged but also a more complex position than the Foundling Museum in respect to the way that museums may explore and represent childhood. This is because the V&A Museum of Childhood is, perhaps, the largest such museum in the world and is the UK's national museum of childhood, housing the nation's finest and largest childhood collections. As a branch of the Victoria and Albert Museum, the V&A Museum of Childhood benefits from the global reputation and name recognition associated with its parent. The museum also benefits from its own access to the collections of the larger Victoria and Albert Museum. Operating within the public sector, the V&A Museum of Childhood receives approximately 85 per cent of its core funding from the Victoria and Albert Museum grant-in-aid (state funding, via the Department for Media, Culture and Sport).

The V&A Museum of Childhood's subject matter, scale, location and reputation have all contributed to burgeoning visitor numbers, which in the year to the end of March 2012 reached 443,000 – a dramatic increase when compared with visitor numbers of 145,000 per annum at the turn of the millennium. In tandem with this growth, the museum's programme and visitor experience are constantly improving. There is evidence of increasing demand among the population for the high-quality family and inter-generational visits that the museum is satisfying. More recent promotion of the museum's national status, and its association as part of the Victoria and Albert Museum, is broadening its audience demographic, with visitors coming from further afield. And in the current difficult economic climate, the free entry to the museum is a significant attraction. Its location in the vibrant East End ensures the participation of a broad and diverse local audience. Indeed, recent market research indicates that ethnic minorities comprise 25 per cent of the museum's visitors, and those in lower socioeconomic groups comprise 20 per cent; these are particularly high rates of participation for these groups within the UK national museum sector more generally.

The V&A Museum of Childhood is also in a somewhat more complex position than the Foundling Museum. This is as a result of its status as a national museum and its broad associated responsibilities. Related to this, there is a tension between its role as either a museum *of* childhood or as a museum *for* children. There is a further tension that arises as a consequence of the name and implicit hierarchy of V&A Museum of Childhood, with the parent museum's status as the world's largest museum of decorative arts and design tending to influence the acquisition and display strategies of the Museum of Childhood.

These complexities are, to some extent, accidents of history. A brief outline of the V&A Museum of Childhood's development and its roots in South Kensington will illuminate the museum's current position – much as the brief history of the Foundling Hospital and the Foundling Museum has illuminated the emerging identity of that museum.

The Great Exhibition of the Works of Industry of all Nations of 1851 was, despite its inclusive title, intended to demonstrate Britain's industrial might and technological capacity to the rest of the world. The Great Exhibition was organized by the Royal Society for the Encouragement of Arts, Manufactures and Commerce and, in particular, by Prince Albert and Henry Cole. Housed in an iron frame building covered in glass, situated in Hyde Park and known as the Crystal Palace, the exhibition yielded, inter alia, both an immediate profit and a legacy of exhibits.

In the wake of the Great Exhibition and with continued inspiration and leadership from Prince Albert and Henry Cole, the South Kensington Museum was opened in 1857. It was housed in a building with an iron frame, walls of green and white striped corrugated iron and a glass roof constructed by Charles Young and Company. The 'Brompton Boilers', as the decidedly unlovely building became known as a result of its resemblance to three adjacent boilers, contained diverse collections. These included Henry Cole's Marlborough House Museum of Ornamental Art as well as a trade collection, patent models and various educational items and materials. The museum was a success with the general public, and was soon extended with the addition of further buildings.

In 1864 the Department of Practical Art and its Superintendent Henry Cole proposed that similar museums should be established in north, east and south London. However, only in the east of the city was Cole's proposal received with enthusiasm. Land was purchased in Bethnal Green, with contributions from the Corporation of London and local businesses including the brewers Truman, Hanbury, Buxton & Co. and Charringtons, as well as Thomas Twining. Parts of the South Kensington building, including the 'Brompton Boilers', were moved to the site in late 1867 and a new red brick exterior was designed by J.W. Wild with Henry Scott, Head of the South Kensington Design office. Further buildings were designed for Bethnal Green but never constructed. Mosaic panels, designed by Frank Moody and representing agriculture, art and science, were added to the exterior, whilst the interior mosaic black and white floor that still survives today was laid by female inmates of Woking Gaol.[2]

The Bethnal Green Museum, as it was then named, was opened by the Prince of Wales on 24 June 1872 as a branch of the South Kensington Museum, with the intention of sharing with the deprived East End the contents of the parent institution. It was an immediate success, with approximately 1.5 million visitors in its first year. Early exhibits included elements of the art and science collections, along with food and animal related exhibits. The Bethnal Green Museum later housed other collections, including, temporarily, Richard Wallace's eighteenth-century French art collection, before the Wallace Collection was permanently established in Manchester Square. The museum was also midwife to other major museums, including the National Portrait Gallery, which emerged from the 1885 National Portraits Exhibition, and the Tate Gallery, founded in 1897 following the Royal Academy's Chantrey Bequest Exhibition at the Bethnal Green Museum in 1896. With the redistribution of the science collections to other nearby sites, the South Kensington Museum was reorganized to focus on art and design. The announcement of its change of name to the Victoria and Albert Museum coincided with the laying of the foundation stone of the Aston Webb building in 1899.

For the Bethnal Green Museum, the metamorphosis into a museum more specifically focused on childhood began under Arthur Sabin, Curator during the early 1920s. Sabin had a remit to reorganize the museum and, inspired by the children's exhibition organized at the Victoria and Albert Museum in 1915 by its then Director (1909–1924) Sir Cecil Harcourt Smith, Sabin developed and exhibited collections relating to childhood with the intention of making them accessible to children. Paintings, for example, were hung at a lower level than usual. Talks, guides and lecturers were provided for school parties. A classroom was created in 1925 and teachers were employed by the museum. Queen Mary donated a large collection of toys to the museum in the same decade, with other significant donors including Mrs T.T. Greg and Mrs Walter Tate. These collections laid the foundations of the V&A Museum of Childhood's current toy collection (Burton 1997: 45).

The Second World War interrupted the museum's development. The East End of London was subject to heavy bombing and the V&A Museum of Childhood operated as a British Canteen, serving the general public in that guise until 1950. When the museum re-opened, the emphasis on childhood and children was initially relaxed. A small collection of childhood-related objects was displayed alongside the Victoria and Albert Museum's circulation of exhibitions to the Bethnal Green site.

Childhood-related objects and displays remained popular during the postwar period. When Roy Strong became Director of the Victoria and Albert Museum (1973–87), the Bethnal Green Museum was re-launched as the Museum of Childhood in 1974.

Figure 14.4 Mr F. Wilson, guide lecturer, teaching a school party, c.1926. © V&A.

All childhood-related collections housed at South Kensington were then transferred to Bethnal Green and any extraneous items were returned from Bethnal Green to South Kensington. The V&A Museum of Childhood's collections have continued to expand, with acquisitions from toy manufacturers, private donations and as a result of the museum's funded acquisition programme. Since 1974 the museum has aspired to advance beyond merely exhibiting a collection of toys representing and exploring childhood in its myriad aspects and to a greater breadth and depth than any comparable institution in the world (Wood 2012: 11).

Where the Foundling Museum is multi-stranded and complex but also very specific in its focus, the V&A Museum of Childhood, as the nation's museum of childhood, has a broad remit and one that must be fulfilled within the context and constraint of limited resources. The material cultures of childhood and children are already vast. However, as these continue to expand, along with the ethnic and cultural diversity evident in British society, this is increasingly challenging for a museum endeavouring to preserve, explore, represent and make increasingly accessible the nation's material cultures relating to children.

The V&A Museum of Childhood also seeks to welcome and address children. Children, in family or in school groups, comprise approximately 60 per cent of the museum's annual visitors. Formal education programmes related to the UK National Curriculum and other educational and creative programmes are at the heart of the museum's day-to-day activities. And thus, in addition to the challenge of fulfilling the role and remit of a national museum of childhood, the V&A Museum of Childhood must also at least partially function as a museum *for* children.

As a branch of the Victoria and Albert Museum – which markets itself as 'the world's greatest museum of art and design' – the museum operates within the broad parameters established by its parent, including a focus on objects and a tradition of connoisseurship. It benefits from access to the collections of the larger Victoria and Albert Museum but is also partially defined by the nature, scope and ambitions of such collections. The relationship between the V&A Museum of Childhood and its parent underpins the museum's focus on the material culture of childhood, perhaps even at the cost of a deeper engagement with the social history of childhood.

In his book, *Vision and Accident: The Story of the V&A*, Anthony Burton, a former senior member of the Victoria and Albert Museum staff, hints at the way in which such complexities are handled internally. The Victoria and Albert Museum and V&A Museum of Childhood are, and have been throughout their intertwined histories, guided by vision, passion, leadership and clearly articulated strategy. But that is not to eliminate accident or happenstance, whether this be the accidents of history that have largely determined the nature of the museums' collections, or the contemporary accidents and contingencies that endlessly disrupt museum directors' 'best laid schemes' (Burton 1999).

Recent initiatives at the V&A Museum of Childhood

Having reviewed the histories of the Foundling Museum and the V&A Museum of Childhood in order to explore and contrast those museums' representations of childhood and children's history, this chapter now explores the vision, intentions and objectives that underpin recent and current initiatives at the V&A Museum of Childhood (while recognizing that there remains scope for accidents aplenty). These initiatives, focused on the extension and refurbishment of the building and on the refreshed display and interpretation of the collections, have sought to improve accessibility, expand the museum's audiences, enhance visitors' experience of the museum and to broaden and deepen audiences' exploration of the museum's representation of and engagement with childhood and children's history.

Since the Bethnal Green Museum's re-launch as the Museum of Childhood in 1974, its collections have expanded significantly, in terms of both volume and quality. However, by the early twenty-first century there had been virtually no investment in the building's structure since its opening in 1872. Under the Directorship of Diane Lees (2000–8), the museum undertook two phases of a Masterplan devised with the architects Caruso St John and intended to transform the museum's physical accessibility and facilities. The key achievements of Phases 1 and 2, completed in April 2003 and December 2006, respectively, were the repair and refurbishment of the building and the re-modelling of the historic Central Hall to include a new shop, café and information desk.

Second, galleries were redesigned and the use of space enhanced throughout the building, allowing for the improved dispersal of visitors on arrival, particularly large school groups. A new entrance and forecourt were also introduced, providing step-free access to the museum and improved circulation, along with other features to enhance visitor experience such as the addition of new toilet facilities and a new lift near the entrance serving all floors. Finally, all learning facilities were upgraded, with the creation of both an enlarged, well-resourced Learning Centre with increased capacity for teaching and school visits and a Community Gallery, with the aim of increasing visitor numbers and further enhancing visitor experience.

These projects sought principally to secure the fabric of the V&A Museum of Childhood and to make it more accessible, especially to children (and never underestimate the importance of a museum's shop, café and toilets!). The museum then undertook detailed research, consultation and planning before implementing a new interpretation strategy to make the content of the museum more accessible. That strategy introduced elements of display and programming particularly aimed at attracting school visits. For example, one of the four main galleries, the Moving Toys Gallery, was created precisely to address elements of the UK's National Curriculum. The History of Toys, exploring their production and significance, has been a significant component of the curriculum for Key Stage 1 in primary schools and the Moving Toys Gallery specifically explores these issues, as well as touching on other aspects of the curriculum including art and design, history, science and mathematics. School groups are a crucial audience for the V&A Museum of Childhood. The museum is committed to supporting life-long learning and recognizes the value of engaging children when they are young, in order to expand their social, cultural, historical and intellectual horizons.

New, child-friendly interpretation panels were introduced with reduced volumes of simplified text and display cases were lowered to improve accessibility for children. 'Dwell spots' were created for school groups or families to congregate and for interpretation assistants to deliver activities linked to the permanent collections. Finally, a range of interactive activities were introduced, especially for younger children who learn through play. These were mainly low-tech and designed to engage with elements of the adjacent permanent collections. For example, dressing-up clothes were placed beside the children's clothing display, rocking horses alongside moving toys and, most popular, a sandpit was located alongside the Good Times and Holidays exhibits.

In 2008 I was appointed Director of the V&A Museum of Childhood. During the last four years the museum has operated within a challenging local and national context. In particular, London and especially the diverse, economically deprived (including high levels of child poverty) east of the city, where the museum is located, has been preparing for the 2012 Olympic Games. The Olympics will have a dramatic impact on the East End, which will experience a raised profile and expectations as the world focuses on this part of London during the games. Regeneration and the upgrading of the business, transport and cultural infrastructure may have a lasting, positive impact on this dynamic but underprivileged part of London. Meanwhile, since 2010 the Conservative/Liberal Democrat coalition government has tightened public expenditure, with museums being hit with budget cuts of varying but significant degrees.

My strategic vision has been to consolidate and build on the museum's recent initiatives and successes, whilst also leading it in new directions. First, I have sought to position the museum decisively as the V&A *national* Museum of Childhood,

Figure 14.5 Museum of Childhood interactive. © V&A.

strengthening the bond with the parent and also reinforcing the museum's national status. The museum benefits from access to the collections of its parent, and operates within the public sector and thus receives the bulk of its funding from the Victoria and Albert Museum grant-in-aid. These factors, in conjunction with its status as a branch of the Victoria and Albert Museum, the world's largest museum of decorative arts and design, enhances name recognition and has contributed to the significant increase in visitor numbers since 2000 discussed above.

Second, I have sought to broaden and deepen the museum's programming, activities and visitor experience. One significant initiative will be the broader and deeper representation of childhood through history in all its aspects, including difficult aspects of childhood experience. The museum's displays have sometimes given a rather 'rose-tinted' view of childhood, focusing primarily on the history of toys. If the museum is to represent a more authentic view of childhood then both positive and negative elements of historical and contemporary childhood must be explored and represented. Toys and play are, after all, only one aspect of childhood experience and the museum aims to explore other areas that might include education, child labour, poverty, the child in the family and the child in the world.

The V&A Museum of Childhood also intends to explore how each generation defines or (re-)invents childhood. It is intended that the museum's permanent galleries should be redisplayed to include those areas noted in the previous paragraph and to provide a broader and deeper representation of childhood. The provision of layered, contextual information will ensure that adults and older children are addressed, whilst multi-media, interactive and visual techniques are intended to engage, in particular, younger children. The museum will make increasing use of personal stories to draw visitors of all ages in on a more emotional level. And crucially, the child's own voice will be represented, underlining that children have participated actively in society throughout history and have not simply been passive. It will be important to ensure that this initiative ensures accessibility at an appropriate level for each of the museum's diverse audiences, from children of all ages to adult visitors, including scholars, artists and childcare practitioners.

The intention to broaden and deepen subject matter underpins the museum's forthcoming exhibition, 'Modern British Childhood 1948–2012' (the dates of the last two London Olympic Games). The exhibition will explore the broad social, political and cultural parameters of British childhood, including health, education and family and will interpret them firmly within a social historical context. A relatively small number of objects will animate these themes and the major changes to the position and landscape of the child during the last 60 years. Some of the objects are not obviously beautiful or aesthetic but are, nevertheless, full of meaning and thought-provoking. An example of such an object in the exhibition is a small milk bottle, just one third of a pint. Bottled milk was available to all school children under 18 after the establishment of the British welfare state. Such an object evokes powerful memories amongst those who received bottled milk, and represents and embodies the positive aspirations of post-Second World War Britain to nourish its young, with the milk of the nation being given in both literal and metaphorical senses to its children.

Third, I have sought to raise and expand the V&A Museum of Childhood's intellectual agenda, with the ambition for the museum to become a centre for ideas relating to childhood and the material culture of childhood. An example of this would be the museum's major research partnership with Queen Mary College, University of London. The joint project, entitled 'The Child in the World', includes three Arts and Humanities Research Council-funded Collaborative Doctoral Awards. The research investigates the changing ways in which children in Britain have understood their relationship with the wider world through their everyday lives, spanning the period from approximately 1870 to the present. It will analyse a wide range of material held by the V&A Museum of Childhood, with three areas of inquiry on 'Children, Home and Empire', 'Children, Migration and Diaspora' and 'Children and Global Citizenship'. The research outcomes from the Child in the World project will have a direct impact on the redisplay of the museum's collections, as well as contributing to its continuing learning and community work. The aim is for this and other scholarly partnerships to have a wider impact on the museum, its staff and visitors, in developing a culture of research and advancing the intellectual agenda for all. Such partnerships and projects strengthen the museum's position within the academic community and encourage debate about historical and contemporary childhood, enabling the V&A Museum of Childhood to participate and contribute to these at local, national and international levels.

Fourth, and in addition to broadening and deepening the museum's programming, activities and visitor experience, is the commitment to continuing to improve accessibility for its wide and diverse audience. The museum's new Audience Development Strategy identifies four primary groups: families, schools, community and 'interested adults'. Each audience is targeted in specific ways that may include temporary exhibitions and smaller displays, and is supported by a comprehensive Learning Programme and an artist-led Community Programme.

The Museum's Community Programme works with local schools, community groups and other educational institutions. It seeks to break down barriers to education by involving participants in learning who are not traditional museum visitors and who may have limited educational and employment opportunities. The museum undertakes two major projects each year. Participating groups receive an introductory talk and tour from one of the museum's curators before taking part in a series of participatory, creative workshops led by a team of freelance artists over several weeks. Some projects involve trips to other cultural institutions. Each group produces new work for a six-month public exhibition in the museum's Front Room Gallery, a prestigious gallery space located at the front of the V&A Museum of Childhood. An example of a Community Programme exhibition is 2010's *Sense of Place*. Three visiting artists from Bangladesh and India taught traditional craft skills to children of South Asian descent and the children's work was displayed alongside that of the visiting artists. With the museum being located in East London, an area of conspicuous cultural diversity and socioeconomic challenge, it is committed to addressing and providing for the local community, as well as for its wider audiences.

Fifth, the V&A Museum of Childhood's Contemporary Programme has facilitated the commissioning and display of the work of contemporary artists and designers engaged with themes of childhood or the visual representation of children and childhood. The museum's first contemporary art commission was 2010's *Institute of Play*. The artist Colin Booth, whose practice is rooted in the white aesthetic and bold, utopian forms of early Modernist art, architecture and design, created an installation on the museum's Marble Floor made from over 2,000 wooden building blocks. Booth's work was embedded alongside an historical survey of children's play bricks and architectural toys dating back to the 1830s. Building bricks are some of the earliest toys with which children begin to play independently and for some sculptors, designers and architects, such as the famous Modernist Frank Lloyd Wright, that impact is lifelong. The installation supported the Contemporary Programme's objective to produce important, thought-provoking work for and about children.

Finally, I have conducted a review of the museum's Acquisitions Policy, which forms part of the V&A's Collecting Plan. Whilst some areas of the museum's collections are extensive and rich in their breadth and quality, others require attention. The Acquisitions Policy has been adjusted to achieve a better-balanced, multi-faceted representation of childhood, with priorities including visual representations of childhood, social history, history of education, early years and contemporary childhood objects. This is consistent with broadening and deepening the museum's programming, activities and visitor experience and it is important that the museum's Acquisitions Policy supports its other initiatives.

The upsurge of serious interest in childhood and the increasing recognition of the multi-faceted centrality of childhood to individuals, communities and societies present museums of childhood with immense opportunity and equally immense challenges. The V&A Museum of Childhood has the opportunity, ambition and capacity to become the international leader in childhood collections, with a breadth and depth of material relating to childhood and children's history unmatched by other institutions. This is a challenge but a welcome and important one. The museum also has the opportunity, ambition and capacity to participate in public policy, academic and other professional engagement with historical and contemporary childhood. The universality of childhood confers responsibility upon the institution – and others like it – and confronts the museum with a huge range of childhood experience and material to accommodate, represent and begin to understand. The understanding of childhood is central to our human endeavour to understand ourselves and the world in which we live. And museums of childhood will contribute significantly to that endeavour.

Notes

1   As the Foundling Museum's website explains: 'These were pinned by mothers to their baby's clothes and upon entry, the Hospital would attach them to the child's record of admission. As foundling babies were given new names, these tokens helped ensure correct identification, should a parent ever return to claim their child. The children were not allowed to keep their tokens, which were frequently everyday objects, such as a coin or button. The Hospital gradually evolved a more sophisticated administrative system, whereby mothers were issued with

receipts. So the practice of leaving tokens died out at the beginning of the nineteenth century' (http://www.foundlingmuseum.org.uk/collections/the-foundling-hospital-collection/).

2 Freeman, C. (2009) 'History of the Museum', online. Available www.museumofchildhood/ about-us/history-of-the-museum (accessed 10 January 2012).

References

Association of American Museums (http://www.aam-us.org/) (accessed 20 February 2012).

Brookshaw, S. (2009) 'The Material Culture of Children and Childhood: Understanding Childhood Objects in the Museum Context', *Journal of Material Culture* 14: 365–83.

Burton, A. (1997) *Bethnal Green Museum of Childhood*, London: V&A Publications.

Burton, A. (1999) *Vision and Accident*, London: V&A Publications.

Freeman, C. (2009) 'History of the Museum', online. Available www.museumofchildhood/ about-us/history-of-the-museum (accessed 10 January 2012).

Museums Association UK (www.museumsassociation.org/about) (accessed 10 February 2012).

Roberts, S. (2006) 'Minor Concerns: Representations of Children and Childhood in British Museums', *Museum and Society*, 4(3): 152–65.

Wood, S. (2012) *Museum of Childhood: A Book of Childhood Things*, London: V&A Publications.

Chapter 15

Children as collectors of cultural heritage

Leland Stanford, Jr and his museum

Karen Sánchez-Eppler

The concept of cultural heritage implies generational transmission, the past handed on to the future. Children powerfully embody this temporal loop: childhood evokes the most deeply known individual experience of the past and children serve as the promissory and emblem of futurity. This essay uses the figure of one particular, if far from representative, California child to assess the generational stakes of cultural heritage and of the practices of collection and preservation that establish museums. Joseph Roach insists on the importance of recognizing the commingled actions of 'looking back' and 'movement forward' – of 'memory' and 'invention' – for understanding any kind of performance (2010: 1082). This seems paradigmatically true for the performances of progress and promise at stake for both childhood and California. As the son of one of the 'Big Four' investors who at enormous personal profit built the transcontinental railroad, Leland Stanford, Jr (1868–84) belongs to a family that epitomizes the most extravagant proliferation of industrial and Californian progress (Figure 15.1). Yet through two European tours the boy developed a keen interest in antiquities and began a collection that would serve as the rationale and founding core of the Leland Stanford, Jr Museum. His death in Italy, from typhoid fever, just two months before his sixteenth birthday, makes the memorializing impetus at stake in all museums a specific act of mourning. The role of art and collecting in the education and life of Leland Stanford, Jr and the memorializing function of the Leland Stanford, Jr Museum together elaborate the multiple and sometimes opposing parts childhood plays in the collection, preservation and transmission of cultural heritage.

As Carol Osborne (1986: 90–1) and Wanda Corn (1997: 17–18) both argue, the image of young Leland as a collector ultimately served to legitimate his mother's unlady-like institutional work of building the Leland Stanford, Jr Museum – the largest private museum in the world. After his death, when Jane Stanford had already forged the museum that she considered the most personal and individual of the memorials to her son, remembrances of his life would always stress the boy's natural avidity as a collector, describing him, for example, as collecting pine cones when he was eight years old (Tutorow 1971: 211). Collection theory has tended to use childhood in a similar way to explain and naturalize the act of collecting, and to identify collecting and display as what James Clifford calls 'crucial processes of Western identity formation' (1988: 220; for the paradigmatic status of children's collecting, see 216–19). As

Figure 15.1 Stanford Family, 1880, Stanford Historical Photograph Collection, item no. 8312, Special Collections, Stanford University Library.

Jean Baudrillard avers, 'it is invariably *oneself* that one collects' (1994: 12). In these terms theories of collection will often evoke oedipal patterns, or ascribe to the objects collected the sorts of compensatory, mediating capacity that D.W. Winnicott (1971) finds in 'transitional objects'.[1] Such accounts, of course, present the collector as an adult and figure collecting as an effort to reclaim a lost repletion associated with childhood itself. In this way the objects gathered are 'used most often to evoke a voluntary memory of childhood', as Susan Stewart explains, both

> in souvenirs, such as scrapbooks, of the individual life history or in the larger antiquarian theme of the childhood of the nation/race. This childhood is not a childhood as lived; it is a childhood voluntarily remembered, a childhood manufactured from its material survivals.
>
> (1993: 145)

But the life of Leland Stanford, Jr prompts the question: what if it is a child who gathers such souvenirs of the past? What happens to such theories when 'a childhood as lived' includes, as it did for young Leland, digging up Ohlone stone implements on the grounds of his family horse farm or purchasing antiquities while travelling in Europe with his parents?

Interior decorating and the education of an heir

An only child, Leland Dewitt Stanford was born 14 May 1868, 18 years into his parent's marriage at a point when their economic, political, and social prestige was already long established. His parents, Leland and Jane Stanford, both came from comfortable, middle-class families in Albany, New York. Leland Stanford had first travelled to California in 1852 and his wife joined him three years later. Jane Stanford sewed curtains and covered crates with cloth to make chairs for their first California house. The extraordinary speed of the Stanfords' rise to prominence was characteristic of the Gold Rush years, and testimony to the period and region's lax legal borders between economic and political power. During a single month in the summer of 1861 Leland Stanford was nominated for governor of California on the Republican ticket, elected President of the Central Pacific Railroad, and the couple purchased one of the finest houses in Sacramento. On 10 May 1869 Stanford himself drove the 'last spike' on the transcontinental track, and shortly after young Leland's first birthday the family travelled across the country by rail – in their own luxuriously furnished private car – to show off their baby to the family back in Albany. It was only after the birth of their child and the highly profitable completion of the transcontinental rail that the Stanfords became art collectors. Undoubtedly, the swift and enormous change their railroad investments made in the size of their already substantial fortune was the most significant impetus for the Stanfords' new interest in art and culture, and many other recent California tycoons responded to their new wealth with similar purchases. But it is also clear that the birth of this boy so late in the Stanfords' marriage had a profound impact on how they thought about their money and on how they spent it (Bancroft 1952; Clark 1931; Tutorow 1971; Berner 1935; Nagel 1985).

In 1872, when Leland was four years old, the Stanfords expanded their two-storey, eight-room, Sacramento home into a four-storey, 44-room mansion with a dining hall large enough to seat 200 guests. Having bought the house and lot in 1861 for $8,000 they spent $45,000 on renovations. Much of the art they purchased for it was produced by artists working in California and featured Western scenes, and although the original house had been built in an Italianate style, the Stanford renovations tended to feature local motifs: they used redwood for panelling in many of the new rooms and in the grand dining hall they ordered railroad locomotives carved in the wood of the cabinetry and etched on the crystal lamps (Wenzel 1940: 249–53; Strazdes 1994). As a child in this house Leland really was a boy with trains on everything.

By the time Leland turned seven the Stanfords had begun construction on a far more elaborate mansion atop Nob Hill in San Francisco, and with this house their California décor became thoroughly infused with a refined European, even global, style. If the Stanfords' extraordinary wealth was a token of progress, the new house they built with it suggests that progress, especially industrial progress, has a long history and deep connections to the past: in Roach's terms, their 'moving forward' manifested itself in things that 'look back'. Instead of Western landscapes and loco-motives, these builders of the powerful new iron world decorated their Nob Hill house in a manner that evoked distant eras of refinement. If such old world graces were useful in asserting the Stanfords' social and economic power, they were deemed similarly productive for the education of their son.

The Stanfords' desire to garner an old world pedigree with the furnishing of their mansion is a fascinating if familiar story of the intricate relationship between economic and cultural capital. 'Capitalism', as Arjun Appadurai observes 'is itself an extremely complex cultural and historical formation, and in this formation commodities and their meanings have played a critical role' (1986: 49). Appadurai's efforts to trace the 'social life of things' defines 'luxury goods' as things whose 'principal use is rhetorical' (1986: 38). For the Stanfords, and even for young Leland, the adoption of this rhetoric was an explicit and self-conscious choice. The family's 1876 trip east to make arrangements for the interior decoration of their new San Francisco palace looked to older forms of social aristocracy for models in cultural display, but there is more evidence of self-confidence than of subservience in their purchases. The exquisite ornamentation that the New York decorating firm Pottier and Stymus elaborated for the Stanfords bypassed New York in constructing a historically and geographically diverse imperium. Each of the mansion's public rooms reflected a different national and temporal theme: India for the reception room, Pompeii for the drawing room (Figure 15.2), Turkey for the dining room, Italy for the family parlour, Flanders for the billiard room, the library in the ornate curves of Louis XIV, while the companion art gallery adopted the neo-classical lines of Louis XVI. As Diana Strazdes observes, it is the transportation empire of the railroad and the steamship that 'connects continents . . . and brings culture'. In 1874 the Big Four had organized the Occidental and Oriental Steamship Company as a subsidiary of the Central Pacific Railroad (Strazdes 2001: 214, 231, 237–8).

Figure 15.2 The 'Pompeiian Room' of the Stanfords' San Francisco mansion designed by Pottier and Stymus. Photograph 1878. Stanford Visual Resource Center, item no. 16456, Special Collections, Stanford University Library.

During the family's 1876 trip east the Stanfords attended the Philadelphia Centennial Exhibition, which was a world tour of its own. In this sense their visit to the Centennial merged with the home decoration intentions of their trip. The catalogue *Gems of the Centennial Exhibition* understood this event as in itself a demonstration of Americans' aesthetic discernment:

> The critical knowledge of the fine arts has made very noticeable advances in America within the last twenty years. The extension of the facilities to travel, the growing number of wealthy Americans, the awakening of new cravings caused by leisure and more complex social relations, the rapid ripening which comes after certain density of population has been reached, have all conduced to this.
>
> (Ferris 1877: 130–1)

If this account closely reflects the rapid changes in the Stanfords' position, it also suggests how the Centennial Exhibition itself can be seen as the nation's own equivalent to the Stanford mansion – for the Centennial, like the Nob Hill house, merges travel, wealth, leisure and more complex social relations in asserting America's increased economic and cultural status. The Centennial celebrated American progress, even as that success tended to be measured by explicitly European standards. Thus a visit to the art galleries in Memorial Hall was hailed as a 'grand sight' that would educate and dazzle 'the millions who have been denied the opportunity of a continental travel' (Anon 1876). For all their wealth, the Stanfords were still among those Americans who lacked such an opportunity, for though they crossed the continent in the luxury of their own personal railroad car they had not as yet crossed the Atlantic.

If the Stanfords visit to the Centennial can be understood as part of their burgeoning interest in European and ancient cultures, it also marks their continuing pride in the promise and splendour of the American West. Two of the paintings displayed at the Centennial Exhibition belonged to the Stanfords and young Leland certainly had an opportunity to tour Memorial Hall and see his family's California landscapes exhibited there. It seems equally probable that this railroad family visited the Main Exhibition Building and Machinery Hall with displays that included American locomotives (Ingram 1876: 214–16). The Stanfords are also likely to have visited the 'Indian Exhibition' in the United States Building with its teepee and totem poles. The Indians of California were well represented in the artefacts on display and images of this exhibit suggest that it was particularly attractive to children (Zegas 1976: 165; Trennert 1974: 118–29). The Stanford family's experience of the Centennial thus simultaneously fuelled an interest in old world culture and confirmed pride in American industry and the American West.

Leland, Jr was fascinated by California's indigenous peoples. Shortly after the Stanfords built their San Francisco mansion they purchased farmland south of the city 'partly', as Norman Tutorow phrases it, because Governor Stanford wanted 'to give his son the appreciation for farm life that he had acquired as a boy and partly to take up serious breeding and training of race horses' (1971: 161). The Stanfords' Palo Alto stock farm and country house were located on the sites of ancient Ohlone villages. Archaeologists now believe that this land had been continually occupied by Native peoples for nearly 5,000 years; the present grounds of Stanford University contain over 60 pre-contact Muwekma-Ohlone sites, with the greatest density along the San Francisquito creek where the Stanfords' house was located (Bean 1994; Johnston 1998). In his explorations on the Palo Alto farm, young Leland dug up at least half a dozen stone mortars and pestles.[2] Stephen Powers' efforts to collect artefacts along the Pacific Coast for the Philadelphia Centennial garnered many similar objects (Zegas 1976: 170–1). Powers' 1877 reports on his findings stressed the vast size and unusual density of the Native population of California before the arrival of the Spanish missions, and the decimation that followed. He described the sound of acorns being 'pounded up in stone mortars . . . the monotonous thump, thump of the pestles' as the central sound of village life in this region (Powers and Powell 1877: 49). In 1874 Hubert Bancroft published the first volume of his monumental documentary history of the *Native Races of the Pacific States*, devoted to the 'Wild Tribes' of California. Bancroft described this project as 'intended to embody all facts that have been preserved concerning these people at the time of their almost simultaneous discovery and disappearance' (1874: xi) and his compendium of sources included detailed reports on the use of stone mortars (1874: 406–8). Both of these studies present themselves as accounts of cultures and peoples who if not yet fully vanquished and vanished (Powers had spent the summers of 1871 and 1872 visiting Indian villages), were understood to be on the brink of disappearance. Thus Leland dug up these artefacts of California's autochthonous past precisely during the years when the first serious American studies of these tribes were published, and when the mythos of the vanishing Indian was accruing a specific scholarly and Californian iteration. While it seems quite unlikely that Leland looked into these scholarly tomes, he probably was aware in a more general way of the local practices described in these studies, such as the central place of acorns in the Ohlone diet and the role of these stone implements in the preparation of acorn porridge and acorn bread. He surely knew too, that the objects he was finding on the land of the Stanfords' new stock farm were remnants of Native ways of life threatened, if not eradicated, by the very tracks of progress on which his family's fortune had been laid.

Governor Stanford's horse-training programme at the Palo Alto stock farm included hiring Eadweard Muybridge to photograph his horses in motion, so as to better understand their gait, and that project too appeared to intervene in time. The series of cameras with electrical triggers that Muybridge deployed along the Stanfords' racetrack is now recognized as one California site of origin for the motion-picture industry. Thus the photographs shot at Palo Alto, like the transcontinental railroad that financed this experiment, were technologies that, as Rebecca Solnit argues, 'had changed the perception of time and space and the nature of vision and embodiment' (2003: 219). Among the photographer's 1878 studies of Palo Alto horses in motion are a series of images of Leland, Jr on his pony 'Gypsy'. Printing the images on glass slides, Muybridge could project them in swift succession through a magic lantern making boy and pony canter across the wall (Prodger 2003: 115). Thus the boy himself participated in these artistic and scientific efforts to alter the experience of time and motion.

A young collector of old things

In 1880, when the Stanfords made their first European tour, Leland, Jr thus arrived in the old world already with insight into the volatility of time and with a sense of what it was like to find the past underneath his feet. Jane Stanford reported to her husband on their son's interest in historical sites:

> He is very anxious to go to Waterloo to the old battlefield [. . .] He read up about the battle last eve. I sent and got a book and the first thing on waking he said he had dreamed of finding bullets in the ground and he wanted to go and stand on the very spot where Wellington had stood. And another bright thing he said, 'Mama it is not what you see there but it is what you take there that makes it interesting. Otherwise it would not be anything but a wheat field perhaps'. I think Leland is far ahead of his years in good sense.
>
> (Nagel 1985: 27)

Leland's desire to 'stand on the very spot where Wellington had stood' seeks in that place what Pierre Nora calls '*lieux de mémoire*'. Nora postulates that interest in such sites of memory – in places and objects that seem to hold and preserve the past – is itself a symptom of the dissolution of 'real environments of memory', of the breaks in communal continuity that have accompanied industrialization, nationalism, modernization, and the concomitant fraying of traditional ways of carrying and transmitting the past (Nora 1989: 7). Nora's account intimates that Leland's wish to go to Waterloo, like his Palo Alto collection of Ohlone artefacts, might be best understood as a response to the ways in which the boy's own life was a whirl of mobility and innovation. In any case, Leland clearly knew that his relationship to the past was subjective as well as eager: 'it is not what you see there but it is what you take there that makes it interesting.' Leland does not seem to have found the dreamed of bullets at Waterloo, but he did collect some on the battlefields of the more recent Franco-Prussian war, and the proprietor of one of the hotels where they stayed gave the boy 'several bullets picked up by himself on the field of Wörthe in 1840' (Stanford, Jr, 4 August 1881: box 1, folder 11; Nash 1886: pt 2).

Jane Stanford's report of this incident as a mark of Leland's 'good sense' suggests how much the older Stanfords were evaluating and even experiencing their European travel through its effects on their son. The trip was certainly motivated by their goals for Leland 'and for his future. This is what brought us abroad for his education' his father explained (Clark 1931: 384). The long European tradition of the Grand Tour had become, by the eighteenth century, something of a coming-of-age ritual for elite young men in their late teens and twenties, notoriously full of cultural but also sexual adventure (Black 2003: 118–31). The notion that such travel should be undertaken by an 11-year-old boy and his parents was a decidedly American adaptation, and in a sense really an invention of the new California millionaires. Wealthy east coast families had generally emulated the European pattern of the tour itself and sent their sons, and by the mid-nineteenth century their marriageable daughters, to the old world to add finishing touches to their already highly cultured educations. A few of the most established of the east coast social elite had such longstanding European connections that they considered travelling in Europe with their children 'as the most natural thing in the world', as Foster Rhea Dulles says of the attitude that took both Theodore and Franklin Roosevelt to Europe as young boys (1964: 127). But unlike families who were transmitting to their offspring cultural experiences the adults already knew well, neither of Leland's parents had crossed the Atlantic before they made this 1880 voyage with their child – thus Governor and Mrs Stanford were gaining cultural knowledge and refinement together with and through the education of their boy. Seven years earlier Phoebe Hearst, whose husband had made his fortune in the Comstock silver mines, similarly made her first trip to Europe in the company of her 10-year-old son, William. She took the boy on a second tour in 1878 where, as she proudly put it, he developed 'a mania for antiquities' that his mother shared, a mania ultimately manifest in the plethora of 'Hearst Castle', the fantastic mansion that William Randolph Hearst would build in San Simeon, California (Macleod 2008: 101). Somehow, on the west coast of America, this traditional rite-of-passage had become a family affair, and especially it seems a bonding adventure for mothers and sons: Governor Stanford soon returned to the US leaving Jane Stanford and 12-year-old Leland to travel together in Germany, Belgium, Italy and France: 'Leland felt responsible for his mother's entertainment', Bertha Berner writes of their travels and notes that 'Mrs. Stanford cherished very pleasant memories of that period' (1935: 29).

The itinerary of the American Grand Tour was quite well established by the middle of the nineteenth century. Though east coast elites remained a significant strand of tourism, Americans abroad now included a large spectrum of 'new types' both in terms of wealth and of geography (Dulles 1964: chapters 6, 8, 10). Indeed the Californian became a kind of quintessential figure for the American traveller of the post-Civil War era: Mark Twain's immensely popular *Innocents Abroad* was initially published in *The Daily Alta California* (1867–68); the 'powerful specimen of an American' that Henry James creates in Christopher Newman hails from San Francisco and serenely believes that 'Europe was made for him, and not he for Europe' (1877: loc 17 and 802).

'The world, to his sense', James observes of Newman, 'was a great bazaar, where one might stroll about and purchase handsome things' (1877: loc 805). On his own more childish stroll of accumulation, young Leland, his tutor recounts 'conceived the idea of bringing away from each place where a halt was made, some object of local interest that would recall the circumstances of his stay', and along with things found and purchased items, Leland also accumulated a large collection of little 'album' and 'ricordo' booklets from virtually every place they visited (Nash 1886: pt 1; Stanford Family Library 1795: boxes 7 and 31). In this sense, Leland's initial collecting began as souvenirs, objects preserved, as Susan Stewart puts it, to 'authenticate the experience of the viewer' and through which 'external experience is internalized' (1993: 134). Stewart's account of how such objects function, inverts in provocative ways Leland's own sense of the subjective aspects of his historical tourism: the mementos he collects materialize his imaginings of past eras and events, at the same time as they authenticate and internalize his experiences of European travel. It proves impossible to disentangle Leland's interest in accessing the past from his interest in preserving traces of his own pleasurable excursions into history.

Jane Stanford next took Leland to Italy, long the essential core of the Grand Tour. Italy was also, of course, deeply familiar, not just in the general way that classicisms 'ubiquity' and 'authority' permeated American culture of the period (Winterer 2007: 2), but also in the specific ways that it had already come to provide a potent idiom for California's splendour and the Stanfords' affluence. The most elaborate spaces in the Stanford's San Francisco mansion were the 'Pompeiian' drawing room and the central rotunda decorated with mosaics. Jane Stanford drew such comparisons herself in letters to her husband: 'the soft skies and climate remind me of dear California, and the aspect of the country too. But how young we are compared to this', she wrote from Naples (Nagel 1985: 30). Casting such links in explicitly generational terms, she discounts the Ohlone remnants of America's ancient past and presents the Stanfords' California 'we' as in itself an emblem of youth.

Girded by this sense of generational distance, Jane Stanford stoked her son's enthusiasm for Italy: 'I have read a good deal to him about Rome and Naples   also the last days of Pompeii – aloud', she wrote her husband. When they reached the ruins of Pompeii, during a period in March 1881 when Vesuvius was active – 'the red light issuing and the clouds of smoke' – the pleased mother reported that their boy was indeed 'wild with interest' (Nagel 1985: 29). In a blank book where Leland practised his German, pasted sundry stamps, and pressed leaves, he took sloppy, badly spelled notes in pencil of the things he saw in the ruins:

> Pompay
> saw stepping stones and chariot ruts of the weles
> hall of justice
> persones room
> public fountain
> stone woren away from drinking found 250 dead people
>
> (1881: box 1, folder 9)

In a letter to his father the boy turns his jotted phrases into more careful sentences:

> My Dear Papa
>   I have been to Pompei since I wrote you last. It is a wonderful sight, to see all the old ruins and the beautiful paintings on the walls, some as bright as if first done, the ruins show that some of the houses were very fine, the streets are all paved and show the weare of the chariot wheels. The fountains in the streets and show indentations where the hands rested of the many who stopped to drink, we went to one house that jhas just been cleared out, and the frescoes are beautiful the men were carrying the old ashes and debris that has laid here for centuries out of the rooms in small baskets, the guide though he watched us very closely allowed me to take a piece of frescoe that had fallen from the wall on the floor.
>
> (1881: box 1, folder 2)

Time and perspective appear remarkably fluid in Leland's writing. The lack of a grammatical subject in his jotted notes conflates what he 'saw' with what archaeologists had 'found', while his letter casts the viewer as more passive and emphasizes all the things 'the ruins show'. Temporal distance shrinks as ancient things appear 'as bright as if first done', and even the most transient and inconsequential of actions (the passage of a carriage, the resting of a hand at a fountain's edge) prove astoundingly durable. At Pompeii it is the repetitive acts of many, not the singular individual – not a Wellington – that most fascinates this boy. Yet Leland's report of his excursion to Pompeii offers clear evidence of the way collecting functions to individuate him in precisely the possessive terms Clifford and Baudrillard critique. When Leland picks a bit of fallen rubble from the floor the meaning of his act is very different from the identical gestures performed by those labouring 'men' filling their 'small baskets' with 'old ashes and debris'.

Leland's evident glee in making off with a piece of fresco acknowledges his collecting as a kind of infraction, the sort of activity the guide is there to prevent, and yet one that the boy has been 'allowed'. Such permission is not inevitable, and Leland's journal and letters from his travels often report moments in which adults are sceptical, indeed suspicious, of his interest in ancient things. A month later, for example,

Leland browsed in an 'antiquities store' in Paris where he notes in his 'Log Book' the saleswoman 'did not like one touch a thing in her store & was rather cheeky so I went off'; his comment shows him to be rather annoyed that the woman did not recognize the boy as the potential customer he in fact was (26 April 1881: box 1, folder 11). As both these instances suggest, hierarchies of age and class map each other in complex ways. Thus the tone of Leland, Jr's letter from Pompeii implies that the boy expects his father to approve of his naughtiness in collecting artefacts, while his careful writing in contrast to his sloppy notebook jottings makes it clear that he does not expect a similar clemency for his penmanship and spelling. Later accounts of this visit to Pompeii will both claim it as the site of origin for the Leland Stanford, Jr Museum and replace the edge of mischief – of getting away with something – evident in young Leland's telling, with a tenor of parental sanction, even injunction: 'the day at Pompeii, when his mother places a fragment of mosaic in the boy's hand and said, 'Let this be the nucleus of your museum' (Nash 1884: 27).[3] The process of memorialization and hagiography that followed young Leland's death transmutes an act that the boy boastfully depicted as illicit into a sign of filial obedience. Such porosity between the 'naughty' and the 'good' seems characteristic of affluent American childhoods during this period, even if encounters like that in the Paris antique store reveal the precarious limits of such permissiveness. Indeed part of what a privileged American childhood comes to entail during the late nineteenth century is a certain licence for mischief, especially mischief associated with acquisition or cultural prestige. It is, after all, Leland's good taste in valuing this piece of fresco that makes his theft into something guides would allow and parents would celebrate.

A similar dynamic structures the very concept of collecting antiquities which James Clifford notes 'at least in the West, where time is generally thought to be linear and irreversible, implies a rescue of phenomena from inevitable historical decay and loss' (1988: 231). Clifford's work critiques 'the retrospective bias of Western appropriations of the world's cultures', but interestingly, for him too, the figure of the child collector proves the most potent instance of collection 'as an exercise in how to make the world one's own' (1988: 222, 218). In Clifford's account the originary space of childhood thus retains its explanatory power, even as he deconstructs both the systems that attribute an originary allure to 'ancient' and 'primitive' cultures and the possessive practices of collecting and displaying these materials. Leland's record of his experiences in Pompeii show him learning these cultural patterns of acquisition – behaviours very actively fostered by the adults around him – and they make clear the ways in which Leland's own interest and engagement serve to focus and make meaningful adult encounters with the old.

A museum for a precious boy

By the time Leland reached Paris he had begun to augment these found tokens of his tour with purchased items. On Palo Alto stock farm paper he drew ledger lines and kept careful accounts of his expenditures ranging from a franc spent on 'soda water' or 'candy' to the purchase of a wide variety of antique military gear: the helmet of a 'garde de Paris' for 12 francs and that of a 'Gurassier' for 25. On 18 October he spent more than 100 francs on military outfits, and the next day recorded spending 4 francs and 50 centimes to have them disinfected (1881: box 1, folder 10). An earlier letter to his father from a trip to Lyon and Marseilles described 'a little girl picking lice out of a boys head' and adds 'it is awful dirty in this part of France' (1880: box 1, folder 1). These lessons in curating cultural heritage reveal acquisition, record-keeping, sanitation, and preservation as the prerogatives and privileges of wealth.

Back in San Francisco Leland assembled a museum in three attic rooms of the Stanford's Nob Hill mansion. 'The ensuing summer was spent by him in the way he loved best', his tutor Henry Nash recalled, 'partly in out-door country life and partly in the classification and arrangement of his collection' (1884: 28). Photographs of this space show heterogeneous objects in which the conventional organizing categories of time, place, medium, genre, use, and value are largely disregarded. The Ohlone implements Leland dug up in Palo Alto and the bit of fresco from Pompeii mingle with European religious art, rock specimens, stuffed birds, and a large arsenal of antique weaponry (Figure 15.3). Clearly taking pride in their boy's collecting practices the Stanfords not only ceded these rooms to him but had an elegant glass topped display case made to furnish Leland's Museum. Thus this 'San Francisco residence Museum' epitomizes what Walter Benjamin recognized as the confluence of childhood and affluence in the act of collecting:

> As Benjamin was probably the first to emphasize, collecting is the passion of children, for whom things are not yet commodities and are not valued according to their usefulness, and it is also the hobby of the rich, who own enough not to need anything useful and hence can afford to make 'the transfiguration of objects' (Schriften I, 416) their business.
>
> (Arendt 1969: 41)

But if what childhood and the rich have in common is a proclivity to disregard use, the doubling of these traits in Leland's collecting may actually serve to invert that structure and make the useless useful – casting the activities that Leland 'loved best' as a fitting apprenticeship to dominion. 'The collector's attitude', as Benjamin put it, 'is in the highest sense, the attitude of an heir' (1969: 66) and the multiple strands of antiquity implicit in the varied artefacts Leland collected and his presumed inheritance of the Stanford fortune merge issues of cultural heritage with the inheritance of things, power, money, and prestige.

The Stanfords settled in New York for the winter and Leland spent time studying the classical collections at the new Metropolitan Museum of Art. Founded in 1870 and its Central Park building only opened in 1880, the Metropolitan Museum was younger than Leland himself, and the Stanfords had fortified their position among the east coast elite by being early and generous donors (Osborne 1986: 15). The museum's first director, Luigi Palma di Cesnola, personally showed Leland the antiquities he had excavated in Cyprus (Osborne 1986: 15, 46; Nash 1884: 27) and as the family prepared for a second trip abroad Cesnola wrote the boy letters of introduction to the

Figure 15.3 'San Francisco residence Museum' is written on the back of this photograph. The archives offer no explanation, but the arrows and numbers drawn on this image may have been made in the planning process for replicating these rooms in the Leland Stanford, Jr Museum. Stanford Historical Photograph Collection, item no. 8673, Special Collections, Stanford University Library.

directors of major museums in Europe: 'I know very well that I need only say that he is a friend of mine to secure for him a kind reception and all the facilities he may wish in order to visit and intelligently inspect the wonderful treasures of your Museum' (22 Sept. 1883: box 1, folder 8). Such intimate ties between elite children and the burgeoning new encyclopaedic museums of the late nineteenth century are not unique to Leland (Higonnet 2009: 5). Young Teddy Roosevelt, for example, set up a museum of natural specimens in his family's New York mansion and would donate 12 mice, a turtle, four bird eggs, and a red squirrel skull from his collection to New York's new Museum of Natural History when it opened in 1877 (Brinkley 2009: 30, 45).

Leland was now 15, and the collecting he undertook during this second European tour was far more focused and serious – 'I only make a collection of Egyptian, Greek and Roman', he explained to his Aunt Kate from Venice (Dec. 1883: box 1, folder 7) – and it was also far more abundantly funded: 'I bought a good many antiquities for my Museum and Papa gave me 4000 francs for its support', he wrote to a friend from Naples (11 Feb. 1884: box 1, folder 7). Leland copied and deciphered hieroglyphics in the Louvre with the help of the young Egyptologist Georges Daressy (Osborne 1986: 47). In January 1884 the Stanfords visited Heinrich Schliemann and the renowned amateur archaeologist gave Leland a collection of 'little earthenware nuts with a hole bored through the centre' that he had excavated 'in the 6th city of Troy, at a depth of sixty-three feet from the surface'. Leland's 'tastes', as Henry Nash asserts, 'had made a great step from the arms and trophies of war of his earlier collection to these historical and ethnological antiquities' (Nash 1886: pt 3).

Carol Osborne rightly observes that 'it is difficult to predict which of a child's adolescent interests will take hold in maturity' (1986: 91) and Leland Stanford, Jr's death in Florence on 13 March 1884 poignantly forecloses such questions. The Stanfords created Leland Stanford Junior University and Museum as memorials to their cherished boy that institutionalized cultural transmission: 'the children of California shall be our children' (Elliott 1937: 13). In this circuit of cultural heritage the child's place is as much origin as telos: Leland's childhood collections of ancient things had not only served to educate this boy, providing a command of cultural inheritance to match his family's power and wealth, his education had also served to instruct his parents. The Stanfords encountered and claimed a cultured past together with and through the education of their 'darling boy'. Anne Higonnet describes how 'the personal art collection museum' of the late nineteenth century was 'born out of opposition to the national or municipal encyclopaedic museum' (2009: 9). For Jane Stanford, in contrast, what was most personal about the Leland Stanford, Jr Museum might well have been its encyclopaedic scope: the largest private museum in the world with the phrase 'progress and civilization' inscribed on the frieze and murals of Cyprus and Egypt flanking the door (Figure 15.4). This grand historical sweep marshalled the authority of the past to express personal memories and grief. Among the first arrangements the Stanfords made for the Leland Stanford, Jr Museum was the purchase of 5,000 duplicate items in the Metropolitan Museum's Cyprian collection, those treasures of antiquity Cesnola had shown Leland in 1882 (Osborne 1986: 49). Thus the museum sought to transmit cultural heritage through the preservation and display of Leland's

Figure 15.4 Leland Stanford, Jr Museum in 1905. It was at the time the largest private museum in the world, and the largest museum in the American west. Stanford Historical Photograph Collection, item no. 9721, Special Collections, Stanford University Library.

own cultural education: 'the various objects which Leland Stanford, Jr. first collected and which gave him his first idea of a Museum', his tutor explained, 'stand exactly as he left them in 1882. As he arranged the case so it will remain' (Nash 1886: pt 2). And the case does remain on display even though the 1906 San Francisco earthquake reduced much of the Leland Stanford, Jr Museum, including the Cyprian collection, to rubble – like the Ohlone villages, Waterloo, and Pompeii.

Notes

1 Werner Muensterberger's heavy-handed and reductionist account of collecting as a manifestation of oedipal desires and castration fears makes such arguments easy to dismiss (1994). For more nuanced accounts of collecting as an effort to deny the threats of castration and death see as well as Baudrillard's piece many of the other essays in Elsner and Cardinal's influential collection, especially those of Mieke Bal, John Forrester, and Naomi Schor (1994).
2 The documentation of the Stanford family collection is poor, but Herbert C. Nash does document 'several Indian mortars and pestles dug up at Palo Alto' (1886: pt 2). The Stanford University Archeology Center has 11 items whose provenance can definitely be traced to Leland, Jr, including six lithic mortars and pestles: Object IDs 15112, 15114, 15118, 15119, 15120, 15121.

3 This version comes from Herbert C. Nash, the boy's tutor, who was hired by Jane Stanford during this period in Italy. Nash's employment did not begin until after this visit to Pompeii, so his account here stems from family lore, or a sense that it is what his employers would want to hear, rather than from direct observation. Nash was much valued by the Stanfords and remained immensely loyal to the family. After Leland, Jr's death he served as personal secretary to Governor Stanford and later as Librarian for Stanford University. He produced the memorial volume for Leland Stanford, Jr and the first catalogue for the Leland Stanford, Jr Museum.

References

Anon. (1876) Centennial Letter. *New Hampshire Sentinel.*

Appadurai, A. (1986) Introduction: Commodities and the Politics of Value. In *The Social Life of Things: Commodities in Cultural Perspective.* New York: Cambridge University Press.

Arendt, H. (1969) Introduction: Walter Benjamin: 1892–1940, in W. Benjamin *Illuminations: Essays and Reflections*, first edition, New York: Schocken Books, pp. 1–58.

Bancroft, H.H. (1952) *History of the Life of Leland Stanford, a Character Study*, Oakland, CA: Biobooks.

Bancroft, H.H. *et al.* (1874) *The Native Races of the Pacific States of North America*, New York: D. Appleton and Company.

Baudrillard, J. (1994) The System of Collecting. In J. Elsner and R. Cardinal, eds. *The Cultures of Collecting*, London: Reaktion Books, pp. 7–24.

Bean, L.J. ed. (1994) *The Ohlone Past and Present: Native Americans of the San Francisco Bay Region*, Menlo Park, CA: Ballena Press.

Benjamin, W. (1955) *Schriften*, Frankfurt am Main: Suhrkamp Verlag.

Benjamin, W. (1969) *Illuminations: Essays and Reflections*, first edition, New York: Schocken.

Berner, B. (1935) *Mrs. Leland Stanford: An Intimate Account*, Stanford, CA: Stanford University Press.

Black, J. (2003) *Italy and the Grand Tour*, New Haven, CT: Yale University Press.

Brinkley, D. (2009) *The Wilderness Warrior: Theodore Roosevelt and the Crusade for America*, New York: Harper Collins.

Clark, G.T. (1931) *Leland Stanford, War Governor of California, Railroad Builder and Founder of Stanford University*, Stanford, CA: Stanford University Press.

Clifford, J. (1988) *The Predicament of Culture: Twentieth-Century Ethnography, Literature, and Art*, Cambridge, MA: Harvard University Press.

Corn, W. (1997) Art Matronage in Post-Victorian America. In *Cultural Leadership in America: Art Matronage and Patronage.* Fenway Court Series. Boston, MA: Isabella Stewart Gardner Museum, pp. 19–24.

Dulles, F.R. (1964) *Americans Abroad: Two Centuries of European Travel*, Ann Arbor: University of Michigan Press.

Elliott, O.L. (1937) *Stanford University: The First Twenty-Five Years*, Stanford, CA: Stanford University Press.

Elsner, J. and Cardinal, R. eds. (1994) *The Cultures of Collecting*, London: Reaktion Books.

Ferris, G.T. (1877) *Gems of the Centennial Exhibition: Consisting of Illustrated Descriptions of Objects of an Artistic Character, in the Exhibits of the United States, Great Britain, France, Spain, Italy, Germany, Belgium, Norway, Sweden, Denmark, Hungary, Russia, Japan, China, Egypt, Turkey, India, etc., etc., at the Philadelphia International Exhibition of 1876*, New York: Appleton.

Higonnet, A. (2009) *A Museum of One's Own: Private Collecting, Public Gift*, Pittsburgh, PA: Periscope Pub.

Ingram, J.S. (1876) *Centennial Exposition Described and Illustrated: Being a Concise and Graphic Description of this Grand Enterprise Commemorative of the First Centenary [!] of American Independence*, Philadelphia: Hubbard Bros.

James, H. (1877) *The American*, Boston, MA: Osgood; 1994. *The American*, Public Domain Books.

Johnston, T. (1998) Those Who Came Before. *Stanford Magazine*. Available at: http://www.stanfordalumni.org/news/magazine/1998/marapr/articles/before.html.

Macleod, D.S. (2008) *Enchanted Lives, Enchanted Objects: American Women Collectors and the Making of Culture, 1800–1940*, Berkeley: University of California Press.

Muensterberger, W. (1994) *Collecting: An Unruly Passion: Psychological Perspectives*, Princeton, NJ: Princeton University Press.

Nagel, G.W. (1985) *Iron Will: the Life and Letters of Jane Stanford*, Stanford, CA: Stanford Alumni Association.

Nash, H.C. (1884) *In Memoriam, Leland Stanford, Jr.*, [San Francisco?]: n.p.

Nash, H.C. (1886) *The Leland Stanford Jr. Museum: Origin and Description*, Palo Alto, CA: The Museum.

Nora, P. (1989) Between Memory and History: Les Lieux de Mémoire. *Representations*, (26), pp. 7–24.

Osborne, C.M. (1986) *Museum Builders in the West: the Stanfords as Collectors and Patrons of Art, 1870–1906*, Stanford, CA: Stanford University Museum of Art, Stanford University.

Powers, S. and Powell, J.W. (1877) *Tribes of California*, Washington, DC: Govt. print off.

Prodger, P. (2003) *Time Stands Still: Muybridge and the Instantaneous Photography Movement*, Stanford, CA: Iris & B. Gerald Cantor Center for Visual Arts at Stanford University.

Roach, J. (2010) Performance: The Blunders of Orpheus. *PMLA*, 125(4), pp. 1078–86.

Solnit, R. (2003) *River of Shadows: Eadweard Muybridge and the Technological Wild West*, New York: Viking.

Stanford, Jr, L. (1871–93) Leland Stanford, Jr Papers. Special Collections, Stanford University Library.

Stanford Family Library (1795–1902) Special Collections, Stanford University.

Stewart, S. (1993) *On Longing: Narratives of the Miniature, the Gigantic, the Souvenir, the Collection*, Durham, NC: Duke University Press Books.

Strazdes, D. (1994) The Visual Rhetoric of the Leland Stanford Mansion in Sacramento. *Stanford University Museum of Art Journal*, 14–15, pp. 13–24.

Strazdes, D. (2001) The Millionaire's Palace: Leland Stanford's Commission for Pottier & Stymus in San Francisco. *Winterthur Portfolio*, 36(4), pp. 213–43.

Trennert, Jr, R.A. (1974) A Grand Failure: The Centennial Indian Exhibition of 1876. *Prologue*, 6(2), pp. 118–29.

Tutorow, N.E. (1971) *Leland Stanford: Man of Many Careers*, Menlo Park, CA: Pacific Coast Publishers.

Twain, M. (1867–68) The Holy Land Excursion. Letter from 'Mark Twain'. Special Travelling Correspondent to the Alta. *Daily Alta Californian*.

Wenzel, C. (1940) Finding Facts about the Stanfords in the California State Library: An Address before the California Historical Society Delivered at the Stanford Mansion in Sacramento on June 16, 1940. *California Historical Society Quarterly*, 19(3), pp. 245–55.

Winnicott, D.W. (1971) *Playing and Reality*, New York: Basic Books.

Winterer, C. (2007) *The Mirror of Antiquity: American Women and the Classical Tradition, 1750–1900*, Ithaca, NY: Cornell University Press.

Zegas, J.B. (1976) North American Indian Exhibit at the Centennial Exposition. *Curator*, 19(2), pp. 162–73.

Chapter 16

Home and hearth
Representing childhood in
fin de siècle Russia

Rebecca Friedman

Over the past decade or so, there has been increasing interest in the habits, values and practices of everyday life in tsarist, Soviet and post-Soviet Russia. Collaborative projects, conferences and scholarly endeavours have sprung up in Russia, in the United States, in Europe and in the interstices of cyberspace. In a number of notable cases, scholars who spent their childhoods in Moscow, St Petersburg or elsewhere in Russia are documenting for outside observers – including scholars, students and communities – how they, and those around them, grew up and managed in the everyday under the harsh conditions of Soviet – and in some cases post-Soviet Russian – life. One central aspect of these explorations is childhood. From Ilya Utekhin's St Petersburg *kommunalka* (communal apartment) on-line museum, to Olga Matich's virtual St Petersburg entitled *Mapping St Petersburg*, to the Russian State University of the Humanities' (Moscow) project on representations of childhood, viewers and readers are invited in to learn, remember and understand the contours of childhoods and daily lives of the past.[1]

Each of these projects invites us to contemplate Russian, Soviet and/or post-Soviet cultural heritage, whether through the spatial narrative of life in St Petersburg as seen through the window of a *tramvai* right before the revolution or within a virtual apartment museum, which includes audio, video and textual materials of Soviet and post-Soviet daily life. In these two cases – the Map of St Petersburg trope and the Virtual Communal Apartment (both projects funded by the National Endowment of the Humanities Digital Humanities Initiative) – the websites become a prism through which visitors can reflect upon the meanings of the past for the present. Ilya Utekhin's *kommunalka* is worth describing further. The Virtual Communal Apartment is itself an exhibitionary space, 'an on-line ethnographic museum'. Utekhin, now an anthropologist at Colgate University in the United States, himself grew up in a St Petersburg *kommunalka* – a very widespread communist era domestic experiment where many families of residents shared common spaces (kitchen, washroom, bathroom) and individual families had their own room (usually one, but sometimes two), for sleeping, etc. In the virtual museum, viewers are able to create their own personalized excursions through the communal apartment, encouraging users to integrate their own selves within the world of the past. In the interviews on-line Utekhin mentions his own son's childhood experiences in the apartment.

Childhood, as a means of reflecting on past spaces and practices, may signify for viewers both a nostalgia for what is lost and an embracing of the present moment. There is a link, however tentative, between the experiences and representations of childhood and modernity in these exhibitions. Viewers might ask themselves, how can Russian society remake itself in the twenty-first century into a modern, 'normal' European state? Childhood, it seems, is one key place to start. Moreover, by creating exhibitionary spaces of everyday life of the past and now its cultural heritage, post-Soviet audiences are invited to reflect upon the meaning of the past in the present. And, in the Russian case, this is no small task as society is still grappling with how to imagine itself in a post-Soviet world. This current nostalgia for Soviet childhood itself is part of a larger phenomenon in Russia today. Scholars have mused about this for some time since the collapse of the communist regime, pointing out that 'nostalgia is a longing for a home that no longer exists or has never existed' (Boym 2001: xiii). This, no doubt, is true for many today as it was for those in the past. Just as members of the waning elite at the end of the nineteenth century looked to the manor house with nostalgic tears, so too do many today imagine themselves longing for the Soviet past. Childhoods are central to these longings. There is much work to be done on the present-day nostalgia for the imperial past. It manifests, at least in part, in a longing for the luxury and space of the early nineteenth and eighteenth centuries. Vladimir Nabokov alludes to this in his *Speak Memory: An Autobiography Revisited* (1967).

Childhood, modernity and material culture in the early twentieth century

This search for meaning in the past, present and future through representations of childhood is not unique to our contemporary times. These linkages between child-hood and modernity can be found in the final years of tsarist rule, when Russia seemed to be embarking on a new, more modern, path. Just as in the present moment, child-hood is displayed in a museum in Ukraine called the Museum of Soviet Childhood[2] or in a virtual museum on-line, as a measure of social progress and nostalgic reflec-tion upon the past, so was it at the start of the last century. In Kiev in 1910, there appeared a large-scale exhibition on 'Childhood and Work', which reflected growing concerns about how to integrate notions of childhood and children themselves into Russia's rapidly industrializing urban environments. The two-month long exhibition in Kiev focused on nursery education in one of the 'centres of the pre-revolutionary kindergarten movement'. Childhood was attracting increasing amounts of attention among professionals, artists and ordinary citizens of the Russian empire, in Kiev and elsewhere. This exhibition reified the increasingly popular association between 'the appropriate treatment of children' and civilized values (Kelly 2007: 25). By display-ing childhood for all to see, professionals were asserting how past and present prac-tices reflect future achievements. Several observers of this display highlighted the centrality of children and their proper childhoods to Russia's modern achievements. For example, in a time of tremendous economic and social upheaval, Russian pro-fessionals – lawyers, doctors, teachers, journalists, among others – understood that children were central to Russia's success on the European stage. Against the backdrop of Russia's rapid urbanization and industrialization in the final decade or so of the nineteenth century, professionals understood that childhood had to be safeguarded to keep pace with Europe. This meant, for example, both highlighting the innocence and unique nature of childhood and formulating laws and theories about protecting children from the onslaught of industrial change, whether through labour laws or medical practice (Kelly 2007: 25–6).

As scholar Catriona Kelly observes, in her magnum opus on Russian/Soviet childhood, there emerged, both within the exhibition and within society at large, a 'cult of childhood' in the decade or so before the Bolsheviks' rise to power (Kelly 2007: 25). This so-called 'cult of childhood', at least according to one contemporary observer, 'is the glory and the distinguishing characteristic of our age' (Kelly 2007: 25). At the start of the twentieth century, this focus on childhood included many areas, from an interest in the child's unique abilities and strengths, to on-going discussions of children's art or child psychology. These emergent emphases manifested in numerous ways in varying fields, from educational advocates who wanted more 'child centered' education to those in the legal profession who advocated for children's rights (Kelly 2007: 25). Although, ultimately, many of these struggles, including those for legal rights, especially those that were not premised upon the power of the patriarch, would not be satisfied until 1917, discussions and definitions about what was seen as a desirable childhood were already coalescing. At the time of the 'Children and Work' Exhibition, childhood was being imagined as a distinct phase of life and the treatment of children themselves as a reflection of the civilized nature of Russian society writ large. Although normative understandings of childhood would later change with the Soviet state-sponsored campaigns, the central importance of childhood as a reflection of national and imperial progress in Russia remained a constant.

The early twentieth century was, of course, the age of mass politics, mass movement and mass society across Europe; Russia was no exception, albeit on a smaller scale. In the final decades of tsarist rule, Russia found itself in the midst of the process of urbanization and industrialization and all that entailed in everyday life. As increasing numbers of Russians migrated to the cities and took up residence in urban dwellings (and, of course, retained ties to the village), they found themselves embroiled in a growing print culture and a burgeoning consumer society, replete with new notions of childhood and intimate life. Even as Russia was confronted by wars and a series of revolutions from the 1890s through the 1910s, writers, readers and advertisers were preoccupied with creating a bourgeois European aesthetic when it came to the domestic realm and to children within its boundaries.

The proper raising of children stood at the centre of debates and discussions about Russia's path to modernity. Professionals of various kinds – from educators to lawyers to psychiatrists to journalists – advised and prescribed notions of proper childhood for those families who were newly arrived to Russia's capital cities (Kelly 2007: 25). This preoccupation is reflected in the quantity of ink spilled in debates over the question of how to raise children and how to understand childhood. These debates about the meaning and content of a 'children's world' manifested in a number of arenas, including discussions of psychology, leisure pursuits and pedagogy. Perhaps the very diversity of opinion (questions of rebellion versus autonomy or growth of consumer culture versus free artistic expression) was itself an indication of how central childhood was to debates about modern society and daily life. Despite the divergence of opinions on how to move forward, most of those people engaged in questions about the emergence of a 'children's world' agreed that 'children's needs and psychic world were different from those of adults' (Kelly 2007: 57).[3]

It was precisely in this era that reformers and activists and intellectuals fostered a new emphasis on childhood as a distinct stage of life (as opposed to imagining children as little adults) (Kelly 2007: 25–60). This vision of childhood had multiple manifestations in these turbulent decades. Given the emerging consensus that children's needs and 'psychic world' were distinct from that of the adults around them, there was a collective sense that children should 'live in safety, steeping themselves in imaginative experiences, and gaining an education' (Kelly 2001: 178). At the same time, industrialization brought with it new factory-made goods and new notions of consumption and shopping. In Moscow and St Petersburg, shopping became a leisure activity – at least for the reasonably well-off – for the first time. Many members of the urban, middle classes, looked to their children (and whether their needs were met) as a measure of their own material success. Children – and fantasies about childhood – occupied centre stage for the new Russian adult consumer at the turn of the century. This new consumer culture aimed at children was exemplified by the appearance of specialist stores with goods for children, whether clothing, toys, products for the nursery or otherwise. The material culture of childhood – objects produced with a child user in mind (whether toys or clothes or furniture) – expanded as one aspect of this growing and modern consumer culture. Although discussions in the Russian press covered many aspects of children's lives, one particular area of interest within lifestyle magazines was the decoration of a child's domestic space. This chapter will explore, in particular, popular journals of the era in order to understand how representations of childhood, and especially those within the familial and domestic arenas, were created and employed by new urban actors, whether journalists, advertisers or others, who were implicated in the creation of a modern consumer society (even if only rhetorically and/or for the privileged few). In doing so, a new cultural heritage of childhood was created through new forms of material culture and aspirations about what childhood entailed. This new culture would work its way, decades and decades later, into new exhibitionary spaces – ideologically transformed in the Soviet and post-Soviet contexts – representing children's cultural heritage. However, in the context of the early twentieth century, few Russian families could actually afford to acquire many of these new objects.

It is worth noting that although Russia experienced the drive toward modernity later than many nations in Europe, and inevitably differently, Russia's embracing of childhood as a marker of modernity resonated with trends to the west. This was especially true in regards to ideologies governing the domestic realm of Russia's newly urbanized, educated elites. Of course, as we shall see, such bourgeois-like aesthetics of childhood and hearth, did not survive intact after 1917. In an era of the overt politicization of daily life, childhood and home were at the centre of communist plans to transform society from the bottom up. Their success, however, is another story.

Women's magazines and representations of modern childhood

Women's magazines, including those with an emphasis on child rearing, saw a boom in the early twentieth century (on women journalists and women's publishing, see Norton and Gheith (2001)). Although the majority of the women's publications hoped either to politicize women or to inspire them to fashion (see Ruane 2009), there were those that showcased an attachment to the domestic realm and its internal order both in terms of the rearing of children and the cleanliness of the space. In particular, the ones that were more focused on daily life and aimed at the middle classes included most prominently *Zhurnal dlia khoziaek* or *Journal for Homemakers* (1912–26, with a hiatus during the civil war), *Zhurnal dlia zhenshchin* or *Journal for Women (*1914–26, with a hiatus during the civil war) and *Zhenshchina* or *Woman* (1907–09 and 1913–16). All three journals had columns or sections expressly reserved for homemakers and for mothers, who were to raise modern children to participate in the newly urbanized environment in which they lived. To do this, they were required to consult scientific experts, sometimes clearly engaged in a pseudo science, and learn about up-to-date domestic technology and childcare wisdom. The stakes in organizing the home and raising children in such a way were high and thus the power granted to women was significant.

By interrogating the texts that represent and prescribe norms of childhood within the home, this chapter highlights how private, intimate, familial space was defined by actors outside of its boundaries, whether advertisers, advice columnists or scientific experts. Norms of childhood were not – or not only – confined to the domestic, and beholden to inward concerns. Instead, childhood was imagined as a reflection of, and in interaction with, the world outside – whether the market place, the department store or the homemaker's magazine. Domestic space emerges as a site 'for public and cultural interaction, a space which outsiders or strangers can enter, a site of encounter' (Bryden and Floyd 1999: 12–13). Within this space, childhood and its representations remained central.[4]

Articles and columns within Russian women's publications decried the inadequate job that parents were doing in raising their children. Rather than suggesting that institutions, whether schools or institutes, take over though, experts called anew on parents to retool themselves and create an appropriate environment at home where modern, appropriate understandings of childhood could flourish. There was a growing consensus about the ways in which children's upbringing was in a state of flux, perhaps crisis. 'Today's school system is far from adequate . . . even though parents increasingly rely on it.' Schools, this expert states in an 1883 issue of the magazine *Drug Zhenshchin* (*Women's Friend*), do not impart to children 'a firmness of characters, a strength of conviction, correct human relations with those close to you . . . These are qualities which should be the basis of both *vospitanie* (upbringing)'. Such qualities, the article continues, 'in a person must be fostered at home and in one's family'. Ultimately, this particular article argues that families are not doing their jobs, and urges parents to read, inform themselves and work harder to properly raise their children and respect their 'fragility' and show constant respect for 'their individuality'. There is the belief that children are yet uncorrupted and that their innocence should be preserved: 'Children, like unspoiled nature, are fair/just and sincere.' Yet, he/she needs limits and must not be allowed to become 'a small tyrant' at home (July 1883: 111–19). Parents were directly implicated in the failure to provide the necessary conditions for their children. A 'dirty' and 'noisy' household and a 'disorderly' room will breed discontent and 'pessimism' among children, one expert advises (*Zhurnal dlia khoziaek* 15 Apr. 1913: 3). What these types of warnings implied, was that missteps in creating a proper domestic order could have grave consequences for children and others within.

These critiques were not incidental. One of the main foci of advice literature and prescriptive magazines was hygiene, especially when it came to children, including cleanliness and healthfulness. In the inaugural edition of the publication *Woman*, a magazine with multiple sections ('Women's World', 'Woman-Mother', 'Woman-Homemaker', 'Woman-Worker', etc.), the editors featured an article in the 'Woman-Homemaker' section entitled 'The Dread of Air'. The author explicates the urgent need for fresh air wafting through the corridors of any home: 'Homemakers do not understand what clean air is, how rich it is in oxygen and how important it is for our health and our internal order and external cleanliness' (*Zhenshchina* 15 Dec. 1907: 1). This, and many other pieces, urged women to educate themselves on the latest domestic scientific principles and to appreciate the connection between 'fresh air', moral standards and a healthy childhood.

Members of the family, including most prominently the children, were to be fed healthy and sanitary food prepared by the mother in the kitchen. The kitchen in women's magazines, thus, held a place of particular prominence, when it came to gadgetry and domestic science. In an early issue of *Zhenshchina* there appeared a lengthy description of how to set up and care for the kitchen. All of the advice, both in terms of which material objects to purchase and how to approach food preparation, centred on health, technology and the modern. With the enumeration of each machine required of a modern kitchen – whether a meat grinder or a 'press' to clean potatoes – authors placed a real emphasis on hygiene and efficiency. The writers decried that 'all serious housewives must possess the correct implements and tools in the kitchen to run a proper household' (*Zhenshchina* 1 Jan. 1908: 4). Prominent among the objects required for the kitchen were certain types of dishes, pots and pans. Authors advised, for instance, that women purchase 'cast iron dishes' because of their ease of cleaning (see Cohen 2009). They added that 'the bright, sparkling copper and pewter dishes of the past inevitably were more ornate than today's kitchenware', but today's were easier to clean and thus more 'hygienic' and appropriate (*Zhenshchina* 1 Jan. 1908: 4). The achievement of this domestic order included purchasing power.

Advice and direction about the creation of a hygienic atmosphere outside the kitchen included special objects and items targeted specifically for children's use.

When it came to children, the stakes were always raised. One such example, and there are many, was a series of linked articles in *Journal for Homemakers*, on the 'children's room and its impact on the well-being of children'. In this 1913 issue, the editors focused on the relationship between a properly ordered and hygienic domestic life and a child's emotional and psychological well-being. They consulted experts, parents and readers, who wrote in to the publications with their own experiences. In this issue (and elsewhere), both writers and readers engaged the language of science to express concerns and offer instructions regarding the child's room. A scientifically based vocabulary underpinned the emphasis on sunshine and airiness. In one particular column on proper care for the child's room, the author indicates that according to 'scientific studies' moisture in the air could lead to the growth of bacteria and poor health.

Many of the articles and letters emphasized the close connection between the decorum of the child's space and his/her physical and emotional well-being (*Zhurnal dlia khoziaek* 15 Apr. 1913: 3–4). In response to a question sent in by a reader, one author pointed out, in particular, the connection between the aesthetic charms and decoration of a child's room and the happiness of the child. He wrote:

> Simplicity, hygiene and the absence of superfluous things are essential for a child's room . . . Everything in a child's room should be light and subtle. You do not need heavy furniture . . . You should be able to put your feet up comfortably on the furniture and all must be bright . . . Any pictures must be carefully chosen and must be simply and aesthetically pleasing . . . Toys must inspire the children to orderliness and caution . . . All must understand that the child's room must be the sunniest and brightest room in the home. Where there is sun – there is no illness, say the Japanese.
>
> (*Zhurnal dlia khoziaek* 15 Apr. 1913: 20)

Experts, in these publications, frequently ruminated over the set-up and meaning of a child's domestic space. This was the most crucial task for any homemaker, including purchasing the correct objects and placing them in the most advantageous position.

Although there are many examples, in a 1918 issue of *Journal for Homemakers*, scientists and other 'experts' compile didactic advice in a piece called: 'The Hygiene of a Child's Room'. The exact reasoning goes as follows: 'A child must occupy the absolute best room in the house . . . From a psychological perspective, sun in a child's room is even more important . . . a dark room would cause sadness in the heart of a child' (*Zhurnal dlia khoziaek* Oct./Nov. 1918: 1–2). The advice continued to suggest that families acquire appropriately styled furniture and toys in order to safeguard a child's future well-being.

Aesthetics, too, were part of the equation. Sleeping quarters were particularly implicated in these discussions. One such article contained an illustration of a suite of rooms: the 'bedroom', 'the sleeping room', the 'children's room' (all from *Zhenshchina* 'Woman-Homemaker' 1 Jan. 1908: 9–10). The 'children's room' does not seem to be a sleeping quarters, but rather contains chairs and a table and some toys on the floor. When setting up the sleeping quarters for children, readers wrote in to warn homemakers that they must be aware of the 'evil/harmful' (*vrednyi*) old customs that were long followed vis-à-vis the set-up of a house, and especially the bedroom. An eye for the future and the modern is central here. 'The custom of making the most spacious and light room for the living room and the darkest and most crowded for the bedroom' is one of those old customs. 'This is a habit of all people across classes – poor and wealthy . . . an intransigent custom' and sometimes a destructive one, as the following expert surmised: 'During dreams a person needs fresh air more than anything . . . because of the kind of breathing we do in our sleep' (*Zhenshchina* 'Woman-Homemaker' section 15 Dec. 1907: 5). Children, it seemed, were meant to sleep in the brightest and airiest room in the house. Experts believed that a well-equipped, clean room was an indicator of healthfulness and modernity. In addition, there had to be enough space to allow for proper distance and healthfulness. Propriety was clearly at risk:

> You must arrange it [sleeping quarters] so that not too, too many people sleep in a single bedroom. In general, each adult person must have more or less 24 kv. Funta [24 sq. feet] and each child 16 [sq. feet]. Therefore in a room that is 10 feet long and 10 feet wide, you should sleep no more than 4 adults or 6 children.
> (*Zhenshchina* 'Woman-Homemaker' section 15 Dec. 1907: 8)

Interestingly enough in these discussions about how to arrange a child's domestic space, there is no indication of the gender of the child, either in the textual descriptions or the visual representations.

Readers frequently wrote in to express their concerns about the relationship between the interiors of their homes and the health of their children. In one 'Letters from Readers' column in *Journal for Homemakers*, a reader wrote in and asked: 'How do you design your home so that you feel good and cosy in it, so that you establish a corner where you can hide and forget about anything unpleasant?' (*Zhurnal dlia khoziaek* 15 Apr. 1913: 19–20). This exchange is fascinating because the reader poses the question of how to establish a home that is shielded from the outside world at the very moment that the marketplace intruded upon the home in the form of advertisements, consumer products and in its advice columns. The editors' answer to this query revolved around two characteristics: cosiness and beauty. The goal is to achieve 'a harmony in the room'. It is therefore 'very important to choose the tone and colour of the room. The tone and the colour are the two most important elements in setting the mood of the room'. On the question of 'tone' the editorial response included the following:

> The general rule is that the bedrooms and the child's room must have a bright tone. The office and living room can be darker, the dining room should be nicely done in middle tones. But, I myself personally prefer the dining room to be darker shades.
> (*Zhurnal dlia khoziaek* 15 Apr. 1913: 19–20)

There also appeared a lot of advice on how to decorate the walls and which colours to choose. Readers advised that the bedroom should be blue-grey, the child's room should be a soft pink/rose, the living room should be dark red, the office dark grey, and the dining room should be brown, the colour of oak. Moreover, 'the furniture must be the simplest you can find . . . and the curtains, the least likely to collect dust on them' (*Zhurnal dlia khoziaek* 15 Apr. 1913: 19–20). The curtains, like the rest of the interior, were required to be clean, hygienic and dust free. These are all markers of a pan-European and US movement toward a modern aesthetic that favoured simplicity over decorativeness due to, at least in part, the practicality of dust collection. Furniture styles, too, were dictated by health concerns. Furniture in the new style was made from wood so as to collect less dust. To ensure these practices, advertisers created ads for products on the back pages of these publications.

Women's magazine prescriptions for hygienic childhood included advertisements for childcare products and objects for children. Advertisers and others who occupied the emergent civil sphere of the city were weighing in on how to raise future generations. Given concerns over health and hygiene so characteristic of the age, many of the products for children highlighted the need to create proper personal hygiene habits, from children's soaps to toothpaste, to lines of products aimed at baby care (these ads can be found in any number of publications, including the ones under discussion here: *Zhenshchina*; *Zhurnal dlia zhenshchin*; *Zhurnal dlia khoziaka*; *Zhenskii mir*, etc.). Although such ads appear in a number of women's publications across the spectrum, one in particular stands out. Each issue of the upscale and glossy lifestyle magazine *Capital City and Countryside* over its four-year run, contains a wealth of advertisements for modern products in general, some of which were aimed at children. Of products on display, a significant number were aimed at children, whether shampoo, soap or clothing stores. This magazine offered a future of prosperity, technology and modernity of everyday life, so much touted and echoed in women's publications of the age, which were magazines aimed at women of the middle classes who were themselves in charge of creating hygienic and modern homes and childhoods for their families. Clothing, too, was another arena of consumption for children. Children's clothing was integral to this new consumer emphasis. In some cases, magazines had ads for clothing stores that featured children's clothing and in other cases there were simply pictures of children in the latest fashions, sometimes imported and other times native to Russia. A typical example of this can be found in the inaugural issue of *Woman*, which contains an entire section called 'Latest Fashions'. Within this section, pictures of children's outfits, segregated by age, featured quite prominently. One dress was for a girl aged 8–10 years and another 4–5 (*Zhenshchina* 'Posledniia Modyi' No. 1, 1907/8: 10–11). The proliferation of advertisements for children's products stretched well beyond any one glossy publication, to include examples in many of the women's magazines discussed above. These magazines routinely contained numerous ads for children's soaps, clothing, furniture or specialty shops. In this sense, Russia was in step with much of the rest of Europe.

Throughout Europe, by the middle of the nineteenth century, it was a common expectation that there would be a separate space within homes for children to learn, play and to sleep. Whether in Paris or London or urban centres elsewhere in Europe, child-size objects could be purchased to fill those spaces (Flanders 2003: 43, 70). The nature of those objects, from furniture to linens, was not incidental. Children's spaces and possessions had to be clean, orderly and hygienic. Not simply a matter of ridding the house of dust, hygiene concerns included the 'extermination of vermin . . . the protection from dirt of various kinds . . . the proper regulation of light' and the proper placement of objects in the home (Flanders 2003: 67). These same concerns preoccupied professionals within Russia at the start of the twentieth century. As Russians made their way to Moscow and St Petersburg, they found themselves influenced by a bourgeois aesthetic that became integrated into Russian domestic culture.

Despite the fact that most Russians at the turn of the century had no material access to the domestic objects required of familial life, writers and journalists continued to present their readers with this new set of consumer desires. In the Russian context, timing was everything. The advertisers and editors/writers intruded on the domestic sphere, just as it was being established in Russia's new urban centres. And, although this new domestic aesthetic was an unattainable fantasy for many, the very image itself – of a bourgeois hygienic home and childhood – remained fixed in the Russian imagination. When the Bolsheviks came to power in 1917 and attacked head on bourgeois practices, they found a nascent consumer culture reflected, at least in part, in normative definitions of the domestic realm and childhood. The creation of revolutionary ideas about family, home and everyday life included the rejection and ultimate condemnation of these norms. In this sense, Bolsheviks were to overturn this emergent heritage of childhood as they attempted to create a new one, more in line with socialist and communist ideals.

No set of norms, however, simply disappears overnight, even within a regime so committed to creating new Soviet men, women and children. As scholars have shown, and continue to show, the practices and ideologies surrounding late nineteenth-century childhood were difficult to erase completely, and experienced many rebirths over the course of the next century.[5] Yet, fundamentally, the Bolshevik project included, at least initially, an impulse to abolish the family unit and raise children for the state and of the state. The emphasis on childhood became less individualistic and more collective, in terms of education, leisure and everyday children's pursuits. In practical terms, however, it was to prove impossible to fully implement such Bolshevik ideologies.

Scholarship in recent years has emphasized the degree to which such consumer practices continued to resurface during the decades of communist rule, at some points more overtly than others, of course. Indeed despite the Bolsheviks' explicit goal of transforming domestic and familial practices to abolish the individual, 'private' home and family configuration, successes were only temporary (and indeed nominal) in this realm. The association between childhood, modernity and science of hygiene re-emerged with a vengeance after Stalin's death and especially in the early years of the highly politicized arena of the domestic sphere in the context of the Cold War. Susan Reid describes how 'the discipline of . . . domestic science' replete with an emphasis on hygiene and child-rearing took on new meaning at the height of the Cold War in the 1950s. Not only did the home occupy centre stage, but so did hygiene. Housewives, as they were called, were urged to pay close attention to 'domestic science' and 'the rules of food hygiene' as they fed their children (Reid and Crowley 2002: 229). Part of the Soviet effort to assert its place alongside, or ahead, of the United States included shaping the lives of Soviet children through hygienic domestic practices. The image of the Soviet Union was implicated in notions of childhood and the home. Images of childhood, home and modernity were, arguably, intertwined throughout the Soviet and now post-Soviet era.

The content and contours of children's material culture, and therefore the memorialization of childhood through cultural heritage objects and sites, has shifted across time and space, from the early twentieth century through to today. We have moved from the early emphasis on hygiene and taste within the individual family, to the more revolutionary ideals characteristic of the early Bolshevik era through late Soviet re-embracing of a more bourgeois, although officially collectivist, understanding and, finally, to the post-Soviet moment, with all of the contradictions that we find ourselves with today: at once materialist and nostalgic.

If the late tsarist era positioned childhood and the child in a modern context, in part, through the creation of a new material culture of childhood, then toys are central to this story. Toys provide a telling case study for the larger narrative of children's constantly shifting material world. The story is a fairly predictable one. In the pre-revolutionary age there was an increased emphasis on making toys available and on creating the consumer desire to possess multiple types of toys (through shop window displays and advertisements). By contrast, in the early Soviet period, there was a suspicion of 'frivolous' items intended specifically 'for the young' and so even the more well-off families had fewer items available for children to play with. Although it is worth noting that in Moscow's Toy Museum – an institution that was established in Moscow in 1918 and moved in 1921 to the town of Sergiyev-Posad, on Moscow's Golden Ring, because of the town's role in late nineteenth-century toy production (including the famous Russian wooden nesting matryoshka doll) – there were often 'displays of suitably hygienic and edifying toys', but individual families had scarce access to such objects (Kelly 2007: 443). During the period of the New Economic Policy (1921–28), when private capitalistic initiatives were officially sanctioned and consumer products began to reappear, on a small scale, more toys saw the light of day. Under Stalin, though, the pendulum swung drastically in the other direction, and the everyday scarcity impacted children's material world. After the Second World War, the so-called 'toy famine' subsided (Kelly 2007: 445). In each mini-era these objects and the memory of them take on new meaning. Today, in the post-Soviet era, where society continues to actively wrestle with the past, there have appeared several museums (including those virtual ones discussed at the start of this chapter) which struggle with how to present childhood and children's heritage as a reflection of the past and as a statement about the present and the future direction of post-Soviet society.

Post-Soviet realities and representations of childhood: the cultural heritage piece

How is childhood of the past imagined and represented today? Is it commodified or (re)presented in a way that reminds us of the pre-Soviet past? What do the contemporary projects tell us about how it has been remade, at least in part, through a kind of bittersweet nostalgia that combines a longing for the past with an awareness of its remoteness? One such manifestation of this tension, perhaps, is the opening of 'The Museum of Soviet Childhood' in Sevastopol in the Black Sea Region, which was reported on *Euronews*. On its website, the creators of the museum explain that the games are from the Soviet era, which in general tended to be both educational in nature and functional in appearance, and cost only 15 kopeks, the price of a game in Soviet times. (Visitors are even provided with Soviet-era coins to insert in the machines in order to play.) The website promises: 'The joy of playing a game on an arcade machine is no longer a matter of the past: the twelve arcade machines in question are not museum exhibits but functioning machines. One can buy a token – the cost 0.5 hrivna – and remember his childhood.'[6]

The children's objects themselves, in addition to the video games, are meant to elicit positive sentiment about the past. Whether 'old open reel and cassette recorders, or vinyl disks', or replicas of Kalashnikov machine guns (a popular toy for boys in the Soviet period) all of the museum's objects are meant to inspire audiences of adults to recall their childhoods and all to reflect nostalgically on the past. This is not a museum aimed at children, but one for adults who want to remember their past. The museum's creator is not subtle about this goal. The creator and owner of *Lukomoire* park, where the museum resides, Nikolay Pomogalov reports on the website that:

> There are a lot of museums that expose the Soviet totalitarianism and negative sides of the Soviet way of live, but I believe that our life also had good sides that we are nostalgic about. I can read it in the eyes of our visitors. Moreover, some donate us pieces from the Soviet times, things from their youth and childhood. Every day we have more and more new exhibits. I didn't expect that the idea would have such a success.[7]

Whether represented in a 2012 Museum of Childhood or a 1910 exhibition about children and work, the displays concerning dominant cultural norms of childhood continue to insist that audiences reflect upon their lives and values and continue to reflect society's view of itself. The nostalgia that adult viewers might feel today as they put their hands on a Soviet-era joy stick or the pride that passers-by sensed as they gazed on the 1910 display, underline the fact that childhood – its meanings and its memories – have played an integral part in how Russian, Soviet and post-Soviet actors have imagined themselves and their place in the world.

Notes

1 On the Virtual Communal Apartment, see http://kommunalka.colgate.edu/index.cfm; on Mapping St Petersburg see http://petersburg.berkeley.edu/index.html; and on the project in Moscow see http://childcult.rsuh.ru/section.html?id=8640.
2 http://www.lukomorie.net.ua/index.php/en/museum/museum-of-soviet-childhood.
3 Kelly has an excellent and extended discussion of these debates and divergences in chapter 1 of *Children's World* (Kelly 2007).
4 On this see the work of Jeremy Aynsley, especially the issue of the *Journal of Design History* devoted to domestic interiors, with some emphasis on the role that magazines played (Aynsley and Berry 2005).
5 There is a growing body of scholarship on domestic interiors during the Soviet era. See, for instance, the work of Susan Reid, among others.
6 http://www.lukomorie.net.ua/index.php/en/museum/museum-of-soviet-childhood.
7 http://www.lukomorie.net.ua/index.php/en/museum/museum-of-soviet-childhood. There is also a Museum of Soviet Arcade Games in Moscow. On this see: http://15kop.ru/en/.

References

Dom i khoziastvo
Drug Zhenshchin
   Issue 7: Jul. 1883.
Zhenshchina
   Issue 1: 15 Dec. 1907/8.
   Issue 2: 30 Dec. 1907/8.
   Issue 3: 1 Jan. 1908.
Zhurnal dlia khoziaek
   Issue 8: Apr. 15 1913.
   Issue 10–11: Oct./Nov. 1918.
Zhurnal dlia zhenshchin

Aynsley, J. and Berry, F. (eds) (2005) 'Publishing the Modern Home: Magazines and the Domestic Interior 1870–1965', *Journal of Design History* 18(1): 1–5.
Boym, S. (2001) *The Future of Nostalgia*, New York: Basic Books.
Brydon, J. and Floyd, I. (1999) *Domestic Space: Reading the Nineteenth Century Interior*, Manchester: Manchester University Press.
Cohen, D. (2009) *Household Gods: The British and their Possessions*, New Haven, CT: Yale University Press.
Flanders, J. (2003) *Inside the Victorian Home: A Portrait of Domestic Life in Victorian England*, New York and London: WW Norton.
Kelly, C. (2001) *Refining Russia: Advice Literature, Polite Culture, and Gender from Catherine to Yeltsin*, New York and London: Oxford.
Kelly, C. (2007) *Children's World: Growing Up in Russia, 1890–1991*, New Haven, CT: Yale University Press.
Norton, B. and Gheith, J. (2001) *An Improper Profession: Women, Gender, and Journalism in Late Imperial Russia*, Durham, NC: Duke University Press.
Reid, S. and Crowley, D. (2000) *Style and Socialism: Modernity and Material Culture in Post-War Eastern Europe*, London: Berg.
Reid, S. and Crowley, D. (2002) *Socialist Spaces: Sites of Everyday Life in the Eastern Bloc*, London: Berg.
Ruane, C. (2009) *The Empire's New Clothes*, New Haven, CT: Yale University Press.

Chapter 17

Material culture in North African children's play and toy heritage

Jean-Pierre Rossie

Introduction

A community's play and toy culture is part of the system by which its worldview and mode of life are transferred to new generations. In this sense, children's play and toy cultures worldwide belong to the heritage of humanity, both tangible and intangible heritage. The communicative role in the transmission of this cultural heritage occurs not only between adults and children, but also between children themselves, including from older to younger children. This communication includes the non-verbal and verbal transmission of knowledge, beliefs, attitudes, behaviour, skills, sensibilities and emotions. Communities are changing social groups and the speed of such changes, including to the experiences and play of children, has arguably increased in recent decades. In considering the play heritage of North African children, this chapter will argue that children's play activities and their toys are an excellent indicator of continuity and change in the broader socio-cultural environment.

North African children's play and toy heritages are clearly linked to the cultural and social contexts of the families and communities in which the children grow up. Many play and toy making activities are inspired by the adult world, stage familial realities and reflect children's participation in everyday life. Yet this does not mean that children remain passive in this process. On the contrary, they are interpreting the adult world in the light of the changes that more strongly affect North African families in villages and urban neighbourhoods. Close attention to the issue of creativity in play also reveals that children's conformity or non-conformity in relation to adult models varies from one playgroup to another, from one play activity to another and even between individual children. The utility and functionality of children's play is important in relation to their informal and formal training and integration into their family and society. However, the children whose games and toys I discuss do not consciously play to become socially adapted nor to gain skills, but engage in play for the well-being and pleasure it gives them.

In this chapter, some aspects of material culture in the play and toy making activities of children from Morocco and the Tunisian Sahara will be explored. In order to contextualize the play activities described, I commence with a discussion of socio-cultural aspects of children's play and toy cultures such as socialization, age, gender and children's relationships with their family and community. The ways in which children delineate spaces in their pretend games shall then be considered, followed by an overview of the toys they create for such play activities.

In these regions children's toys were – and in Moroccan rural areas still are – largely self-made toys often lasting only for the duration of play. Moreover, creating toys often signals the commencement of a game and it may happen that the playful destruction of the self-made toys ends the play activity. As toys are given meaning through their use in play settings, in this chapter toys will be analysed not solely as objects but also as instruments for playing.

Most of the material discussed here was collected through personal research in northern Africa over several decades.[1] This includes data obtained through fieldwork undertaken in the Tunisian Sahara (1975, 1977) and in Morocco (1992–2011). It was during my first fieldwork trip to the Ghrib in southern Tunisia that I became especially interested in children's games and toys. Later this developed into broader research on material, cultural and social aspects of North African children's toy and play cultures. While working from my hometown of Ghent in Belgium, I scrutinized the relevant bibliography and analysed the large collection of North African and Saharan toys in the Musée de l'Homme in Paris.[2] The major importance of these bibliographical and museographical data lies in their potential for developing a broader historical and comparative analysis of the material culture of play, spanning from the early 1900s until today and covering the geographic area from Morocco to Tunisia and from the Mediterranean Sea to the southern border of the Sahara.

The territory of the Ghrib extends from the southern limit of the South Tunisian salt lake onto the Algerian border and is part of the Grand Erg Oriental, an immense sandy desert. The Ghrib, a Muslim population, were estimated at about 4,400 persons in 1975. From the 1920s until recently, their economy was based on semi-nomadism, combining dromedary, goat, sheep and donkey breeding with agriculture in the oases. Since the 1970s, there has been a gradual transition from nomadism to sedentariness in the oases on the border of the salt lake. Nowadays, the Ghrib have almost completely settled in the oases, especially the oasis of El Faouar which has expanded into an important urban centre. Through this process of settlement and urbanization, the Ghrib have lost their renown as dromedary-breeders and many of their traditions (Claus 1983, 1997).

In Morocco my fieldwork has been located in the central and southern regions. The children observed in this fieldwork belong to Muslim families, ranging from poor to middle class, and living in settled communities. With the exception of larger towns such as Marrakech, Kenitra and Tiznit, they live in villages and rural centres. Most information comes from the Anti-Atlas Mountains where research started in 2002 in the provinces of Tiznit and Sidi Ifni, two coastal towns south of Agadir where tourism is of some importance. In the Anti-Atlas villages subsistence is based on agriculture, often according to age-old methods, with a focus on olive, argan and fruit trees as well as livestock. In small towns, the need for casual labour, and positions in the craft industry, commerce, transport and public service have created additional employment opportunities. Modernization has not left the Moroccan rural towns and villages unaffected, and the satellite antenna and mobile phone are omnipresent. Even in small rural centres, shops offer the possibility of using computers and the internet. Much information on play obtained in rural areas refers to Amazigh-speaking children but otherwise the children speak Moroccan Arabic.[3]

The age of the children studied ranges from about three to fourteen years, and as a male researcher I rarely have access to infants living within the domestic women's sphere. Children are mostly the source of information but the memories of adolescents, adults and older people have also been used. Using this range of sources offers information on changing play and toy making practices over time, and opens up the possibility of identifying contrasts between children's and adults' points of view.

The cultural heritage of African children and their play and toy practices have received scant scholarly attention. Several studies of black African children's play heritages have been conducted by Charles Béart (1955), F. Klepzig (1972), David Lancy (1996), Chantal Lombard (1978) and Heide Sbrzesny (1976), but the play cultures of specifically North African children have been largely neglected (Rossie 2008: 24–5, 44). Given this lacuna, the work of play scholars researching primarily in Western contexts, such as Julia Bishop (Bishop and Curtis 2001), Gilles Brougère (2003), Julie Delalande (2001), Sudarshan Khanna (1996) and Brian Sutton-Smith (1986, 1997) has been instrumental in the conceptual framing and analysis of my research. I am also indebted to the Bernard van Leer Foundation (2012) for the stimulating information contained in their numerous publications on early childhood.

Socio-cultural aspects of play and toy making

Children's play activities and toys reflect the direct influence of their physical and human environment. Undoubtedly children living in a nomadic settlement in the desert recreate in their play activities their experiences of this environment and way of life, just as children in a village or town do. When making toys, the mineral and vegetal material used is defined by the physical milieu but children also have waste material at their disposal. Children's games also reflect the economic structures of their society, but as they mostly make their toys themselves these remain outside commercial exchanges.

From approximately six years of age sexual differentiation becomes very pronounced in the play of North African children. At that age boys leave the playgroups often controlled by older girls to form their own playgroups. Especially in their pretend play girls and boys represent the everyday life of either their female or male relatives. Observation shows that Moroccan boys and girls of six years or older continue to form mixed playgroups, but in these cases the players are most often siblings, cousins or close neighbours.

Within their playgroups boys certainly enjoy more freedom than girls. Boys are allowed to travel much further from home than girls, with the distance broadening as the boys become older. Another difference between boys and girls, which grows more pronounced from about eight years of age, is the time available to play. This is due to the greater integration of girls in household tasks and the stricter control they are subjected to, with both factors related to the patriarchal family system. Some play activities belong to girls as well as boys, although these may be played separately in gender-specific groups. While the play of older girls and boys is generally segregated, there are indications that this separation can be surmounted, especially by girls. A specific example was observed in a confrontation between three seven-year-old Sidi Ifni boys and a girl of similar age watching them discuss the organization of a feast. When the girl asked to enter the boys' playgroup they refused and she left temporarily. However, when she returned and offered to clean the play space she was allowed to participate (Rossie 2011: slides 28, 50).

Older girls, and sometimes older boys, play an important role in the play of children aged from two to five years. One of the common tasks of older girls is to look after the little ones and in doing so they regularly play with them. When a girl looks after several smaller children she may organize a playgroup, with the children engaging in parallel or collaborative play. It is also not uncommon to witness an older girl or boy making a toy for a small child. In general, older children play an important role in the transmission of local play and toy culture to younger children. Once they are about six years old, children progressively free themselves from this supervision and constitute their own playgroups mostly with peers and often, although not exclusively, with children of the same sex. From this time on, the role of peers from the same family or from the local neighbourhood becomes crucial in learning how to play and to make toys, as well as in children's socialization and personality development.

In North African society, adults seldom interfere in children's play and toy making activities, except when the adults are being disturbed or in the case of a physically or morally dangerous situation. Moreover, the Moroccan school system does not yet seem to use children's culture in general, or the local play and toy culture in particular, as a pedagogical tool. This seeming adult indifference to children's play heritage does not imply that playful interactions between adults and babies and toddlers are non-existent. Adolescents or adults have been observed constructing toys for children. Moroccan examples include baby rattles made by a mother or grandmother, tambourines made by a mother or father or small windmills made by a father or older man (the tambourine and windmill being linked, respectively, to the Ashura feast and the feast of the birthday of the Prophet Mohammed).

My recent research has emphasized children's creativity, stressing that every hand-made toy and every play activity is a manifestation of the child's individuality, although taking place within a given ecological and socio-cultural context. North African children's creativity in using natural and waste materials to make toys has been increasingly supplemented by the use of imported objects, including plastic dolls which are then dressed as a play activity. Self-motivation seems to be an important aspect of children's development, with play and toy making activities offering very favourable circumstances for autonomous action (Rossie 2008: 364–71). Children are not only receivers of culture but, through play, are also the producers of culture.

Children in North Africa are not limited to tradition in their play, but easily integrate new themes and objects related to local, national or global change. Examples include construction of toys resembling a petrol station, restaurant, supermarket and home for poor or handicapped people as part of a game. Nowadays, small tents and houses used in games may be equipped with imitations of modern utensils, televisions, remote control panels, satellite dishes and mobile phones. In one Anti-Atlas mountain village, girls and boys created mobile phones with clay to use in games which otherwise contain traditional structures such as small houses (Rossie 2011: slide 61). In this context, it is interesting to notice that changes in toys can occur in two contrasting ways. The first is by using local material and techniques to create toys referring to new or non-traditional items, for example when making a toy mobile phone in clay or a tractor of cactus pieces. The second is in using new materials and techniques to modify existing toys, such as using a piece of polystyrene as the head for an otherwise traditional doll or using candy and gift wrappings to create dresses for dolls.

External influences on Moroccan children's toy and play heritage is not a purely modern phenomenon: the selling of toys from the European toy industry dates from as early as 1915. Yet change to the physical and social places where play takes place certainly became more rapid after the Second World War. The swift speed of urbanization and the consequent desertion of villages may strongly impede children's opportunities to explore nature and to use natural materials and objects. Crowded streets replace open air and unstructured play areas. The roles of adults in the workplace and at home have also changed, and consequently this has shaped how children interpret adult roles in their pretend play.

There is no doubt that recent modes of communication in particular have influenced the play culture of Moroccan children. Boys have been observed enacting aggressive play sequences copied from contemporary action films. Both a girls' game and a boys' game in Sidi Ifni demonstrated the influence of television programmes, especially the broadcast of news; in both cases, the Israeli-Palestinian conflict was evoked in play. Boys were also seen to be role-playing as a technician or crew member of a Moroccan television production team; in other words, they were pretending to make a television programme. Girls equipped their dollhouse with a miniature television set and satellite antenna or used a self-made digital photo camera in their play. As the mobile phone has quickly entered the life of Moroccan adults since about 2000, children have integrated this new item of technology in their play activities. The influence of socio-economic change and globalization is perhaps stronger in boys' play than in girls' play, which remains more closely tied to family life. This becomes especially visible in toys created for games linked to transportation, such as cars, trucks, tractors, engines, trains, helicopters and airplanes (Rossie 2011: slides 12, 14, 16, 23, 28, 52, 58).

The growing influence of the global toy industry is easily observed during the annual fairs held in Moroccan towns and villages. In contemporary markets and small shops in North Africa, there are now many toys manufactured in China, alongside a continuing proliferation of second-hand toys. Working-class Moroccan families in both urban and rural areas are active consumers of this cheap range of industrially produced and recycled toys. This commercialization of toys has influenced social behaviour, introducing a new practice whereby adults give children toys as a gift. In general terms, the predominance of self-made toys is declining in towns, with the exception of toy cars or toy weapons made by boys. Moreover, the traditional self-made doll has been almost forgotten amongst many children in towns. Nevertheless, there remain many children, largely but not exclusively in rural areas, who construct hand-made toys for their play, although they may use non-traditional materials.

Today continuity and change are both important factors in the toy and play heritage of Moroccan children from rural areas and in the towns. However, the balance between both forces is tipping in the face of globalization and the dominance of the toy industry. Slowly but surely, the diversity of self-made toys is being supplanted by the greater uniformity of industrially made toys, and children's creativity in toy making is being influenced by designs from the global toy industry.

Children creating spaces for play activities

North African children often place limitations on spaces as play areas in which they enact scenes from both their immediate, experienced world and also from the outside world seen on television and conveyed through other media. The boundaries of these spaces are sometimes only mentally delineated, but regularly children use physical means to do so. Some of these physical boundaries include natural objects such as earth, mud, clay, stones and branches. However, waste objects such as pieces of textile, wood, cardboard, iron and plastic, or even a used van, may also serve this purpose. These play spaces can be small but sometimes they are rather spacious. Traditionally and in Anti-Atlas villages today, babies are normally confined to the home, but as soon as they can walk they are integrated in children's playgroups situated outside the home: in open-air spaces, wastelands, mountain slopes, riversides, fields, streets, construction grounds and parks, but rarely in a home yard or schoolyard. These outdoor spaces are thus the places where games and other play activities occur.

Ghrib and other nomadic or semi-nomadic girls build miniature tents resembling the tents used by their parents (Figure 17.1). These tents are the stages for girls' games related to the domestic and female world, such as dinner and household play but more often to celebrate a wedding. Small colourful carpets made of yarn, or textile strips wrapped around a cross-shaped reed frame are displayed in the tents. Data collected between 1930 and 1960 record that girls among the Tuareg and the Moors populations created small enclosure mats or sleeping mats with grassy stalks and straps of leather or palm-fibres regularly decorated with geometric designs. Other self-made toys such as cushions, beds, utensils, dolls and animals completed the setting (Rossie 2008: 59–63). In 1999 Fernando Pinto Cebrián (Rossie 2008: 63) wrote that girls of the Sahrawi population often enacted their mothers' role as wife and mistress of the family tent, and that adults saw this game as necessary for the girls to learn all that relates to traditional family living in the desert. These observations were mirrored by my own research into the Ghrib girls of the 1970s. Outside the Sahara it is rare to witness children building toy tents, though a girls' playgroup building such tents in two Anti-Atlas villages has been recently noted. In one village a boy aged six years also made a tent when playing with a few girls. The tripod used as a frame is covered with a piece of textile, plastic or empty cement sack (Rossie 2008: 55–75). One girl modernized her tent by putting a piece of polystyrene on top of the tripod to represent a parabolic TV satellite dish (Rossie 2011: slide 59).

Figure 17.1 Ghrib girls making an enclosure before their tent, Tunisian Sahara, 1975.

North African children enjoy representing miniature buildings (Rossie 2008: 76–158). In 1975 Ghrib girls delineated small houses with mud or dug a 'house' in the sand for household and doll play, and Ghrib boys created a mosque or other constructions with wet sand (Rossie 2011: slide 10). Moroccan girls and boys continue to do this quite often with stones and sometimes with mud (Rossie 2011: slides 15, 19, 40, 49, 56). In one example children assembled several small houses into a children's village at some distance from the real village (Rossie 2011: slide 20). In such miniaturized constructions of houses and villages, children enact and interpret many aspects of the adult world they daily observe. Moroccan girls not only make small houses for doll and household play. They also build them to represent a wedding feast, a poor, wealthy or emigrant's family house, an animal shed, a restaurant, a supermarket and other domestic and commercial structures (Rossie 2011: slides 7, 19, 34, 43). Boys seem to delineate small houses less often than girls because the home and household traditionally belongs to the female sphere in Moroccan society. Moroccan boys are more likely to construct toy cattle areas and cattle sheds, gardens, farms, shops, restaurants, garages and a petrol station; places that refer more to the male world (Rossie 2011: slides 41, 48, 50).

Self-made toys for pretend play

Children from Morocco and the Tunisian Sahara made dolls, animals, utensils, musical instruments, and toys related to the male and female spheres, to hunting, fighting, transport, communication, feasts and rituals. Making dolls, mostly female dolls, is done by girls and sometimes by small boys playing together with the girls. The word used for a female doll or a male doll is *tislit* or *isli* and *arusa* or *aris*, respectively, in Amazigh and Arabic languages. These words, translated as bride and bridegroom, reveal the great importance and prestige of the figure of the bride in the minds of young girls and their parents. There appears to be no traditional word meaning 'doll' except for borrowings from Spanish and French (*munika, pupiya*). These local names are not arbitrary choices. They are inspired by the kind of pretend games girls prefer to play with the dolls, namely the celebration of a wedding with its ceremonies, rituals, dinner, music, singing and dancing. Looking for a bride, negotiating marriage by parents, preparing the dowry and organizing the betrothal become part of the pretend play. The emotional moment when a bride leaves her family to go to her husband's family may also be enacted. Different dolls have a role to play in such complex and long lasting, but not necessarily continuous, play activities. Female roles such as a mother, an aunt, a sister, other family member, a cook, a servant, a mistress of ceremony, a henna specialist and a local or foreign visitor may be represented (Figure 17.2). In this kind of make-believe play, as in other forms of pretend play, girls enact, interpret, integrate, accept, make fun of and even oppose what they observe, experience, hear or learn from adults, older children and peers. Older boys may also make dolls but mostly to represent male figures such as a dancer or a mule-driver (Rossie 2011: slides 11, 19).

The female dolls vary significantly according to size, frame, used material, head type, face and decoration. Yet, they are often similar among girls of the same community, region or even population. At the same time individual creativity is undoubtedly apparent. To make and decorate dolls a great diversity of material is used: mineral material (stones, clay), animal material (dried dung, bones, hair, leather, wool), vegetal material (leaves, reed, branches, fruits, ears of maize), textile material (rags, threads), metallic material (wires, sheets), plastic material (flasks, sheets, threads) and ornaments. For some time in towns, but more recently in villages, second-hand dolls

Figure 17.2 Reconstruction of a scene of village girls' wedding play, Anti-Atlas, Morocco, 2004.

imported from Europe or cheap Chinese plastic dolls have been preferred, though girls make dolls dresses in the local fashion. Bridegroom dolls and child dolls also exist but they are seldom seen.

Although boys, especially Tuareg boys, made (and possibly still make) male dolls, they prefer to create animals with clay or clayish earth, vegetables, leaves, nuts and waste material. Making toy dromedaries, horses, donkeys, mules, cattle, livestock, birds, lizards and scorpions for playing games of hunting, animal breeding, caravanning and transport were and still are favourite games of rural boys (Rossie 2005a/b; 2011: slides 12, 16, 19, 21, 56). However, some kinds of traditional toys have declined. In the Sahara there has been a tradition, of at least two thousand years, of adults and children constructing toy animals, mostly dromedaries and horses, in a manner whereby their front legs are united in one trunk, from fired clay – though this is rare today (Rossie 2005b: 75, 90, 141–6; Rossie 2011: slide 57).

Making toy utensils with clay, earth, slaked lime and waste material is largely a girls' job but younger boys may also perform the task. They use these toys most often for dinner and doll play. Almost all kinds of utensils are miniaturized: cups, bowls, plates, tajines, pots, pans, kettles, cooking devices, spoons, forks, ladles and jugs. Some are quite rudimentary, especially those made by small girls, but others are well shaped and functional (Rossie 2008: 159–99; 2011: slides 5, 34, 40, 49, 56). In the Anti-Atlas villages, a special technique is occasionally used to glaze toy pottery, and this is a technique transmitted within girls' playgroups from the older to the younger girls. Girls first cut off a piece of a specific cactus plant and collect the white liquid that flows out of it. After the girl has fired her toy pottery in the family oven she immerses each item in the 'milk' before leaving it to dry overnight. This gives the pottery a shiny glaze that gradually fades with time.

Girls also play by enacting female occupations, such as fetching water, collecting firewood, grinding corn, making bread, preparing oil, washing the linen, spinning, weaving and dressing up (Rossie 2008: 201–34). To do so they make specific toys, often with clay or clayish earth, representing jars, spoons, pots, wells, hand mills for grinding corn or making oil, ovens, spindles, looms and decorative items such as jewellery and spectacles (Rossie 2011: slides 5, 22, 35, 56). Again, waste material and cheap plastic toys are increasingly replacing these self-made utensils (Rossie 2011: slides 34, 35). In 1975 I observed a Ghrib girl in the Tunisian Sahara making a horizontal loom with sticks and scraps of wool threads: an example of a play activity purposely being used by a mother to teach her ten-year-old daughter how to arrange the threads correctly so that she could make a small textile (Rossie 2008: 226–7). Another example of a play activity preparing girls for a specific Anti-Atlas woman's task is the making of argan oil produced from the kernels of the argan tree fruits. Village girls in that region use mud and straw, clay or argan pasta to produce a whole series of utensils, equipment and furniture such as hand mills, portable ovens, plates, receptacles and small three-legged chairs (Rossie 2008: 217–21).

Although younger boys may make toys related to female occupations, boys certainly create many more toys referring to male occupations such as hunting, fishing, fighting, breeding animals, gardening, working in the fields, building, transporting and trading (Rossie 2008: 235–69; 2011: slides 7, 26, 41). Boys make toys representing weapons, wells, drinking and milking devices, miniature gardens, copies of ploughs, pairs of scales, and goods to sell. Although these are mainly boys' games, occasionally girls also play them. A typical toy constructed by older boys and seen in both small and large towns, such as Sidi Ifni or Marrakech, is the local skateboard with ball bearings as wheels (Figure 17.3). Learning to make such a skateboard is transmitted in boys' playgroups.

Girls as well as boys like to sing and make music, especially by banging instruments to beat time (Rossie 2008: 270–300). Small children seem to master rhythm well, although some have more talent for this than others. Girls play handclapping games more often than boys, as well as round games or stage dances accompanied by singing (Rossie 2011: slide 32). Boys have been observed creating a rhythm band and playing wind and string instruments made with natural and waste material (Rossie 2011: slide 33). These self-made instruments include drums, different types of flutes, bagpipes, guitars and violins inspired by those that traditional musicians use. One night in 2005 I observed a twelve-year-old boy in Sidi Ifni who made a drum kit with large milk powder tins, using the tin lids as cymbals.

Figure 17.3 Boys making a skateboard, Sidi Ifni, 2005.

North African children play whenever they have the time and inclination to do so, but some festivities are special occasions for play and toy making activities. Ashura is an important period for children, comparable to the Saint Nicholas traditions and Christmas festivities. Ashura falls on the tenth day of the first month of the Muslim lunar calendar, with festivities lasting for ten days from the beginning of the month. Girls make a specific type of doll, traditionally with a tibia bone from a sheep sacrificed on Aïd el-kebir, the tenth day of the pilgrimage month (Rossie 2005a: 49, 187–90). Today in Morocco during Ashura, parents and other members of the family usually buy toys for children or give them some money. Water pistols and guns for boys and beauty sets for girls are popular cheap toys imported from China. Alongside plastic musical instruments, however, remain the traditional ones made by artisans. Boys and girls use these musical instruments especially for their door-to-door quests organized during Ashura.

Other typical play activities for that period are related to the elements of water and fire. Before the introduction of water guns children made a reed-pump similar to a cycle-pump. One can still see Sidi Ifni children throwing 'water bombs' – plastic bags filled with water – at each other. They also set fire to a long piece of steel wool. Once the end of the piece becomes red hot the child turns it around quickly. When performed skilfully, numerous sparks fly out (Rossie 2008: 311–17, 321). In Tiznit, located about 100 km south from Agadir, older boys and young men still celebrate the traditional masquerade. For this week-long event starting after Ashura they create masks and huge animals used for the nightly parade. The masks are often strikingly expressive and artistically rendered (Rossie 2008: 317–21; 2011: slides 38, 39).

Conclusion

This chapter on material culture in play and toy heritage stresses its importance in the development of North African children, and in their induction into the values of their community. Children's culture is an integral part of the tangible and intangible heritage of humanity, representative of both the social and physical constraints of children's lives but also their active participation in creating the society and culture in which they grow up. The study of children's play offers opportunities to more closely understand the cultural and social organization of a community, imbued as it is with familial and community norms.

Research across different decades clearly demonstrates that unique North African play and toy heritages are disappearing under the combined assault of the school, the media, the toy industry and a more consumerist society, which increasingly influence the families of even the remotest mountain villages. It is therefore an urgent task to study the material culture of North African play in more detail. In order to preserve and make more widely available visual and written documentation on North African and Saharan children's games and toys, in 2005 I donated my research documentation to the Musée du Jouet of Moirans-en-Montagne in France, along with a collection of 641 Moroccan toys (1992–2005) and twenty-nine Ghrib toys (1975) that were used for a significant exhibition running from 2006 until the renovation of this museum

(2010–12, Rossie 2011: slides 77, 78). It is in this museum that my original slides, digital photographs and some videos of North African children's play and toy making activities are safeguarded. To the Centro per la Cultura Ludica of Turin in Italy I donated about 250 toys of Moroccan Anti-Atlas children, which were used by the centre for a remarkable display that opened in November 2010 (Rossie 2011: slides 79, 80). In 2011 I donated forty toys made by Anti-Atlas girls and boys to Museum Victoria in Melbourne, Australia. These international donations were undertaken in an effort to disseminate documentations of Moroccan children's toy heritage as widely as possible.

In November 2009 I created an exhibition and related seminars in Morocco on Moroccan children's play and toy culture in a youth centre of the *Fondation Orient-Occident* in the coastal town Safi (Rossie 2011: slides 70–74). The next phase in these attempts to preserve this cultural heritage, particularly in its own communities, is to create a new collection of Anti-Atlas children's toys with the collaboration of local Moroccan researchers Khalija Jariaa and Boubaker Daoumani. This task is now more urgent than ever before, as even in Anti-Atlas villages traditional toy making activities are vanishing. This collection might one day form the basis for a Moroccan child museum.

The Moroccan 'Charte Nationale de l'Education et de la Formation' stipulates that the educational system is rooted in the cultural heritage of the country. It respects the variety of its regional components, safeguards and develops their specificity (1999). On the basis of this aspiration, it may be hoped that Moroccan children's culture in general and their play and toy culture in particular will become incorporated into this effort to link the educational system to local realities. Using children's heritage not only offers a possibility to valorize and develop the cultural heritage of the country but also to diminish the cleavage between home and school and between teachers and pupils. Using children's play and toy making activities from Morocco and the Tunisian Sahara for pedagogical and socio-cultural purposes has shown the vast potential of this aspect of cultural heritage (Rossie 2011: slides 63–69, 75, 76).

Acknowledgements

I am indebted to Gilbert J.M. Claus for his contribution to my research among the Ghrib and to Khalija Jariaa and Boubaker Daoumani for their help in my research in the Moroccan Anti-Atlas. I also want to thank Gareth Whittaker for editing the text of this chapter.

Notes

1 Trained as a social worker then as an Africanist, children and youth have been a constant research interest throughout my career, possibly linked to my involvement in the scout movement first as youngster then as scoutmaster. As a researcher of the Belgian National Foundation for Scientific Research (1970–78) in 1973 I completed my doctoral thesis on 'Child and Society. The Process of Socialization in Patrilineal Central Africa'. As this research was based on an extensive use of documents, I strongly felt the need to do fieldwork. I commenced research on children's socialization among the Ghrib in 1975.

2 Aside from my fieldwork, sources used for this research include analysis of the large collection of Saharan and North African toys of the Musée de l'Homme in Paris (now in the
Musée du Quai Branly, http://www.quaibranly.fr) and the information gathered in the
related ethnographic, linguistic and general bibliography. Detailed information, maps and
many photographs are found in my books of the collection *Saharan and North African Toy
and Play Cultures* available on http://www.sanatoyplay.org and on http://www.scribd.com
(Jean-Pierre Rossie).
3 Information on the different populations and locations mentioned here can be found in the
introduction of Rossie, J.-P. (2008) available on http://www.sanatoyplay.org.
Amazigh is the indigenous term nowadays used to replace the word Berber, which has a
negative connotation as it refers to the concept barbarian. In central Morocco Tamazight is
spoken and in southern Morocco Tashelhit. Moroccan Arabic is locally called Darija.

References

All publications of Jean-Pierre Rossie are available on the website http://www.sanatoyplay.
org.

Béart, C. (1955) *Jeux et jouets de l'Ouest Africain*, Dakar: Mémoires de l'Institut Français d'Afrique
Noire, no. 42, 2 volumes.
Bernard van Leer Foundation (2011) See http://www.bernardvanleer.org (viewed 12.1.2012).
Bishop, J.C. and Curtis, M. (eds.) (2001) *Play Today in the Primary School Playground: Life, Learning
and Creativity*, Buckingham, Philadelphia: Open University Press.
Brougère, G. (2003) *Jouets et compagnie*, Paris: Stock.
Charte Nationale de l'Education et de la Formation (1999) In *Première Partie, Principes Fondamen-
taux*, available on http://www.takween.com/charte.html (viewed 11.1.2012).
Claus, G.J.M. (1983) 'The Pastoral Ghrib of the Northwestern Tunisian Sahara. Causes and
Effects of the Transition from Nomadism to Sedentariness', in *Liber Memorialis Prof. Dr. P.J.
Vandenhoute 1913–1978*, Gent: Rijksuniversiteit te Gent, pp. 129–43.
——(1997) 'Grossesse, naissance et enfance. Us et coutumes chez les Bédouins Ghrib du Sahara
tunisien', in *Conception, naissance et petite enfance au Maghreb*, Les Cahiers de l'IREMAM, 9/10,
Aix-en-Provence: Institut de Recherches et d'Etudes sur le Monde Arabe et Musulman.
Delalande, J. (2001) *La cour de récréation. Contribution à une anthropologie de l'enfance*, Collection Le
Sens Social, Rennes: Presses Universitaires de Rennes.
Khanna, S. (1996) *Joy of Making Indian Toys*, New Delhi: National Book Trust India.
Klepzig, F. (1972) *Kinderspiele der Bantu*, Meisenheim am Glan: Verlag Anton Hain.
Lancy, D.F. (1996) *Playing on the Mother-Ground: Cultural Routines for Children's Development*, New
York; London: The Guilford Press.
Lombard, C. (1978) *Les jouets des enfants baoulé. Essais sur la créativité enfantine dans une société rurale
africaine*, Paris: Quatre Vents Editeur.
Pinto Cebrián, F. (1999) *Juegos Saharauis para Jugar en la Arena. Juegos y Juguetes Tradicionales del
Sáhara*, Madrid: Miraguano S.A. Ediciones.
Rossie, J-P. (2004) *Games of Physical Skill from the Tunisian Sahara and Morocco: Anthropological
Research and Physical Education for Peace*, SITREC, Stockholm: Royal Institute of Technology.
——(2005a) *Saharan and North African Toy and Play Cultures: Children's Dolls and Doll Play*, Stock-
holm: Royal Institute of Technology.
——(2005b) *Saharan and North African Toy and Play Cultures: The Animal World in Play, Games and
Toys*, Stockholm: Royal Institute of Technology.

—— (2008) *Saharan and North African Toy and Play Cultures: Domestic Life in Play, Games and Toys*, Stockholm: Royal Institute of Technology.

—— (2011) *North African and Saharan Children's Play and Toy Making Activities: Creativity, Transmission between Children, Change and Sociocultural Applications*, PowerPoint created for a presentation at the Department of Education, Brunel University, London.

Sbrzesny, H. (1976) *Die Spiele der !Ko-Buschleute, unter besonderer Berücksichtigung ihrer socialisierenden und gruppenbindenden Funktionen*, Münich/Zürich: R. Piper & Co. Verlag.

Sutton-Smith, B. (1986) *Toys as Culture*, New York; London: Gardner Press Inc.

—— (1997) *The Ambiguity of Play*. Cambridge, MA; London: Harvard University Press.

Index

Aboriginal Children's Play Project 43
ACFC *see* Australian Children's Folklore
  Collection
Ahrends, Burton and Koralek (ABK;
  architects) 199
Albert, Prince Consort 231
Alcott, Louisa May 92
Alexander, C. 85, 88, 99–100
Alexander, P.F. 87
Amanda Levete Architects 202
American Journal of Play 219
Angus, P. 202
Anne Frank House Museum 12
Appadurai, A. 243
'Arab Spring' 34
architectural heritage 11; *see also* Foundling
  Museum; school buildings in England
Arendt, H. 251
Ariès, P. 6, 85, 148, 210
Ashford, Daisy 86, 87
Association of American Museums 223
Auckland Museum 213, 214–15
Austen, Cassandra 87–8
Austen, Jane 85–6, 87–8, 101
Australia 159–72; *Bringing Them Home
  Report* 160, 164–5; child workers 127,
  136–8, 138*f*; colonial children
  161–3, 168; colonialism 159–65;
  commemoration 159, 162–3, 165–7,
  169–71; education 48, 161; Forgotten
  Australians 160, 167–9; Former
  Child Migrants 160, 161, 167–70;
  Indigenous peoples 159, 163–7, 171n1;
  lost children 162–3; museums of
  childhood 216, 218;
  national inquiries 160, 164, 168;
  Native Title Act (1993) 164; playlore
  collections 1–2, 42–4; Point Arthur

Historic Site 161; research on play
  44–52; Stolen Generations 160, 163–4,
  165–7; World Heritage Education (WHE)
  Programme 27; *see also* heritage making
Australian Children's Folklore Collection
  (ACFC) 42–3, 44
Australian National Maritime Museum 1
  69

Bancroft, H.H. 245
Bates, R.J. 131
Batten, B. 159
Baudrillard, J. 240, 242, 249
Baxter, J.E. 8
Benjamin, W. 251
Bernard van Leer Foundation 272
Berner, B. 248
Bethnal Green Museum 231, 232
Birch, D. 86, 101n2
Bishop, J. *et al.* 62, 66, 70–1
Bodleian Library, Oxford 59
Bokova, I. 28, 34–5, 37
Booth, Colin 238
Boston Children's Museum 216
Boym, S. 258
Bradford, F. 8
Braybrooke, N. 88
Bristol Aeroplane Company 193
British Commonwealth and Empire
  Museum, Bristol 120
British Library 59
British Museum 154
Brockhouse, J. 196–7
Bromberg, M. 179
Brontë, Anne 96, 98, 99
Brontë, Branwell 94, 95–9, 96*f*, 97*f*, 100
Brontë, Charlotte 86, 92, 94, 95–6, 96*f*,
  98–101

Brontë, Emily 95–6, 96f, 98, 99, 100
Brontë Parsonage Museum 85
Brooklyn Children's Museum 216, 224
Brooklyn Historical Society 127, 133–4
Brookshaw, S. 209, 211, 212
Brown, G. 160, 168
Bruce, Mary Grant 86
Brueghel, P. 40
Bryden, I. 261
Burn, A. 66
Burton, A. 215, 219, 233

Calverk, K. 122
Canada: child migrants 168, 170, 171;
    Indigenous children 171; museums of
    children 213–14
Capital City and Countryside (magazine) 265
Capitol Children's Museum, Washington
    DC 177
Carroll, Lewis 89–92, 90f
Carter, B. 185–6
Caruso St John (architects) 234
Centro per la Cultura Ludica, Turin,
    Italy 281
Cesnola, Luigi Palma di 251, 253
Chamberlin, Powell and Bon
    (architects) 196f, 202
Chapman University 175, 176f
Charlesworth, H. 11–12
Chawla, L. 33–4
child workers 33, 126–41; 'child rescue'
    bodies 131; exploitation of 126–7,
    129–30; Foundling Hospital and
    Museum 228, 229; heritage site
    experiences 127, 134–5; photographic
    exhibitions 127, 133–4; policy
    agendas 126, 128–9; right to work 129;
    studies of 128, 130; traditional
    installations 127, 130–1, 136–8; V&A
    Museum of Childhood 130–1
childhood 108, 109, 224; cultural heritage
    of 4, 13–14; historiography of 5–7;
    material culture of 7–8, 209, 210–11, 212,
    223, 233; memories of 108–9, 115–19,
    210; sentimentalizing of 210–12
Childhood, Tradition and Change
    project 47–52, 47f
childlore 55; see also Children's Playground
    Games and Songs in the Age of New
    Media project; playlore
children: contemporary representations
    of 3–5; cultural heritage of 4,
13–14; as designers of museums 14;
    historiography 5–7; innocence of
    113–14, 262; material culture of 8, 212,
    219, 223; as museum visitors 4–5, 9,
    107
children as collectors of cultural heritage
    see Leland Stanford, Jr Museum
children as writers see literary juvenilia
children's museums 215, 216–19, 233;
    definition 9, 223–4
Children's Playground Games and Songs
    in the Age of New Media project 52, 55,
    56–72; allusion, synthesis, mimicry and
    parody 70–1; categorization 59, 60f;
    children's involvement in project 61;
    clapping games 62, 66, 67–8t, 71; dance
    routines 62–5, 69–71; documentary
    film 58; ephemerality 71–2; ethnographic
    studies 57–8, 61–6, 69–72; Game-
    Catcher 58–9; inter-disciplinarity 61;
    multimodal performance 66–70, 67–8t;
    Opie archive 56–7; Playtimes website 59,
    60f, 61; proxemics 69; social context 65;
    transformation and creativity 71
City Gallery, Melbourne 136–8, 138f
clapping games 62, 66, 67–8t, 71, 279
Clark, G.T. 247
Cleeve Barr, A.B. 194
Clemons, F. 8
Clifford, J. 240, 249, 250
Cohen, D. 94, 95
Cole, Henry 231
Coleman, K. 152
Coleridge, Hartley 95, 98
collection theory 240, 242
Collins, T. 198
Colombia: intangible heritage 30
colonialsm 156–65, 168
Conrad, Joseph 98
contemporary representations of
    children 3–5
Cooper Marcus, C. 11
Coram, Thomas 226, 227
Corinium Museum, Cirencester 154–5
Corn, W. 240
creative writing see literary juvenilia
creativity 71, 273
Croatia: intangible heritage 30
Crowley, D. 266–7
Crowley, M. (later Medd) 194, 195, 196,
    197–8
cultural genocide 164–5

cultural heritage 2–3; of childhood 4, 13–14; of children 4, 13–14; contemporary representations of children 3–5; cultural values 110–11, 114; and human rights 11–12, 31–5; playlore as 40–2; *see also* intangible cultural heritage
cultural rights 31, 32, 33
Cunningham, H. 108

dance routines 62–5, 69–71
Daressy, G. 253
Darian-Smith, K. 50
Davey, G. 44
Davies, R.L. 194–5
Davin, A. 128–9
De Quincey, Thomas 98
DeMause, L. 6, 148
Dickens, Charles 86–7, 92, 126, 128
discovery centres *see* children's museums
Dodgson, Charles Lutwidge (Lewis Carroll) 89–92, 90*f*
dolls 7, 211, 276–8
dolls' houses 8
Douglas, N. 41, 46
Doyle, Dick (Richard Doyle) 92, 93*f*
Drug Zhenshchin (*Women's Friend*) 261–2
Dudok, Willem 193
Duff, Jane 163
Dulles, F.R. 247

EC *see* European Commission
Edinburgh Museum of Childhood 211, 212, 215–16
Edith Cowan University Museum of Childhood, Perth 216, 218
education: in ancient Rome 151–2, 153; in Australia 48, 161; gender segregation in 48; right to education 32; *see also* Japan's superior students; school buildings in England
Egypt and the 'Arab Spring' 34
electronic games 50, 58–9, 219
Eliot, T.S. 92
Elliott, O.L. 253
English Heritage 191
ethnic minorities 33; migrant experience 111, 117–18; *see also* Australia
ethnographic studies 41, 46, 57–8, 61–6, 69–72
Eureka!, Halifax, UK 224
European Commission (EC) 33, 36 7

European Jewish Children's Aid (EJCA) 182

Factor, J. 10, 44, 45, 46–7, 50
Fass, P. 13, 210
Ferris, G.T. 244
Finnegan, R. 65–6
Flanders, J. 266
Fleming, Marjory 86
Floyd, J. 261
folklore *see* childlore; playlore
Fondation Orient-Occident, Safi, Morocco 281
Forster, J. 87
Forum UNESCO: Universities and Heritage (FUUH) 28–9
Foundling Hospital, London 226–7, 226*t*, 229
Foundling Museum, London 222, 224, 228*f*; history 227–8; representations of childhood 156, 228–30
Fujin no tomo (The Lady's Companion) 75, 77, 80, 82
Furedi, F. 50
Futatsugi Shōji 80

games 40, 41, 45–6, 48, 57
Gaskell, Elizabeth 92
gender: in ancient Rome 150; in play of North African children 272–3, 278–9; roles 7; segregation in school 48
Getzels, J. W. 87
Ghetto Fighter's House, Nahariyah, Israel 175, 177
Gibson, D. 196–7
Gill, T. 42, 50
Gold, Natalie 184
Goldfinger, Ernö 192, 201
Goldsmith, Rev. J. 98
Gomme, B. 41, 46
Graham, B. 3
Great Exhibition, London (1851) 231
Greg, Mrs T.T. 232
Gropius, W. 198
Grossinger News 179
Grundy, I. *et al.* 88, 89

Hall, D.C. 193
Hammond, D. 58
Handel, G.F. 226, 227, 229
Hani, M. 77
Harcourt Smith, Sir Cecil 232
Harper, S. 171

Harris, Rhian 218
Harty, J. 95
Hearst Castle 247
heritage, concept of 108
heritage making 4–5, 107–23;
   childhood 108, 109; children's own
   visit 119–22; cultural values 110–11,
   114; heritage 108; identity 111–12, 122;
   intergenerational communication 110;
   learning museum performance 112;
   memories of childhood 108–9,
   115–19; methodology 109; migrant
   experience 111, 117–18; nostalgia 108–9,
   115, 116–17, 118, 268; political use
   of the innocent child 113–14; 'taking
   the children' 107, 109–13; tradition
   of visiting 112–13; understanding the
   past 109–10, 113–14, 117
High School Musical (film) 62–3, 69, 70
Highland Museum of Childhood 224
Higonnet, A. 253
Hillabold, S. 89
Hinchcliffe, E. 194
Hine, Lewis 133–4, 135*f*
historiography of children and
   childhood 5–7
Hizme, Irene G. 179–81
Hodges, D.J. 217
Hogarth, William 226, 227, 228
Holocaust child survivors 12, 175–88;
   adoption 179–82; foster care 183–4;
   JFCS summer camp 185–6; life with
   relatives 182–3; memorials 175, 176*f*,
   177; museum exhibitions 177, 188;
   optimistic accounts 177–8, 187, 187*f*;
   postwar reality 178–87; reunion with
   parents 184–5
Hook, Hope 86
Hooper, W. 94, 95
Howard, D. 44, 45*f*, 46, 48, 49, 50
Howard, J. 163, 166
Howard, P. 3
Hudson, D. 90
Huizinga, J. 99
human rights: and cultural heritage 11–12,
   31–5; and romanticism 12–13

ICOMOS (International Council on
   Monuments and Sites) 33
identity 13, 111–12, 122, 210, 240, 242
Imperial War Museum, London 222, 225
imperialist ideology 98, 114; in Brontë

juvenilia 98–9; colonialism 156–65,
   168
Indigenous people's rights 31, 167; *see also*
   Australia
Indonesia: Patrimonito International Work
   Camps 25, 27, 27*f*, 28*f*
the innocent child 113–14, 262
intangible cultural heritage 9–10;
   oral traditions and expressions 40;
   performing arts 40; play 40–1;
   rituals 40; social practices 40; traditional
   craftsmanship 40–1; UNESCO
   Convention 3, 22, 29–31, 36, 40–1
International Council on Monuments and
   Sites (ICOMOS) 33
International Slavery Museum,
   Liverpool 119–20
Ishiguchi Gitarō 80

Jackson, Michael 63–4
Jackson, P.W. 87
Jalland, P. 162
James, H. 248
Japan's superior students 11, 74–84;
   criticisms of preparatory education 81;
   educationally obsessed mothers 75–9;
   mass media portrayals of 74–5; museums
   of educational history 74; parental
   school visits 77, 78, 80; parent–teacher
   meetings 77–8, 81; private tutors 82–3;
   Seishi Elementary School 80–1; starting
   school 77; teachers as allies of education
   mothers 79–83
Jenkins, H. 113, 122
Jensen, N. 119
Jewish Family and Children Services
   (JFCS) 185–6
Jewish Labor Committee 178–9
John Pardey Architects 202
Johnson, E. 87
Johnson-Marshall, S. 194, 195, 196
Jordan: World Heritage Education (WHE)
   Programme 27
Jordanova, L. 217
Journal of Social Care Work 183
Juvenilia Press 86

Katō, S. 81
Kay, J. 198
Kelly, C. 6, 258, 259, 260, 267
Kerouac, Jack 95
Khawajkie, E. 24

Kids in Museums 155
Kimura, H. 79–80
Kirby, P. 129–30
Kitchin, John 196
Knapp, M. and H. 10, 41
Kobayashi Saburō 81
Korczak, Janusz 177
Korea, Republic of: International Youth
    Culture Camp 29
Kraftl, P. 13
Kress, G. 66
Kvisterøy, I. 24, 25
Kyoto's Municipal Museum of School
    History 74

Larkin, Philip 88
Lavalette, M. 128, 129
Lawrence, C. 155
Lee, M. 195, 196
Lee, N. 4
Lees, Diane 234
Leland Stanford, Jr Museum 9, 240–55;
    Grand Tour 246–50; interior
    decorating 243–5; Leland as a young
    collector 245–51, 253; Leland's
    education 246–7, 253, 255n3;
    museum 251–4, 252f, 254f; Palo Alto
    farm 245–6; Stanford family 241f, 242–3;
    death and memorials 253
Levy, Amy 92
Lewis, C.S. 94–5
libraries 85–6
Life Magazine 177–8, 179, 181
Lindsay, P. 45–6, 52
literary juvenilia 8–9, 85–102; book
    making 9, 86–9, 94–101; creative
    imitation 86–7, 91; imaginary kingdoms
    (paracosms) 92, 94–101; in libraries 85–
    6; magazine making 89–92
Locke, T. 198
Lowenthal, D. 2–3
Lucretius 148
Lydon, J. 134
Lynch, K. 33
Lyons Israel Ellis (architects) 200, 201, 201f

McCord Museum, Montreal 213–14
MacKeith, S. 94, 95
McKinty, J. 47f
McMaster, J. 85, 88
McRainey, D.L. 14
Makishi masquerade 30

Malkin, Thomas 98
Marsh, K. 46, 65
Martin, B. 194
Mary of Teck, Queen 232
Masaru, I. 75
Mason, S.C. 198–9
mass media: influences on playlore 48,
    56; portrayals of ancient Rome 155;
    portrayals of Japanese students 74–5;
    see also Children's Playground Games and
    Songs in the Age of New Media project
material culture 223; in ancient Rome
    153–4; of childhood 7–8, 209, 210–11,
    212, 223, 233; of children 8, 212, 219,
    223; see also literary juvenilia; toys
Mayall, B. 4, 129
Mayor, F. 28
Medd, D. 194, 195, 197–8
memories of childhood 108–9, 115–19, 210
Metropolitan Museum of Art, New
    York 251
Midgley, P. 87
Millman, Isaac 181–2
Mitchell, G. 58
Moe Folklife Project 46
Moffatt, D. 34
Montessori, M. 198
Moorhouse, E. 197
Morris, H. 198
Morris, W. 200
Morrow, V. 129
Morss, J.R. 4
Muensterberger, W. 254n1
multimodal performance 66–70
Murray, Patrick 211, 215–16
Musée du Jouet, Moirans-en-Montagne,
    France 280–1
Museum of London 155
Museum of New Hampshire History 134,
    135f
Museum of Soviet Chilhood,
    Sevastopol 268
museum representations 7, 209–20,
    222–39; children's museums 9, 215,
    216–19; conceptual issues 222–5; material
    culture 7–8, 209, 210–11, 212; museums
    of childhood 9, 156, 211, 212–13,
    215–16, 217–19, 228–30; museums
    of children 213–15; sentimentalizing
    childhood 210–12
Museum Victoria, Melbourne, Australia 1–
    2, 42, 43–4, 48, 281

Museum Voor Het Onderwijs, the Hague 216
museums: children as designers 14; children as visitors 4–5, 9, 107; interactive activities 119, 135, 155, 177, 216–17, 218, 228, 235; learning museum performance 112; tradition of visiting 112–13; *see also* children's museums; heritage making; material culture; museums of childhood; museums of children
Museums Association 222–3
museums of childhood 211, 212–13, 215–16, 217–19; conceptual issues 9, 222–5; *see also* Foundling Museum; V&A Museum of Childhood
museums of children 213–15
music 279–80; *see also* Children's Playground Games and Songs in the Age of New Media project
Muybridge, E. 246

Nabokov, V. 258
Nagel, G.W. 246
Nardinelli, C. 128, 129
Nash, H.C. 250, 251, 253, 254, 254n2, 255n3
National Child Labor Committee (NCLC, US) 133, 134
National Learning Centre, Washington DC 216–17
National Library of Australia 42, 48
National Museum of Australia 169
National Museums Liverpool (UK) 169
National Trust 224
National Trust Museum of Childhood 126–7, 224
Nepal: intangible heritage 30
New Zealand: museums of children 213, 214–15
Newsom, J. 194
Nieuwenhuys, O. 126
Nora, P. 246–7
North African children's play and toy heritage 270–82; creativity 273; festivals 280; gender differentiation 272–3, 278–9; the Ghrib of Tunisia 271, 275–6, 276f, 278; Moroccan Muslim children 271–5, 276, 279, 279f, 280, 281; music 279–80; self-made toys for pretend play 271, 274–5, 276–80, 277f; socio-cultural aspects 272–5; spaces

for play activities 275–6, 276f; toy exhibitions 280–1; toy making 273–4
Norway: Norwegian Agency for Development Cooperation (Norad) 24, 25; World Heritage Education (WHE) Programme 25, 26f
nostalgia 108–9, 115, 116–17, 118, 210–11, 258, 268
Novick, Rabbi W. 179, 180

Oeuvre de Secours aux Enfants (OSE) 181
Opie, I. 41, 46, 49, 55, 56–7, 58, 59, 70
Opie, P. 41, 55, 56–7, 58, 59, 70
oral-formulaic tradition 65
oral traditions and expressions 40, 45, 46, 48, 55; *see also* Children's Playground Games and Songs in the Age of New Media project
O'Reilly, E. 89
Osborne, C.M. 240, 253

Palmer, D. 45–6, 52
paracosms 92, 94–101
Parker, D. 66
Parkhurst, H. 198
Pascoe, C. 50
Patrimonito *see* World Heritage Education (WHE) Programme
Patt, E. 178
Pavlic, B. 24
Pearson, E. 198
Peckham, R.S. 3
performing arts 40, 48, 49–50; *see also* Children's Playground Games and Songs in the Age of New Media project
Philadelphia Centennial Exhibition 244–5
Pierrepont, Lady Mary (*later* Wortley Montagu) 88–9
Pinto Cebrián, F. 275
Pitt Rivers Museum, Oxford 59
Play and Folklore (journal) 44
playground games and songs *see* Children's Playground Games and Songs in the Age of New Media project; playlore
'playing house' 7
playlore 10, 40–53; *for* and *about* children 42–3; Australian research 44–52; behaviour management strategies 50–1; *of* children 42; collecting and displaying playlore 1–2, 42–4; as cultural heritage 40–2; electronic and online play 50, 58–9; ethnic diversity 48;

playlore (*cont.*):
  games 40, 41, 45–6, 48, 57; new media
  and technologies 48, 56, 58; oral
  traditions and expressions 40, 45, 46, 48,
  55; pedagogical strategies 51; performing
  arts 40, 48, 49–50; play spaces 50;
  rituals 40; rules 51–2; safety 50, 51;
  social practices 40, 51; story games 49;
  traditional craftsmanship 40–1; *see also*
  Childhood, Tradition and Change project;
  Children's Playground Games and Songs
  in the Age of New Media project
Please Touch Museum, Philadelphia 216
Plow, H. 186
Pludermacher, S. and R. 181
Pollock, L.A. 6
Pomogalov, N. 268
Powers, S. 245
Praed, Rosa 92
proxemics 69

Quarry Bank Mill, Manchester 134, 135–6,
  136*f*

Rasmussen, K. 10–11
Rawson, B. 152, 153
Read, P. 165
Reid, S. 266–7
Rescue Children Inc. 177, 179, 180
Rhône-Poulenc Foundation 24
Richards, C. 61–2
Roach, A. 167
Roach, J. 240, 243
Roberts, S. 211
Robinson, K. 135
Robinson, T. 128
Rogers, C.R. 91
Roman children and childhood 144–56;
  agency of children 153–4; definition
  of childhood 148; *delicia/deliciae* 153;
  education 151–2, 153; evidence 147–9;
  familia 149–50; funerary altars 144, 145*f*,
  146*f*, 150–2; gender 150; ideas of ancient
  Rome 144–7, 156; infant mortality 148–
  9; marriage 150; material culture 153–4;
  media portrayals of 155; museum
  exhibitions 153–6; slave children 149,
  152–3, 155, 156
Roosevelt, T. 247, 253
Rosen, M. 61
Rosenblum, W. 133, 134
Rosenzweig, R. 111

Roud, S. 61
Rudd, K. 160, 163, 167
Russell, H. 46, 51
Russian representations of childhood
  257–69; early 20th century 258–66;
  Bolshevik ideology 266; Soviet
  era 266–7; post-Soviet realities
  and representations 268; children's
  rooms 263–4, 265–6; nostalgia 258, 268;
  on-line museums 257; toys 267; women's
  magazines and representations of modern
  childhood 261–6
Russick, J. 14

Sabin, Arthur 232
safety 50
SAHD (Students Association for Heritage
  Defence) 29
Saint, A. 201
Samuel, R. 115
Sánchez-Eppler, K. 9
Sanders, V. 89
Scherrer Hicks (architects) 202
Schleimann, H. 253
Schlereth, T.J. 7, 8, 211
school buildings in England 11, 190–204;
  Victorian buildings 191–2; 1930s 192–3;
  1945–70 191, 192, 193–200, 195*f*; 1990s
  onwards 191; art in schools 194, 199;
  Brutalism 200, 201, 201*f*; comprehensive
  schools 199–200; conservation and
  re-use of postwar schools 201–4;
  Education Act (1944) 192, 199, 201;
  National Heritage Listing 191, 192,
  201, 202, 203; Nottinghamshire and
  CLASP 196–7; open planning 197–9,
  200; Plowden Report (1967) 197–8;
  prefabrication 193–7, 199; primary
  schools 191, 192, 194–5, 195*f*, 196*f*, 197–
  9; secondary schools 191, 192, 195, 196,
  197, 198, 199–200; village schools 197–8
self-identity 13
Serkess, Leonard 186
Shaheed, F. 32–3
Sheffield Museums 225
Shepherd, B.W. 218, 219–20
Shore, Emily 88
Shozawa, J. 79–80
Shufu no tomo (The Housewife's
  Companion) 78, 82
Silvey, R. 94
Sirindhorn, Princess Maha Chakri 31

sites and spaces of childhood 10; children's rooms at home 263–4, 265–6; places of children *vs.* children's places 10–11; play spaces 50, 275–6; 'Wild Child' exhibition, Auckland Museum 214–15
slavery 119–21, 131, 149, 152–3, 155, 156
Smiets, R. 29–30
Smithson, A. and P. 200, 201
social context 40, 51, 65, 272–5
Sofaer Derevenski, J. 8
Soldo, J.J. 92
Solnit, R. 246
South Kensington Museum, London 231–2
Spock, Michael 216
Statius 153
Stewart, S. 242, 248
Stillman, C.G. 193
Stone, P. 24, 25
Strazdes, D. 243
Strong, Margaret Woodbury 211
Strong Museum of Play 211, 218–19
Strong, Roy 232
Studart, D.C. 216
Students Association for Heritage Defence (SAHD) 29
Suetonius 148
Sutton-Smith, B. 41, 219
Suzuki, T. 80
Swain, S. *et al.* 160

Takizawa, M. 76
Tate, Mrs Walter 232
Taylor, R. 66
Tenzer, H. 179
Thelen, D. 111
Thomas Coram Foundation 227, 228
Thompson, E.P. 128
Titchen, S. 24
Tolley, A.T. 88
Tooley Foster (architects) 202
Torney, K. 163
toys 7–8; in ancient Rome 154; museum collections 209, 211, 215–16, 234–5; in North Africa 271, 273–5, 276–81; in Russia 267
Truman, H.S. 181
Turner, Ethel 86
Turner, I. 44, 45
Tutorow, N.E. 245
Twain, M. 248

UNESCO (United Nations Educational, Scientific and Cultural Organization) 21–37; Associated Schools Project Network (ASPnet) 23, 24; cultural rights 31, 33; Forum UNESCO: Universities and Heritage (FUUH) 28–9; Goodwill Ambassadors 30–1; 'Growing Up in Cities' project 33–4; Intangible Heritage Convention 3, 22, 29–31, 36, 40–1; International Centre for the Study of the Preservation and Restoration of Cultural Property (ICCROM) 27; Memory of the World programme 36, 42; World Heritage Centre (WHC) 23; World Heritage Convention 3, 23, 36, 170–1; World Heritage Education (WHE) Programme 22, 23–8; 'young people' 21, 28
UNICEF (United Nations Children's Fund): Child Friendly Cities initiative 14; child trafficking 156; child workers 126; formation of 12
United Kingdom: child migrants 160, 161, 168; child workers 126–7, 128–9, 130–3, 134–6, 136*f*; children's museums 216, 217–18, 224; colonial children 161–3, 168; museums of childhood 211, 212, 215–16; Roman childhood in museum exhibitions 154–5; *see also* Children's Playground Games and Songs in the Age of New Media; Foundling Museum, London; heritage making; school buildings in England; V&A Museum of Childhood
United Nations: *Convention on the Rights of the Child* (1989) 12, 31, 34, 101n1, 170; Declaration on the Rights of Indigenous Peoples (2008) 167; Genocide Convention (1948) 165; *International Covenant on Economic, Social and Cultural Rights* (1966) 32; *State of World Population Report* (2008) 30; *see also* UNESCO; UNICEF
United Service for New Americans (USNA) 182
United States: child workers 127, 133–4, 135*f*; children's museums 177, 216–17, 218–19, 223–4; Holocaust Memorial Museum 177; museums of childhood 211, 218–19; *see also* Leland Stanford, Jr Museum
Upfal, A. 88
Utelkhin, I. 257

V&A Museum of Childhood 5, 223*f*, 224,
230–9, 232*f*; accessibility 234–5, 237;
Children at Work 130–1; collections 225,
225*t*, 238; Community Programme 237;
Contemporary Programme 237–8;
history 215, 216, 230–3, 234; interactive
activities 234–5, 235*f*; learning 234–5,
237; recent initiatives 233–8;
research 237; role 217–18, 219, 230, 233,
234–6
Van Leeuwen, T. 66, 69
Vaughan, Iris 86, 87
Ventris, M. 195
Virginia Historical Society 134

Ward, C. 129
Ware, S.A. 166
Waugh, Evelyn 92
Webb, D. 58, 59, 60*f*
Weeks, J. 194–5
Wells, H.G. 88
Wertsch, J.V. 108
Whiteley, Opal 86
William Boyd Childhood Collection 1–2
Wilson, F. 232*f*
Winchester Discovery Centre 131–3
Winnicott, D.W. 101, 242

women's magazines: Japan 75, 77, 78, 80,
81–2; Russia 261–6
Wood, Sir Robert 193
Woolf, Virgina 89
World Heritage Education (WHE)
Programme 23–8; educational resource
kit 24, 25, 26*f*, 35; establishment 24;
international/regional forums 24, 25,
27, 27*f*, 28*f*, 34; Patrimonito 22, 24, 28,
35; regional workshops 25, 27; summer
camps 25, 26*f*; 'young people' 28
Wortley Montagu, Lady Mary 88–9
writings of children *see* literary juvenilia
Wulman, L. 178, 179

Yad Vashem 175
Yasujirō, O. 74
Yorke, Rosenberg and Mardall
(architects) 202
Yoshimitsu, M. 74–5

Zelizer, V.A. 129
Zhenshchina (*Woman*) 261, 262, 263–4, 265
Zhurnal dlia khoziaek (*Journal for
Homemakers*) 261, 262, 263, 264–5
Zhurnal dlia zhenshchin (*Journal for Women*) 261
Zimmerman, L. J. *et al.* 36